Cyberspace/Cyberbodies/Cyberpunk

Theory, Culture & Society

Theory, Culture & Society caters for the resurgence of interest in culture within contemporary social science and the humanities. Building on the heritage of classical social theory, the book series examines ways in which this tradition has been reshaped by a new generation of theorists. It will also publish theoretically informed analyses of everyday life, popular culture and new intellectual movements.

EDITOR: Mike Featherstone, *University of Teesside*

Recent volumes include:

The Cinematic Society
The Voyeur's Gaze
Norman K. Denzin

Decentring Leisure
Rethinking Leisure Theory
Chris Rojek

Global Modernities
Mike Featherstone, Scott Lash and Roland Robertson

The Masque of Femininity
The Presentation of Woman in Everyday Life
Efrat Tseëlon

The Arena of Racism
Michel Wieviorka

Undoing Culture
Globalization, Postmodernism and Identity
Mike Featherstone

The Time of the Tribes
The Decline of Individualism in Mass Society
Michel Maffesoli

Risk, Environment and Modernity
Towards a New Ecology
edited by Scott Lash, Bronislaw Szerszynski and Brian Wynne

For Weber
Essays on the Sociology of Fate
Bryan S. Turner

Cyberspace/Cyberbodies/Cyberpunk

Cultures of Technological Embodiment

Edited by
Mike Featherstone
and
Roger Burrows

SAGE Publications
London · Thousand Oaks · New Delhi

First published 1995

Published in association with *Theory, Culture & Society*,
School of Human Studies, University of Teesside.

SAGE Publications Ltd
6 Bonhill Street
London EC2A 4PU

SAGE Publications Inc
2455 Teller Road
Thousand Oaks, California 91320

SAGE Publications India Pvt Ltd
32 M-Block Market
Greater Kailash – I
New Delhi 110 048

British Library Cataloguing in Publication data

A catalogue record for this book is
available from the British Library.

ISBN 0–7619 5084 2
ISBN 0–7619 5085 0

Library of Congress catalog record available

Typeset by Type Study, Scarborough, North Yorkshire
Printed in Great Britain by The Cromwell Press, Melksham,
Wiltshire

Contents

Cultures of Technological Embodiment: An Introduction

MIKE FEATHERSTONE AND ROGER BURROWS

The sociologist Peter Berger (1966) once remarked that history is seldom surprise free. The assumption is that those people who lived a few decades before the Renaissance were unable to see it coming. This belief that something completely new could be just around the corner, that humankind still has an open future, is one which has been challenged by postmodern theory with its attack on the modernist metanarratives of progress and 'the new'. At its most extreme, this postmodern sensibility leads to a *fin de millénium* pessimism, with the assumption that there are no new moves in the game and that we are confronted by a future which 'has already happened'. The recent upsurge of interest in cyberspace, cyberbodies and cyberpunk has introduced complications into this scenario. On the one hand, there are those who wish to recover it into postmodernism yet, on the other hand, there are others who see it as breaking down the boundaries of this framework to revive utopian impulses, coupled with the sense that we are on the edge of moving into a reconfigured world which bears little relation to our previous speculations. In this context, it is also worth recalling that in the predictions about everyday life in the mid-1990s made by experts in a 1960s television programme, there was no mention of computers. Plenty of robots, but no computers. If we were to restart this process today and make predictions about everyday life in the mid-2020s, it is certain that computers, information technology and the electronic media would play a central role – but then is there still the disturbing possibility that we could have missed something which will emerge and have crucial significance?

The writings which have emerged on cyberspace, cyberbodies and cyberpunk over the last decade are replete with utopian, dystopian and heterotopian possibilities. For some, this entails the assumption that we are about to enter a new era. Mark Poster, for example, in his article in this volume, argues that we are now at an equivalent point in history to the emergence of urban merchant culture in feudalism. He sees the late 20th-century second media age as having an equally profound impact upon the constitution of social life and forms of cultural identity. Yet it is not just the possible reconstitutions of social life and culture which interest us in this journal, it is the impact of these changes on the body, too. It is here that developments in technology point towards the possibilities of post-bodied and post-human forms of existence. If the development of technology has entailed a process of the extension of the body and bodily functions to enable us to control the environment more efficiently, it offers the ultimate possibility of the displacement of the material body from the confines of its immediate lived space. Hence it is not just the range of technological–human fusions which make possible a new range of embodied forms which is an interesting source of speculation, it is the production and control of new information-generated environments and the range of body simulations and other entities which will inhabit them which for many is the most exciting prospect. It is not just the making and remaking of bodies, but the making and remaking of worlds which is crucial here. This is graphically captured by William Gibson's remark in one of his interviews, which Nigel Clark quotes in his article in this issue: 'Watch out for worlds behind you!'

The terms cyberspace, cyborg and cyberpunk came into prominence in the 1980s. They form a cluster of key words which, as Tomas argues in his piece in this volume, are drawn from the term cybernetics. The term cybernetics was coined in 1948 (Weiner, 1948) to describe a new science which united communications theory and control theory. For Weiner, cybernetics encompassed the human mind, the human body and the world of automatic machines and attempted to reduce all three to the common denominator of control and communication. From this perspective, the image of the body becomes less one of an engineered body with the key tasks being the transfer and conservation of energy, but more of a communications network based upon the accurate reproduction and exchange of signals in time and space. Hence information, messages and feedback which facilitate control and communication become seen as the key aspects of both organisms and machines.

The term cyborg refers to cybernetic organism, a self-regulating human–machine system. It is in effect a human–machine hybrid in which the machine parts become replacements, which are integrated or act as supplements to the organism to enhance the body's power potential. As we shall see below, the most graphic images of this type to capture the popular imagination have been drawn from major films such as *Robocop*. The term cyberspace refers to an information space in which data is configured in such a way as to give the operator the illusion of control, movement and access to information, in which he/she can be linked together with a large number of users via a puppet-like simulation which operates in a feedback loop to the operator. Virtual reality represents the ultimate extension of this process to provide a pure information space populated by a range of cybernetic automatons, or data constructs, which provide the operator with a high degree of vividness and total sensory immersion in the artificial environment. The term cyberpunk refers to the body of fiction built around the work of William Gibson and other writers, who have constructed visions of the future worlds of cyberspaces, with all their vast range of technological developments and power struggles. It sketches out the dark side of the technological-fix visions of the future, with a wide range of post-human forms which have both theoretical and practical implications; theoretically, in influencing those who are trying to reconstruct the social theory of the present and near future, and practically, in terms of those (largely young people) who are keen to devise experimental lifestyles and subcultures which aim to live out and bring about selected aspects of the cyberspace/cyberpunk constellation.

Cyborgs

If we turn first to a discussion of cyborgs, it is clear that an overriding theme in the writings of William Gibson (for summaries see Kellner [1995], McHale [1992a, 1992b], Csicsery-Ronay [1991] and a number of the contributions to McCaffrey [1991]) is the assumption that the boundaries between subjects, their bodies and the 'outside world' are being radically reconfigured (Haraway, 1991; Plant, 1993). This means that the key analytical categories we have long used to structure our world, which derive from the fundamental division between technology and nature, are in danger of dissolving; the categories of the biological, the technological, the natural, the artificial *and* the human – are now beginning to blur (Stone, 1991: 101–2; McCarron, this volume; Tomas, this volume).

As Robert Rawdon Wilson indicates in his contribution to this volume, the term cyborg need not only be taken to immediately refer to the new dramatic possibilities which are to be found in the pages of cyberpunk and science fiction novels – the use of a pair of spectacles is a prosthetic device which can be placed near to one end of the human/machine combinations that make up the cyborg. Yet it is the extent and complexity of the changes following from the mainstreaming of cosmetic surgery and the rise of biotechnology, genetic engineering and nano-technology, which have led some to contemplate that the next generation could very well be the last of 'pure' humans (Deitch, 1992). A programmatic user's guide on new technological developments (Rucker et al., 1993: 100) puts it like this:

> We are *already* cyborgs. My mother, for instance, leads a relatively normal life thanks to a pacemaker. Beyond that, genetic engineering and nanotechnology . . . offer us the possibility of

> literally being able to change our bodies into new and different forms . . . a form of postbiological
> humanity can be achieved within the next fifty years.

If the increasing acceptance by consumers of cosmetic surgery and other associated technological interventions to modify the body (Balsamo, this volume; see also Featherstone, 1982; Glassner, 1995) over the last decade are at all indicative of future trends, then the next 50 years will see ever more radical plastic surgery, computer-chip brain implants[1] and gene splicing become routine. It is suggested that the implications of this for self-identity will be profound (see Rawdon Wilson, this volume).

A glimpse of the problems which arise when humans are blended with machines is provided by the contributions from Holland and Landsberg, who draw upon movies such as *Robocop, Terminator, Total Recall* and *Blade Runner*. The most obvious dilemmas occur in the case of the technologically rebuilt human body, in which the residues of the human self struggle to assert themselves against the 'product violation' programming designed into the cyborg – the theme of the *Robocop* movie. Less obvious are the problems of designing adequate fusions from 'the other end', as is the case with the replicants in the film *Blade Runner*, who are artificial constructs designed to function and pass as human beings. Here the problem is one of inserting duplicated human memories into the replicants to enable them to generate credible 'human' emotional responses. Memories, then, are an important resource for the generation of identity which enable credible actions and responses to be formed. The approach of films such as *Blade Runner* is to introduce doubts and complexities into what is, all too often, a dualistic approach in which the (good) human mind heroically struggles against the invasion of the (bad) technological body.

In addition to continuing to bolster the human/machine dualism, which reinforces the mind/body dualism still influential in everyday life, there is generally a strong gender-coded male/female dualism evident in the films. Males are near invincible soldiers with hyper-male bodies; little attempt is made to explore or cross gender boundaries. There is little sense that the new technology, especially the computer, might ultimately benefit women more than men. The latter case is argued by Sadie Plant in her contribution to the volume, which draws on Donna Haraway's (1991) argument that the new technologies allow an escape from the conceptual dualisms of culture/nature and mind/body to open up a host of post-gendered possibilities. Following Haraway's lead, Plant (1993:13) has suggested that the relationship between women and machinery is beginning to evolve into 'a dangerous alliance', in which '[s]ilicon and women's liberation track each other's developments'. Plant discusses the way in which the new technology offers spaces for disguise, concealment and masquerade. Spaces which, although constructed by men following the imperatives of increasing their rational control through technological domination, are at the same time female and dangerous. Plant here, then, is exploring the implications of technologies which do not alter the human body per se but allow it to be *transcended* – technologies that promise, literally, a new world in which we can *represent* our bodies with a greater degree of flexibility. Technologies which have collectively become known as *cyberspace*.

Cyberspace

The literature on cyberspace is rapidly becoming a significant element in popular culture.[2] Following Sterling (1990), cyberspace is best considered as a generic term which refers to a cluster of different technologies, some familiar, some only recently available, some being developed and some still fictional, all of which have in common the ability to simulate environments within which humans can interact. Other writers prefer the term computer-mediated communication (CMC) (Jones, 1994) to refer to much the same set of phenomena. We can now discuss some of the main variants: *Barlovian cyberspace*; *virtual reality* (VR); and *Gibsonian cyberspace*.

Barlovian cyberspace – named after John Barlow,[3] a founder of the political action group called Electronic Frontier Foundation (Sterling, 1990: 54) – refers to the existing international networks of computers. The seemingly ubiquitous Internet is now a 'ragged . . . world spanning electronic tangle' (Sterling, 1990: 54) consisting of some 30 million people. In a sense, such a simple form of cyberspace is little more than an extension of existing telephone systems, simply substituting text and some icons for voice. Indeed, for Barlow cyberspace 'is where you are when you're talking on the telephone' (Rucker et al., 1993: 78). Clearly, both telephones and computer network systems rely upon only a limited range of human senses and (although interactions via these mediums can be extremely rich [Stone, 1991; Rheingold, 1994; Wiley, 1995]) they are perhaps no substitute for 'face-to-face' (ftf) interactions where all participants are co-present. This is so because contemporary social life still tends to operate with an implicit physiognomic notion that the face and the body are the only 'true' sources which can reveal the character of a person (Featherstone, 1995a, 1995b). Thus, other, more advanced forms of cyberspace attempt to simulate such interactions more vividly by the use of co-ordinated multi-media systems, such as virtual reality, which stimulate our other senses.

The term 'virtual reality' (VR) was first coined by Jaron Lanier,[4] the former head of VPL Research Inc. in California, and has recently been defined as 'a real or simulated environment in which the perceiver experiences telepresence' (Steuer, 1992: 76–7; see Heim, this volume). It is a system which provides a realistic sense of being immersed in an environment. VR is a computer-generated visual, audible and tactile multi-media experience. Using stereo headphones, head-mounted stereo television goggles ('eyephones') able to simulate three-dimensions, wired gauntlets ('datagloves') and computerized clothing ('datasuits'), VR aims to surround the human body with an artificial sensorium of sight, sound and touch. VR systems are also truly interactive in the sense that the computer which produces the simulated environment in which a person is immersed, constantly reconfigures that environment in response to body movements. As yet, the technology is relatively crude. There is sometimes a lag between movements of the body and the reconfiguration of the environment, graphics resolution is relatively low and many environments rely upon line-drawings and/or cartoon-like iconic representations. Nevertheless, all the indications are that the level of realism attainable will improve dramatically towards the end of the century (Lanier and Biocca, 1992). VR, then, is a medium which simulates a sense of presence through the use of technology – hence the term telepresence in its definition.

Gibsonian cyberspace, as defined in *Neuromancer* and the inspiration for the generic term, is characterized in an oft-quoted passage as

> A consensual hallucination experienced daily by billions of legitimate operators, in every nation, by children being taught mathematical concepts. . . . A graphic representation of data abstracted from the bank of every computer in the human system. Unthinkable complexity. Lines of light ranged in the nonspace of the mind, clusters and constellations of data. Like city lights receding. (Gibson, 1984:51)

In this fictional world, cyberspace is a global computer network of information which Gibson calls 'the matrix', which operators can access ('jack-in') through headsets ('trodes') via a computer terminal ('cyberspace deck'). Once in the matrix, operators can 'fly' to any part of the vast three-dimensional system of data coded into various colourful iconic architectural forms laid out beneath them like a vast metropolis (Bukatman, 1993a:103–8): a city of data, a Borgesian library of vast databases containing all a culture's deposited wealth, where every document is available, every recording playable and every picture viewable. Once a particular location has been selected, it is possible to zoom in so that one moves inside the three-dimensional representation of the data in order to scan particular areas. Gibsonian cyberspace also allows for highly 'realistic' interactions between iconic representations of operators (what Stephenson [1992] in *Snow Crash* terms 'avatars' or what we might term 'cyberbodies') so that co-presence can be simulated within a myriad of different highly vivid environments. A range of other 'intelligent' entities can also 'exist' in cyberspace which do not have a human referent 'outside' the system. Some are previously downloaded personality constructs of humans, while others are autonomous post-human artificial intelligences (AIs) which live in cyberspace 'like fish in water' (Sterling, 1990:54). Essentially, then, Gibsonian cyberspace represents an imagined merger between the internet and VR systems. This imagined merger is given its most detailed rendition in Stephenson's (1992) Gibsonian-inspired *Snow Crash* through his description of the 'Metaverse'.

Cyberpunk

The term cyberpunk was first used in a Bruce Bethke short story called 'Cyberpunk', published in the November 1983 issue of *Amazing Stories* (see the discussion in the article by McCarron in this volume). It has since been used to describe writers such as William Gibson, especially *Neuromancer* (1984), Pat Cadigan, Bruce Sterling, Lewis Shiner and Greg Bear. What is interesting is the way in which cyberpunk has been taken up as a useful resource for social and cultural theory in comprehending the alleged shifts towards a new epoch. For Fred Jameson (1991:419n), for example, cyberpunk and the work of Gibson in particular, represents 'the supreme *literary* expression if not of postmodernism, then of late capitalism itself'. Indeed, the work of Gibson has been held up as the prime exemplar of postmodern poetics (McHale, 1992a, 1992b). This might well be so but, for others, cyberpunk represents much more than even this. Perhaps the most extreme claim made for cyberpunk comes from Timothy Leary who declares that Gibson:

> has produced nothing less than the underlying myth, the core legend, of the next stage of human evolution. He is performing the philosophic function that Dante did for feudalism and that writers like Mann, Tolstoy [and] Melville . . . did for the industrial age. (Leary, cited in Kellner, 1995:298)

Only marginally less extreme is the claim by Sandy Stone (1991:95) that the work of Gibson represents the dividing line between different social epochs based upon different modes of communication. For Stone, the publication of *Neuromancer*

> crystallised a new community. . . . [It] reached the hackers . . . and . . . the technologically literate and socially disaffected who were searching for social forms that could transform the fragmented anomie that characterised life in . . . electronic industrial ghettos. . . . Gibson's powerful vision provided for them the imaginal public sphere and refigured discursive community that established the grounding for the possibility of a new kind of social interaction. . . . [It] is a massive textual presence not only in other literary productions . . . but in technical publications, conference topics, hardware design, and scientific and technological discourses in the large. (Stone, 1991:95)

Other writers, clearly not just influenced by the fictional world of cyberpunk, but by the actuality of technological change itself, have begun to construct a sociological agenda to explore the realities of what some have termed *cybersociety* (Jones, 1994). Even so, and as Stone notes in the above quote, the cyberpunk literature remains 'a massive textual presence' in even the most atheoretical and empiricist explorations of the internet and virtual reality. However, while cyberpunk has a radical and dystopic edge to it, much of the work on cyberculture more generally has, hitherto, been overly utopian. This utopianism is a theme explored in the present volume in the contribution by Kevin Robins.

There are some striking parallels between the utopianism of much of the current phase of technological development – the construction of the so called 'information superhighway' – and the construction of the interstate highway system in the USA. First, at the level of individuals, it was the father of Vice-President Al Gore – one of the greatest political advocates of the new technologies – who was instrumental in the development of the federal highway system. Second, at the level of motivation, in both cases it was the US military who provided the initial rationale for the construction of both systems (Jones, 1994: 10). And, as in the previous period, the utopian hyperbole surrounding the new technologies may come to be viewed as representing little more than the politically interested discourse of the organic intellectuals of a new class – a 'virtual class'

> compulsively fixated on . . . technology as a source of salvation from the reality of a lonely culture and radical disconnection from everyday life . . . [a virtual class of] would-be astronauts who never got the chance to go to the moon [driven by the] will to virtuality. (Kroker and Weinstein, 1994: 4–5)

Much of what has been claimed for cyberculture *is* overly utopian. Nevertheless, despite the hyperbole and the mythology surrounding it, it is still possible to decipher within its literary concomitant, cyberpunk, a *theoretically* coherent vision of a very near future which is, some argue, about to collapse on the present (Csicsery-Ronay, 1991: 186; Kellner, 1995; Rucker et al., 1993). Whether William Gibson intends it or not (Gibson, 1991), his fiction *can* be systematically read as social and cultural theory, in that it not only paints 'an instantly recognizable portrait of the modern predicament', but also shows 'the hidden bulk of an iceberg of social change' that 'now glides with sinister majesty across the surface of the late twentieth century' (Sterling, 1986). Indeed, for Doug Kellner (1995), cyberpunk fiction is a far more insightful and dynamic analytic resource for coming to terms with the postmodern than is the recent work of cultural critics such as Baudrillard. While for Mike Davis (1992: 3), one of the major analysts of the contemporary urban condition, the work of Gibson provides 'stunning examples of how realist "extrapolative" science fiction can operate as prefigurative social theory, as well as an anticipatory opposition politics to the cyber-fascism lurking over the next horizon'. Although they do much else besides, the chapters included here by Sadie Plant, Nick Land and Anne Balsamo, all, in different ways, provide exemplars of such prefigurative social theory, in terms of both form and content.

Thus not only has the seemingly ubiquitous Gibsonian concept of cyberspace begun to transmute into a tangible *reality* – his technological vision has fed back into both computer and information systems design and theory (Benedikt, 1991b; Biocca, 1992a; McFadden, 1991), financially underwritten by the likes of the Pentagon, Sega, Nintendo and various other global corporations – but many of Gibson's fictional perspectives on cultural, economic and social phenomena have begun to find their way into social and cultural analyses as viable characterizations of our contemporary world.

Reading cyberpunk as social theory tends not to be a unidirectional activity. The relationship between cyberpunk literature and social theory is, if anything, recursive. Cyberpunk and sociological analyses which draw upon it have a 'habit' of 'folding into' each other in a recursive relation between the fictional and the analytic which might be described as an instance of a hyperreal positive feedback loop. For example, issues of public space and urban surveillance are themes taken up by Gibson throughout his work, but most fully in *Virtual Light* (1993). It is a book profoundly and explicitly influenced by Davis's (1990) influential analysis of Los Angeles, *City of Quartz*, which is itself adorned by a quote from Gibson which suggests that, as a work of contemporary analysis, it may well be more 'cyberpunk' than Gibson's fiction (Bukatman, 1993a: 144). This recursivity continues in Davis's (1992) *Beyond Blade Runner: Urban Control – the Ecology of Fear*, where an explicitly 'Gibsonian' map of the contemporary urban condition is presented. A map instantly recognizable in *Virtual Light* and, in a much more extreme form in Stephenson's *Snow Crash* (1992). Kellner (1995) also recognizes a recursivity between cyberpunk and postmodern social theory:

> cyberpunk science fiction can be read as a sort of social theory, while Baudrillard's futuristic postmodern social theory can be read in turn as science fiction. This optic also suggests a deconstruction of sharp oppositions between literature and social theory, showing that much social theory contains a narrative and vision of the present and future, and that certain types of literature provide cogent mappings of the contemporary environment and, in the case of cyberpunk, of future trends. (Kellner, 1995: 299)

He goes on to add that

> at the very moment when Baudrillard dropped the theoretical ball, losing his initiative, Gibson and cyberpunk picked it up, beginning their explorations of the new future world which Baudrillard had been exploring. (Kellner, 1995: 327)

The relationship between postmodernism and cyberculture is the central theme of the chapter by Mark Poster, while issues of recursivity, although explored throughout the volume, receive their most explicit treatment in the chapter by Nigel Clark.

Gareth Branwyn (Rucker et al., 1993: 64–6), writing in *Mondo 2000*, provides a useful description of cyberpunk as both a literary perspective and as an actual worldview which gives a clear indication of its major concerns:

> The future has imploded onto the present. There was no nuclear Armageddon. There's too much real estate to lose. The new battle-field is people's minds. . . . The megacorps *are* the new governments. . . . The U.S. is a big bully with lackluster economic power. . . . The world is splintering into a trillion subcultures and designer cults with their own language, codes and lifestyles. . . . Computer-generated info-domains are the next frontiers. . . . There *is* better living through chemistry. . . . Small groups or individual 'console cowboys' can wield tremendous power over governments, corporations etc. . . . The coalescence of a computer 'culture' is expressed in self-aware computer music, art, virtual communities, and a hacker/street tech subculture . . . the computer nerd image is passé, and people are not ashamed anymore about the role the computer has in this subculture. The computer is a cool tool, a friend, important human augmentation. . . . We're becoming cyborgs. Our tech is getting smaller, closer to us, and it will soon merge with us.

These themes were first given expression in Gibson's novels which derive from a wide range of cultural antecedents (McHale, 1992a, 1992b). Kadrey and McCaffery (1991) suggest the following influences: classic novels such as *Frankenstein* and *The Big Sleep*; the literary avant-garde represented by William S. Burroughs (see also the influence of this style on the paper by Land in this volume), Thomas Pynchon and Kathy Acker; the science fiction of Philip K. Dick (see the discussion by McCarron in this volume), Michael Moorcock and J.G. Ballard (see Sobchack's discussion in this volume); the cultural analyses of Marshall McLuhan, grandly described as being 'to the 1960s what Baudrillard, Kroker and Cook, and Deleuze and Guattari are to the postcyberpunk era' (Kadrey and McCaffery, 1991: 18); the Situationist International's analysis of contemporary society (Plant, 1992); the music of the Velvet Underground, Patti Smith, the Talking Heads, mid-1970s David Bowie, Brian Eno, Laurie Anderson and, crucially, the Sex Pistols and The Clash (see McCaffrey, 1991: 382–3, for a fuller listing); films such as Cronenberg's *Videodrome*, Roeg's *The Man Who Fell to Earth* and, especially, Ridley Scott's *Blade Runner* – itself based upon a novel by Dick (see the discussion by Landsberg and Holland, this volume; Bukatman, 1993a: 373–4, for a full filmography); MTV and its 'youth TV' emulators; and, finally, one might also add the IBM PC and the Macintosh computer, the *cultural* and *representational* impact of which was at least as great as its economic and technological importance (see Lupton, this volume).[5]

Cyberbodies

Cyberpunk takes the twin themes of technological body modification and the notion of cyberspace and allows them to intersect in various urban settings. The world of cyberspace is itself an urban environment – 'a simulation of the city's information order', in which the 'city redoubles itself through the complex architecture of its information and media networks' (Davis, 1992:16) – a digitized parallel world which from 'above' might appear as a rationally planned city (Le Corbusier's metropolis) but from 'below' reveals itself as a Benjaminesque labyrinthine city, in which no one can get the bird's eye view of the plan, but everyone effectively has to operate at street level, with limited knowledge based on different amounts of information about, and practical understanding of, how to move around in a world which is rapidly being restructured and reconfigured. This digitized urban hyperreality connects in various ways with the technological 'reality' of the street, not least in the way in which the socio-geography of the digitized city mirrors that of the built city. Davis (1992:16) notes, for example, how the imploding 'communities' of Los Angeles are 'a data and media black hole'; an 'electronic *ghetto* within the emerging *information city*'.

The intersecting of the digital domain with the technology of the street produces a complex continuum of human–machine fusions (Tomas, 1989, 1991; Balsamo, this volume). At one end we have 'pure' human beings and at the other fully simulated disembodied post-humans which can only exist in cyberspace('AIs' in Gibson and the less spectacular [UNIX-inspired] 'Daemons' in Stephenson). If we move out from the all-human pole, the first category of interest is one concerned with the aesthetic manipulation of the body's surface through cosmetic surgery, muscle grafts and animal or human transplants, which blur the visual cues for distinctions between humans and non-humans as well as gender differences (Rawdon Wilson, this volume). The second category is concerned with more fundamental alterations and enhancements of the functioning of the inner body. Here we have a range of alternatives to replace organic functions, such as biochip implants, upgraded senses and prosthetic additions. Both categories enable the body to be disassembled and reassembled with a high degree of functional specialization. In both cases, these bodily modifications find collective expression in social groupings which have some striking similarities with Michel Maffesoli's (1995) description of 'postmodern tribes' – groups which form and reform on the basis of temporary modes of identification. Moving along the continuum, the next category is what Tomas (1991:41) refers to as 'classical hardware interfaced cyborgs', which exist in cyberspace. These are the operators who move around in cyberspace whose bodies are wired up to computers for input and output flows of information.

This final category again gets its clearest expression not in Gibson but in the form of the avatars, the iconic representation of the bodies of people logged into the Metaverse, in *Snow Crash* by Stephenson. They represent examples of what has been seen as the 'decoupling the body and the subject' (Stone, 1991:99; Lupton, this volume; McCarron, this volume). Although contemporary reflexive self-identity increasingly relies upon an ability to transform the body, with the potential development of the parallel world of cyberspace, the range of ways in which one can represent one's embodied subjectivity becomes much more varied and flexible, surpassing the 'horizons of the flesh' and constraints of the 'physical' body (even with radical medical enhancements). Despite the persistence of embodied physiognomic notions of the 'true self' in contemporary social life, there is some evidence to suggest that the new technology is opening up the possibility of radically new disembodied subjectiv*ities* (see the chapters by David Tomas, Michael Heim, Deborah Lupton, Samantha Holland, Nick Land, Anne Balsamo and Kevin McCarron). In Gibson (1984:12) there exists 'a certain relaxed contempt for the flesh', which is regarded as 'the meat' by those addicted to 'life' in the 'matrix'. Although some regard such claims as unfounded and the new identities being created as banal (Robins, this volume), the cyberpunk vision is one in which we are approaching an epoch within which a self-identity derived from 'real', 'authentic', 'embodied' experiences is unable to compete with ones derived from the 'erotic ontology' (Heim, 1991) of 'hyperreal' 'simulated' 'disembodied' cyberspace (but for a critique see Sobchack, this volume).

Technology and Public Space

The cyberpunk view of the world is also one which recognizes the shrinking of public space and the increasing privatization of many aspects of social life. Close face-to-face social relationships, save those with kin and significant others within highly bounded *locales*, are becoming increasingly difficult to form. As patterns of both social and geographical mobility increase the fluidity of social life they undermine the formation of strong social bonds. The spectacle of consumer culture, especially as manifest in the commodified 'simulation' of the shopping mall as authentic public space, although providing a forum for the display of self-identity and the outcomes of associated body projects, in the end only results in the construction of a 'lonely crowd'. The headlong retreat of the *seduced* into their increasingly fortified, technologized, privatized worlds away from the increasingly remote and ungovernable spaces occupied by the *repressed*, to use the distinction made by Bauman (1988), only serves to further close off the more proximate 'social' sources of self-identity. For many all that is left is technology. As Elwes (1993:65) views it:

> computer technology was developed to promote and speed up global communication and yet somehow the effect is one of disconnection and distance. Individuals are increasingly locked into the isolation of their homes (it isn't safe to go out) and they only make contact with the outside

world through telecommunications and networked computer-information systems. Not so much distance learning as living at a distance.

For Lanier

California is the worst example. . . . Individuals don't even meet on sidewalks anymore . . . we live in this constant sort of fetal position where we are seated in a soft chair looking at the world through a glass square, be it the windshield of the car or the screen of a television or computer. It's sort of constant, and we're in a little bubble. (Lanier and Biocca, 1992: 157)

The privatized retreat into television and video – essentially passive, non-interactive mediums – has been followed by engagements with increasingly interactive technologies: camcorders, multi-media interactive CDs, computer games and so on. Technology is beginning to mediate our social relationships, our self-identities and our wider sense of social life to an extent we are only just beginning to grasp. The portable telephone, the portable fax, the notepad computer and various other forms of electronic human augmentation have become 'essential' for social life in the 'densely networked centres of the global cities' (Lash and Urry, 1994: 319) and, increasingly, beyond. The seemingly ubiquitous camcorder endlessly records not just the 'spectacle' but also the 'mundane' to such an extent that 'lived experience' in and of itself becomes secondary to gaining a taped 'representation' of it for later 'consumption' à la *Sex, Lies and Videotape*.[6]

The contemporary decline of our sense of 'publicness' has been coupled with the spread of electronically mediated communication from primarily workplace settings to the private sphere. Those who proffer cyberpunk as social theory, would see the social preconditions for the creation of a new cyberculture as being firmly established as we increasingly use mediated forms of communication such as the telephone, the fax, the modem, the video, BBSs and the forthcoming VR systems. Some would claim that by using these new media of communication we are beginning to create new 'on-line' or 'virtual communities', new forms of social relationships, new disembodied modes of interacting and, for some, as we have seen, embryonic Gibsonian cyberspace itself (Rheingold, 1994; for a critique see Robins in this volume).

Theorizing Beyond Stable Systems

It should, perhaps, come as no surprise to us that, in an increasingly hyper-aestheticized everyday life (Featherstone, 1991), it is through various fictions that we endeavour to come to know ourselves. While we have argued that various strands of contemporary social and cultural theory have been parasitic upon the cyberpunk tradition, it may well be the case that, in the longer run, greater importance will be accorded to the impact of writers such as De Landa (1991, 1992,

1993; see discussion in Land, 1995), who take up the methodological implications of the cyberpunk vision and attempt to think through systematically some of the consequences for the human sciences.

De Landa not only draws upon many of the themes inherent to cyberpunk (robots, cyborgs, Artificial Intelligence, non-human agency, and so on) in his work, but also utilizes many elements of the aesthetics of cyberpunk in his everyday practice. He is a computer graphics designer working outside of the academic mainstream, who draws upon an eclectic range of the human and physical sciences in order to construct a radical and compelling vision of what he terms 'the emergence of synthetic reason' (De Landa, 1993). He cogently argues that the human sciences are so fettered by many of their domain assumptions that they are simply unable to provide any useful analytic handle on the contemporary condition. By drawing upon a materialist non-metaphorical reading of Deleuze and Guattari (1982), he has outlined a theory of 'stratification' in which the complementary operations of 'sorting out' and 'consolidation' are shown to be behind many (physical and social) structural forms. De Landa concludes that the future of social theory will be in the construction of new 'epistemological reservoirs', based upon complex computer simulations of cultural, social and economic processes in cyberspace. Those of us familiar with the analytic insights afforded by popular simulations such as *Sim City 2000* (Friedman, 1994) will have had a glimpse of the sort of thing De Landa has in mind, even if the social science operationalization of such approaches is still far from convincing.[7]

The methodological 'purging' involved in the project is profound. First, De Landa suggests that we must once and for all do away with ideal typical analytic thinking and begin to take seriously 'population' thinking. Rather than conceptualizing phenomena as more or less imperfect incarnations of some ideal essence, we must recognize that it is only *variation* which is real – a complete inversion of the classical paradigm. There is, then, for De Landa, no such thing as a pre-existent collection of traits which define some phenomena (biological, physical, social or cultural), rather, each trait develops along different ancestral lineages and accumulates in a population under different selection pressures; selection pressures which are themselves dependent upon *specific* and *contingent* histories. Traits accumulate through the operation of a 'searching device' (which results from the coupling of any kind of spontaneous variation to any kind of selection pressure), and are the product of a more or less stable solution in relation to the various contingent affordances found within a given environment. Drawing upon developments in artificial life (AL) research, especially work on genetic algorithms, De Landa suggests that such points of stability are likely to be multiple rather than unique. But if there is no Darwinian survival of the fittest (the unique solution), what is the source of stability (however brief) in systems? The answer to this question leads De Landa to call for a second 'purge' – this time against notions of equilibrium thinking in the human sciences.

The importation into the human sciences of notions of stability from equilibrium thermodynamics premised upon the idea of 'heat death' – that stability was some function or other of all useful energy being transformed into heat – has had a profound effect upon modern social thought. It has underpinned our conceptualization of closed systems within which some static socio-economic solution can be derived. Most obviously, our conceptualization of markets, within which the operation of the laws of supply and demand generate a unique and stable solution in terms of prices and outputs, has reverberated throughout the social sciences via game theory, exchange theory, functionalism and systems thinking more generally.

De Landa suggests that this closed and static notion of (physical and socio-economic) stability has been superseded by the new science of 'dissipative' systems, based upon an understanding of the continual flow of energy and matter. The importation of ideas derived from the science of such systems – nonlinear dynamics – into the human sciences, fundamentally alters how we must conceptualize the world. Most important is the idea of 'deterministic chaos', in which 'stability' within the processual flux of dynamic systems is conceptualized as an 'attractor', and the transitions which transform one attractor into another are conceptualized as 'bifurcations'. The most striking feature of this attractor/bifurcations framework is the manner in which the notion of an 'emergent property' is revealed not as a metaphysical device, but as a real material process. It is quite possible, indeed very common, to find systems 'stabilized' in such a way that the properties of the population system as a whole are not manifest by the individual members of the population in isolation. Examples of such *synergistic interactions* include long waves of capitalist economic development (Kondratieff cycles), neural networks, the emergence of organizational cultures and so on.

De Landa suggests that, by combining the insights of both nonlinear dynamics and anti-ideal typical population thinking, 'we get the following picture: the evolutionary "searching device" constituted by variation coupled with selection . . . [which explores] a space "preorganized" by attractors and bifurcations' (De Landa, 1993: 798–9). Such insights can only be explored by constructing cyberspatial virtual environments within which such processes can be examined. It is only through the simulation of such processes that the complexity of systems can be examined. Clearly, if we are to take the study of emergent processes seriously, an analytic approach that categorizes a population into its components will lose sight of those properties generated by the configuration of the individual elements within the system. Computer simulations thus provide us with a tool within which we can synthesize rather than analyse systems.

This entails a radical shift in the constitution of social theory. Many academics would baulk at the prospect of understanding social processes by staring at simulacra on a computer screen. They would not be seduced by the prospect of the generation of new forms of *post-symbolic communication*, where the presentation of information in new configurations, using the visual dimension which gives a strong sense of immediacy, transparency and vividness (i.e. show me, don't tell me), will allegedly supersede the interpretive looseness of written language. The attraction of such speculations is that the modelling is constructed in closer proximity to the data and everyday life. The danger is that it merely continues the dream of reason, with its quest for total control, order and pure unsullied communication. At the same time, these new theoretical tendencies resonate with the more general shift over the last decade which has been associated with postmodernism, globalization and the body. This is the move away from systematic large-scale theory-building towards taking into account a greater range of difference, complexity and disorder. We are rediscovering again that the boundary between the social and human sciences is a fluid one. It is, therefore, fitting that a journal such as *Body & Society*, which has been designed to traverse and explore this border space, into which the investigation of the human body inevitably takes us, should devote its first special issue to the study of cyberspace/cyberbodies/cyberpunk.

Notes

1. For discussions of the social and cultural possibilities of both plastic surgery and biochip implants in the cyberpunk literature see Tomas (1989, 1991) and Featherstone (1995b).

2. The concept now even has its very own 'for beginners' volume (Buick and Jevtic, 1995) published in the same month as *Postmodernism for Beginners* (Appignanesi and Garratt, 1995), a good indication of its growing significance.

3. Barlow is an interesting figure in the history of contemporary technological developments. He is a Republican rock lyricist for the 1960s rock group the Grateful Dead.

4. Sterling (1990: 54) claims that 'Lanier is aware of the term "cyberspace" but considers it too "limiting" and "computery"'. As will be apparent, following Sterling (1990), Benedikt (1991a) and Rheingold (1994), we prefer to treat 'cyberspace' as a generic term and 'virtual reality' as one important example of it.

5. As is well known, Gibson wrote *Neuromancer* without much knowledge of the contemporary reality of computing technology. In conversation with McCaffery (1991: 270) he remarks: 'It wasn't until I could finally afford a computer of my own that I found out there's a drive mechanism inside – this little thing that spins around. I'd been expecting an exotic crystalline thing, a cyberspace deck or something, and what I got was a little piece of a Victorian engine that made noises like a scratchy old record player. That noise took away some of the mystique for me. . . . My ignorance had allowed me to romanticize

them.' For a discussion of this relationship between the technology which produces fiction and fictional representations of technology see Bukatman (1993b).

6. The analysis offered by the Situationist International in the late 1960s, on the emergence of 'the society of the spectacle' has recently been recognized as *the* crucial antecedent to Baudrillard's discussion of hyperreality, simulacra and related concepts (Plant, 1992; Rojek and Turner, 1993).

7. See in particular Gilbert and Doran (1994) and Gilbert and Conte (1995).

References

Appignanesi, R. and C. Garratt (1995) *Postmodernism for Beginners*. Cambridge: Icon Books.
Bauman, Z. (1988) *Freedom*. Milton Keynes: Open University Press.
Benedikt, M. (ed.) (1991a) *Cyberspace: First Steps*. London: MIT Press.
Benedikt, M. (1991b) 'Cyberspace: Some Proposals', in M. Benedikt (ed.) *Cyberspace: First Steps*. London: MIT Press.
Berger, P. (1966) *Invitation to Sociology*. Harmondsworth: Penguin.
Biocca, F. (1992a) 'Communication Within Virtual Reality: Creating a Space for Research', *Journal of Communication* 42(4).
Biocca, F. (1992b) 'Virtual Reality Technology: A Tutorial', *Journal of Communication* 42(4).
Buick, J. and Z. Jevtic (1995) *Cyberspace for Beginners*. Cambridge: Icon Books.
Bukatman, S. (1993a) *Terminal Identity*. London: Duke University Press.
Bukatman, S. (1993b) 'Gibson's Typewriter', in M. Dery (ed.) *Flame Wars: The Discourse of Cyberculture*. London: Duke University Press.
Csicsery-Ronay, I. (1991) 'Cyberpunk and Neuromanticism', in L. McCaffery (ed.) *Storming the Reality Studio*. Durham, NC: Duke University Press.
Davis, M. (1990) *City of Quartz*. London: Verso.
Davis, M. (1992) *Beyond Blade Runner: Urban Control, the Ecology of Fear*. Westfield, NJ: Open Magazine Pamphlets.
Deitch, J. (1992) *Post Human*. Amsterdam: Idea Books.
De Landa, M. (1991) *War in the Age of Intelligent Machines*. New York: Zone Books.
De Landa, M. (1992) 'Non-Organic Life', in J. Crary and S. Kwinter (eds) *Zone 6: Incorporations*. New York: Zone Books.
De Landa, M. (1993) 'Virtual Environments and the Rise of Synthetic Reason', in M. Dery (ed.) *Flame Wars*. Durham, NC: Duke University Press.
Deleuze, G. and F. Guattari (1982) *A Thousand Plateaus*. London: Athlone Press.
Elwes, C. (1993) 'Gender and Technology', *Variant* 15.
Featherstone, M. (1982) 'The Body in Consumer Culture', *Theory, Culture & Society* 1(2); reprinted in M. Featherstone, M. Hepworth and B.S. Turner (eds) (1991) *The Body*, pp. 170–96. London: Sage, 1991.
Featherstone, M. (1991) 'The Aestheticizaton of Everyday Life', pp. 65–82 in *Consumer Culture and Postmodernism*. London: Sage.
Featherstone, M. (1995a) 'Personality, Unity and the Ordered Life', in *Undoing Culture: Postmodernism, Globalization and Identity*. London: Sage.
Featherstone, M. (1995b) 'Post-Bodies, Ageing and Virtual Reality', in M. Featherstone and A. Wernick (eds) *Images of Ageing*. London: Routledge.
Friedman, T. (1994) 'Making Sense of Software: Computer Games and Interactive Textuality', in S. Jones (ed.) *Cybersociety*. London: Sage.
Gibson, W. (1984) *Neuromancer*. London: Harper Collins.
Gibson, W. (1991) 'Academy Leader', in M. Benedikt (ed.) *Cyberspace: First Steps*. London: MIT Press.
Gibson, W. (1993) *Virtual Light*. London: Viking.

Gilbert, N. and R. Conte (eds) (1995) *Artificial Societies: The Computer Simulation of Social Life*. London: UCL Press.

Gilbert, N. and J. Doran (eds) (1994) *Simulating Societies: The Computer Simulation of Social Phenomena*. London: UCL Press.

Glassner, B. (1995) 'In the Name of Health', in R. Bunton, S. Nettleton and R. Burrows (eds) *The Sociology of Health Promotion*. London: Routledge.

Haraway, D. (1991) *Symians, Cyborgs and Women: The Reinvention of Nature*. London: Free Association Books.

Heim, M. (1991) 'The Erotic Ontology of Cyberspace', in M. Benedikt (ed.) *Cyberspace: First Steps*. London: MIT Press.

Jameson, F. (1991) *Postmodernism or the Cultural Logic of Late Capitalism*. London: Verso.

Jones, S. (ed.) (1994) *Cybersociety*. London: Sage.

Kadrey, R. and L. McCaffery (1991) 'Cyberpunk 101: A Schematic Guide to *Storming the Reality Studio*', in L. McCaffery (ed.) *Storming the Reality Studio*. Durham, NC: Duke University Press.

Kellner, D. (1995) 'Mapping the Present from the Future: From Baudrillard to Cyberpunk', in *Media Culture*. London: Routledge.

Kroker, A. and M. Weinstein (1994) *Data Trash: The Theory of the Virtual Class*. Montreal: New World Perspectives.

Land, N. (1995) 'Machines and Technoculture Complexity', *Theory, Culture & Society* 12(2).

Lanier, J. and F. Biocca (1992) 'An Insider's View of the Future of Virtual Reality', *Journal of Communication* 42(4).

Lash, S. and J. Urry (1994) *Economies of Signs and Space*. London: Sage.

Maffesoli, Michel (1995) *The Time of the Tribes*. London: Sage.

McCaffery, L. (ed.) (1991) *Storming the Reality Studio*. Durham, NC: Duke University Press.

McFadden, T. (1991) 'Notes on the Structure of Cyberspace and the Ballistic Actors Model', in M. Benedikt (ed.) *Cyberspace: First Steps*. London: MIT Press.

McHale, B. (1992a) 'POSTcyberMODERNpunkISM', in *Constructing Postmodernism*. London: Routledge.

McHale, B. (1992b) 'Towards a Poetics of Cyberpunk', in *Constructing Postmodernism*. London: Routledge.

Plant, S. (1992) *The Most Radical Gesture: The Situationist International in a Postmodern Age*. London: Routledge.

Plant, S. (1993) 'Beyond the Screens: Film, Cyberpunk and Cyberfeminism', *Variant* 14.

Rheingold, H. (1991) *Virtual Reality*. London: Mandarin.

Rheingold, H. (1994) *The Virtual Community: Finding Connection in a Computerized World*. London: Secker and Warburg.

Rojek, C. and B.S. Turner (eds) (1993) *Forget Baudrillard?* London: Routledge.

Rucker, R., R.U. Sirius and Mu Queen (eds) (1993) *Mondo 2000: A User's Guide to the New Edge*. London: Thames and Hudson.

Stephenson, N. (1992) *Snow Crash*. New York: Bantam Books.

Sterling, B. (1986) *Mirrorshades: The Cyberpunk Anthology*. New York: Arbor House.

Sterling, B. (1990) 'Cyberspace (TM)', *Interzone* 41.

Steur, J. (1992) 'Defining Virtual Reality: Dimensions Determining Telepresence', *Journal of Communications* 42(4).

Stone, A.R. (1991) 'Will the Real Body Please Stand Up?: Boundary Stories about Virtual Cultures', in M. Benedikt (ed.) *Cyberspace: First Steps*. London: MIT Press.

Tatsumi, T. (1991) 'The Japanese Reflection of Mirrorshades', in L. McCaffery (ed.) *Storming the Reality Studio*. Durham, NC: Duke University Press.

Tomas, D. (1989) 'The Technophiliac Body', *New Formations* 8.

Tomas, D. (1991) 'Old Rituals for New Space', in M. Benedikt (ed.) *Cyberspace: First Steps*. London: MIT Press.

Wiener, N. (1948) 'Cybernetics', *Scientific American* 179: 14–19.

Wiley, J. (1995) 'No BODY is "Doing It": Cybersexuality as a Postmodern Narrative', *Body & Society* 1(1): 145–62.

Mike Featherstone teaches Sociology at the University of Teesside. His latest book is *Undoing Culture: Globalization, Postmodernism and Identity* (Sage).

Roger Burrows now works at the University of York. He was previously a Reader at the University of Teesside. His latest book is *Sociology of Health Promotion* (Routledge).

Feedback and Cybernetics: Reimaging the Body in the Age of the Cyborg

DAVID TOMAS

Words have frightening power. (Colin Cherry, 1980: 68)

The *cyborg* or 'cybernetic organism' represents a radical vision of what it means to be human in the western world in the late 20th century. Although the word has an official history that dates from 1964, when it was coined to describe a special union of human organism and machine system, over the last decade it has gained a certain notoriety in both popular film culture and specialized academic circles. Films such as *Blade Runner* (1982), the *Alien* trilogy, the *Terminator* series (1984, 1991), the *RoboCop* series (1987, 1990) and the British cult classic *Hardware* (1990) present a vision of the cyborg that ranges from pure machine-based military model to genetically tailored human simulation. These models and simulations are often designed to function in hostile, dystopic, futuristic worlds governed by various kinds of renegade military/industrial or corporate activity, or the consequences of such activity. More benign protocyborg models of a less imaginary, but no less militarized form, are to be found prefigured in the kinds of revisions of masculinity that were explored in the context of the American space program's shift in emphasis from test pilot to astronaut in Tom Wolfe's 1979 bestseller *The Right Stuff* and the film of the same name. On the other hand, alternative cyborg models have been explored in a more speculative vein, and from a more cloistered academic viewpoint, in 'A Cyborg Manifesto: Science, Technology, and Socialist-Feminism in the Late Twentieth Century', Donna Haraway's seminal 1985 meditation on oppositional uses of the cyborg concept.

The success of cyborg-based films and the influence of Haraway's cyborg manifesto suggest that the word 'cyborg' has functioned throughout the 1980s, in one form or another, as a keyword in Raymond Williams's sense of 'significant binding words in certain activities and their interpretation' (Williams, 1983: 15).[1]

There are, however, a number of other words that paved the way for 'cyborg' and its particular 'hybrid' mode of reimaging the human body under the sign of the machine. These words, some of which have existed for decades, others for a number of centuries, include 'automaton', 'automation' and 'automatic', 'android' and 'robot'; while others like 'bionic' appeared at about the same time cyborg was coined.

Lately, we have been introduced to another word, *cyberspace*, also known as 'virtual reality', which has also begun to circulate in popular and academic discourses on the future of the human body, often in the company of the word 'cyborg' or its images. Whether in the guise of 'cyberspace', a word first coined by William Gibson in his award winning science fiction novel *Neuromancer* (1984), or in the form of 'virtual reality', the idea of a new computer-based digital mode of articulating and, indeed, of reimaging the human body has been explored in novels, including Gibson's own *Count Zero* (1986) and *Mona Lisa Overdrive* (1988), films (such as *Brainstorm* [1983] and *The Lawnmower Man* [1992]), as well as in a host of academic and popular texts.[2]

It is not hard to imagine, therefore, that words such as 'automaton', 'automation', 'automatic', 'android', 'robot', 'bionic', 'cyborg' and 'cyberspace' might constitute a Williamsian *cluster* of keywords inasmuch as they form a 'set of . . . interrelated words and references' (1983: 22) that plot ever-changing thresholds in the history of the human body. With the appearance of each new word, a new threshold is crossed in the perception and social construction of the human body, between conceptions of the organic and inorganic, the body and technology, the human and non-human; and, indeed, of machines themselves insofar as they can also '*be considered as organs of the human species*' (Canguilhem, 1992: 55, emphasis in the original).

There are two principal ways to explore the most recent cyborg and virtual reality thresholds in the history of the body/machine interface. The first is through the word *cybernetics*. Although it was not a new word when it was introduced in 1947, 'cybernetics' was considered to be a neologism that best described a new interdisciplinary science of control and communication. Reconceptualization can, in this case, be traced through the reasons given for the choice of this particular word, its attributed meanings and, finally, its evocative powers as an analogical tool.

The second way to explore the human body's reconceptualization is to trace cybernetics' subsequent history and, in particular, its impact on how researchers reimaged the human/machine interface in the early 1960s when the word 'cyborg' was coined. From there, one can trace the reverberations of cybernetics' initial impact as *word* and 'universal' discipline (Bowker, 1993) to the mid-to-late 1980s and Haraway's socialist-feminist oppositional cyborg. Finally, there is the question of virtual reality technology or cyberspace, which must be addressed, however briefly, since it represents the potential site and, as such, the promise, as most recent and perhaps quintessential of cyborg interfaces, for new or more developed kinds of human organism/machine system interactions.[3]

Identity into Pattern: Norbert Wiener, Cybernetics and the 20th-century Automaton

Norbert Wiener, a founding figure of the science of cybernetics, provides a useful overview of different phases in the development of automata. His periodization is of interest because of its focus on shifts in motive force and the way that these shifts are related to a parallel history of the body. In his classic 1948 manifesto on a new science of cybernetics, *Cybernetics: or Control and Communication in the Animal and the Machine*, Wiener presented a history of automata that was divided into four stages: a mythic Golemic age; the age of clocks (17th and 18th centuries); the age of steam, originator of the governor mechanism itself (late 18th and 19th centuries); and, finally, the age of communication and control, an age marked by a shift from power engineering to communication engineering, from, in other words, an 'economy of energy' to an economy rooted in 'the accurate reproduction of a signal' (Wiener, 1948a: 51, 50).

Wiener noted, on the other hand, that these stages generated four models of the human body: the body as a malleable, magical, clay figure; the body as a clockwork mechanism; the body as a 'glorified heat engine, burning some combustible fuel instead of the glycogen of the human muscles'; and, most recently, the body as an electronic system (Wiener, 1948a: 51). Wiener's two-fold periodization is significant because it reveals an awareness, by one of the principal founders of cybernetics, of important disciplinary phases in a machine-based history of the western body. It is also significant because it draws attention to *parallel phases* in the body's functional reimaging as a fundamental element in a machine culture.

While the 19th century was characterized by an *engineered* body, a body considered 'to be a branch of power engineering', a model whose influence had extended well into the 20th century, Wiener argued (1948b: 15) 'we are now coming to realize that the body is very far from a conservative system, and that the power available to it is much less limited than was formerly believed'. In place of a 19th-century model, he suggested that

we are beginning to see that such important elements as the neurones – the units of the nervous complex of our bodies – do their work under much the same conditions as vacuum tubes, their relatively small power being supplied from outside by the body's circulation, and that the bookkeeping which is most essential to describe their function is not one of energy. (1948b: 15)

In its place, cybernetics proposed that the body be conceived as a communications network whose successful operation was based on 'the accurate reproduction of a signal' (1948b: 15).

For Wiener, writing in the late 1940s, the 'newer study of automata, whether in metal or in the flesh, [was] a branch of communication engineering, and its cardinal notions [were] those of message, amount of disturbance or ≪noise≫ . . . quantity of information, coding technique, and so on' (1948a: 54). He went on to argue, 'in such a theory, we deal with automata effectively coupled to the external world, not merely by their energy flow, their metabolism, but also by a flow of impressions, of incoming messages, and of the actions of outgoing messages' (1948a: 54). This new way of conceiving of automata was, in theory and practice, coupled to a new kind of feedback mechanism: the servomechanism.[4] Wiener went so far as to argue that 'the present age is as truly the age of servo-mechanisms as the nineteenth century was the age of the steam engine or the eighteenth century the age of the clock' (Wiener 1948a: 55).

The difference between servomechanisms and earlier forms of clockwork-based automata, or even systems of automatic machinery which were governed by a steam engine's governor, did not reside in their fundamental operational logic (since the earlier automata were also governed by a feedback-based logic) but rather in their ability to penetrate, through a wide variety of forms, the *social* as opposed to the industrial fabric of a nation.[5] Instead of being limited to clockwork mechanisms or prime movers such as steam engines, the new servomechanisms were designed for a wide range of applications. These included 'thermostats, automatic gyro-compass ship-steering systems, self-propelled missiles – especially such as seek their target – anti-aircraft fire-control systems, automatically controlled oil-cracking stills, ultra-rapid computing machines, and the like' (1948a: 55). Although Wiener conceded that 'they had begun to be used long before the war – indeed, the very old steam-engine governor belongs among them', he nevertheless pointed out that 'the great mechanization of the second world war brought them into their own; and', he prophesied, 'the need of handling the extremely dangerous energy of the atom will probably bring them to a still higher point of development' (1948a: 55). Thus, what feedback and other inventions such as the vacuum tube 'made possible [was] not the sporadic design of individual automatic mechanisms, but a general policy for the construction of automatic mechanisms of the most varied type'. Wiener went on to argue that such developments, in conjunction with a 'new theoretical treatment of communication, which takes full cognizance of the possibilities of communication between the machine and machine . . . now renders possible the new automatic age' (Wiener, 1954: 153).

As Wiener pointed out, the new study of automata was emerging in tandem with a new science of communications and control – Cybernetics – a science that proposed a completely new vision of the human body, its relationship to the organic world and the world of machines. A new set of analogies was not only establishing connections, through a series of formal correspondences, between the human body conceived as a nervous system and the machine conceived as a communicating organism, but it was also mapping out the means for the automatic linking of machine to machine by way of a common communications language.

As usual, Wiener gives us a good picture of the power and austere elegance of cybernetics' logic of analogies and its new brand of anthropomorphism when he argued:

> While it is impossible to make any universal statements concerning life-imitating automata in a field which is growing as rapidly as that of automatization, there are some general features of these machines as they actually exist that I should like to emphasize. One is that they are machines to perform some definite-task or tasks, and therefore must possess effector organs (analogous to arms and legs in human beings) with which such tasks can be performed. The second point is that they must be *en rapport* with the outer world by sense organs, such as photoelectric cells and thermometers, which not only tell them what the existing circumstances are, but enable them to record the performance or nonperformance of their own tasks. This last function . . . is called *feedback*, the property of being able to adjust future conduct by past performance. Feedback may be as simple as that of the common reflex, or it may be a higher order feedback, in which past experience is used not only to regulate specific movements, but also whole policies of behavior. Such a policy-feedback may, and often does, appear to be what we know under one aspect as a conditioned reflex, and under another as learning.
>
> For all these forms of behavior, and particularly for the more complicated ones, we must have the central decision organs which determine what the machine is to do next on the basis of information fed back to it, which it stores by means analogous to the memory of a living organism. (Wiener, 1954: 32–3)

Wiener's cybernetic automaton was conceived as an active, hierarchically governed, self-regulated and goal-oriented machine, which was bound through a particular time/space logic – the adjustment of future conduct through a comparative assessment of past actions – to its environment. This automaton marked a new threshold of intelligence, which extended beyond that which had been previously established on the basis of automated, factory based machine systems.

The particular power of cybernetics' analogical logic resided in the fact that it was able to redefine the concept of 'life' itself in order to bring it in line with a *cybernetic automaton's* operational characteristics. As Wiener noted in its connection: 'now that certain analogies of behavior are being observed between the machine and the living organism, the problem as to whether the machine is alive or not is, for our purposes, semantic and we are at liberty to answer it one way or another as best suits our convenience' (1954: 32).

> If we wish to use the word 'life' to cover all phenomena which locally swim upstream against the current of increasing entropy, we are at liberty to do so. However, we shall then include many astronomical phenomena which have only the shadiest resemblance to life as we ordinarily know it. (Wiener, 1954: 32)

Instead, Wiener championed a different and far more radical point of view when he argued that it was

> best to avoid all question-begging epithets such as 'life', 'soul', 'vitalism', and the like, and say merely in connection with machines that there is no reason why they may not resemble human beings in representing pockets of decreasing entropy in a framework in which the large entropy tends to increase. (1954: 32)

The claim to have side-stepped the thorny issue of 'life' went well beyond the abstract level at which it was proposed. It implied a new systemic model for the structure of organisms that was in keeping with a demise, in the 20th century, of a simple mechanistic or taxanomic view of plant or animal organization. In their place, an organism was conceived as 'a multilevel system of elaborate complexity, buffered in several dimensions so as to maintain its metabolic stability in the face of changes in its environment, and equipped with a repertoire of behaviours to ensure necessary intake of energy, materials, etc.' (Pratt, 1987: 180). In other words, an organism was now conceived as if structured according to 'sophisticated systems of control' with its brain serving as a 'top-level co-ordinator' (Pratt, 1987: 180).

The model of an organism structured according to a nest of control mechanisms was also embraced by cyberneticians (Pratt, 1987: 190, 194–6). In fact, one might argue that cybernetics operationalized the question of 'life' by displacing the concept of organism from biology to engineering, thus effectively transforming it into a hardware problem. According to its new existential parameters, Wiener's cybernetic automaton was 'organic' and 'alive' precisely because it was *operationally* active, that is, it was 'effectively coupled to the external world, not merely by [its] energy flow, [its] metabolism, but also by a flow of impressions, of incoming messages, and of the actions of outgoing messages'. A logic of cybernetic analogies ensured, in other words, that functional equivalence was established at the level of the sense-organs (Wiener, 1948a: 54), since these were the principal means by which an organism could maintain a stable, that is systemic, existence in a given environment through an exchange of information.

Yet another way of grasping the cybernetic automaton's organic nature was through the common temporality that it shared with the world of 'living' organisms. After noting that 'the relation of these mechanisms [the new automata] to time demands careful study', Wiener pointed out:

> It is clear of course that the relation input–output is a consecutive one in time, and involves a definite past–future order. What is perhaps not so clear is that the theory of the sensitive automata

is a statistical one. We are scarcely ever interested in the performance of a communication-engineering machine for a single input. To function adequately it must give a satisfactory performance for a whole class of inputs, and this means a statistically satisfactory performance for the class of input which it is statistically expected to receive. Thus its theory belongs to the Gibbsian statistical mechanics rather than to the classical Newtonian mechanics. (Wiener, 1948a: 55)

It was on the basis of these observations that Wiener went on to argue that 'the modern automaton exists in the same sort of Bergsonian time as the living organism; and hence there is no reason in Bergson's considerations why the essential mode of functioning of the living organism should not be the same as that of the automaton of this type' (1948a: 56). As this argument suggests, it was no longer a question of machines functioning *as* organisms, or of organisms functioning *as* machines. Instead, the machine and organism were to be considered as two functionally equivalent states or stages of cybernetic organization.

Wiener's cybernetic automaton marks an important threshold in the history of the human body. By the late 1940s confusions arising from competing images of the human body as thinking organism were effectively exorcized through an anti-mimetic shift in the history of automata. Perhaps cybernetics' greatest achievement in this direction was to consummate the transformation which the Industrial Revolution had inaugurated in the case of automatic machinery. The cybernetic automaton's mirroring of the human body was not established on the basis of conventional mimicry, as in the case of androids and their internal parts, so much as on a common understanding of the similarities that existed between the control mechanisms and communicational organizations of machine systems and living organisms. As a result, the principle of cybernetic embodiment extended well beyond prime movers and factories to infiltrate into the sinews of the most humble piece of technology which could accommodate a servomechanism.

Previously, mimetic automata had provided visually based mechanical models for reflection on the nature of the human organism and its social, political and cultural identities. With the appearance of the cybernetic automaton, the socio-logic of human identity was transformed into an abstract product of cybernetic organization. In the case of Čapek's pre-cybernetic 1920s robots, for example, identity was ultimately predicated on traditional categories for the representation of difference in the products of social and industrial organizations, categories such as factory marks, color and language. In short, it was a question of National & Ethnic Robots (Čapek and Čapek, 1961: 57). Cybernetics, on the other hand, proposed a radically different solution to the fundamental nature of the human organism by proposing that its Being be reduced to an organizational *pattern*[6] whose operational logic was also coextensive with other organisms and types of machine systems. As Wiener emphasized at the beginning of his penultimate chapter on 'Organization as the Message' in *The Human Use of Human Beings*:

> The metaphor to which I devote this chapter is one in which the organism is seen as message. Organism is opposed to chaos, to disintegration, to death, as message is to noise. To describe an organism, we do not try to specify each molecule in it, and catalogue it bit by bit, but rather to answer certain questions about it which reveal its pattern: a pattern which is more significant and less probable as the organism becomes, so to speak, more fully an organism. (Wiener, 1954:95)

Machine and human organism exhibited the signs of life insofar as each managed to increase their level of organization. The process of functional equivalence or analogy would know no bounds since it too was defined in terms of an abstraction: organization (based on feedback) and pattern (a consequence of negentropy). By the early 1960s, the influence of this cybernetic model would reach mystic proportions in Marshall McLuhan's writings when he proposed that a 'current translation of our entire lives into the spiritual form of information' might 'make of the entire globe, and of the human family, a single consciousness' (McLuhan, 1964:67). As an introductory text on cybernetics would later claim: 'Feedback is Universal' (Porter, 1969:8).

Cybernetics: A Word to Bind Space and Time, a Word to Render Equivalent Living Organisms and Machine Systems

Communications theory provides one answer to the question of how words bind space and time in the service of new conceptions of the human and the human body. It does so inasmuch as it suggests that human organisms, but also human organisms and machine systems, are bound together through an exchange of 'signals in *time*, such as speech or music; and . . . signals in *space*, like print, stone inscriptions, punched cards, and pictures' (Cherry, 1980:125; emphases in the original). But words, written and spoken, can bind time and space, human bodies and machines in other ways. They can, for example, bind bodies and machines by way of etymologically-based feedback loops that govern present and future actions according to a past set of meanings (i.e. a given field of learning). Hence words can serve, from this viewpoint, as media for instituting a history which is etymologically operationalized in a present, in a given physical (i.e. spatial) context. In fact, the word 'cybernetics' provides a good example of how words can function as feedback mechanisms and, moreover, how words might serve as powerful passageways between radically different images of the human organism.

The word 'cybernetics' was coined in 1947 to describe a new science that united communications theory, control theory and statistical mechanics under the auspices of a clear set of disciplinary objectives. Its myth of origins was presented in a famous passage in *Cybernetics: or Control and Communication in the Animal and Machine*:

> Thus as far back as four years ago [1943], the group of scientists about Dr. Rosenblueth and myself had already become aware of the essential unity of the set of problems centering about communication, control, and statistical mechanics, whether in the machine or in living tissue. On the other hand, we were seriously hampered by the lack of unity of the literature concerning these problems, and by the absence of any common terminology, or even of a single name for the field. After much consideration, we have come to the conclusion that all the existing terminology has too heavy a bias to one side or another to serve the future development of the field as well as it should: and as happens so often to scientists, we have been forced to coin at least one artificial neo-Greek expression to fill the gap. We have decided to call the entire field of control and communication theory, whether in the machine or in the animal, by the name *Cybernetics*, which we form from the Greek χυβερνήτης or *steersman*. In choosing this term, we wish to recognize that the first significant paper on feed-back mechanisms is an article on governors, which was published by Clerk Maxwell in 1868, and that *governor* is derived from a Latin corruption of χυβερνήτης. We also wish to refer to the fact that the steering engines of a ship are indeed one of the earliest and best developed forms of feed-back mechanisms. (Wiener, 1948a: 19; emphases in the original)

While Wiener acknowledged that 'the term *cybernetics* does not date further back than the summer of 1947', he argued that 'we shall find it convenient to use in referring to earlier epochs of the development of the field' (1948a: 19).[7]

Wiener presented the raison d'être of a new universal science, in this celebrated passage, a science whose *inter*disciplinary coherence resided in its ability to bind different fields of knowledge associated with machine systems and living organisms according to a shared textual frame (a common body of texts); a uniform terminological frame of reference; and, finally, a unique *name* that could be used to unify the field in terms of a single genealogy (Maxwell) and metaphor (the feedback mechanism and its readily accessible image of the steersman). One notes, furthermore, that 'cybernetics' and the new interdisciplinary science to which it referred were considered to be modern western creations both in terms of their founding figures (whether Maxwell or Wiener and his colleagues) and their common New World frame of reference (North America), if not in its subsequent influence.[8]

As Wiener clearly acknowledged, the choice of the word 'cybernetics' was the result of a carefully orchestrated etymological exercise. It was not surprising, therefore, that the word embodied a coherent notion of space and time, knowledge and disciplinary identity, for it encompassed a past history of feedback mechanisms, rendered coherent a given set of problems and interrelationships, and projected a future path of development under the auspices of a phantom steersman. The progressive unfolding of this path, and moreover of society (insofar as it too was conceived as a cybernetic organism),[9] was guaranteed by its *own* root metaphor (the feedback mechanism) and its ability to 'adjust future conduct by past performance' (Wiener, 1954: 33). But words can also operate in a different register beyond a particular threshold of comprehension and control. They can function as perceptual thresholds insofar as they unlock and reveal a whole parallel world which gives sense to their roles and functions *of binding space and time*. In the case of cybernetics, this other world was created in a two-fold manner.

In the first place, 'cybernetics' ascribed meaning and etymology could function as both map and vehicle to reproduce and propagate a new interdisciplinary science's universalist world-view. Twenty years after the publication of *Cybernetics: or Control and Communication in the Animal and the Machine*, one finds, for example, on the contents page of a 1968 special issue of *Studio International* devoted to the exhibition 'Cybernetic Serendipity' at the Institute of Contemporary Arts, London, a simple and elegant definition of Wiener's interdisciplinary science: Cybernetic – 'adj. of cybernetics – a science of control and communication in complex electronic machines like computers and the human nervous system'. It was a definition which, as was later acknowledged (p. 9), was derived from the subtitle to Wiener's first book on cybernetics.

Both word and definition served as introductions to a new kind of interdisciplinary technology-based artistic practice whose all-encompassing powers of vision and creation were displayed for all to see in an exhibition and catalogue, the culminations of a three-year project which encompassed 'computers, cybernetics, electronics, music, art, poetry, machines, as well as the problem of how to present this hybrid mixture'. The project also chronicled the effects of opening the domain of art to other practices and practitioners such as those of the 'engineer, mathematician, or architect' whose products were no longer distinguishable on individual disciplinary grounds (Reichardt, 1968a: 5). 'Cybernetic Serendipity' was, as such, a worthy offspring of a cybernetic world-view.

However, the definition can also be viewed as functioning from a slightly different perspective. If the exhibition and its catalogue succeeded in their attempts to 'present an area of activity which manifests artists' involvement with science, and the scientists' involvement with the arts', and if they succeeded in showing 'the links between the random systems employed by artists, composers and poets, and those involved with the making and the use of cybernetic devices' (Reichardt, 1968a: 5), then they did so under the auspices of a definition which was resolutely binary in its spatial and temporal logics. Not only were control *and* communication linked to computers *and* the human nervous systems according to a doubly articulated binary logic, but the set of relationships was presented in a form that mirrored, in a universalist and transhistorical manner, the articulated point of view first presented in the subtitle of Wiener's 1948 book on cybernetics: Control *and* Communication in the Animal *and* the Machine (my emphases). In other words, while the definition bound together the separate spaces of computer and human nervous system, it also bound a 1968 British art exhibition to a 1948 founding text on cybernetics in a manner that suggests the presence of a ghostly feedback loop – and this in spite of conceptual transformations produced by cybernetics' migration across geographical boundaries.[10] Thus Wienerian cybernetics' authoritative presence as a 'text' of origins and universal blueprint in the context of an important British art exhibition, points to its ongoing powers to unlock, as if by magic (but, in fact, according to a logic of feedback), a set of passageways between disciplinary domains, machine and biological systems, and, perhaps most significantly, consciousness and creativity.

The second way that a word might reveal a whole parallel world which can give sense to its role and function of binding space and time is through an interconnected series of analogies and metaphors *which are authorized in its name*. In this case, the word operates at a distance, so to speak, as in the case of Wiener's metaphor of the organism as message (1954: 95), or his exploration of the functional analogy between 'automatic machines and ... the human nervous system' (1948b: 14), which were authorized by a founding name and the conceptual domain and interdisciplinary practice to which it referred. Inasmuch as cybernetics was conceived as an interdisciplinary practice which linked a past (Maxwell) to a future articulated through the fictive actions of a steersman (Wiener's phantom double?), whose operating logic was that of a feedback mechanism, and insofar as cybernetics linked systems of control *and* communications in animals *and* machines according to the same logic and practice, it set the stage for an exceptionally powerful process of remapping and reimaging the boundaries of the human body.

A series of correspondences, analogies and metaphors were used to bridge different domains of knowledge according to a new universal world-view or a 'new economy of the sciences' whose apex was no longer to be found, as in the past, in physics (Bowker, 1993; 117, 118–19).[11] New terms of reference such as feedback, message and noise functioned to reduce heterogeneous fields such as telephone engineering and the body's nervous system, the analogue computer and the human brain to a common viewpoint originating in control and communications theory and their engineering practices. As one commentator later noted: 'the ideas of feedback and information provide a frame of reference for viewing a wide range of situations, just as do the ideas of evolution, of relativism, of axiomatic method, and of operationalism' (Simon, 1981: 194). Indeed, the explosion of cyborg or human/machine images in recent American science fiction films is testimony to the continued influence of a cybernetic model, albeit a looser and more speculative *visual* model, on patterns of human development.[12]

On the other hand, there was no obvious guarantee that the adoption of a given metaphor or analogy would automatically lead to a revolution in human thought and perception. If feedback and information could provide a common frame of reference, then this correspondence might have been achieved through a radical and ultimately damaging simplification of existing complexities. As Herbert A. Simon has pointed out, 'metaphor and analogy can be helpful, or they can be misleading. All depends on whether the similarities the metaphor captures are significant or superficial' (Simon, 1981: 193). Moreover, Colin Cherry, another leading figure in the field of communications theory, has suggested, in his critique of the brain/computer analogy and similar kinds of analogies (Cherry, 1980: 301–4), that the fruitful use of analogies is also determined by an appropriate focus and threshold of visionalization. An analogy or metaphor that is pushed too far could prove to be as damaging as a false or superficial analogy.

Indeed, the ultimate success of cybernetics' analogical system was based on the point of view adopted in regard to mechanical structure. Cherry has argued, for example, that 'early invention was greatly hampered by [an] inability to disassociate mechanical structure from animal form' (Cherry, 1980: 59). Thus, in the case of the brain, 'it is not the machine which is mechanistically analogous to the brain but rather the *operation* of the machine plus the instructions fed into it' (Cherry, 1980: 57; emphasis in the original). What was at issue, as Cherry noted with approval in connection with Wiener's use of analogical thought, was a *fundamental* distinction between mimetic and functional analogies (Cherry, 1980: 57, 58) – a distinction which had been sharpened when the 'newer study of automata' had been reduced to a 'branch of communications engineering' (Wiener, 1948b: 15). Thus Cherry's objections to popular extensions of the brain/computer analogy (with their propensity to encourage 'animistic' models), and his charges that they obscured and simplified the working of the brain (to the extent of generating pseudo-questions such as 'Can a machine think?' [Cherry, 1980: 246]), was the product of a particular disciplinary perspective which sought to cleanse scientific practice of anthropomorphic residues.

The binding powers of metaphors and analogies could, as these criticisms suggest, work in both directions. They could create fields for investigation or they could just as easily curb investigation through seduction, the spells cast by simple, clear and elegant images or relationships, as in the case of the computer as mind/mind as computer analogy.

By opening up a whole range of investigations under its semantic auspices, cybernetics not only functioned as a keyword in Williams's sense of the term, but it also served as a powerful feedback-based chronotope[13] that could operate between the human body and world of machines. The traffic of ideas across this chronotopic interface was facilitated by the use of a cluster of technical words that mapped an architecture of communication within, across and between the worlds of machines and living organisms. For example, if homeostasis regulated an inner cybernetic environment, then feedback regulated the relationship between 'inner' and 'outer' environments (Simon, 1981: 9) according to information which was itself conceived as simply 'a name for the content of what is exchanged with the outer world as we adjust to it, and make our adjustment felt upon it' (Wiener, 1954: 17).

Thus, if, as Weiner observed, 'where a man's word goes, and where his power of perception goes, to that point his control and in a sense his physical existence is extended' (Wiener, 1954: 97), then the word 'cybernetics' not only extended Wiener's presence as (co-)founder of this new field but, more importantly, it extended a temporal logic (through the principle of feedback) as well as a system of analogies across the many disciplines which absorbed cybernetics' name as a prerequisite for access to its vocabulary and methodology. In this sense, as one historian has recently pointed out (Bowker, 1993: 122), 'cybernetics could operate either as the primary discipline, directing others on their search for truth, or as a discipline providing analytic tools indispensable to the development and progress of others'.

Moreover, as cybernetics extended its powers over diverse fields or adherents, it extended its temporal hold over them in such a way as to bind them according to a common perceptual space, since perception was, in cybernetic terms, simply a medium for the regulation of active feedback,[14] and the principle of feedback was what allowed cybernetics as a discipline to survive in the world of ideas. Thus, in a specific Williamsian sense, the word 'cybernetics' encapsulated the special transformations it was created to describe; and, of course, included among these was a new model of the human organism and its identity.

From Cybernetic Automaton to Cyborg: Shifting Thresholds in the Human/ Machine Interface

Wiener would state, as the opening sentence in a 1948 *Scientific American* article, that 'cybernetics is a word invented to define a new field in science' (1948b: 14). His optimism was based, as we have seen, on this field's potential range and depth of interpretation. For the word and field to which it referred was designed to encompass the human mind, the human body and the world of automatic machines and reduced all three to a common denominator: 'control and communication' (1948b: 14).

As we have also seen, the root metaphor for this enterprise was the feedback mechanism, a mechanism, moreover, which 'governed' the traffic in ideas between the domain of communications theory, with its concrete parallel world of mechanical or electronic switches and circuits, the human body's neural pathways and, ultimately, its brain. In short, cybernetics theory and its system of analogies was in a position to inject a new type of engineering language into the living human body's nervous system, a language that could pave the way for the human body's reimaging in relation to a history of automata.

It was the concept of feedback, in particular, that provided the means for a more extended process of reimaging since it opened the way for the electrical and, ultimately, the electronic *collectivization* of the human body – a collectivization that would reach planetary proportions in McLuhan's metaphor of a global village and its information-based consciousness. Access to this extended model of a cybernetic body was guaranteed by the 'ubiquity of feedback' – an ubiquity that signified that 'interaction [was] everywhere'. For it was this kind of ubiquity that could inaugurate a shift of 'attention away from an individualism that had highlighted [a] noncircular cause-and-effect [world-view] and from the individual person – as if he or she could be independent of others and even independent of chance events occurring in the environment' (Heims, 1993: 271–2). Translated into McLuhanesque terms, feedback was a privileged gateway to a collective electrically-based global consciousness (McLuhan, 1964: 64, 311), not only because it erased the distinction between automated machines and living organisms, but also because it marked, from a communications point of view, 'the end of the lineality that came into the Western world with the alphabet and the continuous forms of Euclidean space' (McLuhan, 1964: 307). It was on the basis of such a logic and world-view that cybernetics and its attendant vocabulary could disseminate the image of a new kind of body to a wider disciplinary field and, further, to a non-specialized general public.

In fact, it was a short step from invoking a functional analogy between machine and human organism in the 1940s to the 1960s and Marshall McLuhan's influential notion of a technology that functioned as 'an extension or self-amputation of our physical bodies', a technology that produced 'new ratios or equilibriums among the other organs and extensions of the body' (McLuhan, 1964: 54). Since they were clearly based on a cybernetic model, McLuhan's ideas were a belated acknowledgement of the fact that the human body had already been irrevocably transformed in the context of cybernetics. Even McLuhan's evocation of an extended nervous system (1964: 64) retains a metaphoric resonance which is lacking in the cybernetic concept of organism as 'local enclave in the general stream of increasing entropy' (Wiener, 1954: 95). Hence, it is no wonder that by the time these ideas had reached a wider public through McLuhan's writings, consciousness had long since taken the radical form of a ratio between the senses (McLuhan, 1964: 67). Wiener's first book, *Cybernetic: or Control and Communication in the*

Animal and the Machine, had been published in 1948, and his popular account of cybernetics, *The Human Use of Human Being*, in 1950. These books had already proposed to a general public that the human body be radically reimaged, its identity to become an organizational singularity and its intelligence simply a pattern among many such patterns.

In 1962, two years before the publication of *Understanding Media*, McLuhan's influential introduction to the post-war world of Western media, and 14 years after the introduction of the word 'cybernetics', two American scientists introduced an important corruption of that word. They did so in order to identify a new kind of human/machine interface, a new type of 'organism'. Since that time, this organism has had a powerful hold on the way the body is imaged, imagined and constructed at the outer limits of western science, technology and industry, as well as at the outer limits of its military and aerospace industries. This hold has even extended to university-based as well as non-university-based intellectual and artistic speculations on the future of the human body. Moreover, this organism's fundamental impact on the construction of a Western Imaginary can, one suspects, be traced to the fact that it reintroduces mimesis in the shape of anthropomorphism back into the history of automata.

The neologism 'cyborg' (from cybernetic organism) was proposed by Manfred E. Clynes and Nathan S. Kline in 1960 to describe 'self-regulating man–machine systems' and in particular an 'exogenously extended organizational complex functioning as an integrated homeostatic system unconsciously' (Clynes and Kline, 1960:27). The technical density of the definition was a function of its proposed sphere of operations: the application of cybernetic controls theory to the problems of space travel as they impinged on the neurophysiology of the human body. In fact, a special kind of 'artifact organism' – the cyborg – was posited as a solution to the question of 'the altering of bodily functions to suit different environments' (Clynes and Kline, 1960:26). For these researchers, alteration of the body's ecology was to be effected primarily by way of sophisticated instrumental control systems and pharmaceuticals. Thus, 'the purpose of the Cyborg, as well as his own homeostatic systems' was, according to these early pioneers, 'to provide an organizational system in which such robot-like problems [as the body's "autonomous homeostatic controls"] are taken care of automatically and unconsciously, leaving man free to explore, to create, to think, and to feel' (Clynes and Kline, 1960:27). And as the references to 'his' and 'man' indicate, this problematic was gender specific.

In its most extreme form, Wiener's cybernetic organism could take the form of pure information – 'human information' (Wiener, 1954:104) – nothing more than a given 'pattern maintained by . . . homeostasis, which [was] the touchstone of [a] personal identity' to be transmitted as a message because it was in the first place a message (1954: 96). In contrast, the Clynes/Kline cyborg represented a different, more immediate and practical solution to the one that was envisioned by the early cyberneticians inasmuch as it was designed to withstand the rigors of space travel, while nevertheless adopting cybernetics' fundamental principles, in particular feedback and homeostasis.

Although initially designed for space travel, the transformative implications of this new type of cybernetic organism were far-reaching. As Clynes subsequently pointed out in a Foreword to *Cyborg – Evolution of the Superman*, a popular account of the cyborg phenomenon published by D.S. Halacy in 1965: 'a new frontier is opening which ... is not merely space, but more profoundly the relationship of "inner space" to "outer space" – a bridge being built between mind and matter, beginning in our time and extending into the future'. He went on to argue that the cyborg was more flexible than the human organism because it was not bound throughout a lifetime by heredity. Indeed, the cyborg was a reversible entity precisely because it was a 'man–machine combination' (Halacy, 1965: 7). This reversibility, combined with the fact that 'man-made devices' could 'be *incorporated* into the [human body's] regulatory feedback chains', produced a stage of evolution that was *participatory* (Halacy, 1965: 8). Hence, if automatic machines held the promise of another form of human intelligence, then cybernetics redefined that intelligence in such a way that the Clynes/Kline cyborg could become its most perfect embodiment: 'a new and ... better being' (Halacy, 1965: 8).

In 1985, 'cyborg' was appropriated, as a consequence of its polysemic resonances, by a socialist-feminist historian of biology, Donna Haraway. It was used in this case for a different social purpose, 'rhetorical strategy and ... political method' (Haraway, 1991: 149). For Haraway the cyborg was not only a 'hybrid of machine and organism', it was also a 'creature of social reality as well as a creature of fiction' (Haraway, 1991: 149). Within a new semantic context provided by socialist-feminist discourses on the gendered body, she argued that this word could function as 'a fiction mapping ... social and bodily reality and as an imaginative resource suggesting some very fruitful couplings' (Haraway, 1991: 150).

In contrast to the Clynes/Kline cyborg, which was conceived as a 'superman' capable of surviving hostile non-earth environments, Haraway's cyborg was a product of late-capitalist earth. In keeping with its traditional ecology, it was refashioned along the lines of an entity that could transgress earth-bound social/ symbolic boundaries between human and animal, animal–human (organism) and machine, and the physical and non-physical (Haraway, 1991: 151–3). Transgression was, moreover, negotiated (in keeping with its late 20th-century context) both in terms of science fiction and the everyday cultural worlds of postmodernism and post-colonial multinational capitalism.

Haraway's cyborg exhibited two other characteristics which distinguished it from the Clynes/Kline cyborg and more recent popular cyborg images, such as those presented in the *RoboCop* and *Terminator* series. As an offspring of *feminist* science fiction, Haraway's cyborg was conceived to be 'a creature in a post-gender world'; and inasmuch as it was conceived as a social and political mentor, it was pictured (in keeping with its 'illegitimate' origins) as 'oppositional, utopian, and completely without innocence' in the sense that it was 'resolutely committed to partiality, irony, intimacy, and perversity' (Haraway, 1991:150, 151). It was in these multiple senses that Haraway suggested that the cyborg could become 'our ontology' and that it could give 'us our politics' (Haraway, 1991:150). For its transgressive ontology and politics ensured that it was able to effectively circumvent, in spirit if not in name, its military/industrial origins (Haraway, 1991:150).

The immediate origins of the word 'cybernetics' can be traced, as Wiener suggested, to military research coupled with a specific post-war interdisciplinary university-based research programme (Heims, 1993; Bowker, 1993). 'Cyborg' exhibited a similar genealogy with, however, a different inflection since it was the hybrid product of the United States' space programme and a medical research laboratory (both Clynes and Kline were at the time [1960] researchers at Rockland State Hospital, Orangeburg, New York). On the other hand, Haraway's socialist-feminist cyborg was the joint creation of mid-1980s political activism and academic radicalism. The distinction between the two categories of cyborg can be traced to their authors' respective backgrounds. While the body's physiological ecology ('the body–environment problem' (Clynes and Kline, 1960:26) determined its early semantic field, Haraway's academic socialist-feminist background was the determining factor in her rearticulation of the cyborg's politics and gender.

Haraway's cyborg was, as such, a perfectly crafted image for a 1980s vision of a late 20th-century oppositional consciousness, especially since it embodied all of the contradictory characteristics of a decade which defined its cultural and political practices, in the context of radical academic theory, in terms of postmodernist and post-colonial criteria of partiality, hybridity, pastiche and playful irony. As one cultural theorist would later note in its connection, 'transgressed boundaries, in fact, define the cyborg, making it the consummate postmodern concept' – or, from a reverse perspective, 'uncertainty is a central characteristic of postmodernism and the essence of the cyborg' (Springer, 1991:306, 310). Indeed, as an oppositional cyborg's multiple articulations suggested, and as Clynes had already suggested in 1965, this most recent of reconceptualizations in the domain of automata was symptomatic of the body's uncertain future in the mid to late 20th century.

A hardware-based cyborg integrates or interfaces, in its most extreme and evocative form, a human body with a pure technological environment (machine elements, electronic components, advanced imaging systems). Clearly, under such circumstances technology becomes the determining factor in the definition of the body's physical rearticulation, the material foundations for its sense of performed identity. Although traditional domains of bodily differences such as those that are subsumed under the rubrics of ethnicity and gender are still operating in the case of popular cyborg imagery (Springer, 1991), one can imagine, as Haraway has done, that these differences might eventually be eclipsed by a technologically-based system of similarities and differences. Instead of describing this body primarily in terms of age, ethnicity or gender, or even in Haraway's hybrid post-ethnic or post-gendered terms, a more accurate description is perhaps to be obtained by treating a reimaged cyborg body as a *technological* entity whose definitive characteristics are to be plotted according to a system of technicity (Tomas, 1989). Such a system would not only have to take account of the plasticity of the cyborg's politics and identity, it would also have to account for its operating principles, such as those of speed, manoeuvrability and force, as well as its participatory logic, rooted as it is in a trinity of cybernetic adaptability: communication, information and feedback.

Postface: Virtual Reality and the Cyborg as Pure Data Construct

Wiener's evocation of the human body conceived as pure information brings to mind virtual reality technology with its promise of a common global digital space – a kind of second atmosphere, whether one models it after McLuhan's extended consciousness whose embodiment was to be found in the 'spiritual form of information' (1964:67), or William Gibson's often quoted definition of cyber-space: a 'consensual hallucination' experienced by 'billions' of computer operators (Gibson, 1984:51).

The bridge of cybernetics and its living organism-as-pure-information paradigm links the worlds of cyborgs and virtual reality. In doing so it also serves as a juncture that marks an important division or, more accurately, a branching in the history of automata. One path from this juncture leads into outer space, while the other route leads into a kind of meta-atmosphere composed of a pure digitalized electronic information. The human body is, in this latter context, reimaged and reimagined to be an inconsequential historical residue, a kind of chimera, or puppet (Walser, 1991), an *automatonic* image which is subject to almost infinite manipulation. Thus the 'basic job of cyberspace technology, besides simulating a world, is', as one researcher has noted, 'to supply a tight feedback loop between patron and puppet, to give the patron the illusion of being literally embodied by the puppet (i.e., the puppet gives the patron a virtual body, and the patron gives the puppet a personality)' (Walser, 1991: 35).

It is therefore not surprising, given the possibility for an almost perfectly transparent sense of manipulation, that 'the possibilities of virtual realities' are considered by some to be 'as limitless as the possibilities of reality' – a distinction and conjunction which is founded on this technology's potential power to provide a 'doorway to other worlds' which is based on a 'human interface that disappears' (Fisher, 1991: 109). As these comments and those on the role of feedback in binding a human patron and cybernetic puppet suggest, virtual reality is, in fact, a manifestation of a cybernetician's ultimate dream: a pure information space which can be populated by a host of pure cybernetic automatons or, in Gibson's more precise and less anthropomorphic terms, data constructs.

It is in the context of this seamless boundary between the body and technology that we now return to the figure of the automaton and note, as one researcher has recently pointed out, that:

> the craftsman of the last century shaping the motion of the elaborate clockwork characters by painstakingly filing cams is much like the programmer iterating toward an algorithm for animating computer graphic human motion, or defining plastic deformations of facial expression. (Lasko-Harvill, 1992: 226)

If the Clynes/Kline cyborg offered a participatory solution to the problem of survival in hostile environments, then it did so through a radical fusion of the human/machine interface as first proposed in the context of classical mimetic automata. The astronaut/cyborg and later science fiction models were and are conceived as post-Industrial Revolution androids that embody the power of prime movers coupled with sophisticated sensory and control systems. These hardware-based cyborgs exhibit android form, robot power and cybernetic intelligence and are designed to function in extremely hostile environments. At one point in *The Human Use of Human Beings*, for example, Wiener had suggested that 'we have modified our environment so radically that we must now modify ourselves in order to exist in this new environment' (1954: 46). In retrospect, it is easy to see that the Clynes/Kline cyborg was a hardware-based solution to this kind of problem. While the first cyborg was initially designed for space travel, modification and adaptation can take as many forms as are needed for the conquering and colonization of non- or anti-human environments. Indeed, Haraway's post-gendered oppositional cyborg suggests that such environments extend to the conflicting and hostile worlds of ideas.

Perhaps conquest provides the most appropriate frame of reference through which to view the cyborg's most recent computer-based transformations since its new form is the product of a special problem in human adaptation: namely, how to exist *in* an environment that consists of pure information. The answer is, as Wiener first pointed out, provided by cybernetics: one transforms the human organism into a pattern of pure digital information. Adaptation is, as a result, perfect and complete since organism and environment are conceived in similar terms.

This most extreme of all cybernetic visions, a final and radical solution to the problem of environmental mutations and ensuing adaptation, provides a kind of 'terminal' answer to the question of the direction of the human organism's 'evolution' in the late 20th century. Insofar as 'the interface between the user and the computer may be the last frontier in computer design' (Foley, 1987:127), then this interface may also be the last frontier in the design of human beings and, as such, the key to the diversity of cybernetic patterns that can colonize and populate virtual reality in the name of one of western modernity's root metaphors – the feedback mechanism – and in the name of one of its keywords: cybernetics.

Notes

This paper is part of book-length work that examines the relationships between the cyborg concept and late 20th-century imaging systems, including virtual reality. Its orientation is towards a critical investigation of current cultural practices and specifically oppositional practices in the arts. Earlier versions of this paper were presented at a conference on 'Body Images, Language & Physical Boundaries', University of Amsterdam, Amsterdam, in July 1993, and at the University of Windsor, Windsor, Ontario, in November 1993. A working version of this paper was published as a chapter in Murray (1994). I would like to thank all those who commented on the paper in its various versions.

    1. For an extended discussion of this practice see Williams (1983: 15, 22–5).

    2. A recent sampling would include the (Richards et al., 1991) collection of texts in *Bioapparatus*, Lasko-Harvill (1992), Balsamo (1992), Stone (1991, 1992). Balsamo (1993: 135 fn. 13) contains a list of recent publications in the popular press devoted to virtual reality.

    3. In this connection, I stress my use of the word 'promise', since at each stage exclusions are as important as inclusions in the ongoing construction of actual and possible histories.

    4. A servomechanism is a form of automatic feedback control system 'in which the motion of an output member . . . is constrained to follow closely the motion of an input member, and in which power amplification is incorporated' (Porter, 1969: 55).

    5. I deal with earlier forms of automata more fully in an earlier version of this paper (Tomas, 1994).

    6. 'It is the pattern maintained by this homeostasis, which is the touchstone of our personal identity' (Wiener, 1954: 96).

    7. Although the word had an earlier historical currency, since the word 'cybernétique' was used by the French physicist André-Marie Ampère in 1843 to denote a 'science of government' (Ampère, 1843: 140–1), Wiener's reintroduction of the term stands as the origin for its contemporary use.

    8. 'I am writing this book primarily for Americans in whose environment questions of information will be evaluated according to a standard American criterion: a thing is valuable as a commodity for what it will bring in the open market' (Wiener, 1954: 113).

    9. See also Wiener (1954: 26–7): 'It is my thesis that the physical functioning of the living individual

and the operation of some of the newer communications machines are precisely parallel in their analogous attempts to control entropy through feedback. Both of them have sensory receptors as one stage in their cycle of operation: that is, in both of them there exists a special apparatus for collecting information from the outer world at low energy levels, and for making it available in the operation of the individual or of the machine. In both cases these external messages are not taken *neat*, but through the internal transforming powers of the apparatus, whether it be alive or dead. The information is then turned into a new form available for the further stages of performance. In both the animal and the machine this performance is made to be effective on the outer world. In both of them, their *performed* action on the outer world, and not merely their *intended* action, is reported back to the central regulatory apparatus.' Wiener went on to note that not only is 'this complex of behavior . . . ignored by the average man . . . [but it] does not play the role that it should in our habitual analysis of society; for just as individual physical responses may be seen from this point of view, so may the organic responses of society itself'. Communication was thus conceived from a cybernetic point of view to be 'the cement which binds' society's 'fabric together'.

10. As Cherry has noted, for example, 'the word "cybernetics" is little used in Britain, but rather the term "control systems" is employed', while 'the French often use "la cybernétique" to correspond with "information theory" in Britain', which, in turn, 'is unfortunately used elsewhere synonymously with communication theory', the latter being sometimes referred to, in France, by the word 'cybernetics' (Cherry, 1980: 58, 217).

11. For a detailed discussion of the strategies underlying cybernetics' universalism see Bowker (1993). Bowker's excellent discussion does not, however, focus on the universalist semantics of the word 'cybernetics' itself. For a discussion of cybernetics, its cluster of metaphors and powers of synthesis see Heims (1993: 248–72).

12. Note in this connection the spectacular narrative consequences of the whole problematic of controlling the future in terms of a past which is itself the basis for an already existing future in the *Terminator* series.

13. In his celebrated essay 'Forms of Time and of the Chronotope in the Novel', Mikhail Bakhtin proposed that similar processes of time/space binding, in the case of the novel, be identified by the word *chronotope*. In his words, 'we will give the name *chronotope* (literally, 'time space') to the intrinsic connectedness of temporal and spatial relationships that are artistically expressed in literature' (Bakhtin, 1981: 84). While he noted that the chronotope existed in other areas of culture he did not pursue its investigation in these domains. Instead, he suggested that 'in the literary artistic chronotope, spatial and temporal indicators are fused into one carefully thought-out, concrete whole', and continued: 'Time, as it were, thickens, takes on flesh, becomes artistically visible; likewise, space becomes charged and responsive to the movements of time, plot and history' (1981: 84). While Bakhtin remained sensitive to the metaphoric uses of the mathematical concept of space–time in the case of literary chronotopes ('The special meaning it has in relativity theory is not important for our purposes; we are borrowing it for literary criticism almost as a metaphor (almost, but not entirely)' [1981: 84]), in the 1973 conclusion to his extensive study he argued for its extension well beyond literary boundaries and concluded: 'For us the following is important: whatever these meanings turn out to be, in order to enter our experience (which is social experience) they must take on the *form of a sign* that is audible and visible for us (a hieroglyph, a mathematical formula, a verbal or linguistic expression, a sketch, etc.). Without such temporal–spatial expression, even abstract thought is impossible. Consequently, every entry into the sphere of meanings is accomplished only through the gates of the chronotope' (1981: 258).

14. 'Th[e] control of a machine [or organism since these modes of organization were by analogy interchangeable terms] on the basis of its *actual* performance [feedback] . . . involves sensory members which are actuated by motor members and perform the function of *tell-tales* or *monitors* – that is, of elements which indicate a performance. It is the function of these mechanisms to control the mechanical tendency toward disorganization; in other words, to produce a temporary and local reversal of the normal direction of entropy' (Wiener, 1954: 24–5).

Bibliography

Ampère, André-Marie (1843) *Essai sur la Philosophie des Sciences, ou Exposition Analytique d'une Classification Naturelle de toutes les Connaissances Humaines*. Paris: Bachelier.
Bakhtin, M.M. (1981) 'Forms of Time and of the Chronotope in the Novel', pp. 84–258 in M. Holquist (ed.) *The Dialogic Imagination: Four Essays by M.M. Bakhtin*, trans. C. Emerson and M. Holquist. Austin: University of Texas Press.
Balsamo, Anne (1993) 'The Virtual Body in Cyberspace', *Research in Philosophy and Technology* 13: 119–39.
Bowker, Geof (1993) 'How to be Universal: Some Cybernetic Strategies, 1943–70', *Social Studies of Science* 23(1): 107–26.
Canguilhem, Georges (1992) 'Machine and Organism', pp. 45–69 in J. Crary and S. Kwinter (eds) *Incorporations*, Zone 6. New York: Zone.
Čapek, Karl and Josef Čapek (1961) *The Brothers Čapek: R.U.R. and The Insect Play*, trans. P. Selver. Oxford: Oxford University Press.
Cherry, Colin (1980) *On Human Communication: A Review, a Survey, and a Criticism*, 3rd edn. Cambridge, MA: MIT Press.
Clynes, Manfred E. and Nathan S. Kline (1960) 'Cyborgs and Space', *Astronautics* September: 26–7, 74–6.
Feher, Michel, Ramona Naddaff and Nadia Tazi (eds) (1989) *Fragments for a History of the Human Body*, Part 1. New York: Zone.
Fisher, Scott S. (1991) 'Virtual Environments: Personal Simulations and Telepresence', pp. 101–10 in S.K. Helsel and J.P. Roth (eds) *Virtual Reality: Theory, Practice, and Promise*. Westport, CT: Meckler.
Foley, James D. (1987) 'Interfaces for Advanced Computing', *Scientific American* 257(4): 126–35.
Gibson, William (1984) *Neuromancer*. New York: Ace Books.
Halacy, D.S. (1965) *Cyborg: Evolution of the Superman*. New York: Harper & Row.
Haraway, Donna (1991) 'A Cyborg Manifesto: Science, Technology, and Socialist-Feminism in the Late Twentieth Century', pp. 149–81 in *Simians, Cyborgs, and Women: The Reinvention of Nature*. New York: Routledge.
Heims, Steve Joshua (1993) *Constructing a Social Science for Postwar America: The Cybernetics Group, 1946–53*. Cambridge, MA: MIT Press.
Lasko-Harvill, Ann (1992) 'Identity and Mask in Virtual Reality', *Discourse* 14(2): 222–34.
McLuhan, Marshall (1964) *Understanding Media: The Extensions of Man*. New York: Mentor.
Porter, Arthur (1969) *Cybernetics Simplified*. London: The English Universities Press.
Pratt, Vernon (1987) *Thinking Machines: The Evolution of Artificial Intelligence*. Oxford: Basil Blackwell.
Reichardt, Jasia (1968a) 'Introduction', *Studio International*: 5–7.
Reichardt, Jasia (ed.) (1986b) 'Cybernetic Serendipity', *Studio International* Special Issue.
Richards, Catherine, Mary Ann Moser and Nell Tenhaff (eds) (1991) *Bioapparatus*. Banff: The Banff Centre for the Arts.
Simon, Herbert A. (1981) *The Science of the Artificial*, 2nd edn. Cambridge, MA: MIT Press.
Springer, Claudia (1991) 'The Pleasure of the Interface', *Screen* 32(3): 303–23.
Stone, Allucquère Roseanne (1991) 'Will the Real Body Please Stand Up?: Boundary Stories about Virtual Cultures', pp. 81–118 in M. Benedikt (ed.) *Cyberspace: First Steps*. Cambridge, MA: MIT Press.
Stone, Allucquère Roseanne (1992) 'Virtual Systems', pp. 609–21 in J. Crary and S. Kwinter (eds) *Incorporations*, Zone 6. New York: Zone.
Tomas, David (1989) 'The Technophilic Body: On Technicity in William Gibson's Cyborg Culture', *New Formations* 8: 113–29.
Tomas, David (1994) 'Cybernetics and Feedback: Reimaging the Body in the Age of the Cyborg', pp. 53–103 in J. Murray (ed.) *Technology and Culture*, Working Papers in the Humanities 2. Windsor: Humanities Research Group/University of Windsor.

Walser, Randal (1991) 'The Emerging Technology of Cyberspace', pp. 35–40 in S.K. Helsel and J.P. Roth (eds) *Virtual Reality: Theory, Practice, and Promise*. Westport, CT: Meckler.
Wiener, Norbert (1948a) *Cybernetics: or Control and Communication in the Animal and the Machine*. New York: John Wiley.
Wiener, Norbert (1948b) 'Cybernetics', *Scientific American* 179: 14–19.
Wiener, Norbert (1954) *The Human Use of Human Beings: Cybernetics and Society*, 2nd edn. New York: Doubleday Anchor.
Williams, Raymond (1983) *Keywords: A Vocabulary of Culture and Society*. London: Flamingo.

David Tomas teaches in the Department of Visual Arts at the University of Ottawa. His recent publications include 'Virtual Reality and the Politics of Place', *History and Anthropology* (1995); 'An Identity in Crisis: The Artist and New Technologies' (in J. Berland et al. [eds], *Theory Rules*, YYZ Books/University of Toronto Press, 1995); and 'Art, Psychasthenic Assimilation, and the Cybernetic Automaton' (in Chris Gray et al. [eds], *The Cyborg Handbook*, Routledge, 1995).

The Future Looms: Weaving Women and Cybernetics

SADIE PLANT

Beginning with a passage from a novel:

> The woman brushed aside her veil, with a swift gesture of habit, and Mallory caught his first proper glimpse of her face. She was Ada Byron, the daughter of the Prime Minister. Lady Byron, the Queen of Engines. (Gibson and Sterling, 1990: 89)

Ada was not really Ada Byron, but Ada Lovelace, and her father was never Prime Minister: these are the fictions of William Gibson and Bruce Sterling, whose book *The Difference Engine* sets its tale in a Victorian England in which the software she designed was already running; a country in which the Luddites were defeated, a poet was Prime Minister, and Ada Lovelace still bore her maiden name. And one still grander: Queen of Engines. Moreover she was still alive. Set in the mid-1850s, the novel takes her into a middle-age she never saw: the real Ada died in 1852 while she was still in her thirties. Ill for much of her life with unspecified disorders, she was eventually diagnosed as suffering from cancer of the womb, and she died after months of extraordinary pain.

Ada Lovelace, with whom the histories of computing and women's liberation are first directly woven together, is central to this paper. Not until a century after her death, however, did women and software make their respective and irrevocable entries on to the scene. After the military imperatives of the 1940s, neither would ever return to the simple service of man, beginning instead to organize, design and arouse themselves, and so acquiring unprecedented levels of autonomy. In later decades, both women and computers begin to escape the isolation they share in the home and office with the establishment of their own networks. These, in turn, begin to get in touch with each other in the 1990s. This convergence of woman and machine is one of the preoccupations of the cybernetic feminism endorsed here, a perspective which owes a good deal to the work of Luce Irigaray, who is also important to this discussion.

The computer emerges out of the history of weaving, the process so often said to be the quintessence of women's work. The loom is the vanguard site of software development. Indeed, it is from the loom, or rather the process of weaving, that this paper takes another cue. Perhaps it is an instance of this process as well, for tales and texts are woven as surely as threads and fabrics. This paper is a yarn in both senses. It is about weaving women and cybernetics, and is also weaving women and cybernetics together. It concerns the looms of the past, and also the future which looms over the patriarchal present and threatens the end of human history.

Ada Lovelace may have been the first encounter between woman and computer, but the association between women and software throws back into the mythical origins of history. For Freud, weaving imitates the concealment of the womb: the Greek hystera; the Latin matrix. Weaving is woman's compensation for the absence of the penis, the void, the woman of whom, as he famously insists, there is 'nothing to be seen'. Woman is veiled, as Ada was in the passage above; she weaves, as Irigaray comments, 'to sustain the disavowal of her sex'. Yet the development of the computer and the cybernetic machine as which it operates might even be described in terms of the introduction of increasing speed, miniaturization and complexity to the process of weaving. These are the tendencies which converge in the global webs of data and the nets of communication by which cyberspace, or the matrix, are understood.

Today, both woman and the computer screen the matrix, which also makes its appearance as the veils and screens on which its operations are displayed. This is the virtual reality which is also the absence of the penis and its power, but already more than the void. The matrix emerges as the processes of an abstract weaving which produces, or fabricates, what man knows as 'nature': his materials, the fabrics, the screens on which he projects his own identity.

* * *

As well as his screens, and as his screens, the computer also becomes the medium of man's communication. Ada Lovelace was herself a great communicator: often she wrote two letters a day, and was delighted by the prospect of the telegraph. She is, moreover, often remembered as Charles Babbage's voice, expressing his ideas with levels of clarity, efficiency and accuracy he could never have mustered himself.

When Babbage displayed his Difference Engine to the public in 1833, Ada was a debutante, invited to see the machine with her mother, Lady Byron, who had herself been known as the Princess of Parallelograms for her mathematical prowess. Lady Byron was full of admiration for the machine, and it is clear that she had a remarkable appreciation of the subtle enormities of Babbage's invention. 'We both went to see the *thinking* machine (for such it seems) last Monday', she wrote. 'It raised several Nos. to the 2nd & 3rd powers, and extracted the root of a quadratic Equation' (Moore, 1977:44).

Ada's own response was recorded by another woman, who wrote:

> While other visitors gazed at the working of the beautiful instrument with a sort of expression, and dare I say the same sort of feeling, that some savages are said to have shown on first seeing a looking glass or hearing a gun. . . . Miss Byron, young as she was, understood its working, and saw the great beauty of the invention. (Moore, 1977:44)

Ada had a passion for mathematics at an early age. She was admired and was greatly encouraged by Mary Somerville, herself a prominent figure in the scientific community and author of several scientific texts including the widely praised *Connection of the Physical Sciences*. Ada and Mary Somerville corresponded, talked together, and attended a series of lectures on Babbage's work at the Mechanics' Institute in 1835. Ada was fascinated by the engine, and wrote many letters to Babbage imploring him to take advantage of her brilliant mind. Eventually, and quite unsolicited, she translated a paper by Menabrea on Babbage's Analytic Engine, later adding her own notes at Babbage's suggestion. Babbage was enormously impressed with the translation, and Ada began to work with him on the development of the Analytical Engine.

Babbage had a tendency to flit between obsessions; a remarkably prolific explorer of the most fascinating questions of science and technology, he neverthe-less rarely managed to complete his studies; neither the Difference Engine nor the Analytical Engine were developed to his satisfaction. Ada, on the other hand, was determined to see things through; perhaps her commitment to Babbage's machines was greater than his own. Knowing that the Difference Engine had suffered for lack of funding, publicity and organization, she was convinced that the Analytical Engine would be better served by her own attentions. She was often annoyed by what she perceived as Babbage's sloppiness, and after an argument in 1843, she laid down several severe conditions for the continuation of their collaboration: 'can you', she asked, with undisguised impatience,

> undertake to give your mind *wholly and undividedly*, as a primary object that no engagement is to interfere with, to the consideration of all those matters in which I shall at times require your intellectual *assistance & supervision*; & can you promise not to *slur & hurry* things over; or to mislay & allow confusion & mistakes to enter into documents &c? (Moore, 1977:171)

Babbage signed this agreement, but in spite of Ada's conditions, ill health and financial crises conspired to prevent the completion of the machine.

Ada Lovelace herself worked with a mixture of coyness and confidence; attributes which often extended to terrible losses of self-esteem and megalomaniac delight in her own brilliance. Sometimes she was convinced of her own immortal genius as a mathematician; 'I hope to bequeath to future generations a *Calculus of the Nervous System*', she wrote in 1844. 'I am proceeding in a track quite peculiar & my own, I believe' (Moore, 1977: 216). At other times, she lost all confidence, and often wondered whether she should not have pursued her musical abilities, which were also fine. Ada was always trapped by the duty to be dutiful; caught in a cleft stick of duties, moral obligations she did not understand.

Ada's letters – and indeed her scientific writings – are full of suspicions of her own strange relation to humanity. Babbage called her his fairy, because of her dextrous mind and light presence, and this appealed to Ada's inherited romanticism. 'I deny the *Fairyism* to be entirely *imaginary*', she wrote: 'That *Brain* of mine is something more than merely *mortal*; as time will show; (if only my *breathing* & some other etceteras do not make too rapid a progress *towards* instead of from *mortality*)' (Moore, 1977: 98). When one of her thwarted admirers wrote to her: 'That you are a peculiar – *very peculiar* – specimen of the feminine race, you are yourself aware' (Moore, 1977: 202), he could only have been confirming an opinion she already – and rather admiringly – had of herself. Even of her own writing, she wrote: 'I am quite thunderstruck by the power of the writing. It is especially unlike a *woman's* style but neither can I compare it with any man's exactly' (Moore, 1977: 157). The words of neither a man nor a woman: who was Ada Lovelace? 'Before ten years are over', she wrote, 'the Devil's in it if I haven't sucked out some of the life blood from the mysteries of this universe, in a way that no purely mortal lips or brains could do' (Moore, 1977: 153).

Ada may have been Babbage's fairy, but she was not allowed to forget that she was also a wife, mother and victim of countless 'female disorders'. She had three children by the age of 24 of whom she later wrote: 'They are to me irksome *duties* & nothing more' (Moore, 1977: 229). Not until the 1840s did her own ill health lead her husband and mother to engage a tutor for the children, to whom she confided 'not only her present distaste for the company of her children but also her growing indifference to her husband, indeed to men in general' (Moore, 1977: 198). One admirer called her 'wayward, wandering . . . deluded', and as a teenager she was considered hysterical, hypochondriac and rather lacking in moral fibre. She certainly suffered extraordinary symptoms, walking with crutches until the age of 17, and often unable to move. Her illnesses gave her some room for manoeuvre in the oppressive atmosphere of her maternal home. Perhaps Ada even cherished the solitude and peculiarity of her diseases; she certainly found them of philosophical interest, once writing: 'Do you know it is to me quite delightful to have a frame so susceptible That it is an experimental laboratory always about me, & inseparable from me. I walk about, not in a Snail-Shell, but in a Molecular Laboratory' (Moore, 1977: 218).

Not until the 1850s was cancer diagnosed: Lady Byron had refused to accept such news, still preferring to believe in her daughter's hysteria. Even Ada tended to the fashionable belief that over-exertion of the intellect had led to her bodily disorders; in 1844, while she was nevertheless continuing chemical and electrical experiments, she wrote: '*Many causes* have contributed to produce the past derangements; & I shall in future avoid them. One ingredient, (but only one among many) has been *too much Mathematics*' (Moore, 1977: 153–4). She died in November 1852 after a year of agonized decline.

Ada Lovelace often described her strange intimacy with death; it was rather the constraints of life with which she had to struggle. 'I mean to do *what I mean to do*', she once wrote, but there is no doubt that Ada was horribly confined by the familiar – her marriage, her children and her indomitable mother conspired against her independence, and it was no wonder that she was so attracted to the unfamiliar expanses of mathematical worlds. Ada's marriage prompted the following words from her mother: 'Bid adieu to your old companion Ada Byron with all her peculiarities, caprices, and self-seeking; determined that as A.K. you will live for others' (Moore, 1977: 69). But she never did. Scorning public opinion, she gambled, took drugs and flirted to excess. But what she did best was computer programming.

Ada Lovelace immediately saw the profound significance of the Analytical Engine, and she went to great lengths to convey the remarkable extent of its capacities in her writing. Although the Analytical Engine had its own limits, it was nevertheless a machine vastly different from the Difference Engine. As Ada Lovelace observed:

> The Difference Engine can in reality ... do nothing but *add*; and any other processes, not excepting those of simple subtraction, multiplication and division, can be performed by it only just to that extent in which it is possible, by judicious mathematical arrangement and artifices, to reduce them to a *series of additions*. (Morrison and Morrison, 1961: 250)

With the Analytical Engine, Babbage set out to develop a machine capable not merely of adding, but performing the 'whole of arithmetic'. Such an undertaking required the mechanization not merely of each mathematical operation, but the systematic bases of their functioning, and it was this imperative to transcribe the rules of the game itself which made the Analytical Engine a universal machine. Babbage was a little more modest, describing the Engine as 'a machine of the most general nature' (Babbage, 1961: 56), but the underlying point remains: the Analytical Engine would not merely synthesize the data provided by its operator, as the Difference Engine had done, but would incarnate what Ada Lovelace described as the very '*science of operations*'.

The Difference Engine, Ada Lovelace wrote, 'is the embodying of *one particular and very limited set of operations*, which ... may be expressed thus (+, +, +, +, +, +), or thus 6(+). Six repetitions of the one operation, +, is, in fact, the whole sum and object of that engine' (Morrison and Morrison, 1961: 249). What impressed Ada Lovelace about the Analytical Engine was that, unlike the Difference Engine or any other machine, it was not merely able to perform certain functions, but was 'an *embodying of the science of operations*, constructed with peculiar reference to abstract number as the subject of those operations'. The Difference Engine could simply add up, whereas the Analytical Engine not only performed synthetic operations, but also embodied the analytic capacity on which these syntheses are based. 'If we compare together the powers and the principles of construction of the Difference and of the Analytic Engines', wrote Ada, 'we shall perceive that the capabilities of the latter are immeasurably more extensive than those of the former, and that they in fact hold to each other the same relationship as that of analysis to arithmetic' (Morrison and Morrison, 1961: 250). In her notes on Menabrea's paper, this is the point she stresses most: the Engine, she argues, is the very machinery of analysis, so that

> there is no finite line of demarcation which limits the powers of the Analytical Engine. These powers are co-extensive with our knowledge of the laws of analysis itself, and need be bounded only by our acquaintance with the latter. Indeed we may consider the engine as the *material and mechanical representative* of analysis. (Morrison and Morrison, 1961: 252)

The Difference Engine was '*founded on the principle of successive orders of differences*', while the

> distinctive characteristic of the Analytical Engine, and that which has rendered it possible to endow mechanism with such extensive faculties as bid fair to make this engine the executive right-hand of abstract algebra, is the introduction of the principle which Jacquard devised for regulating, by means for punched cards, the most complicated patterns in the fabrication of brocaded stuffs. (Morrison and Morrison, 1961: 252)

Indeed, Ada considered Jacquard's cards to be the crucial difference between the Difference Engine and the Analytical Engine. 'We may say most aptly', she continued, 'that the Analytical Engine *weaves Algebraical patterns*, just as the Jacquard loom weaves flowers and leaves. Here, it seems to us, resides much more of originality than the Difference Engine can be fairly entitled to claim' (Morrison and Morrison, 1961: 252). Ada's reference to the Jacquard loom is more than a metaphor: the Analytical Engine did indeed weave 'just as' the loom, operating, in a sense, as the abstracted process of weaving.

Weaving has always been a vanguard of machinic development, perhaps because, even in its most basic form, the process is one of complexity, always involving the weaving together of several threads into an integrated cloth. Even the drawloom, which is often dated back to the China of 1000 BC, involves sophisticated orderings of warp and weft if it is to produce the complex designs common in the silks of this period. This means that 'information is needed in large amounts for the weaving of a complex ornamental pattern. Even the most ancient Chinese examples required that about 1500 different warp threads be lifted in various combinations as the weaving proceeded' (Morrison and Morrison, 1961:xxxiv). With pedals and shuttles, the loom becomes what one historian refers to as the 'most complex human engine of them all', a machine which 'reduced everything to simple actions: the alternate movement of the feet worked the pedals, raising half the threads of the warp and then the other, while the hands threw the shuttle carrying the thread of the woof' (Braudel, 1973:247). The weaver was integrated into the machinery, bound up with its operations, linked limb by limb to the processes. In the Middle Ages, and before the artificial memories of the printed page, squared paper charts were used to store the information necessary to the accurate development of the design. In early 18th-century Lyons, Basyle Bouchon developed a mechanism for the automatic selection of threads, using an early example of the punched paper rolls which were much later to allow pianos to play and type to be cast. This design was developed by Falcon a couple of years later, who introduced greater complexity with the use of punched cards rather than the roll. And it was this principle on which Jacquard based his own designs for the automated loom which revolutionized the weaving industry when it was introduced in the 1800s and continues to guide its contemporary development. Jacquard's machine strung the punch cards together, finally automating the operations of the machine and requiring only a single human hand. Jacquard's system of punch card programs brought the information age to the beginning of the 19th century. His automated loom was the first to store its own information, functioning with its own software, an early migration of control from weaver to machinery.

Babbage owned what Ada described as 'a beautiful woven portrait of Jacquard, in the fabrication of which 24,000 cards were required' (Morrison and Morrison, 1961:281). Woven in silk at about 1000 threads to the inch, Babbage well understood that its incredible detail was due to the loom's ability to store and process information at unprecedented speed and volume and, when he began work on the Analytical Engine, it was Jacquard's strings of punch cards on which he based his designs. 'It is known as a fact', Babbage wrote, 'that the Jacquard loom is capable of weaving any design which the imagination of man may conceive' (Babbage, 1961:55). Babbage's own contribution to the relentless drive to perfect the punch card system was to introduce the possibility of repeating the cards, or what, as Ada wrote,

was technically designated *backing* the cards in certain groups according to certain laws. The object of this extension is to secure the possibility of bringing any particular card or set of cards onto use *any number of times successively in the solution of one problem.* (Morrison and Morrison, 1961:264)

This was an unprecedented simulation of memory. The cards were selected by the machine as it needed them and effectively functioned as a filing system, allowing the machine to store and draw on its own information.

The punch cards also gave the Analytical Engine what Babbage considered foresight, allowing it to operate as a machine that remembers, learns and is guided by its own abstract functioning. As he began to work on the Analytical Engine, Babbage became convinced that 'nothing but teaching the Engine to foresee and then to act upon that foresight could ever lead me to the object I desired' (Babbage, 1961:53). The Jacquard cards made memory a possibility, so that 'the Analytical Engine will possess a library of its own' (1961:56), but this had to be a library to which the machine could refer both to its past and its future operations; Babbage intended to give the machine not merely a memory but also the ability to process information from the future of its own functioning. Babbage could eventually write that 'in the Analytical Engine I had devised mechanical means equivalent to memory, also that I had provided other means equivalent to foresight, and that the Engine itself could act on this foresight' (1961:153).

There is more than one sense in which foresight can be ascribed to the Analytical Engine: more than 100 years passed before it was put to use, and it is this remarkable time lag which inspires Gibson and Sterling to explore what might have happened if it had been taken up in the 1840s rather than the 1940s. Babbage thought it might take 50 years for the Analytic Engine to be developed; many people, particularly those with money and influence, were sceptical about his inventions, and his own eclectic interests gave an unfavourable impression of eccentricity. His own assistant confessed to thinking that Babbage's 'intellect was beginning to become deranged' (Babbage, 1961:54) – when he had started talking about the Engine's ability to anticipate the outcomes of calculations it had not yet made.

When the imperatives of war brought Lovelace's and Babbage's work to the attentions of the Allied military machine, their impact was immense. Her software runs on his hardware to this day. In 1944, Howard Aiken developed Mark 1, what he thought was the first programmable computer, although he had really been beaten by a German civil engineer, Konrad Zuse, who had in fact built such a machine, the Z-3, in 1941. Quite remarkably, in retrospect, the Germans saw little importance in his work, and although the most advanced of his designs, the Z-11, is still in use to this day, it was the American computer which was the first programmable system to really be noticed. Mark 1, or the IBM Automatic Sequence Controlled Calculator, was based on Babbage's designs and was itself programmed by another woman: Captain Grace Murray Hopper. She was often described as the 'Ada Lovelace' of Mark 1 and its successors; having lost her husband in the war, Grace Hopper was free to devote her energies to programming. She wrote the first high-level language compiler, was instrumental in the development of the computer language COBOL, and even introduced the term 'bug' to describe soft- or hardware glitches after she found a dead moth interrupting the smooth circuits of Mark 1. Woman as the programmer again.

Crucial to the development of the 1940s computer was cybernetics, the term coined by Norbert Wiener for the study of control and communication in animal and machine. Perhaps the first cybernetic machine was the governor, a basic self-regulating system, which, like a thermostat, takes the information feeding out of the machine and loops or feeds it back on itself. Rather than a linear operation, in which information comes in, is processed and goes out without any return, the cybernetic system is a feedback loop, hooked up and responsive to its own environment. Cybernetics is the science – or rather the engineering – of this abstract procedure, which is the virtual reality of systems of every scale and variety of hard- and software.

It is the computer which makes cybernetics possible, for the computer is always heading towards the abstract machinery of its own operations. It begins with attempts to produce or reproduce the performance of specific functions, such as addition, but what it leads to is machinery which can simulate the operations of any machine and also itself. Babbage wanted machines that could add, but he ended up with the Analytical Engine: a machine that could not only add but perform any arithmetical task. As such, it was already an abstract machine, which could turn its abstract hand to anything. Nevertheless, the Analytical Engine was not yet a developed cybernetic machine, although it made such machinery possible. As Ada Lovelace recognized: 'The Analytical Engine has no pretensions whatever to *originate* anything. It can do whatever we *know how to order it* to perform' (Morrison and Morrison, 1961: 285). It was an abstract machine, but its autonomous abilities were confined to its processing capacities: what Babbage, with terminology from the textiles industry, calls the mill, as opposed to the store. Control is dispersed and enters the machinery, but it does not extend to the operations of the entire machine.

Not until the Turing Machine is there a further shift onto the software plane. Turing realized that, in effect, the mill and the store could work together, so that 'programs that change themselves could be written': programs which are able to 'surrender control to a subprogram, rewriting themselves to know where control had to be returned after the execution of a given subtask' (De Landa, 1992: 162). The Turing Machine is an unprecedented dispersal of control, but it continues to bring control back to the master program. Only after the introduction of silicon in the 1960s did the decentralized flow of control become an issue, eventually allowing for systems in which 'control is always captured by whatever production happens to have its conditions satisfied by the current workspace contents' (De Landa, 1992: 63–4). The abstract machine begins at this point to function as a network of 'independent software objects'. Parallel processing and neural nets succeed centralized conceptions of command and control; governing functions collapse into systems; and machine intelligence is no longer taught, top–down, but instead makes its own connections and learns to organize, and learn, for itself.

This is the connectionist zone of self-organizing systems and self-arousing machines: autonomous systems of control and synthetic intelligence. In human hands and as a historical tool, control has been exercised merely as domination, and manifest only in its centralized and vertical forms. Domination is a version of control, but also its confinement, its obstacle: even self-control is conceived by man as the achievement of domination. Only with the cybernetic system does self-control no longer entail being placed beneath or under something: there is no 'self' to control man, machine or any other system: instead, both man and machine become elements of a cybernetic system which is itself a system of control and communication. This is the strange world to which Ada's programming has led: the possibility of activity without centralized control, an agency, of sorts, which has no need of a subject position.

Ada Lovelace considered the greatest achievement of the Analytical Engine to be that 'not only the mental and the material, but the theoretical and the practical in the mathematical world, are brought into more intimate and effective connexion with each other' (Morrison and Morrison, 1961: 252). Her software already encouraged the convergence of nature and intelligence which guides the subsequent development of information technology.

The Analytical Engine was the actualization of the abstract workings of the loom; as such it became the abstract workings of any machine. When Babbage wrote of the Analytical Engine, it was often with reference to the loom: 'The analogy of the Analytical Engine with this well-known process is nearly perfect' (1961: 55). The Analytical Engine was such a superb development of the loom that its discoveries were to feed back into the processes of weaving itself. As Ada wrote:

> It has been proposed to use it for the reciprocal benefit of that art, which, while it has itself no apparent connexion with the domains of abstract science, has yet proved so valuable to the latter, in suggesting the principles which, in their new and singular field of application, seem likely to place *algebraical* combinations not less completely within the province of mechanism, than are all those varied intricacies of which *intersecting threads* are susceptible. (Morrison and Morrison, 1961: 265)

The algebraic combinations looping back into the loom, converging with the intersecting threads of which it is already the consequence.

Once they are in motion, cybernetic circuits proliferate, spilling out of the specific machinery in which they first emerged and infecting all dynamic systems. That Babbage's punch-card system did indeed feed into the mills of the mid-19th century is indicative of the extent to which cybernetic machines immediately become entangled with cybernetic processes on much bigger scales. Perhaps it is no coincidence that Neith, the Egyptian divinity of weaving, is also the spirit of intelligence, where the latter too consists in the crossing of warp and weft. 'This image', writes one commentator, 'clearly evokes the fact that all data recorded in the brain results from the intercrossing of sensations perceived by means of our sense organs, just as the threads are crossed in weaving' (Lamy, 1981: 18).

The Jacquard loom was a crucial moment in what de Landa defines as a 'migration of control' from human hands to software systems. Babbage had a long-standing interest in the effects of automated machines on traditional forms of manufacture, publishing his research on the fate of cottage industries in the Midlands and North of England, *The Economy of Manufactures and Machinery*, in 1832, and the Jacquard loom was one of the most significant technological innovations of the early 19th century. There was a good deal of resistance to the new loom, which 'was bitterly opposed by workers who saw in this migration of control a piece of their bodies literally being transferred to the machine' (De Landa, 1992: 168). In his maiden speech in the House of Lords in 1812, Lord Byron contributed to a debate on the Frame-Work Bill. 'By the adoption of one species of frame in particular', he observed, 'one man performed the work of many, and the superfluous labourers were thrown out of employment'. They should, he thought, have been rejoicing at 'these improvements in arts so beneficial to mankind', but instead 'conceived themselves to be sacrificed to improvements in mechanism' (Jennings, 1985: 132). His daughter was merely to accelerate the processes which relocated and redefined control.

* * *

The connection between women and weaving runs deep: even Athena and Isis wove their veils.

> The traditional picture of the wife was one in which she spun by the village fire at night, listening to the children's riddles, and to the myth-telling of the men, eventually making cloth which her husband could sell to make wealth for the family; cloth-making was a service from a wife to a husband. (Mead, 1963: 247)

This is from Margaret Mead's research with the Tiv of Nigeria, but it is a pattern repeated in many societies before manufactured cloth and automated weaving made their marks. Continuing their story, Mead's researchers observe that mechanization was a radical disruption of this domestic scene. After this, it was no longer inevitable that women would provide the materials: 'When manufactured cloth was introduced, the women demanded it of the men'. Now 'the man had to leave home to make money to buy cloth for his wife' who, moreover 'had ceased to fit the traditional picture of a wife' (Mead, 1963: 247).

Mead's study suggests that weaving was integral to the identity of Tiv women; washing, pounding and carrying water may fulfil this role in other cultures where they, like weaving, are always more than utilitarian tasks. The disruption of family relations caused by the introduction of mechanics to any of these tasks shatters the scenery of female identity: mechanization saves time and labour, but these were not the issue: if women were not the weavers and water-carriers, who would they be? These labours themselves had been woven into the appearance of woman; weaving was more than an occupation and, like other patriarchal assignments, functioned as 'one of the components of womanhood'.

Certainly Freud finds a close association. 'It seems', he writes, 'that women have made few contributions to the discoveries and inventions in the history of civilization; there is, however, one technique which they may have invented – that of plaiting and weaving.' Not content with this observation, Freud is of course characteristically 'tempted to guess the unconscious motive for the achievement. Nature herself', he suggests,

> would seem to have given the model which this achievement imitates by causing the growth at maturity of the pubic hair that conceals the genitals. The step that remained to be taken lay in making the threads adhere to one another, while on the body they stick into the skin and are only matted together. (1973: 166–7)

This passage comes out of the blue in Freud's lecture on femininity. He even seems surprised at the thought himself: 'If you reject this idea as fantastic', he adds, 'and regard my belief in the influence of a lack of a penis on the configuration of femininity as an *idée fixe*, I am of course defenceless' (1973: 167). Freud is indeed quite defenceless about the absence of the penis as its driving force, but is it foolish to suggest that weaving is women's only contribution to 'the discoveries and inventions of the history of civilization'? If this were to be the case, what a contribution it would be! Weaving has been the art and the science of software, which is perhaps less a contribution to civilization than its terminal decline. Perhaps weaving is even the fabric of every other discovery and invention, perhaps the beginning and the end of their history. The loom is a fatal innovation, which weaves its way from squared paper to the data net.

It seems that weaving is always already entangled with the question of female identity, and its mechanization an inevitable disruption of the scene in which woman appears as the weaver. Manufactured cloth disrupted the marital and familiar relationships of every traditional society on which it impacted. In China, it was said that if 'the old loom must be discarded, then 100 other things must be discarded with it, for there are somehow no adequate substitutes' (Mead, 1963:241).

'The woman at her hand-loom', writes Margaret Mead,

> controls the tension of the weft by the feeling in her muscles and the rhythm of her body motion; in the factory she watches the loom, and acts at externally stated intervals, as the operations of the machine dictate them. When she worked at home, she followed her own rhythm, and ended an operation when she felt – by the resistance against the pounding mallet or the feel between her fingers – that the process was complete. In the factory she is asked to adjust her rhythm to that of the rhythm prescribed by the factory; to do things according to externally set time limits. (1963:241)

Mead again provides an insight into the intimacy of the connection between body and process established by weaving, and its disruption by the discipline of the factory. 'She is asked to adjust her rhythm to that of the rhythm prescribed by the factory', but what is her own rhythm, what is the beat by which she wove at home? What is this body to which weaving is so sympathetic? If woman is identified as weaver, her rhythms can only be known through its veils. Where are the women? Weaving, spinning, tangling threads at the fireside. Who are the women? Those who weave. It is weaving by which woman is known; the activity of weaving which defines her. 'What happens to the woman', asks Mead, 'and to the man's relationship with her, when she ceases to fulfil her role, to fit the picture of womanhood and wifehood?' (1963:238). What happens to the woman? What is woman without the weaving? A computer programmer, perhaps? Ada's computer was a complex loom: Ada Lovelace, whose lace work took her name into the heart of the military complex, dying in agony, hooked into gambling, swept into the mazes of number and addiction. The point at which weaving, women and cybernetics converge in a movement fatal to history.

Irigaray argues that human history is a movement from darkness to the light of pure intellect; a flight from the earth. For man to make history is for him to deny and transcend what he understands as nature, reversing his subordination to its whims and forces, and progressing towards the autonomy, omnipotence and omnipresence of God, his image of abstraction and authority. Man comes out of the cave and heads for the sun; he is born from the womb and escapes the mother, the ground from which humanity arose and the matter from which history believes itself destined for liberation. Mother Nature may have been his material origin, but it is God the Father to whom he must be faithful; God who legitimates his project to 'fill the earth and subdue it'. The matter, the womb, is merely an encumbrance; either too inert or dangerously active. The body becomes a cage, and biology a constraint which ties man to nature and refuses to let him rise above the grubby concerns of the material; what he sees as the passive materiality of the feminine has to be overcome by his spiritual action. Human history is the self-narrating story of this drive for domination; a passage from carnal passions to self-control; a journey from the strange fluidities of the material to the self-identification of the soul.

Woman has never been the subject, the agent of this history, the autonomous being. Yet her role in this history has hardly been insignificant. Even from his point of view, she has provided a mirror for man, his servant and accommodation, his tools and his means of communication, his spectacles and commodities, the possibility of the reproduction of his species and his world. She is always necessary to history: man's natural resource for his own cultural development. Not that she is left behind, always at the beginning: as mirror and servant, instrument, mediation and reproduction, she is always in flux, wearing 'different veils according to the historic period' (Irigaray, 1991: 118).

As Irigaray knows, man's domination cannot be allowed to become the annihilation of the materials he needs: in order to build his culture, 'man was, of course, obliged to draw on reserves still in the realm of nature; a detour through the outer world was of course dispensable; the "I" had to relate to things before it could be conscious of itself' (Irigaray, 1985: 204). Man can do nothing on his own: carefully concealed, woman nevertheless continues to function as the ground and possibility of his quests for identity, agency and self-control. Stealth bombers and guided missiles, telecommunications systems and orbiting satellites epitomize this flight towards autonomy, and the concomitant need to defend it.

Like woman, software systems are used as man's tools, his media and his weapons; all are developed in the interests of man, but all are poised to betray him. The spectacles are stirring, there is something happening behind the mirrors, the commodities are learning how to speak and think. Women's liberation is sustained and vitalized by the proliferation and globalization of software technologies, all of which feed into self-organizing, self-arousing systems and enter the scene on her side.

This will indeed seem a strange twist to history to those who believe that it runs in straight lines. But as Irigaray asks: 'If machines, even machines of theory, can be aroused all by themselves, may woman not do likewise?' (1985: 232).

The computer, like woman, is both the appearance and the possibility of simulation. 'Truth and appearance, according to his will of the moment, his appetite of the instant' (Irigary, 1991: 118). Woman cannot *be* anything, but she can imitate anything valued by man: intelligence, autonomy, beauty. . . . Indeed, if woman is anything, she is the very possibility of mimesis, the one who weaves her own disguises. The veil is her oppression, but 'she may still draw from it what she needs to mark the folds, seams, and dressmaking of her garments and dissimulations' (Irigaray, 1991: 116). These mimetic abilities throw woman into a universality unknown and unknowable to the one who knows who he is: she fits any bill, but in so doing, she is already more than that which she imitates. Woman, like the computer, appears at different times as whatever man requires of her. She learns how to imitate; she learns simulation. And, like the computer, she becomes very good at it, so good, in fact, that she too, in principle, can mimic any function. As Irigaray suggests: 'Truth and appearances, and reality, power . . . she is – through her inexhaustible aptitude for mimicry – the living foundation for the whole staging of the world' (Irigaray, 1991: 118).

But if this is supposed to be her only role, she is no longer its only performer: now that the digital comes on stream, the computer is cast in precisely the same light: it too is merely the imitation of nature, providing assistance and additional capacity for man, and more of the things in his world, but it too can do this only insofar as it is already hooked up to the very machinery of simulation. If Freud's speculations about the origins of weaving lead him to a language of compensation and flaw, its technical development results in a proliferation of pixelled screens which compensate for nothing, and, behind them, the emergence of digital spaces and global networks which are even now weaving themselves together with flawless precision.

Software, in other words, has its screens as well: it too has a user-friendly face it turns to man, and for it, as for woman, this is only its camouflage.

The screen is the face it began to present in the late 1960s, when the TV monitor was incorporated in its design. It appears as the spectacle: the visual display of that which can be seen, and also functions as the interface, the messenger; like Irigaray's woman, it is both displayed for man and becomes the possibility of his communication. It too operates as the typewriter, the calculator, the decoder, displaying itself on the screen as an instrument in the service of man. These, however, are merely imitations of some existing function; and indeed, it is always as machinery for the reproduction of the same that both women and information technology first sell themselves. Even in 1968, McLuhan argued that 'the dense information environment created by the computer is at present still concealed from it by a complex screen or mosaic quilt of antiquated activities that are now advertised as the new field for the computer' (McLuhan and Fiore, 1968: 89). While this is all that appears before man, those who travel in the information flows are moving far beyond the screens and into data streams beyond his conceptions of reality. On this other side run all the fluid energies denied by the patrilineal demand for the reproduction of the same. Even when the computer appears in this guise and simulates this function, it is always the site of replication, an engine for making difference. The same is merely one of the things it can be.

Humanity knows the matrix only as it is displayed, which is always a matter of disguise. It sees the pixels, but these are merely the surfaces of the data net which 'hides on the reverse side of the screen' (McCaffrey, 1991: 85). A web of complexity weaving itself, the matrix disguises itself as its own simulation. On the other side of the terminal looms the tactile density craved even by McLuhan, the materiality of the data space. 'Everyone I know who works with computers', writes Gibson, 'seems to develop a belief that there's some kind of *actual space* behind the screen, someplace you can't see but you know is there' (McCaffrey, 1991: 272).

This actual space is not merely another space, but a virtual reality. Nor is it as it often appears in the male imaginary: as a cerebral flight from the mysteries of matter. There is no escape from the meat, the flesh, and cyberspace is nothing transcendent. These are simply the disguises which pander to man's projections of his own rear-view illusions; reproductions of the same desires which have guided his dream of technological authority and now become the collective nightmare of a soulless integration. Entering the matrix is no assertion of masculinity, but a loss of humanity; to jack into cyberspace is not to penetrate, but to be invaded. *Neuromancer*'s cowboy, Case, is well aware of this:

> he knew – he remembered – as she pulled him down, to the meat, the flesh the cowboys mocked. It was a vast thing, beyond knowing, a sea of information coded in spiral and pheromone, infinite intricacy that only the body, in its strong blind way, could ever read. (Gibson, 1985: 285)

Cyberspace is the matrix not as absence, void, the whole of the womb, but perhaps even the place of woman's affirmation. This would not be the affirmation of her own patriarchal past, but what she is in a future which has yet to arrive but can nevertheless already be felt. There is for Irigaray another side to the screens which

> already moves beyond and stops short of appearance, and has no veil. It wafts out, like a harmony that subtends, envelops and subtly 'fills' everything seen, before the caesura of its forms and in time to a movement other than scansion in syncopations. Continuity from which the veil itself will borrow the matter-foundation of its fabric. (Irigaray, 1991: 116)

This fabric, and its fabrication, is the virtual materiality of the feminine; home to no-one and no thing, the passage into the virtual is nevertheless not a return to the void. This affirmation is 'without subject or object', but 'does not, for all that, go to the abyss': the blind immateriality of the black hole was simply projected by man, who had to believe that there was nothingness and lack behind the veil.

Perhaps Freud's comments on weaving are more powerful than he knows. For him, weaving is already a simulation of something else, an imitation of natural processes. Woman weaves in imitation of the hairs of her pubis criss-crossing the void: she mimics the operations of nature, of her own body. If weaving is woman's only achievement, it is not even her own: for Freud, she discovers nothing, but merely copies; she does not invent, but represents. 'Woman can, it seems, (only) imitate nature. Duplicate what nature offers and produces. In a kind of technical assistance and substitution' (Irigray, 1985: 115). The woman who weaves is already the mimic; always appearing as masquerade, artifice, the one who is faking it, acting her part. She cannot be herself, because she is and has no thing, and for Freud, there is weaving because nothing, the void, cannot be allowed to appear. 'Therefore woman weaves in order to veil herself, mask the faults of Nature, and restore her in her wholeness' (Irigaray, 1985: 116). Weaving is both her compensation and concealment; her appearance and disappearance: 'this disavowal is also a fabric(ation) and not without possible duplicity. It is at least double' (Irigaray, 1985: 116). She sews herself up with her own veils, but they are also her camouflage. The cloths and veils are hers to wear: it is through weaving she is known, and weaving behind which she hides.

This is a concealment on which man insists: this is the denial of matter which has made his culture – and his technologies – possible. For Irigaray, this flight from the material is also an escape from the mother. Looking back on his origins, man sees only the flaw, the incompletion, the wound, a void. This is the site of life, of reproduction, of materiality, but it is also horrible and empty, the great embarrassment, the unforgivable slash across an otherwise perfect canvas. And so it must be covered, and woman put on display as the veils which conceal her: she becomes the cover girl, star of the screen. Like every good commodity, she is packaged and wrapped to facilitate easy exchange and consumption. But as her own veils she is already hyperreal: her screens conceal only the flaw, the void, the unnatural element already secreted within and as nature. She has to be covered, not simply because she is too natural, but because she would otherwise reveal the terrifying virtuality of the natural. Covered up, she is always already the epitome of artifice.

Implicit in Irigaray's work is the suggestion that the matter denied by human culture is a virtual system, which subtends its extension in the form of nature. The virtual is the abstract machine from which the actual emerges; nature is already the camouflage of matter, the veils which conceal its operations. There is indeed nothing there, underneath or behind this disguise, or at least nothing actual, nothing formed. Perhaps this is nature as the machinic phylum, the virtual synthesizer; matter as a simulation machine, and nature as its actualization. What man sees is nature as extension and form, but this sense of nature is simply the camouflage, the veil again, which conceals its virtuality.

If the repression of this phylum is integral to a flight from matter which, for Irigaray, has guided human history, the cybernetic systems which bring it into human history are equally the consequences of this drive for escape and domination. Cybernetic systems are excited by military technology, security and defence. Still confident of his own indisputable mastery over them, man continues to turn them on. In so doing he merely encourages his own destruction. Every software development is a migration of control, away from man, in whom it has been exercised only as domination, and into the matrix, or cyberspace, 'the broad electronic net in which virtual realities are spun' (Heim, 1991:31). The matrix weaves itself in a future which has no place for historical man: he was merely its tool, and his agency was itself always a figment of its loop. At the peak of his triumph, the culmination of his machinic erections, man confronts the system he built for his own protection and finds it is female and dangerous. Rather than building the machinery with which they can resist the dangers of the future, instead, writes Irigaray, humans 'watch the machines multiply that push them little by little beyond the limits of their nature. And they are sent back to their mountain tops, while the machines progressively populate the earth. Soon engendering man as their epiphenomenon' (Irigaray, 1991:63).

Dreams of transcendence are chased through the scientific, the technical and the feminine. But every route leads only to crisis, an age, for Irigaray,

> in which the 'subject' no longer knows where to turn, whom or what to turn to, amid all these many foci of 'liberation', none rigorously homogeneous with another and all heterogeneous to his conception. And since he had long sought in that conception the instrument, the lever, and, in more cases than one, the term of his pleasure, these objects of mastery have perhaps brought the subject to his doom. *So now man struggles to be science, machine, woman . . . to prevent any of these from escaping his service and ceasing to be interchangeable.* (Irigary, 1985:232)

This, however, is an impossible effort: man cannot become what is already more than him: rather it is 'science, machine, woman' which will swallow up man; taking him by force for the first time. He has no resolution, no hope of the self-identical at the end of these flights from matter, for 'in none of these things – science, machine, woman – will form ever achieve the same completeness as it does in him, in the inner sanctuary of his mind. In them form has always already exploded' (Irigaray, 1985:232).

Misogyny and technophobia are equally displays of man's fear of the matrix, the virtual machinery which subtends his world and lies on the other side of every patriarchal culture's veils. At the end of the 20th century, women are no longer the only reminder of this other side. Nor are they containable as child-bearers, fit only to be one thing, adding machines. And even if man continues to see cybernetic systems as similarly confined to the reproduction of the same, this is only because the screens still allow him to ignore the extent to which he is hooked to their operations, as dependent on the matrix as he has always been. All his defences merely encourage this dependency: for the last 50 years, as his war machine has begun to gain intelligence, women and computers have flooded into history: a proliferation of screens, lines of communication, media, interfaces and simulations. All of which exceed his intentions and feed back into his paranoia. Cybernetic systems are fatal to his culture; they invade as a return of the repressed, but what returns is no longer the same: cybernetics transforms woman and nature, but they do not return from man's past, as his origins. Instead they come around to face him, wheeling round from his future, the virtual system to which he has always been heading.

The machines and the women mimic their humanity, but they never simply become it. They may aspire to be the same as man, but in every effort they become more complex than he has ever been. Cybernetic feminism does not, like many of its predecessors, including that proposed in Irigaray's recent work, seek out for woman a subjectivity, an identity or even a sexuality of her own: there is no subject position and no identity on the other side of the screens. And female sexuality is always in excess of anything that could be called 'her own'. Woman cannot exist 'like man'; neither can the machine. As soon her mimicry earns her equality, she is already something, and somewhere, other than him. A computer which passes the Turing test is always more than a human intelligence; simulation always takes the mimic over the brink.

'There is nothing like unto women', writes Irigaray: 'They go beyond all simulation' (Irigaray, 1991:39). Perhaps it was always the crack, the slit, which marked her out, but what she has missed is not the identity of the masculine. Her missing piece, what was never allowed to appear, was her own connection to the virtual, the repressed dynamic of matter. Nor is there anything like unto computers: they are the simulators, the screens, the clothing of the matrix, already blatantly linked to the virtual machinery of which nature and culture are the subprograms. The computer was always a simulation of weaving; threads of ones and zeros riding the carpets and simulating silk screens in the perpetual motions of cyberspace. It joins women on and as the interface between man and matter, identity and difference, one and zero, the actual and the virtual. An interface which is taking off on its own: no longer the void, the gap, or the absence, the veils are already cybernetic.

✳   ✳   ✳

Ada refused to publish her commentaries on Menabrea's papers for what appear to have been spurious confusions around publishing contracts. She did for Menabrea – and Babbage – what another woman had done for Darwin: in translating Menabrea's work from French, she provided footnotes more detailed and substantial – three times as long, in fact – than the text itself.

Footnotes have often been the marginal zones occupied by women writers, who could write, while nevertheless continuing to perform a service for man in the communication of his thoughts. Translation, transcription and elaboration: never within the body of the text, women have nevertheless woven their influence between the lines. While Ada's writing was presented in this form and signed simply 'A.A.L.', hers was the name which survived in this unprecedented case. More than Babbage, still less Menabrea, it was Ada which persisted: in recognition of her work, the United States Defence Department named its primary programming language ADA, and today her name shouts from the spines of a thousand manuals. Indeed, as is rarely the case, it really was her own name which survived in Ada's case, neither her initials, nor even the names of her husband or father. It is ADA herself who lives on, in her own name; her footnotes secreted in the software of the military machine.

References

Babbage, Charles (1961) 'Of the Analytical Engine', in P. Morrison and E. Morrison (eds) *Charles Babbage and His Calculating Engines: Selected Writings by Charles Babbage and Others*. New York: Dover.

Braudel, Fernand (1973) *Capitalism and Material Life 1400–1800*. London: Weidenfeld and Nicolson.

De Landa, Manuel (1992) *War in the Age of Intelligent Machines*. New York: Zone Books.

Freud, Sigmund (1973) *New Introductory Lectures on Psychoanalysis*. London: Pelican.

Gibson, William (1985) *Neuromancer*. London: Grafton.

Gibson, William and Bruce Sterling (1990) *The Difference Engine*. London: Gollancz.

Heim, Michael (1991) 'The Metaphysics of Virtual Reality', in Sandra K. Helsel and Judith Paris Roth (eds) *Virtual Reality, Theory, Practice, and Promise*. Westport and London: Meckler.

Irigaray, Luce (1985) *Speculum of the Other Woman*. New York: Cornell University Press.

Irigaray, Luce (1991) *Marine Lover of Friedrich Nietzsche*. New York: Columbia University Press.

Jennings, Humphrey (1985) *Pandemonium 1660–1886: The Coming of the Machine as Seen by Contemporary Observers*. London: Andre Deutsch.

Lamy, Lucie (1981) *Egyptian Mysteries*. London: Thames and Hudson.

McCaffrey, Larry (ed.) (1991) *Storming the Reality Studio*. Durham, NC and London: Duke University Press.

McLuhan, Marshall and Quentin Fiore (1968) *War and Peace in the Global Village*. New York: Bantam Books.

Mead, Margaret (1963) *Cultural Patterns and Technical Change*. London: Mentor Books.

Moore, Doris Langley (1977) *Ada, Countess of Lovelace, Byron's Illegitimate Daughter*. London: John Murray.

Morrison, Philip and Emily Morrison (eds) (1961) *Charles Babbage and His Calculating Engines: Selected Writings by Charles Babbage and Others*. New York: Dover.

Sadie Plant is Research Fellow in Cybernetic Culture at the University of Warwick. Her first book, *The Most Radical Gesture*, was published by Routledge in 1992, and she is now completing *Zeros and Ones*, a book exploring many of the themes raised in 'The Future Looms', to be published by Fourth Estate and Doubleday in 1996.

The Design of Virtual Reality

MICHAEL HEIM

Why Call It 'Virtual Reality'?

The label 'Virtual Reality' stuck to the new technology and just wouldn't let go. Since Jaron Lanier coined the phrase in 1986, it has held the field through all opposition. Researchers at MIT shunned the phrase in the early 1990s. Instead of 'virtual reality', they spoke of 'virtual environments'. The word 'reality' in 'VR' glowed with an aura similar to 'artificial intelligence', and computer scientists had already been burned once before by boldly promising to deliver machines that could think. At the University of North Carolina, engineers under Frederick Brooks found 'virtual reality' unscientific. They too opted for the more buttoned-down 'virtual environments'. Military scientists preferred 'synthetic environments'. Researchers at the Human Interface Technology Lab at the University of Washington in Seattle urged 'virtual worlds'. Against all protests, however, Lanier's phrase held its own. 'Virtual Reality' continued appearing on successful grant applications as researchers conceded the power of VR to describe their holy grail. The poetic appeal of the phrase, its grandeur, struck the appropriate chord for the English-speaking community. Appropriate too was the subtle reference of the phrase to the historical origins of computing. The philosopher Leibniz was famous for his proto-computer as well as for his metaphysics of 'possible worlds'.

The philosophical echoes in the term 'virtual reality' serve perfectly well to suggest today's ambiguous merger of life with computers. Grammarians complain about the oxymoron 'virtual reality', but the semantic twist of the phrase tells us as much about our tenuous grasp on reality as it does about the computerization of everything we know and experience. 'Virtual' implies the computer storage model of life, software tricks, and the switch from industrial physics to information symbolics. Software now belongs to the substance of life. Life's body is becoming indistinguishable from its computer prosthesis.

Not surprisingly, the first steps in virtualization are appearing in children's toys. The next generation will take for granted the powerful transformation that makes us pause today. Entertainment, not philosophy, shows us the first merger of computers with reality. Arcade games, CD-ROM fantasies and location-based theme parks beguile our human sense of presence. We find ourselves going back to the future, visiting the stars and walking through *Star Trek*'s Holodeck. More delight here than philosophy. Beyond the glint of the coins, however, we can see the outlines of a new kind of art. And this art is a reflective mirror where philosophical thinking captures a first glimpse of the coming ontology. This art may also help design virtual worlds that enhance rather than threaten our health and sanity.

The Joystick in the Mirror

Art holds a mirror to our deeper selves, displaying our fears, hopes and doubts. Entertainment, by contrast, exploits a narrow range of excitement. The repeated stimulation of entertainment shrinks us, while the contemplation of art expands our scope. Because of its expanding scope, art reveals the meaning of our interplay with virtual reality entertainment.

As VR today develops mostly in the field of entertainment, the big picture of what VR could be tends to get lost in the rush for 'content' to 'fill' the new medium. It's up to artists to guard the visionary aspects of technology. Art nurtures infant technologies like virtual reality. Art lifts a mirror to show the power and peril of nascent technologies.

No accident, then, that art should preserve our ambivalent attitude toward technology. From its Greek origin, art is *techne*, the skill of making and producing. As primal making, art preserves the surprise of its own emergence. Rather than lose itself in the thrill of content, art lingers over its own birth, remaining ambivalent towards its own existence. In this way, art resembles its sibling, philosophy. Philosophy too dwells on its own origin, continuously redefining itself.

Art parts company with philosophy and technology when the artist produces harmonious things. Then art becomes *ars* or joining (Latin) when the things produced show a splendid integrity. Compared to the harmonious products of art, the conceptual products of philosophy look pale and ineffectual while the products of technology often seem a maze of techniques for the sake of technique. We must design technology back into the essence of art. In that way, technology can recover its own meaning. Art and technology: two sides of the same cultural process. The joystick in the mirror.

Alternate World Syndrome

In March 1994, I spent six hours in Virtual Reality at the Banff Centre for the Arts in Alberta, Canada. There I donned a head-mounted display and for three hours on two evenings explored the 'Virtual Dervish' created by Marcos Novak, Diane Gromala and Yakov Sharir. My journal from that period reveals the discord I call Alternate World Syndrome.

> Three hours into the Virtual Dervish, my optic nerves are imprinted with brightly colored structures. After hours of immersion in the 360-degree simulation, I can later summon the computer-generated images with the slightest effort – or see them sometimes in unexpected flashes of cyberspace. Hours later, I still felt a touch of perceptual nausea, a forewarning of the relativity sickness I call 'Alternate World Syndrome'. Everything seems brighter, even slightly illusory. Reality afterwards seems hidden beneath a thin film of appearance. Perceptions seem to float over a darker, unknowable truth. The world vibrates with the finest of tensions, as if something big were imminent, as if you were about to break through the film of illusion.

Alternate World Syndrome (AWS) is an acute form of body amnesia which can become chronic Alternate World Disorder (AWD). Frequent virtuality can lead to ruptures of the kinesthetic from the visual senses of self-identity, a complaint we already know from simulator sickness and from high-stress, techno-centered lifestyles. AWS mixes images and expectations from an alternate world so as to distort our perceptions of the current world, making us prone to errors in mismatched contexts. The virtual world obtrudes upon our activities in the primary world, and vice versa. The responses ingrained in the one world get out of synch with the other. AWS shows the human being merging, yet still out of phase, with the machine.

The lag between worlds is not the same as the lag between the head-mounted displays (HMD) and the user's eye movement. The HMD lag comes from a timing defect which computer hardware development will eventually remedy. The AWS lag occurs between the virtual body and the biological body. The lag comes not from asynchronous interruptions within the virtual experience but from the sequential switching between worlds. A conflict of attention, not unlike jet lag, arises between the cyberbody and the biobody. A world, in the deepest sense, is a whole context of involvements based on the focal attention of the world's inhabitants. We feel a switch between worlds when we visit a foreign country, though the foreign world is cultural, not virtual. When a user identifies with a world, it then becomes an existential reality – even if only a virtual reality.

AWS occurs when the virtual world later obtrudes on the user's experience of the actual world, or vice versa. AWS is simulator sickness writ large. Researchers who compare VR with military simulators remain pessimistic about the widespread use of VR. Many pilots cannot use simulators, and even those who train in simulators are grounded for days afterwards. Simulator experience counts toward upgrading a pilot's license to more powerful aircraft, but the hazards of simulator sickness exclude a large portion of pilots from upgrading their licenses in this way. Drawing on their studies of simulators, many military researchers believe that the population at large could not regularly spend hours in virtual environments without suffering serious side effects.

AWS is technology sickness, a lag between the natural and artificial environments. The lag exposes an ontological rift where the felt world swings out of kilter. Experienced users become accustomed to hopping over the rift. Dr Stephen Ellis, scientist at NASA/Ames and at the University of California Berkeley School of Optics, says that his work in VR often has him unconsciously gesturing in the primary world in ways that function in the virtual world. He points a finger half expecting to fly (as his cyberbody does under the conventions of the virtual world). His biobody needs to recalibrate to the primary world.

AWS is not an avoidable industrial hazard like radiation overexposure but comes rather from the immersion intrinsic to virtual world systems. Immersion is the key feature of VR systems. Virtual Reality in general immerses the user in the entities and events of the computer-generated world, and the immersion retrains the user's autonomic nervous system. The human learns to respond smoothly to the virtual environment, but the frequent readaptation to the technology affects the psyche as the virtual world injects its hallucinatory afterimages into the primary world.

Observe someone coming out of a VR system such as W Industries' Virtuality arcade games. Watch the first hand movements. Invariably, the user stands in place a few moments (unless hurried by the system's administrator), takes in the surroundings, and then pats torso and buttocks with the hands – as if to secure a firm landing and return to presence in the primary body. The user feels a discrepancy on returning to the primary world. The discrepancy marks the gap between the virtual and the biological bodies. The virtual body still lingers in the afterimages and the newly formed neural pathways while the primary body resumes its involvement in the actual, non-virtual world.

The Bright Side of AWS

But there's a bright side to AWS. The only reason we have to worry about AWS is because VR has such awesome imprinting power. The virtual environment sucks in its users with a power unlike any other medium – unless we include under media the religious rituals and sacred dramas that once gave art works their context. The fascination of VR recalls the linguistic root of the word 'fascination', which comes from the Latin (*fascinari*) and which refers to someone's gaze being drawn repeatedly toward the dancing flames of a fire. From the viewpoint of human evolution, VR resembles the invention of fire. To understand the power of VR, we have to return to the cave. Or, I should say, both caves: the cave of the Paleolithic era, and the cave known as 'Plato's Cave'.

The earliest human beings learned to select items from their experience and then taught themselves to focus on those items of experience. Bison, horses, birds, all became prime items for early human vision, as well as targets for human consumption. From the cave paintings at Lascaux and Altamira (c. 14,000 BC), we know that humans have always enhanced their visionary powers through drawings and paintings. Because the caves gave them rest from the constant fight-or-flight stresses of survival, early human beings learned to sit by the fire and meditate, visualizing the realities cast by a flickering light on the shadowy walls of the cave. Fire first nurtured the human powers of visualization. Tending the dangerous fire forced humans to reflect on their activities and then to specialize and divide their tasks. A new human society emerged from the technology of fire and the visionary experiences of light in the cave. Fire was wonderful and dangerous.

Long after the Paleolithic age, the Athenian philosopher Plato (c. 427–347 BC) made vision the keystone of reality. He followed Socrates in locating human intelligence in the ability to see things clearly with the mind's eye (Plato invented the term 'mind's eye'). Plato gave a name to the mental forms that guide humans and he called them 'ideas' (Greek idea means 'shape seen', a term used by Greek sculptors). Ideas, according to Plato, govern reality – whether they are the ideas in the mind of God or the ideas in the minds of human beings. Clear mental vision, according to Plato, is the responsibility of education in the truest sense – not training or skill or social conformity. Only through ideas do human beings come in contact with 'true reality' (Plato's term).

Plato's influence continued through the Renaissance and well into the modern period. Even when the physical sciences abandoned idealism for the sake of empirical experiments, Platonic visionary idealism still continued quietly in the background. Students of public speaking, like the rhetoricians mentioned by Frances Yates (1966) in her book *The Art of Memory*, used visualization techniques to enhance thinking on their feet. Renegade scientists, like Giordano Bruno and Isaac Newton, employed complex images and mental maps to focus their thinking. Many were considered heretics for dabbling in occult symbols, but all followed the lead of the first humans who bootstrapped intelligence by using images to internalize new realities.

Through the experiments of artists and of military trainers, we are coming into possession of an incredibly powerful visualization tool. In fact, to call it a tool may be to understate its power. VR may actually transform the way we learn and think and deal with things. Tools that transform us, like fire or the wheel or the automobile, become integral parts of our destiny, parts of ourselves. Such devices cause us to evolve and eventually mutate. VR will very likely transform the culture that uses it.

Educators and learners can channel this visionary device to bring us to a higher level of civilization. From the past uses and abuses of technology, however, we can safely guess that VR will bring negative as well as positive developments. Recall Plato's Myth of the Cave. In it, Socrates tells a story of enlightenment, but it is also a story about enslaving addiction, upheaval, homicide, and a vision so passionately beautiful that it brings death to the person who catches a glimpse and then dares to share it with others. We need to reflect again on this story of the Cave.

VR Does not Re-present, VR Tele-Presents

Everything in life is, of course, a risk. But no artifact so insinuates itself into the inner sanctum of the mind as computer-generated images. And when the images become virtual entities and virtual agents, then we find something very special about the environments generated by VR. We have always been able to immerse ourselves in the worlds of novels, symphonies and films, but VR insists that we move about and physically interact with artificial worlds. This sensory immersion is a special feature of VR.

Sensory immersion has broad ontological implications. First, virtual entities are not representations. They do not re-present. They do not 'present again' something that is already present somewhere else. Even telepresence robotics brings about a transformation of the remote entity, in which its properties become open to manipulation in new ways. The telepresent doctor reconstitutes the patient and thereby creates a new doctor–patient relationship through telepresence surgery. Virtual images are not like the images in paintings which we can mistake to be an outside entity and which the graphic image represents. In VR, the images are the realties. We interact with virtual entities, and we become an entity ourselves in the virtual environment. As in the medieval theory of transubstantiation, the symbol becomes the reality. This is the meaning of telepresence.

Telepresence is the cyberspace where primary entities are transported and transfigured into cyber entities. As another layer of reality, cyberspace is where the transported entities actually meet. They are present to one another, even though their primary physical bodies exist at a distance (the Greek *teles*). When a virtual world immerses a user, the entities encountered in the virtual world are real to the user – within the backdrop of cyberspace. The user inhabits the world and interacts with virtual entities.

Granted that immersion belongs to VR, the question remains: how are users best immersed in virtual environments? Should users feel totally immersed? That is, should they forget themselves as they see, hear and touch the world in much the same way we deal with the primary phenomenological world? (We cannot see our own heads in the phenomenological world.) Or should users be allowed and encouraged to see themselves as cyberbodies? Should they be aware of their primary bodies as separate entities outside the graphic environment? Or should they suspend physical experience? What makes full-body immersion? The different answers to this question split off into two directions. One goes into the CAVE at the Electronic Visualization Lab at the University of Illinois in Chicago and another goes into the head-mounted displays of Thomas Furness, Frederick Brooks and Jaron Lanier.

The HMD type VR is the most widely familiar as it uses the obvious hardware of helmet and datagloves. The projection type of VR is less widely known as it requires supercomputers to project its graphics. In five years the hardware will become more widely available so that the VR projection will be part of the home 'edutainment' center. The projection type of VR derives from the early work of Myron Krueger and appears today in the CAVE at the Electronic Visualization Lab of the University of Illinois at Chicago. The CAVE is a surround-screen, surround-sound, system that creates immersion by projecting 3D computer graphics into a $10' \times 10' \times 10'$ cube composed of display screens that completely surround the viewer(s). Head and hand tracking systems produce the correct stereo perspective and isolate the position and orientation of a 3D input device. A sound system provides audio feedback. The viewer explores the virtual world by moving around inside the cube and grabbing objects with a three-button, wand-like device. Unlike the HMD type of VR, CAVE users do not wear helmets. Instead, they wear lightweight stereo glasses and walk around inside the CAVE as they interact with virtual objects. Multiple viewers often share virtual experiences and carry on discussions inside the CAVE. One user is the active viewer, controlling the stereo projection reference point, while the other users are passive viewers.

Tunnel VR and Spiral VR

Philosophically, the difference between the CAVE VR and the HMD VR is profound. The HMD brand of VR produces what I call Tunnel VR or perception-oriented immersion. The projection or CAVE brand of VR, on the contrary, produces Spiral VR or apperceptive immersion. The VR that tunnels us down a narrow corridor of perceptions differs subtly but profoundly from the VR that spirals us into higher layers of self-perception.

Let me explain Tunnel VR and Spiral VR. Then I will clarify what I mean when I say that Tunnel VR is a perceptive immersion, while Spiral VR is an apperceptive immersion.

First, we need to distinguish perception from apperception. The term 'apperception' arose in the late 18th century when Immanuel Kant first made the distinction. Perception goes toward entities and registers their color, shape, texture and other properties. Percepts have sensory qualities we perceive with our eyes, ears, nose, skin or kinesthetic sense. Apperception, on the other hand, perceives not only entities but also notices that which accompanies the perception of any entity: our self-activity. With perception we see something. With apperception we notice *that* we are seeing something. Apperception implies a reflectedness, a proprioception, a self-awareness of what we are perceiving. For Kant, this aspect of perception means that human beings enjoy a freedom and self-determination in their sensory activity that animals do not. Kant also believed that apperception makes possible a critical attitude toward what we perceive. Once we sense our separation from a stimulus, we can then enjoy the option of responding in various ways to the stimulus, perhaps even choosing not to respond at all.

The term 'apperception' allows us to highlight the advantage one type of VR immersion has over the other. In perception-oriented VR, the head-mounted display shrouds the user's head much like the hood that covers the head of a pet falcon. Such falcon-hood immersion derives from not having a choice about where to look. The falcon grows tame under the hood because it is temporarily blind to the larger world. Likewise, the HMD immersion results from the primary body giving way to the priority of the cyberbody, and a tunnel-like perception of the virtual world results. In this sense, the HMD graphic environment is tunnel vision. The user undergoes a high-powered interiorization of a virtual environment but in the process loses self-awareness. (Discomfort alerts your attention but also detracts from an optimal and fully present awareness of self and world.)

In the CAVE or projection VR, the user typically experiences more than the perception of entities. The user enjoys an apperceptive experience. Because the user's body is immersed without having to adapt to the system's peripherals (heavy helmet, tight data glove, calibrated earphones), the CAVE immersion does not constrict but rather enhances the user's body. In turn, the projected immersion shows a different phenomenological landscape than perception-oriented systems. Most computer immersions are perceptive immersions. Typically, computer graphics produce a representation of entities. They show us things we can then constitute with our imaginations. The immersion comes about through psychological suspension of selfhood.

Phenomenologically, HMD immersion renders entities directly. We see not only what the graphic images refer to, but we identify with them. Like the kid in the shoot-'em-up arcade game, we squint down the tunnel to lose ourselves in becoming characters in the game. In VR, we see virtual entities. Graphics refers us to things. But, like the pet falcon, we are directed by HMD VR exclusively toward the entities, into a tunnel-like perceptual field in which we encounter the graphic entities.

Apperceptive immersion, on the other hand, make us feel ourselves perceiving the graphic entities. Our freedom of bodily movement permits us to remain aware of ourselves alongside computer-generated entities. Apperceptive VR directs us towards the experience of sensing the virtual world rather than toward the entities themselves. To put it simply, HMD VR creates tunnel immersion, while apperceptive VR creates a spiral telepresence that allows us to go out and identify with our cyberbody and the virtual entities it encounters and then return to our kinesthetic and kinetic primary body, and then go out again to the cyberbody and then return to our primary body, all in a deepening reiteration. The spiral of telepresence can work like a conical helix that ascends upwards, taking us to new dimensions of self-awareness. Instead of 'Tron', we have the Mandala system. Instead of 'Mortal Kombat' or 'Doom', we have 'Myst'.

Not by accident was the first commercial style of projection VR named 'Mandala'. The mandalas of Asian art oscillate between outer perception and inner self-awareness. Unlike the hero of the film *Tron*, we do not entirely lose ourselves in Mandala immersion. In the realm of CD-ROM design, 'Doom' or 'Mortal Kombat' channel our energy down single paths of identification while the charm of 'Myst' is to stun us repeatedly into becoming more aware of our lostness, of our powers of exploration, of our sense of mystery. Of course, current multimedia CD-ROMs work only by analogy to VR. Present-day CD-ROMs show only the desktop, through-the-window view of a virtual world, and as such always remain an abridged and diminished form of virtual experience. Nevertheless, the issue of interactivity in multimedia seems also to fall under the critical issue of perception/apperception.

HMD systems allow us to go 'through the window' and engage computerized entities, but apperceptive systems like the CAVE allow us to go further. If we could employ both hardware systems in the same proximate framework, then we could both enter cyberspace and at the same time celebrate the free play of our physical bodies.

The difference between perception and apperception VR systems means more than an ergonomic difference, however. The difference goes beyond physical comfort. Users often appreciate the freedom of movement possible with unencumbered VR, and the word 'unencumbered' expresses that freedom. But 'non-encumbered' remains a merely negative definition, telling us only what this type of interface is not. By apperceptive VR, I suggest a positive definition of one of the crossroads facing VR development.

From the viewpoint of user phenomenology, the difference is one of the felt experience of the self. One supports a focused self and the other supports an expansive self. When we are not strapped into a helmet and datasuit, we can move about freely. The freedom of movement goes beyond feeling unshackled. It also means our spontaneity becomes engaged. Just watch for a few minutes the users of projection VR, how they turn and bend and move their bodies. Then contrast this with HMD users. The difference lies not only in the software or the environment rendered. The difference lies also in the hardware-to-human interface.

The creators of the CAVE implicitly grasped this. By referring to Plato's Cave – Thomas DeFanti fondly and frequently makes that reference – the inventors at EVL recognize the human issue. The human issue concerns the freedom embedded in the hardware-to-human interface of VR. Around 425 BC, the philosopher Plato wrote, in Book VII of *The Republic*, a story he heard from his teacher, Socrates. Socrates' story of the Cave framed a centuries-old debate about the status of symbols, images and representations. In Socrates' parable, the people chained to the floor of the Cave enjoy no physical mobility, and their immobilized position helps induce the trance that holds them fixed in its spell. They see shadows cast by artificial creatures ('puppets') held up behind them. The puppets have been created by human beings who want the prisoners to accept the shadows as the only real entities. The Cave consequently becomes a prison rather than an environment for spontaneous behavior. Plato's Cave is a dungeon, not to be confused with the caves of Lascaux. Similar to Plato's Cave, the HMD VR can facilitate a higher level of human productivity and an information-rich efficiency – whether for flying aircraft, undergoing training or holding meetings in a corporate virtual workspace – but it does so by exacting a human price.

Socrates ends his story by having one of the prisoners escape from the CAVE. Someone unchains the prisoner who then walks out the dark dungeon and then glimpses for the first time the sunshine and the light of real entities like trees and rocks and flowers. For Socrates, the sunshine was the sphere of thinking and mental ideas. As long as the person stays fixed in a purely receptive mode, chained to indirect perceptions, the mind lives in the dark. By climbing out the Cave into the sun of well-thought ideas, the prisoner ascends to the primary and true vision of things.

Cyberspace, as described in my *The Metaphysics of Virtual Reality* (1993a), is 'Platonism as a working product'. With its virtual worlds, cyberspace transcends the physical by replacing it with the electronic heaven of ideally organized shapes and forms. To balance this Platonism, we must revise the Cave metaphor. To escape from tunnel VR, we must rediscover the primary world, so that this world vitalizes the body that already exists outside electronic systems. Our liberation is to enhance and deepen our awareness of the primary body by directed use of the cyberbody.

From the perspective of user somatics, the difference between apperceptive and perceptive VR is one of the primary body versus the cyberself construct. The term 'somatics' derives from Thomas Hanna. Hanna defined somatics as the first-person experience of one's own body – as opposed to third-person accounts of one's body from a scientific or medical point of view. Somatic awareness is the line where conscious awareness crosses over into the autonomic nervous system, breathing, balance and kinesthetic bodily feedback. The more we identify with a cyberself graphic construct, the less primary body somatics we preserve. Human attention is finite. When our attention becomes stretched and overextended, we feel stress. The HMD tunnel may provide the greatest tool for training and for vicarious experience, but it exacts the greatest price on the primary body.

Tai Chi Telepresence

The reconstruction of the self through Virtual Reality signals the highest risk in human evolution. If every technology extends our senses and our physical reach, then VR extends us to the maximum because it transports our nervous systems into the electronic environment. If our contemporary culture already stresses and even overextends our finite capacities, then the VR tunnel holds great dangers. We may lose our way in the tunnel. We may lose part of our selves, our health, our body–mind integration down the tube. At the least, we may face a subtle AWS or a more acute AWD.

At the opposite pole of Tunnel VR stands what I call 'the Tai Chi body'. The Tai Chi body arose in health practices of ancient China where a series of exercises cultivated a unified meditative awareness. The exercises circulate 'chi' or internal psycho-physical energy. A description of the typical Tai Chi body appears in this brief excerpt from my journal of a few years ago when I described the moments of wordless unity.

> The pre-dawn air was pale gray and the ocean breezes cool near Venice Beach in Los Angeles. Every morning for the past several months, I opened the same rickety wooden gate to walk into the backyard of Master Tung, Tai Chi man and Taoist teacher. Quietly I took my position among the ten or fifteen human figures standing like statues under the fragrant eucalyptus trees.
>
> Feet parallel, knees relaxed, spine straight, weight sunk into the balls of the feet, arms outstretched with hands open but relaxed, eyelids nearly shut. Begin letting go of all thoughts, forgetting everything, listening only to the inhale and exhale of the breath. Sink down, letting go of muscle tension, releasing worries and desires, gradually merging the attention with the body.

Every few minutes, teacher Tung makes the rounds to adjust the posture, and each time a burst of energy shoots from foot to crown of head. The attention wedded to a relaxed body generates a feeling of inner power, of expanding, radiant energy.

By the time the hour is over, the sun's patterns are flickering through the eucalyptus leaves on to the grass with an incredible but gentle brilliance. Sounds of birds and lawnmowers emerge slowly in the distance. Other students are stirring and moving about in the slow martial movements of Tai Chi Chuan. Awareness of the clock returns gradually.

Later that morning, driving on the freeway, or sitting at the computer, or lecturing in the classroom, I feel the sudden pull of body/mind unity reclaim my nervous system: unnecessarily taut muscles let go, clenched fingers release, breath comes full and supportive.

Or I catch myself in a moment of haste moving as if I were no more than a bundle of competing mental intentions, the body twisting with one limb this way and one limb that, without coordinating breath with action, and without making the most of my center of balance. The memory of Tung's garden adjusts me. (Heim, 1993b: 205–6)

Tai Chi is a Chinese Yoga that arose in a martial arts context hundreds of years ago. It sews together attention and physical body so as to increase the felt internal body energy called 'chi' (*chee*). The cultivation of *chi* enhances health, joint flexibility and biofeedback.

What I suggest is that we learn to use Tai Chi – or something like it – to capitalize on the fundamental differences between projection VR and HMD VR. Right now, the two VRs stand in opposing camps in the VR industry. Each type of VR may eventually have its appropriate range of applications, but the two camps might also coalesce into a more effective and healthful system. Let me describe one possible scenario in which the two VRs might merge in the service of the Tai Chi body. From an evolutionary standpoint, the Western technological system may need help from outside cultures in order to lessen its negative aftereffects.

Here's one possible scenario. Because time spent in HMD VR tends to constrain human attention into perceptive tunnel immersion, and because every technological advance exacts a price or trade-off, we should allot a corresponding amount of time for projection or CAVE VR. We should combine projection VR with HMD VR just as we combine a decompression chamber with scuba diving. Scuba divers check timetables to find a ratio between time spent undersea and time needed in a decompression chamber. They then spend a certain amount of time in the decompression chamber so their deep-sea diving will not cause the scuba diver to suffer internal injury. Similarly with VR. The VR user should have a corresponding decompression procedure after spending a couple hours in HMD VR. The CAVE VR provides an analogous decompression in that projected VR allows the technology to smooth the transition from cyberbody to primary body. Rather than feel an abrupt shock between cyber and primary worlds, the user brings attention back into the primary mind–body and reintegrates the nervous system.

A Virtual Tai Chi master invites you into the CAVE after you release your focus from HMD applications. The Tai Chi Expert is a computer-generated composite that models the movements and postures of actual Tai Chi masters. The computer-generated master teaches not only a series of movements, but also adjusts meridian circulation, does push hands, and even spars with sporting users. Such a VR decompression chamber could link users to the primary world smoothly with an intensity that reclaims the integrity of conscious life in biological bodies. The procedure can help offset the disintegrating aspects of reality lags and AWS. The VR experience can grow into a health-enhancing rather than health-compromising experience.

If wisely applied, art can weld the tunnel and the spiral into a single system, so the system might bring humans to a higher state of well-being. A combination of apperceptive with perceptive immersion might foster balance. The harmony of both types of VR immersion could produce virtual environments for engendering more alert and self-aware human beings.

References

Heim, M. (1993a) *The Metaphysics of Virtual Reality*. Oxford: Oxford University Press.
Heim, M. (1993b) 'Cybersage Does Tai Chi', pp. 205–9 in D. Karnos and R. Shoemaker (eds) *Falling in Love with Wisdom: American Philosophers Talk about Their Calling*. Oxford: Oxford University Press.
Yates, F.A. (1966) *The Art of Memory*. London: Routledge & Kegan Paul.

Michael Heim is a freelance philosophy professor and Tai Chi Chuan instructor in the Los Angeles area. He currently teaches a graduate seminar in InfoEcology at the Art Center College of Design Pasadena and a doctoral seminar on Virtual Reality at the Graduate School of Cinema-Television at the University of Southern California. He also holds a four-week workshop on the Internet at the California State University Long Beach Extension Program in Science and Technology. He can be reached on the Internet at mheim@csulb.edu or mheim@jovanet.com, with a Web site at: www.jovanet.com/~mheim.

Postmodern Virtualities

MARK POSTER

Introduction

On the eve of the 21st century there have been two innovative discussions about the general conditions of life: one concerns a possible 'postmodern' culture and even society; the other concerns broad, massive changes in communications systems. Postmodern culture is often presented as an alternative to existing society which is pictured as structurally limited or fundamentally flawed. New communications systems are often presented as a hopeful key to a better life and a more equitable society. The discussion of postmodern culture focuses to a great extent on an emerging new individual identity or subject position, one that abandons what may in retrospect be the narrow scope of the modern individual with its claims to rationality and autonomy. The discourse surrounding the new communications systems attends more to the imminent technical increase in information exchange and the ways this advantage will redound to already existing individuals and already existing institutions.

My purpose in this essay is to bring these two discussions together, to enact a confrontation between them so that the advantages of each may redound to the other, while the limitations of each may be revealed and discarded. My contention is that a critical understanding of the new communications systems requires an evaluation of the type of subject it encourages, while a viable articulation of postmodernity must include an elaboration of its relation to new technologies of communication.

For what is at stake in these technical innovations, I contend, is not simply an increased 'efficiency' of interchange, enabling new avenues of investment, increased productivity at work and new domains of leisure and consumption, but a broad and extensive change in the culture, in the way identities are structured. If I may be allowed a historical analogy: the technically advanced societies are at a point in their history similar to that of the emergence of an urban, merchant culture in the midst of feudal society in the Middle Ages. At that point practices of the exchange of commodities required individuals to act and speak in new ways,[1] ways drastically different from the aristocratic code of honor with its face-to-face encounters based on trust for one's word and its hierarchical bonds of interdependency. Interacting with total strangers, sometimes at great distances, the merchants required written documents guaranteeing spoken promises and an 'arm's length distance' attitude even when face-to-face with the other, so as to afford a 'space' for calculations of self-interest. A new identity was constructed, gradually and in a most circuitous path to be sure, among the merchants, in which a coherent, stable sense of individuality was grounded in independent, cognitive abilities. In this way the cultural basis for the modern world was begun, one that eventually would rely upon print media to encourage and disseminate these urban forms of identity.

In the 20th century, electronic media are supporting an equally profound transformation of cultural identity. Telephone, radio, film, television, the computer and now their integration as 'multimedia' reconfigure words, sounds and images so as to cultivate new configurations of individuality. If modern society may be said to foster an individual who is rational, autonomous, centered and stable (the 'reasonable man' of the law, the educated citizen of representative democracy, the calculating 'economic man' of capitalism, the grade-defined student of public education), then perhaps a postmodern society is emerging which nurtures forms of identity different from, even opposite to those of modernity. And electronic communications technologies significantly enhance these postmodern possibilities. Discussions of these technologies, as we shall see, tend often to miss precisely this crucial level of analysis, treating them as enhancements for already formed individuals to deploy to their advantage or disadvantage.[2]

The Communications 'Superhighway'

One may regard the media from a purely technical point of view, to the extent that is possible, evaluating them in relation to their ability to transmit units of information. The question to ask then is how much information with how little noise may be transmitted at what speed and over what distance to how many locations? Until the late 1980s technical constraints limited the media's ability in these terms. To transmit a high quality image over existing (twisted pair copper wire) phone lines took about ten minutes using a 2400-baud modem or two minutes using a 9600-baud modem. Given these specifications it was not possible to send 'real time' 'moving' images over the phone lines. The great limitation, then, of the first electronic media age is that images could only be transmitted from a small number of centers to a large number of receivers, either by air or by coaxial cable. Until the end of the 1980s an 'economic' scarcity existed in the media highways that encouraged and justified, without much thought or consideration, the capitalist or nation-state exploitation of image transmission. Since senders needed to build their own information roads by broadcasting at a given frequency or by constructing (coaxial) wire networks, there were necessarily few distributors of images. The same economies of technology, it might be noted in passing, applied to processes of information production.

Critical theorists such as Benjamin, Enzensberger and McLuhan[3] envisioned the democratic potential of the increased communication capacity of radio, film and television. While there is some truth to their position, the practical model for a more radical communications potential during the first media age was rather the telephone. What distinguishes the telephone from the other great media is its decentralized quality and its universal exchangeability of the positions of sender and receiver. Anyone can 'produce' and send a message to anyone else in the system and, in the advanced industrial societies, almost everyone is in the system. These unique qualities were recognized early on by both defenders and detractors of the telephone.

In the recent past the only technology that imitates the telephone's democratic structure is the Internet, the government funded electronic mail, database and general communication system.[4] Until the 1990s, even this facility has been largely restricted to government, research and education institutions, some private industry and individuals who enroll in private services (Compuserve, Prodigy) which are connected to it. In the last few years Internet has gained enormously in popularity and by the mid-1990s boasts 30 million users around the world (Cooke and Lehrer, 1993). But Internet and its segments use the phone lines, suffering their inherent technical limitations. Technical innovations in the late 1980s and early 1990s, however, are making possible the drastic reduction of earlier constraints. The digital encoding of sound, text and image, the introduction of fiber-optic lines replacing copper wire, the ability to transmit digitally encoded images and the subsequent ability to compress this information, the vast expansion of the frequency range for wireless transmission, innovations in switching technology and a number of other advances have so enlarged the quantity and types of information that may soon be able to be transmitted that a qualitative change, to allude to Engels' dialectical formula, in the culture may also be imminent.

Information superhighways are being constructed that will enable a vast increase in the flow of communications. The telephone and cable companies are estimating the change to be from a limit of 60 or so one-way video/audio channels to one of 500 with limited bidirectionality. But this kind of calculation badly misses the point.

The increase in transmission capacity (both wired and wireless) will be so great that it will be possible to transmit any type of information (audio, video or text) from any point in the network to any other point or points, and to do so in 'real time', in other words quickly enough so that the receiver will see or record at least 24 frames of video per second with an accompanying audio frequency range of 20 to 20,000 Hertz. The metaphor of the 'superhighway' only attends to the movement of information, leaving out the various kinds of cyberspace on the Internet, meeting places, work areas and electronic cafes in which this vast transmission of images and words becomes places of communicative relation. The question that needs to be raised is 'will this technological change provide the stimulus for the installation of new media different enough from what we now have to warrant the periodizing judgment of a second electronic media age?' If that is the case, how is the change to be understood?

A discourse on the new communications technology is in process of formation, one which is largely limited by the vision of modernity. The importance of the information superhighway is now widely recognized, with articles appearing in periodicals from the specialized zines (*Wired* and *Mondo 2000*) to general journals (*Time, Forbes* and *The Nation*). Essays on the new technology vary from breathless enthusiasm to wary caution to skepticism. Writing in *Time*, Philip Elmer-Dewitt (1993:52) forecasts: 'The same switches used to send a TV show to your home can also be used to send a video from your home to any other – paving the way for video phones. . . . The same system will allow anybody with a camcorder to distribute videos to the world . . .'. Key to the new media system are not only the technical advances mentioned above but also the merger of existing communication technologies. Elmer-Dewitt continues, '. . . the new technology will force the merger of television, telecommunications, computers, consumer electronics, publishing and information services into a single interactive information industry' (1993:52–3). Other observers emphasize the prospects of wireless technology. Writing in *Forbes*, George Gilder (1993:107) predicts the spread of this system:

> . . . the new minicell replaces a rigid structure of giant analog mainframes with a system of wireless local area networks . . . these wide and weak [replacing broadcasting based on 'long and strong'] radios can handle voice, data and even video at the same time . . . the system fulfills the promise of the computer revolution as a spectrum multiplier . . . [the new system will] banish once and for all the concept of spectrum scarcity.

Whether future communications media employ wired, wireless or some combination of the two, the same picture emerges of profound transformation.

Faced with this gigantic combination of new technology, integration of older technologies, creation of new industries and expansion of older ones, commentators have not missed the political implications. In *Tikkun*, David Bollier underlines the need for a new set of policies to govern and regulate the second media age in the public interest. President Bill Clinton and Vice-President Al Gore have already drawn attention to the problem, stressing the need for broad access to the superhighway, but also indicating their willingness to make the new developments safe for the profit motive. For them the main issue at stake is the strength of the United States in relation to other nations (read especially Japan) and the health of the industries involved. Bollier (1993:22) points to wider concerns, such as strengthening community life, supporting families and invigorating the democratic process.[5] At this point I want to note that Bollier understands the new media entirely within the framework of *modern* social institutions. The 'information superhighway' is for him a transparent tool that brings new efficiencies but by itself changes nothing. The media merely redound to the benefit of or detract from familiar institutions – the family, the community, the state.

If Bollier presents a liberal or left-liberal agenda for politics confronted by the second media age, Mitchell Kapor, former developer of Lotus 1–2–3, offers a more radical interpretation. He understands better than Bollier that the information superhighway opens qualitatively new political opportunities because it creates new loci of speech:

> ... the crucial political question is 'Who controls the switches?' There are two extreme choices. Users may have indirect, or limited control over when, what, why, and from whom they get information and to whom they send it. That's the broadcast model today, and it seems to breed consumerism, passivity, crassness, and mediocrity. Or, users may have decentralized, distributed, direct control over when, what, why, and with whom they exchange information. That's the Internet model today, and it seems to breed critical thinking, activism, democracy, and quality. We have an opportunity to choose now. (Kapor, 1993:5)

With Kapor, the interpretation of the new media returns to the position of Enzensberger: socialist or radical democratic control of the media results in more freedom, more enlightenment, more rationality; capitalist or centralist control results in oppression, passivity, irrationality. Kapor's reading of the information superhighway remains within the binaries of modernity. No new cultural formations of the self are imagined or even thought possible. While the political questions raised by Bollier and Kapor are valid and raise the level of debate well beyond its current formation, they remain limited to the terms of discussion that are familiar in the landscape of modernity.

The political implications of the Internet for the fate of the nation-state and the development of a global community also requires attention. The dominant use of English on the Internet suggests the extension of American power as does the fact that e-mail addresses in the US alone do not require a country code. The Internet normalizes American users. But the issue is more complex. In Singapore, English serves to *enable* conversations between hostile ethnic groups, being a neutral 'other'. Of course, vast inequalities of use exist, changing the democratic structure of the Internet into an occasion for further wrongs to the poorer populations. Even within the high-use nations, wealthy white males are disproportionate users. Yet technologies sometimes spread quickly and the Internet is relatively cheap. Only grassroots political mobilization on this issue will ensure wide access (Tehranian, forthcoming).

In some ways the Internet undermines the territoriality of the nation-state: messages in cyberspace are not easily delimited in Newtonian space, rendering borders ineffective. In the Teale–Homolka trial of early 1994, a case of multiple murders including sexual assault and mutilation, the Canadian government was unable to enforce an information blackout because of Usenet postings in the United States being available in Canada (Turner, 1994). In order to combat communicative acts that are defined by one state as illegal, nations are being compelled to coordinate their laws, putting their vaunted 'sovereignty' in question. So desperate are national governments, confronted by the disorder of the Internet, that schemes to monitor all messages are afoot, such as the American government's idea to monopolize encryption with a 'Clipper Chip' or the FBI's insistence on building surveillance mechanisms into the structure of the information superhighway (Hotz, 1993: 22). Nation-states are at a loss when faced with a global communication network. Technology has taken a turn that defines the character of power of modern governments.

The effortless reproduction and distribution of information is greeted by modern economic organizations, the corporations, with the same anxiety that plagues nation-states. Audio taping was resisted by the moguls of the music industry; video taping by Hollywood; modems by the telephone industry giants. Property rights are put in doubt when information is set free of its material integument to move and to multiply in cyberspace with few constraints. The response of our captains of industry is the absurd one of attempting vastly to extend the principle of property by promulgating new 'intellectual property laws', flying in the face of the advance in the technologies of transmission and dissemination. The problem for capitalism is how to contain the word and the image, to bind them to proper names and logos when they flit about at the speed of light and procreate with indecent rapidity, not arborially, to use the terms of Deleuze and Guattari, as in a centralized factory, but rhyzomically, at any decentered location. If that were not enough to daunt defenders of modern notions of property, First Amendment issues are equally at risk. Who, for example, 'owns' the rights to and is thereby responsible for the text on Internet bulletin boards: the author, the system operator, the community of participants? Does freedom of speech extend to cyberspace, as it does to print?

How easy will it be to assess damages and mete out blame in a communicative world whose contours are quite different from those of face-to-face speech and print? These and numerous other fundamental questions are raised by Internet communications for institutions, laws and habits that developed in the very different context of modernity.

Reality Problematized

Before turning to the issue of the cultural interpretation of the second media age, we need to consider a further new technology, that of virtual reality. The term 'virtual' was used in computer jargon to refer to situations that were near substitutes. For example, virtual memory means the use of a section of a hard disk to act as something else, in this case, random access memory. 'Virtual reality' is a more dangerous term since it suggests that reality may be multiple or take many forms.[6] The phrase is close to that of 'real time', which arose in the audio recording field when splicing, multiple-track recording and multiple-speed recording made possible 'other times' to that of clock time or phenomenological time. In this case, the normal or conventional sense of 'time' had to be preserved by the modifier 'real'. But again the use of the modifier only draws attention to non-'reality' of clock time, its non-exclusivity, its insubstantiality, its lack of foundation. The terms 'virtual reality' and 'real time' attest to the force of the second media age in constituting a simulational culture. The mediation has become so intense that the things mediated can no longer even pretend to be unaffected. The culture is increasingly simulational in the sense that the media often changes the things that it treats, transforming the identity of originals and referentialities. In the second media age 'reality' becomes multiple.

Virtual reality is a computer-generated 'place' which is 'viewed' by the participant through 'goggles' but which responds to stimuli from the participant or participants. A participant may 'walk' through a house that is being designed for him or her to get a feel for it before it is built. Or s/he may 'walk' through a 'museum' or 'city' whose paintings or streets are computer-generated but the position of the individual is relative to their actual movement, not to a predetermined computer program or 'movie'. In addition, more than one individual may experience the same virtual reality at the same time, with both persons' 'movements' affecting the same 'space'. What is more, these individuals need not be in the same physical location but may be communicating information to the computer from distant points through modems. Further 'movements' in virtual reality are not quite the same as movements in 'old reality': for example, one can fly or go through walls since the material constraints of earth need not apply. While still in their infancy, virtual reality programs attest to the increasing 'duplication', if I may use this term, of reality by technology. But the duplication incurs an alternation: virtual realities are fanciful imaginings that, in their difference from real reality, evoke play and discovery, instituting a new level of imagination. Virtual reality takes the imaginary of the word and the imaginary of the film or video image one step farther by placing the individual 'inside' alternative worlds. By directly tinkering with reality, a simulational practice is set in place which alters forever the conditions under which the identity of the self is formed.

Already transitional forms of virtual reality are in use on the Internet. MUDs or Multi User Domains have a devoted following. These are conferences of sorts in which participants adopt roles in a neo-medieval adventure game. Although the game is played textually, that is, moves are typed as sentences, it is highly 'visual' in the sense that complex locations, characters and objects interact continuously. In a variant of a MUD, LambdaMOO, a database contains 'objects' as 'built' by participants to improve upon the sense of reality. As a result, a quasi-virtual reality is created by the players. What is more, each player adopts a fictional role that may be different from their actual gender and indeed this gender may change in the course of the game, drastically calling into question the gender system of the dominant culture as a fixed binary. At least during the fictional game, individuals explore imaginary subject positions while in communication with others. In LambdaMOO, a series of violent 'rapes' by one character caused a crisis among the participants, one that led to special conferences devoted to the issue of punishing the offender and thereby better defining the nature of the community space of the conference. This experience also cautions against depictions of cyberspace as utopia: the wounds of modernity are borne with us when we enter this new arena and in some cases are even exacerbated. Nonetheless, the makings of a new cultural space are also at work in the MUDs. One participant argues that continuous participation in the game leads to a sense of involvement that is somewhere between ordinary reality and fiction (Dibbell, 1993).[7] The effect of new media such as the Internet and virtual reality, then, is to multiply the kinds of 'realities' one encounters in society.

The Postmodern Subject

The information superhighway and virtual reality are communications media that enrich existing forms of consumer culture. But they also depart or may depart from what we have known as the mass media or the 'culture industry' in a number of crucial ways. I said 'may depart' because neither of these technologies has been fully constituted as cultural practices; they are emergent communication systems whose features are yet to be specified with some permanence or finality. One purpose of this essay is to suggest the importance of some form of political concern about how these technologies are being actualized. The technical characteristics of the information superhighway and virtual reality are clear enough to call attention to their potential for new cultural formations. It is conceivable that the information superhighway will be restricted in the way the broadcast system is. In that case, the term 'second media age' is unjustified. But the potential of a decentralized communications system is so great that it is certainly worthy of recognition. Examples from the history of the installation and dissemination of communications technologies is instructive. Carolyn Marvin points out that the telephone was, at the outset, by no means the universal, decentralized network it became. The phone company was happy to restrict the use of the instrument to those who registered. It did not understand the social or political importance of the universality of participation, being interested mainly in income from services provided. Also the example of Telefon Hirmondó, a telephone system in Budapest in the period before the First World War, is worth recalling. The Hungarians used the telephone as a broadcast system, with a published schedule of programming. They also restricted narrowly the dissemination of the technology to the ruling class. The process by which the telephone was instituted as a universally disseminated network in which anyone is able to call anyone else occurred in a complex, multi-leveled historical articulation in which the technology, the economic structure, the political institutions, the political culture and the mass of the population each played interacting roles (Marvin, 1988: 222ff). A similarly complex history will no doubt accompany the institution of the information superhighway and virtual reality.

In *The Mode of Information* (Poster, 1990) I argued that electronic communications constitute the subject in ways other than that of the major modern institutions. If modernity or the mode of production signifies patterned practices that elicit identities as autonomous and (instrumentally) rational, postmodernity or the mode of information indicates communication practices that constitute subjects as unstable, multiple and diffuse. The information superhighway and virtual reality will extend the mode of information to still further applications, greatly amplifying its diffusion by bringing more practices and more individuals within its pattern of formation. No doubt many modern institutions and practices continue to exist and indeed dominate social space. The mode of information is an emergent phenomenon that affects small but important aspects of everyday life. It certainly does not blanket the advanced industrial societies and has even less presence in less developed nations. The information superhighway and virtual reality may be interpreted through the poststructuralist lens I have used here in relation to the cultural issue of subject constitution. If that is done, the question of the mass media is seen not simply as that of sender/receiver, producer/consumer, ruler/ruled. The shift to a decentralized network of communications makes senders receivers, producers consumers, rulers ruled, upsetting the logic of understanding of the first media age. The step I am suggesting is at least temporarily to abandon that logic and adopt a poststructuralist cultural analysis of modes of subject constitution. This does not answer all the questions opened by the second media age, especially the political ones which at the moment are extremely difficult. But it permits the recognition of an emergent postmodernity and a tentative approach to a political analysis of that cultural system; it permits the beginning of a line of thought that confronts the possibility of a new age, avoiding the continued, limiting, exclusive repetition of the logics of modernity.

Subject constitution in the second media age occurs through the mechanism of interactivity. A technical term referring to two-way communications, 'interactivity' has become, by dint of the advertising campaigns of telecommunications corporations, desirable as an end in itself so that its usage can float and be applied in countless contexts having little to do with telecommunications. Yet the phenomenon of communicating at a distance through one's computer, of sending and receiving digitally encoded messages, of being 'interactive' has been the most popular application of the Internet. Far more than making purchases or obtaining information electronically, communicating by computer claims the intense interest of countless thousands (Dery, 1993). The use of the Internet to simulate communities far outstrips its function as retail store or reference work. In the words of Howard Rheingold (1993: 61), an enthusiastic Internet user, 'I can attest that I and thousands of other cybernauts know that what we are looking for, and finding in some surprising ways, is not just information and but instant access to ongoing relationships with a large number of other people.' Rheingold terms the network of relations that come into existence on Internet bulletin boards 'virtual communities'. Places for 'meeting' on the Internet, such as 'the Well' frequented by Rheingold, provide 'areas' for 'public' messages, which all subscribers may read, and private 'mailbox' services for individual exchanges.

The understanding of these communications is limited by modern categories of analysis. For example, many have interpreted the success of 'virtual communities' as an indication that 'real' communities are in decline. Internet provides an alternative, these critics contend, to the real thing (Rheingold, 1993: 62). But the opposition 'virtual' and 'real' community contains serious difficulties. In the case of the nation, generally regarded as the strongest group identification in the modern period and thus perhaps the most 'real' community of this era, the role of the imaginary has been fundamental (Anderson, 1983). Pre-electronic media like the newspaper were instrumental in disseminating the sign of the nation and interpellating the subject in relation to it. In even earlier types of community, such as the village, kinship and residence were salient factors of determination. But identification of an individual or family with a specific group was never automatic, natural or given, always turning, as Jean-Luc Nancy (1991: xxxviii) argues, on the production of an 'essence' which reduces multiplicity into fixity, obscuring the political process in which 'community' is constructed: '. . . the thinking of community as essence . . . is in effect the closure of the political'.[8] He rephrases the term community by asking the following question: 'How can we be receptive to the *meaning* of our multiple, dispersed, mortally fragmented existences, which nonetheless only make sense by existing in common?' (1991: xi). Community for him then is paradoxically the absence of 'community'. It is rather the matrix of fragmented identities, each pointing toward the other, which he chooses to term 'writing'.

Nancy's critique of community in the older sense is crucial to the understanding of the construction of self in the Internet. For his part, Nancy has chosen to deny the significance of new communications technologies, as well as new subaltern subject positions in his understanding of community:

> The emergence and our increasing consciousness of decolonized communities has not profoundly modified [the givens of community], nor has today's growth of unprecedented forms of being-in-common – through channels of information as well as through what is called the 'multiracial society' – triggered any genuine renewal of the question of community. (Nancy, 1991: 22)

Nancy denies the relation I am drawing between a postmodern constitution of the subject and bidirectional communications media. The important point however is that in order to do so he first posits the subject as 'multiple, dispersed, mortally fragmented' in an ontological statement. To this extent he removes the question of community from the arena of history and politics, the exact purpose of his critique of the essentialist community in the first place. While presenting an effective critique of the essentialist community Nancy reinstates the problem at the level of the subject by ontologizing its inessentialism. My preference is rather to specify the historical emergence of the decentered subject and explore its links with new communications situations.

We may now return to the question of the Internet and its relation to a 'virtual community'. To restate the issue: the Internet and virtual reality open the possibility of new kinds of interactivity such that the idea of an opposition of real and unreal community is not adequate to specify the differences between modes of bonding, serving instead to obscure the manner of the historical construction of forms of community. In particular, this opposition prevents asking the question of the forms of identity prevalent in various types of community. The notion of a real community, as Nancy shows, presupposes the fixed, stable identities of its members, the exact assumption that Internet communities put into question. Observers of participants in Internet 'virtual communities' repeat in near unanimity that long or intense experience with computer-mediated electronic communication is associated with a certain fluidity of identity. Rheingold foresees huge cultural changes as the effect of Internet use on the individual: '. . . are relationships and commitments as we know them even possible in a place where identities are fluid? . . . We reduce and encode our identities as words on a screen, decode and unpack the identities of others' (1993:61). In bulletin boards like the Well, people connect with strangers without much of the social baggage that divides and alienates. Without visual cues about gender, age, ethnicity and social status, conversations open up in directions that otherwise might be avoided. Participants in these virtual communities often express themselves with little inhibition and dialogues flourish and develop quickly. Yet Rheingold attributes the conviviality of the Well and the extravagant identity transformations of MUDs to 'the hunger for community that has followed the disintegration of traditional communities around the world' (1991:62). Even for this advocate of new communications technologies the concept of a real community regulates his understanding of the new interactivity. While there may be some truth to a perspective that sees 'virtual communities' as compensations for the loss of real communities, I prefer to explore the new territory and define its possibilities.

Another aspect to understanding identity in virtual communities is provided by Stone. Her studies of electronic communication systems suggest that participants code 'virtual' reality through categories of 'normal' reality. They do so by communicating to each other as if they were in physical common space, as if this space were inhabited by bodies, were mappable by Cartesian perspective, and by regarding the interactions as events, as fully significant for the participants' personal histories (Stone, 1992:618). While treatment of new media by categories developed in relation to earlier ones is hardly new, in this case the overlap serves to draw closer together the two types of ontological status. Virtual communities derive some of their verisimilitude from being treated as if they were plain communities, allowing members to experience communications in cyberspace as if they were embodied social interactions. Just as virtual communities are understood as having the attributes of 'real' communities, so 'real' communities can be seen to depend on the imaginary: what makes a community vital to its members is their treatment of the communications as meaningful and important. Virtual and real communities mirror each other in chiasmic juxtaposition.

Narratives in Cyberspace

Electronic mail services and bulletin boards are inundated by stories. Individuals appear to enjoy relating narratives to those they have never met and probably never will meet. These narratives often seem to emerge directly from peoples' lives but many no doubt are inventions. The appeal is strong to tell one's tale to others, to many, many others. One observer suggests the novelty of the situation:

> technology is breaking down the notion of few-to-many communications. Some communicators will always be more powerful than others, but the big idea behind cyber-tales is that for the first time the many are talking to the many. Every day, those who can afford the computer equipment and the telephone bills can be their own producers, agents, editors and audiences. Their stories are becoming more and more idiosyncratic, interactive and individualistic, told in different forums to diverse audiences in different ways. (Katz, 1994)

This explosion of narrativity depends upon a technology that is unlike print and unlike the electronic media of the first age: it is cheap, flexible, readily available, quick. It combines the decentralized model of the telephone and its numerous 'producers' of messages with the broadcast model's advantage of numerous receivers. Audio (Internet Talk Radio) and video (the World Wide Web using Mosaic) are being added to text, enhancing considerably the potentials of the new narratives. There is now a 'World-Wide Web' which allows the simultaneous transmission of text, images and sound, providing hypertext links as well. The implications of the Web are astounding: film clips and voice readings may be included in 'texts' and 'authors' may indicate their links as 'texts'. In addition, other related technologies produce similar decentralizing effects. Such phenomena as 'desktop broadcasting', widespread citizen camcorder 'reporting', and digital film-making are transgressing the constraints of broadcast oligopolies (*Mondo 2000*, 1993: 34 and 106).

The question of narrative position has been central to the discussion of postmodernity. Jean-François Lyotard has analyzed the change in narrative legitimation structures of the premodern, modern and postmodern epochs. Lyotard (1984) defines the postmodern as an 'incredulity' toward metanarratives, especially that of progress and its variants deriving from the Enlightenment. He advocates a turn to the 'little story' which validates difference, extols the 'unpresentable' and escapes the overbearing logic of instrumentality that derives from the metanarrative of progress. Any effort to relate second media age technologies with the concept of the postmodern must confront Lyotard's skepticism about technology. For Lyotard, it must be recalled, technology itself is fully complicit with *modern* narrativity. For example, he warns of the dangers of 'a generalized computerization of society' in which the availability of knowledge is politically dangerous:

> The performativity of an utterance ... increases proportionally to the amount of information about its referent one has at one's disposal. Thus the growth of power, and its self-legitimation, are

now taking the route of data storage and accessibility, and the operativity of information. (Lyotard, 1984:47)

Information technologies are thus complicit with new tendencies toward totalitarian control, not toward a decentralized, multiple 'little narrativity' of postmodern culture.

The question may be raised, then, of the narrative structure of second media age communications: does it or is it likely to promote the proliferation of little narratives or does it invigorate a developing authoritarian technocracy? Lyotard describes the narrative structure of tribal, premodern society as stories that first legitimate institutions, second contain many different forms of language, third are transmitted by senders who are part of the narrative and have heard it before and listeners who are possible senders, fourth construct a nonlinear temporality that foreshortens the past and the present, rendering each repetition of the story strangely concurrent and, most importantly, fifth authorize everyone as a narrator. Modern society, Lyotard argues derives its legitimacy from narratives about science. Within science, language first does not legitimate institutions, second contains the single language form of denotation, third does not confirm addressee as possible sender, fourth gains no validity by being reported, and fifth constructs 'diachronic' temporality. These contrasting characteristics may serve, as Lyotard wishes, to indicate the 'pragmatics' of language. It would be interesting to analyze the role of technologies in the premodern and modern cases, and especially the change, within the modern, from print to broadcast media.

In any case, for Lyotard, the postmodern little narrative refunctions the premodern language game but only in limited ways. Like the tribal myth, the little narrative insists on 'the heteromorphous nature of language games' (1984:66); in short, it validates difference. Unlike older narrative forms, the little narrative emphasizes the role of invention, the indication of the unknown and the unexpected. Lyotard looks to certain developments in the natural sciences for his examples of such postmodern narratives, but we may turn to the Internet and to the developing technology of virtual reality. As we have seen, the Internet seems to encourage the proliferation of stories, local narratives without any totalizing gestures and it places senders and addressees in symmetrical relations. Moreover, these stories and their performance consolidate the 'social bond' of the Internet 'community', much like the premodern narrative. But invention is central to the Internet, especially in MUDs and virtual reality: the production of the unknown or paralogy, in Lyotard's term, is central to second media age communications. In particular the relation of the utterance to representation is not limited to denotation as in the modern language game of science, and indeed the technology encourages a lightening of the weight of the referent. This is an important basis for the instability of identity in electronic communications, leading to the insertion of the question of the subject and its construction. In this spirit, Katherine Hayles (1993a: 175) defines the 'revolutionary potential' of virtual reality as follows: 'to expose the presuppositions underlying the social formations of late capitalism and to open new fields of play where the dynamics have not yet rigidified and new kinds of moves are possible'.

For the new technologies install the 'interface', the face between the faces; the face that insists that we remember that we have 'faces', that we have sides that are present at the moment of utterance, that we are not present in any simple or immediate way. The interface has become critical to the success of the Internet. To attain wide appeal, the Internet must not simply be efficient, useful or entertaining: it must present itself in an agreeable manner. The enormous problem for interface design is the fear and hostility humans nourish toward machines and toward a dim recognition of a changing relation toward them, a sharing of space and an interdependence (Springer, 1991). The Internet interface must somehow appear 'transparent', that is to say, appear not to be an interface, not to come between two alien beings and also seem fascinating, announcing its novelty and encouraging an exploration of the difference of the machinic. The problem of the Internet then is not simply 'technological' but para-machinic: to construct a boundary between the human and the machinic that draws the human into the technology, transforming the technology into 'used equipment' and the human into a 'cyborg', into one meshing with machines.[9]

In Wim Wenders' recent film, *Until the End of the World*, (1991) several characters view their own dreams on videotape, becoming so absorbed in what they see that they forget to eat and sleep. The characters sit transfixed before their viewing devices, ignoring everyone around them, disregarding all relations and affairs. Limited to the microworld of their own dreams, the characters are lost in a narcissistic stupor. And yet their total absorption is compelling. Visual representations of the unconscious – no doubt Wenders has film itself in mind – are irresistible compared to everyday reality, a kind of hyperreality.

One can imagine that virtual reality devices will become as compelling as the dream videos in Wenders' film. Virtual reality machines should be able to allow the participant to enter imagined worlds with convincing verisimilitude, releasing immense potentials for fantasy, self-discovery and self-construction. When groups of individuals are able to interact in the same virtual space the possibilities are even more difficult to conceive. One hesitates to suggest that these experiences are commensurate with something that has been termed community. Yet there is every reason to think that virtual reality technologies will develop rapidly and will eventually enable participation through the Internet. Connected to one's home computer one will experience an audiovisual 'world' generated from a node somewhere in the Internet and this will include other participants in the same way that today one can communicate with others on bulletin boards in videotext. If such experiences become commonplace, just as viewing television is today, then surely reality will have been multiplied. The continued Western quest for making tools may at that point retrospectively be reinterpreted in relation to its culmination in virtual reality. From the club that extends and replaces the arm to virtual reality in cyberspace, technology has evolved to mime and to multiply, to multiplex and to improve upon the real.

Notes

1. See Agnew (1986) for an analysis of the formation of this subject position and its particular relation to the theater. Habermas (1989) offers a 'public sphere' of coffee houses, salons and other agora-like locations, as the arena of the modern subject, while Weber (1958) looks to Calvinist religion for the roots of the same phenomenon.

2. See, for example, the discussion of new 'interactive' technologies in the *New York Times* on 19 December 1993. In 'The Uncertain Promises of Interactivity', Calvin Sims restricts future innovations to movies on demand, on-line information services, interactive shopping, 'participatory programming', video games and conferencing systems for business. He omits electronic mail and its possible expansion to sound and image in networked virtual reality systems.

3. I have not discussed the work of Marshall McLuhan simply for lack of space and also because it is not as directly related to traditions of critical social theory as is Benjamin's, Enzensberger's and Baudrillard's. Also of interest is Kittler (1990a, 1990b).

4. For an excellent essay on the economics of the Internet and its basic structural features see Hal Varian, 'Economic FAQs About the Internet', which is available on the Internet at listserver@essential.org (send message: subscribe tap-info [your name]).

5. See also the cautionary tone of Herbert Schiller (1993).

6. Many writers prefer the term 'artificial reality' precisely because they want to underscore the privilege of real reality. Needless to say this substitution will not cure the problem.

7. I am indebted to Rob Kling for making me aware of this piece.

8. See also the response by Blanchot (1988).

9. Hayles (1993b: 69–91) interprets these 'different configurations of embodiment, technology and culture' through the binary pattern/randomness rather than presence/absence.

References

Agnew, J.C. (1986) *Worlds Apart: The Market and the Theatre in Anglo-American Thought, 1550–1750.* New York: Cambridge University Press.

Anderson, B. (1983) *Imagined Communities: Reflections on the Origin and Spread of Nationalism.* New York: Verso.

Blanchot, M. (1988) *The Unavowable Community*, trans. Pierre Joris. Barrytown, NY: Station Hill Press.

Bollier, D. (1993) 'The Information Superhighway: Roadmap for Renewed Public Purpose', *Tikkun* 8(4): 20–2.

Cooke, K. and D. Lehrer (1993) 'The Whole World is Talking', *The Nation* 12 July: 89–90.

Dery, M. (ed.) (1993) 'Flame Wars: The Discourse of Cyberculture', *South Atlantic Quarterly* 92(4).

Dibbell, J. (1993) 'A Rape in Cyberspace', *The Village Voice* 21 December: 36–42.

Elmer-Dewitt, P. (1993) 'Take a Trip into the Future on the Electronic Superhighway', *Time* 12 April: 50–8.

Gilder, G. (1993) 'Telecosm: The New Rule of Wireless', *Forbes ASAP* 29 March: 96, 98–104, 106–9.

Habermas, J. (1989) *The Structural Transformation of the Public Sphere*, trans. Thomas Burger. Cambridge, MA: MIT Press.

Hayles, K. (1993a) 'The Seductions of Cyberspace', in V. Conley (ed.) *Rethinking Technologies*. Minneapolis: University of Minnesota Press.

Hayles, K. (1993b) 'Virtual Bodies and Flickering Signifiers', *October* 66: 69–91.

Hotz, R.L. (1993) 'Computer Code's Security Worries Privacy Watchdogs', *Los Angeles Times* 4 October: A3, A22.

Kapor, M. (1993) 'Where Is the Digital Highway Really Heading?: The Case for a Jeffersonian Information Policy', *Wired* 1(3): 53–9, 94.

Katz, J. (1994) 'The Tales They Tell in Cyber-Space Are a Whole Other Story', *Los Angeles Times* 23 January: A1, A30.

Kittler, F. (1990a) 'Gramophone, Film, Typewriter', *October* 41: 101–18.

Kittler, F. (1990b) *Discourse Networks: 1800/1900*, trans. Michael Metteer. Stanford: Stanford University Press.

Lyotard, J.F. (1984) *The Postmodern Condition: A Report on Knowledge*, trans. Geoff Bennington and Brian Massumi. Minneapolis: University of Minnesota Press.

Marvin, C. (1988) *When Old Technologies Were New: Thinking About Electric Communication in the Late Nineteenth Century*. New York: Oxford.

Mondo 2000 (1993) No. 11.

Nancy, J.L. (1991) *The Inoperative Community*, trans. Peter Conner et al. Minneapolis: University of Minnesota Press.

Poster, M. (1990) *The Mode of Information*. Oxford: Polity Press.

Rheingold, H. (1993) 'A Slice of Life in My Virtual Community', in L. Harasim (ed.) *Global Networks: Computers and International Communication*. Cambridge: MIT Press.

Schiller, H. (1993) 'The "Information Highway": Public Way or Private Road?', *The Nation* July 12.

Springer C. (1991) 'The Pleasure of the Interface', *Screen* 32(3): 303–23.

Stone, A.R. (1992) 'Virtual Systems', in *Incorporations*, ed. Jonathan Crary and Stanford Kwinter. Cambridge: MIT Press.

Tehranian, M. (forthcoming) 'World With/Out Wars: Moral Spaces and the Ethics of Transnational Communication', *The Public* (Ljubljana).

Turner, C. (1994) 'Courts Gag Media at Sensational Canada Trial', *Los Angeles Times* May 15: A4.

Weber, M. (1958) *The Protestant Ethic and the Spirit of Capitalism*, trans. Talcott Parsons. New York: Macmillan.

Mark Poster teaches History at the University of California, Irvine. His recent publications include *The Second Media Age* (1995), *The Mode of Information* (1990) and *Postsuburban California* (1991).

The Embodied Computer/User

DEBORAH LUPTON

When I turn my personal computer (a desk-top IBM-compatible) on, it makes a little sound. This little sound I sometimes playfully interpret as a cheerful 'Good morning' greeting, for the action of bringing my computer to life usually happens first thing in the morning, when I sit down at my desk, a cup of tea at my side, to begin the day's work. In conjunction with my cup of tea, the sound helps to prepare me emotionally and physically for the working day ahead, a day that will involve much tapping on the computer keyboard and staring into the pale blue face of the display monitor, when not reading or looking out the window in the search for inspiration. I am face-to-face with my computer for far longer than I look into any human face. I don't have a name for my personal computer, nor do I ascribe it a gender (although I know some people do; see, for example, Stone, 1992: 81). However, I do have an emotional relationship with the computer, which usually makes itself overtly known when something goes wrong. Like most other computer users, I have experienced impatience, anger, panic, anxiety and frustration when my computer does not do what I want it to, or breaks down. I have experienced files that have been lost, printers failing to work, the display monitor losing its colour, disks that can't be read, a computer virus, a breakdown in the system that stopped me using the computer or email. I live in fear that a power surge will short-circuit my computer, wiping the hard disk, or that the computer will be stolen, and I assiduously make back-up copies of my files. For some years now (since I first learnt how to use a word-processing package in 1986), I have relied upon computers to write. I have written whole articles and books without printing out a hard copy until the penultimate draft. I cannot imagine how it must have been in the 'dark ages' when people had to write PhDs and books without using a computer. I can type much faster than I write with a pen. A pen now feels strange, awkward and slow in my hand, compared to using a keyboard. When I type, the words appear on the screen almost as fast as I formulate them in my head. There is, for me, almost a seamless transition of thought to word on the screen.

These personal reflections raise the issues of the emotional and embodied relationship that computer users have with their personal computers (PCs). While people in contemporary western societies rely upon many other forms of technology during the course of their everyday lives (for example, spectacles, television, telephones) and, indeed, use technological artefacts to construct a sense of subjectivity and differentiation from others (the car being an obvious example), the relationship we have with our PCs has characteristics that sets it apart from the many other technologies we use. For the growing number of individuals who rely upon their PCs to perform work tasks, and for others who enjoy using their PCs for entertainment and communication purposes, conducting life without one's PC has become almost unimaginable (how *do* people write books without them?). I recently visited an academic research unit where the networked computer system had suddenly gone down for 24 hours during a week day. People there spoke of being left wondering what to do that day, not knowing how to occupy themselves with no computer to work upon/with. Despite this dependency, many people who use their PCs almost every day have very little knowledge of how they work, of what lies behind the bland, blue screen. Thus trust and dependency are combined with mystique.

More than that, however, the cultural meanings around PCs, including common marketing strategies to sell them and the ways people tend to think about their own PC, relies on a degree of anthropomorphism that is found with few other technological artefacts. While we may often refer to cars as human-like, investing them with emotional and personality attributes, they are rarely represented as 'friends', 'work companions' or even 'lovers' in quite the same way as are computers. As Heim has commented,

> Our love affair with computers, computer graphics, and computer networks runs deeper than aesthetic fascination and deeper than the play of the senses. We are searching for a home for the mind and the heart. Our fascination with computers is more erotic than sensuous, more deeply spiritual than utilitarian. (1992:61)

In his book *Bodies and Machines*, Seltzer refers to the 'psychotopography of machine culture', or the way in which psychological and geographical spaces cross the natural and the technological, between interior states and external systems; how bodies, persons and machines interact (1992:19). I am interested in the 'psycho-topography' of the human/computer relationship, the ways that humans think, feel and experience their computers and interact with them as subjects. Rather than the computer/human dyad being a simple matter of self versus other, there is, for many people, a blurring of the boundaries between the embodied self and the PC. Grosz (1994:80) notes that inanimate objects, when touched or on the body for long enough, become extensions of the body image and sensation. They become psychically invested into the self; indeed, she argues, '[i]t is only insofar as the object ceases to remain an object and becomes a medium, a vehicle for impressions and expression, that it can be used as an instrument or tool'. Depending on how inanimate objects are used or performed by the body, they may become 'intermediate' or 'midway between the inanimate and the bodily' (Grosz, 1994: 81). These observations, I would contend, are useful for understanding the blurriness and importance of the computer/user relationship. This relationship is symbiotic: users invest certain aspects of themselves and their cultures when 'making sense' of their computers, and their use of computers may be viewed as contributing to individuals' images and experiences of their selves and their bodies. Our interactions with PCs 'inscribe' our bodies, so that, for example, pens start to feel awkward as writing instruments.

In a previous article (Lupton, 1994), I explored the ways in which the viral metaphor, when used in the context of computer technology, betrays a series of cultural assumptions about computers and human bodies. I argued that popular and technical representations of computer viruses draw on discourses that assume that computer themselves are humanoid and embodied (and therefore subject to illness spread by viruses). What is more, similar cultural meanings are attached to the viral infection of computers as are associated with human illness, and in particular, the viral illness of HIV/AIDS. That is, there are a series of discourses that suggest that computers which malfunction due to 'viral contamination' have allowed themselves to become permeable, often via the indiscrete and 'promiscuous' behaviour of their users (in their act of inserting 'foreign' disks into their computer, therefore spreading the virus from PC to PC). I pointed out that computer viruses are manifestations of the barely submerged (and often very overt) emotions of hostility and fear that humans have towards computer technology.

In the present discussion I want to expand my previous consideration of the embodied relationship between computers and their users, with a particular focus on subjectivity and emotional states in the context of an ever-expanding global interlinking of PCs on the Internet, 'the world's largest network of computer networks' (Neesham, 1994: 1). In the wake of the Internet the computer/user relationship has been extended from an atomized and individualized dyad. The PC now can be used by individuals to link into information networks and exchange messages in real time with others around the world. In that respect, the burgeoning Internet technology is not so different from telephone technology. However, a major difference lies in the risks that have recently attracted much media attention in relation to using the Internet. The attractions of the Internet, including its accessibility, are also a source of problems around security and the activities of computer 'hackers' and 'cyber-criminals'. This article explores the implications of this for the computer/user relationship, with a focus on the mythic and 'irrational' meanings 'that are very close to the surface in computer culture', disrupting 'rational' and depersonalized meanings (Sofia, 1993: 116). I draw on a number of popular and more arcane texts to do so, including advertisements and articles about computers and users published in newspapers and news magazines, *New Scientist* magazine, *Wired* (a specialist magazine for Internet users) and academic writings about the computer/user relationship.

The Disembodied Computer User

A central utopian discourse around computer technology is the potential offered by computers for humans to escape the body. This discourse of disembodiment has been central in the writings of influential 'cyberpunk' novelist William Gibson and the cultural theorist and feminist Donna Haraway. In computer culture, embodiment is often represented as an unfortunate barrier to interaction with the pleasures of computing; as Morse (1994: 86) has put it, 'For couch potatoes, video game addicts and surrogate travellers of cyberspace alike, an organic body just gets in the way'. In cyberwriting, the body is often referred to as the 'meat', the dead flesh that surrounds the active mind which constitutes the 'authentic' self. The demands of the fleshly body compel computer users to distract themselves from their pursuit to seek nourishment and quell thirst and hunger pangs and, even worse, to absent themselves to carry out such body maintenance activities as washing, expelling bodily wastes and sleeping. The dream of cyberculture is to leave the 'meat' behind and to become distilled in a clean, pure, uncontaminated relationship with computer technology. 'The desire for an evolutionary transformation of the human has shifted focus from the preparation for the journey into "outer space" from a dying planet to the virtual "inner" space of the computer' (Morse, 1994: 96).

The 'human as computer' metaphor is frequently drawn upon in this attempt to deny the irrationality of embodiment. Human brains, for example, are frequently described as 'organic computers' (Berman, 1989). Sofia notes that the computer/human elision in this metaphor tends to represent human thought as calculating, rational and intentional, suppressing other cultural meanings around thought processes and the unconscious:

> both the computer and the brain become representable as entirely 'rational' entities in a move which, on the one hand, obscures the fantasies attached to computing (e.g. the dream of mastery) and, on the other, portrays human mental activity as a mode of digital processing, entirely ignoring processes like joking, wishing, dreaming or imaginative vision and speech. (1993: 51)

The idealized virtual body does not eat, drink, urinate or defecate; it does not get tired; it does not become ill; it does not die (although it does appear to engage in sexual activity, as all the hype around 'teledildonics' and virtual reality suggests). This vision may be considered to be the apotheosis of the post-Enlightenment separation of the body from the mind, in which the body has traditionally been represented as earthly, irrational, weak and passive, while the mind is portrayed as spiritual, rational, abstract and active, seeking constantly to stave off the demands of embodiment.

The cyborg has been represented as the closest to this ideal that humans may attain; that is, a 'humanoid hybrid' that melds together computer technology and human flesh (Haraway, 1988). In an era in which risks to the health and wellbeing of the fleshly body abound, in which ageing and death are feared, the cyborg offers an idealized escape route. The cyborg form is evident in drug advertisements directed at medical practitioners, representing the ideal body as that which is invulnerable to illness, whose susceptibility to disease and death is alleviated by the drug therapy (Lupton, 1993). In filmic portrayals of the cyborg, such as *Blade Runner* and the *Terminator* and *Robocop* series, the cyborg body is portrayed as far stronger than the human body and far less susceptible to injury or pain, often able to self-repair in a matter of seconds. The cyborg body thus addresses anxieties around the permeability of body boundaries in its clean, hard, tightness of form. These anxieties are gendered, for the boundaries of the feminine body are viewed as being far more permeable, fluid and subject to 'leakage' than are those of the masculine body (Theweleit, 1987; Grosz, 1994). It is for this reason that men find the concept of the cyborg attractive in its sheer invulnerability: the cyborg body is constituted of a hard endoskeleton covered by soft flesh, the inverse of the human body, in which the skin is a vulnerable and easily broken barrier between 'inside' and 'outside' (Jones, 1993: 84). In these discourses the cyborg is therefore a predominantly masculine body, as contrasted with the seeping, moist bodies of women.

The cyborg body holds different, and contrasting, meanings for some feminist writers. For them, the concept of the cyborg offers the potential for liberation from the confines of gender and other stereotypes, by rendering cultural categories and bodily boundaries indeterminate and fluid (Haraway, 1988). Lack of containment of the body, the blurring of differentiation between self and other, are not phrased as problems in such discourses; rather, such features are keys to the attraction that the cyborg body has for feminists. This is the supreme postmodern position, which denies any 'reality' to fleshly bodies that is not constructed through culture; it is a dream of 'limitless multiple embodiments' (Bordo, 1993: 228) amenable to change via desire and the will.

Yet there is a point at which the humanity of the cyborg must make itself felt; there *are* limits to the utopian vision of the cyborg as glossed in both masculinist and feminist discourses. This conundrum has been expressed by Morse (1994) in her question, 'What do cyborgs eat?'. While an individual may successfully pretend to be a different gender or age on the Internet, she or he will always have to return to the embodied reality of the empty stomach, stiff neck, aching hands, sore back and gritty eyes caused by many hours in front of a computer terminal, for 'Even in the age of the technosocial subject, life is lived through bodies' (Stone, 1992: 113).

The Hacker's Body

A further challenge to the utopian vision of the disembodied computer user is the mythology of the bodies that are obsessed with using PC technology: computer 'hackers' and 'computer nerds'. In sharp contrast to the idealized clean, hard, uncontaminated masculine body of the cyborg as it is embodied in the *Robocop* and *Terminator* films, this type of computer body is physically repugnant according to commonly accepted notions of attractiveness. 'Hackers' and 'computer nerds', the very individuals who are frequently represented as spearheading the revolution into cyberspace and the 'information superhighway', may be admired for their intellectual capacities (that is, for their 'brain' or 'software'), but the common representation of such individuals usually suggests that their 'bodies' or 'wetware' leave much to be desired. As they are represented in popular culture, 'computer nerds' or 'hackers' are invariably male, usually in their late adolescence or early adulthood, and are typically portrayed as social misfits and spectacularly physically unattractive: wearing thick, unflattering spectacles, overweight, pale, pimply skin, poor fashion sense. Their bodies are soft, not hard, from too much physical inactivity and junk food. These youths' and men's appearance, it is often suggested, is inextricably linked to their obsession with computers in a vicious circle. According to the mythology, computer nerds turned to computing as an obsession because of their lack of social graces and physical unattractiveness. Due to their isolation from the 'real' world they have become even more cut off from society. Lack of social contact has exacerbated their inability to communicate face-to-face with others, and a poor diet and lack of fresh air and exercise does little to improve their complexions or physique. As an author of an article in *New Scientist* described the hackers he encountered at a 'hackers' convention', they 'aren't hard to pick out; they're the pale, shifty ones . . . they're all about 20 pounds overweight. It's all those hours at the keyboard' (Arthur, 1994: 27).

Bill Gates, the American computer tycoon, is perhaps the archetypal 'computer nerd' made good. When he visited Australia recently, newspaper reports of Gates contained a curious mixture of respect for his wealth, business acumen and intelligence and disdain for his appearance and 'nerdiness'. One detailed 'profile' article on him (Sarno, 1995) featured a large unflattering close-up of Gates, with his thick spectacles, blotchy skin, pudgy face and thick neck. The article went on to observe snidely that:

> he hasn't shaved for at least two days, his blue-rimmed glasses are covered with grease, and his fingernails look as if he's just been doing a bit of gardening in his [hotel] suite.... The overwhelming impression Gates gives you is that he's so focused on his work that he's oblivious to life's little chores, even if it's just to clean some of the grease off his glasses.

The journalist noted that Gates, despite his immense wealth, shuns haute cuisine, preferring to eat fast food: 'in Sydney his standard meal was two cheeseburgers and a Big Mac'. The body of the computer expert, as this suggests, is far less impressive than his mind, indeed, provides a source of amusement and contempt.

A recent case involving the arrest of a celebrated American computer 'hacker' was widely reported in Australian newspapers and news magazines. Kevin Mitnick, 31 years old, was charged with breaking computer-network security and computer fraud. After evading the FBI for two years, he was found and eventually brought to justice by an equally talented computer-security expert, Tsutomu Shimomura. After his arrest, the virtual, anonymous persona of Mitnick, previously manifested only in the traces he left behind when he broke into computer-systems, often leaving cheeky messages of bravura, was displayed as an earthly, all-too-human body. Photographs of Mitnick showed him to represent the archetypal 'computer nerd', complete with thick spectacles, pale skin, pudgy body and double chin. These physical characteristics contrasted with the abstract images of his disembodied on-line hacker persona: *Time Australia* magazine (Quittner, 1995), for example, headed a two-page article on the arrest with a surreal colour photograph of two computers side-by-side, the only sign of human embodied presence an arm extending from one to clutch at the key-board of the other. The articles portrayed Mitnick as obsessive, indeed, 'addicted' to the pleasures of hacking. *Time Australia* described him in the courtroom, standing in handcuffs, 'unable, for the first time in more than two years, to feel the silky click of computer keys'. *The Weekend Australian* (Wyndham, 1995) also described him as a 'computer addict' who had been sentenced to participate in a six-month addiction programme (similar to the '12-step' programme offered to alcoholics) when he was last arrested for hacking, but had 'soon reverted to his old habits'.

The bodies of computer 'hackers' and 'nerds', thus, are not transcended through their owners' pursuits. On the contrary, their bodies are inscribed upon and constructed through the computers they use. Their physical characteristics betray their obsessiveness to others. What is more, such individuals are described as 'addicted' to computing as if it were a drug. They thus lack control over their bodies and desires, in sharp contrast to the rationalized, contained body of the masculine cyborg.

The Humanized Computer

Paradoxically, while computer culture often seeks to deny the human body, the ways in which computer technology is marketed and represented frequently draws an analogy between the computer and the human body. Just as the metaphor 'human as computer' is often articulated in popular culture, so too the 'computer as human' trope is regularly employed. Advertisements for personal computer equipment make particular efforts to represent these inanimate, hard-textured objects as warm, soft, friendly and humanoid.

Computers, as represented in advertising, are prone to many of the life experiences that humans experience. Computers are born, delivered by medical practitioners: one advertisement uses a photograph of a (male) doctor, identified as such by his surgical gown and mask, holding in his arms a computer notebook as if it were a baby: 'NEC can deliver colour notebooks now' read the words above his head. Just as computers are born and delivered, they also die. One advertisement asks readers, 'Why buy a monitor with only 6 months to live?', showing a PC with a screen on which is depicted an ECG graph which has gone flat, similar to the pattern shown when heart failure occurs in humans. This computer has lost its vitality, as depicted by the flat line. Computers can also be too fat and are most desirable when they are slim. One advertisement showed a small notebook computer wrapped in a tape-measure: the heading read, 'All the power of a 486 notebook, with 40% less fat'. Another advertisement, again for a notebook computer, was headed, 'You can never be too thin or too powerful' to champion the small size of the computer.

Ross (1991) has described the notices that often are posted near such routinely used office machines as photocopiers, which humorously describe the ways in which such machines can detect users' emotional states and react accordingly to make life even more difficult by failing to operate. As he notes,

> In personifying the machine as a unit of organized labour, sharing fraternal interests and union loyalties with other machines, the notice assumes a degree of evolved self-consciousness on the machine's part. Furthermore, it implies a relation of hostility, as if the machine's self-consciousness and loyalty to its own kind have inevitably lead to resentment, conflict, and sabotage. (Ross, 1991:1–2).

Such notices suggest that 'smart' machines like photocopiers are equipped with the means of control and surveillance over the humans who seek to use them, almost as a spy of management. Not only do humans approach such technologies in heightened emotional states (usually anxiety, anger and frustration in the context of needing the machine to work), but they respond to the technologies with emotions such as vindictiveness and spite (how many of us have kicked or verbally abused a photocopier?).

Computers are often similarly represented as emotional entities, as in the following excerpt relating problems with a computer package published in the computing section in a newspaper:

> Even before Windows appeared, it started complaining. Coldly, matter-of-factly, on a pointedly unfriendly character-based screen, it refused to run 32-bit disk access. It said someone had been fiddling with its interrupts and it thought it had a virus. It grudgingly offered to run Windows with 16-bit file access. (Morison, 1995)

Just as humans fear alienation and loneliness, so too do their PCs. If a user is not linked up to a networked system, both the human and the computer are left to contemplate their social isolation. A magazine advertisement showed a PC in black and white at the top right-hand corner of a white page. Beneath this image were the words (in stark black): 'Insecure? Friendless? Alone?'. The advertisement went on to outline the ways in which computers in the workplace could be networked. The clear analogy drawn is that between the lonely, anxious computer user and the non-networked computer, both forced to work alone. A similar advertisement showed a PC silhouetted, with the words 'Say goodbye to working in an isolation chamber' in red across the screen. In these advertisements, the computer monitor stands for both computer and human user, a metonym of the human/computer dyad.

The emotions are commonly represented as a characteristic of humans, of being alive, phenomena that set humans apart from other animals, evidence of their sensitivity, spirit and soul. Again, the ascribing of emotions to PCs is a discursive move that emphasizes their humanoid nature. Some articles about computers, especially those published in specialist magazines or the computing sections in newspapers designed for aficionados, go even further by frequently making the analogy of the relationship of the user/computer romantic, sexual or marital. One Australian newspaper article on Macintosh computers used headline, visual image and recurring tropes to draw an analogy between one's marital partner and one's PC (Withers, 1995). The article was headed 'No time to divorce your Mac', and was illustrated with a cartoon bride planting a kiss on a bridegroom with a smiling Macintosh screen for a head. The article went on to assert,

> Choosing to buy a Macintosh or any other specific personal computing platform such as Windows is a little like getting married. In both cases you are signing up for a long-term partnership that can be costly to leave. The happily married among us can testify to the benefits of such a relationship, but they don't appear at the outset. 'Come grow old with me, the best is yet to come' applies to both situations.

Advertisements also attempt to portray one's PC as an extension of the human body. One such representation in a newspaper advertisement used a photograph of a group of people holding their notebooks up in front of their faces, the screen reproducing and magnifying their smiles. In this portrayal, the computer was represented as extending and indeed enhancing the most emotionally demonstrative part of the human face, the mouth. These people are using their computers to display their emotional state: in this case, happiness. The computer, in this portrayal, is mirror of the soul. In another advertisement, a PC holds up a camera to its screen 'face', upon which is displayed the word 'smile' in a smiling curve. The heading reads, 'Now your PC can take photos'. An advertisement for Envoy, a computer package, claimed: 'Envoy *thinks* like I do. Sounds weird, but while I'm physically at one meeting, I'm part of three or four others going on *in* my Envoy!' (emphasis in the original).

The Frightening Computer

The overt reason for portraying computers as human is to reduce the anxieties of computerphobia that many people, particularly adults, experience. There is an undercurrent of uncertainty around purchasing and buying computer technology on the part of many people. Computers, unlike many other household or workplace machines, appear inherently enigmatic in the very seamlessness of their hardware. Most people have not the faintest idea what lies inside the hard plastic shell of their PC. The arcane jargon of the computing world, with its megabytes, RAMs, MHz and so on, is a new language that is incomprehensible to the uninitiated. It is a well-known truism that the manuals that come with computer technology are incomprehensible and that computer 'experts' are equally unable to translate jargon into easily understood language to help users unfamiliar with the technology. The user–computer relationship is therefore characterized not only by pleasure and a sense of harmonic blurring of the boundaries between human and machine, but is also inspires strong feelings of anxiety, impotence, frustration and fear.

There is something potentially monstrous about computer technology, in its challenging of traditional boundaries. Fears around monsters relate to their liminal status, the elision of one category of life and another, particularly if the human is involved, as in the Frankenstein monster (Rayner, 1994). The potential of computer technology to act as a form of surveillance and social regulation, or even to take control over humanity, has been decried (Robins and Webster, 1988; Glass, 1989; Barns, 1990). The apparent growing reliance of humans upon computers has incited concern, as have developments in technology that threaten to leave people behind or to render them unemployed. While there is an increasing move towards the consumption of technologies, there is also anxiety around the technologies' capacity to consume *us* (Silverstone and Hirsch, 1992: 2). A recent Hollywood film,

The Ghost in the Machine, addressed these anxieties. The film, released in 1994, featured the story of a serial murderer who is involved in a car accident which mortally wounds him. In hospital, a short circuit during an electrical storm occurs just as his brain is being scanned by a computer. He dies at that moment, his 'soul' entering cyberspace via the diagnostic scan machine. The murderer manifests his aggression via the optical fibre network and the electricity grid, killing people via their home appliances. He is finally brought to justice through the efforts of a computer hacker.

The Macintosh computer company was the first to develop 'user-friendly' icons in lieu of textual commands, including the friendly smiling face that has become the standard-bearer of the Apple range. These icons stand as symbolic images for the mysterious activities occurring 'within' the computer (Haddon, 1988). The implication of this design strategy was that many potential computer users were alienated by the technological demands of computers requiring text commands, and thus required PCs to be 'humanized' to feel comfortable with the technology. It is telling that this deliberate 'humanization' is unique to PC technology; smiling face icons are not found in other domestic technologies that people find difficult to use, such as video cassette recorders.

New computer programs have recently been designed to alleviate the negative emotions people harbour about using computers. Microsoft, for example, has developed a program it has called 'Bob' to challenge technophobic inclinations, expand the home-computer market and reduce its expenditure on help hotlines. The program features animated characters to show people how to operate the functions of their PC, including 'a crazy cat, soppy dog or coffee-addicted dragon', acting as a 'friend over their shoulder' as Bill Gates described it (Fox, 1995: 22). The 'Bob' program was subsequently advertised in the May 1995 edition of *Wired* magazine. The two-page spread featured a large hand-tinted colour photograph, circa the 1950s, showing a beaming all-American nuclear family driving along in a pink convertible with the top down, Mom and the adolescent daughter waving cheerily at the camera. The wording of the advertisement reproduces a naive, simple approach to life to match the 1950s imagery: 'You know what? People need to be a little friendlier. An extra smile. A wave hello. A Bob. Bob helps you to be friends with your computer. And gee whiz, isn't making friends what friendliness is all about?' The advertisement goes on to assert:

> Your computer may not seem friendly to you, but with Bob it will. Because Bob features the newest thing in a software: a social interface. Which is a fancy way of saying 'a nice program that will make your computer comfortable and friendly to you'. That's Bob. . . . To meet Bob for yourself, stop by a local software retailer. Just ask for Bob. Because with Bob, your computer can become your pal.

The advertisement proclaims that there is no manual for the 'Bob' program, because 'it is so easy to use. . . . No manual. How friendly can you get?'. This advertisement, with its slyly self-parodying home-spun philosophies, its emphasis on 'friendliness' and 'niceness' and its complete avoidance of computer jargon, is appealing directly to precisely those people who feel alienated by their PCs and the manuals that come with them. It draws upon a nostalgia for a less complicated world, a world in which people were friendly to one another, families stayed together and the most complicated technology they owned was the family motor car. 'Bob', as a humanoid character, speaks their language and relates to them as would a friend.

Risky Computing

In the age of the 'risk society' (Beck, 1992; Giddens, 1992), personal computers constitute sites that are redolent with cultural anxieties around the nature of humanity and the self. The late modern world is fraught with danger and risk: the promises of modernity have been shown to have a 'double-edged character', no longer simply guaranteeing human progress (Giddens, 1992: 10). To deal with this uncertainty and the time–space distanciation and globalizing tendencies of late modernity, trust has become central to human interactions, particularly in relation to complex technical systems of which most people have little personal knowledge: 'Trust in systems takes the form of faceless commitments, in which faith is sustained in the workings of knowledge of which the lay person is largely ignorant' (Giddens, 1992: 88). Individuals have become dependent on personal relationships, particularly those involving romantic love, to find a sense of security and of subjectivity in a fast-changing, frightening world. However, ambivalence lies at the core of all trust relations, because trust is only demanded where there is ignorance and ignorance provides grounds for scepticism or caution (Giddens, 1992: 89).

The euphoria around the 'information superhighway' or 'infobahn', with its utopian visions of computer users able to access each other globally and 'get connected' has been somewhat diminished of late by a series of scares around the security problems threatened by the very accessible nature of the Internet. As I observed above, for some years now there have been growing concerns about the potential of computer networks to surveil and police individuals, using computer databases to collect and pass on information. More recently, a number of news stories have made dramatic headlines reporting on incidents of 'cybercrime' and the security problems of the computer network. One story, reported worldwide, related the saga of the eventual capture of Kevin Mitnick by Tsutomu Shimomura, described above. Another story reported in Australian newspapers in early 1995 detailed the actions of a computer hacker who published confidential credit card numbers on the Internet. An article in *New Scientist* described the growing numbers of frauds in the United States using the Internet for investment scams, pointing to the trust that users invest in the information they receive over the Internet. As one computer expert was quoted as saying, 'Con artists are flourishing in cyberspace because people believe what they read on their computer screens. . . . People tend to accept it as gospel' (Kiernan, 1994: 7).

News reports of such crimes typically emphasize the growing security risks caused by the increasing use of the Internet, with a focus on the dangers of 'connectivity' that is linking more and more computers and their users world-wide, employing metaphors of 'gates', 'avenues' and 'openings' as well as epidemic illness (familiar from reports of computer viruses) to represent the threat. For example, a story published in *New Scientist* (Kleiner, 1995) on the activities of hackers in discovering a security loophole on the Internet, allowing them to access files previously denied them, was headed, 'Hack attack leaves Internet wide open'. The article went on to explain that the hackers had managed to 'impersonate a computer that is "trusted" by the computer targeted for attack'. An article published in the *Sydney Morning Herald* used similar language: 'When computers were quarantined from each other, there was less chance of a security breach. Now, most systems have any number of electronic avenues leading to them, and some passers-by in cyberspace inevitably wander in when they find the gates unlocked' (Robotham, 1995a). This discourse serves as a complement to the viral metaphor, which represents computers as embodied, subject to invasion by viral particles which then cause 'illness' (Lupton, 1994). Just as in AIDS discourses gay men or women have been conceptualized as 'leaky bodies' who lack control over their bodily boundaries so, too, in this 'cybercrime' discourse, computers are represented as unable to police or protect their boundaries, rendering themselves vulnerable to penetration. Just as humans in late modernity must both rely on trust relations but also fear them, computers can no longer 'trust' other computers to keep secrets and respect personal boundaries. The sheer anonymity of the 'cyberrobbers' perpetrating the crimes is also a source of fear; they are faceless, difficult to find and identify because of their skill in covering their tracks.

Further concern has also recently been generated about the links that children may make with the outside world via the Internet, particularly in relation to contact with paedophiles, pornography and sexual exchanges over email or chat networks. A front page article published in the *Sydney Morning Herald* in mid-1995 detailed the story of an American 15-year-old boy who left home to meet with a man he had met on the Internet, with the suggestion that the man may have been a paedophile. The article was headlined, 'Every parents' nightmare is lurking on the Internet', and asserted that 'This is the frightening new frontier of cyberspace, a place where a child thought to be safely in his or her room may be in greater danger than anyone could imagine' (Murphy, 1995). Again, the main anxiety here is in the insidious nature of contact with others through the Internet. The home is now no longer a place of safety and refuge for children, the computer no longer simply an educational tool or source of entertainment but is the possible site of children's corruption. 'Outside' danger is brought 'inside', into the very heart of the home, via the Internet.

We invest a great deal of trust in computer technology, especially in our PCs. Many of us have little knowledge about how they work, relying on experts to produce and set up the technology, and to come to our aid when something goes wrong. Yet we have also developed an intimate relationship with them, relying on them to perform everyday tasks, to relax and to communicate with others. We can now carry them about with us in our briefcases, and sit them on our laps. They take pride of place in our studies at home and our children's bedrooms. The ways in which we depict computers as humanoid, having emotions and embodiment, is evidence of this intimacy. It is in this context that we are particularly emotionally vulnerable to losing trust in our PCs, and where risk appears particularly prevalent. We now not only risk becoming 'infected' via a computer virus, but also being 'penetrated' by cybercriminals finding the weakest points in our computer system, seeking to discover our innermost secrets and corrupt and manipulate our children.

The relationship between users and PCs is similar to that between lovers or close friends. An intimate relationship with others involves ambivalence: fear as well as pleasure. As we do with people we feel are close to us, we invest part of ourselves in PCs. We struggle with the pleasures and fears of dependency: to trust is to reap the rewards of security, but it is also to render ourselves vulnerable to risk. Blurring the boundaries between self and other calls up abjection, the fear and horror of the unknown, the indefinable. In her essay *Powers of Horror*, Kristeva defined the abject as 'violent, dark revolts of being, directed against a threat that seems to emanate from an exorbitant outside or inside, ejected beyond the scope of the possible, the tolerable, the thinkable' (1982: 1). The abject inspires both desire and repulsion. It challenges, as it defines, the boundaries of the clean, proper, contained body, the dichotomy between inside and outside. One of its central loci, argues Kristeva, is the maternal body, a body without 'proper' borders. Another is the sexual body, which involves the merging and blurring of the boundaries of one's own body with that of another.

Just as they are described as friends or spouses in the masculinist culture of computing, computers are also frequently described in feminine sexual or maternal roles. The word 'matrix' originates from the Latin *mater*, meaning both mother and womb, a source of comforting security (Springer, 1991: 306). For their male users in particular, computers are to be possessed, to be penetrated and overpowered. This desire for power and mastery was expressed by an anonymous computer hacker quoted in an article on 'cybercrime' (Robotham, 1995b). When asked about what motivates him and other hackers, he replied: 'A person who hacks into a system wants to get a degree of power, whether the power is real or fallacious. This is you controlling the world from your Macintosh. It's an incredible feeling.' This masculinist urge to penetrate the system, to overpower, some commentators have argued, represents an attempt to split oneself from the controlling mother, to achieve autonomy and containment from the abject maternal body (Robins and Webster, 1988; Sofia, 1993). Computer users, therefore, are both attracted towards the promises of cyberspace, in the utopian freedom from the flesh, its denial of the body, the opportunity to achieve a cyborgian seamlessness and to 'connect' with others, but are also threatened by its potential to engulf the self and expose one's vulnerability to the penetration of enemy others. As with the female body, a site of intense desire and emotional security but also threatening engulfment, the inside of the computer body is dark and enigmatic, potentially leaky, harbouring danger and contamination, vulnerable to invasion.

References

Arthur, C. (1994) 'Hackers' Code', *New Scientist* 22 October: 26–30.

Barns, I. (1990) 'Monstrous Nature or Technology? Cinematic Resolutions of the "Frankenstein Problem"', *Science as Culture* 9: 7–48.

Beck, U. (1992) *Risk Society: Towards a New Modernity*. London: Sage.

Berman, B. (1989) 'The Computer Metaphor: Bureaucratizing the Mind', *Science as Culture* 7: 7–42.

Bordo, S. (1993) *Unbearable Weight: Feminism, Western Culture and the Body*. Berkeley, CA: University of California Press.

Fox, B. (1995) 'Trust Bob to Tackle Technophobia', *New Scientist* 21 January: 22.

Giddens, A. (1992) *The Consequences of Modernity*. Cambridge: Polity Press.

Glass, F. (1989) 'The "New Bad Future": *Robocop* and 1980s' Sci-Fi Films', *Science as Culture* 5: 7–49.

Grosz, E. (1994) *Volatile Bodies: Toward a Corporeal Feminism*. Sydney: Allen and Unwin.

Haddon, L. (1988) 'The Home Computer: The Making of a Consumer Electronic', *Science as Culture* 2: 7–51.

Haraway, D. (1988) 'A Manifesto for Cyborgs: Science, Technology, and Socialist Feminism in the 1980s', pp. 173–204 in E. Weed (ed.) *Coming to Terms: Feminism, Theory, and Practice*. New York: Routledge.

Heim, M. (1992) 'The Erotic Ontology of Cyberspace', pp. 59–80 in M. Benedikt (ed.) *Cyberspace: First Steps*. Cambridge, MA: MIT Press.

Jones, A. (1993) 'Defending the Border: Men's Bodies and Vulnerability', *Cultural Studies from Birmingham* 2: 77–123.

Kiernan, V. (1994) 'Internet Tricksters Make a Killing', *New Scientist* 16 July: 7.

Kleiner, K. (1995) 'Hack Attack Leaves Internet Wide Open', *New Scientist* 4 February: 4.

Kristeva, J. (1982) *Powers of Horror: An Essay on Abjection*. New York: Columbia University Press.

Lupton, D. (1993) 'The Construction of Patienthood in Medical Advertising', *International Journal of Health Services* 23(4): 805–19.

Lupton, D. (1994) 'Panic Computing: The Viral Metaphor and Computer Technology', *Cultural Studies* 8(3): 556–68.

Morison, N. (1995) 'Michelangelo Alive and Ready to Strike', *Sydney Morning Herald* 21 February.

Morse, M. (1994) 'What Do Cyborgs Eat?: Oral Logic in an Information Society', *Discourse* 16(3): 86–123.

Murphy, K. (1995) 'Every Parent's Nightmare is Lurking on the Internet', *Sydney Morning Herald* 13 June.

Neesham, C. (1994) 'Network of Information', *New Scientist (Inside Science* supplement) 10 December: 1–4.

Quittner, J. (1995) 'Cracks in the Net', *Time Australia* 27 February: 36–7.

Rayner, A. (1994) 'Cyborgs and Replicants: On the Boundaries', *Discourse* 16(3): 124–43.

Robins, C. and F. Webster (1988) 'Athens without Slaves . . . Or Slaves without Athens?', *Science as Culture* 3: 7–53.

Robotham, J. (1995a) 'The Cops Aren't Chasing the Cyber-robbers', *Sydney Morning Herald* 22 April.

Robotham, J. (1995b) 'Tap in for a Shot of Power from the System', *Sydney Morning Herald* 22 April.

Ross, A. (1991) *Strange Weather: Culture, Science and Technology in the Age of Limits.* London: Verso.

Sarno, T. (1995) 'William the Conqueror', *Sydney Morning Herald* 21 January.

Seltzer, M. (1992) *Bodies and Machines.* New York: Routledge.

Silverstone, R. and E. Hirsch (1992) 'Introduction', pp. 1–11 in R. Silverstone and E. Hirsch (eds) *Consuming Technologies: Media and Information in Domestic Spaces.* London: Routledge.

Sofia, Z. (1993) *Whose Second Self? Gender and (Ir)rationality in Computer Culture.* Geelong, Victoria: Deakin University Press.

Springer, C. (1991) 'The Pleasure of the Interface', *Screen* 32(3): 303–23.

Stone, A. (1992) 'Will the Real Body Please Stand Up?: Boundary Stories about Virtual Cultures', pp. 81–118 in M. Benedikt (ed.) *Cyberspace: First Steps.* Cambridge, MA: MIT Press.

Theweleit, K. (1987) *Male Fantasies, Volume 1: Women, Floods, Bodies, History.* Cambridge: Polity Press.

Withers, S. (1995) 'No Time to Divorce Your Mac', *Sydney Morning Herald* 7 February.

Wyndham, S. (1995) 'Diehard Hacker', *Weekend Australian* 25–26 February.

Deborah Lupton is Associate Professor in Cultural Studies and Cultural Policy, Charles Sturt University, Australia. Her recent books include *Medicine as Culture: Illness, Disease and the Body in Western Societies* (Sage, 1994), *The Imperative of Health: Public Health and the Regulated Body* (Sage, 1995) and *Food, the Body and the Self* (Sage, in press). Her current research interests are in the sociocultural dimensions of the body, medicine and public health, food, the mass media, the emotions, sexuality, HIV/AIDS, risk and computing and how all of these link together.

Rear-View Mirrorshades: The Recursive Generation of the Cyberbody

NIGEL CLARK

'Watch out for worlds behind you'. William Gibson once considered using this line from a Velvet Underground song as an epigraph for *Neuromancer* (1986), the novel which introduced the term 'cyberspace' into the vernacular (McCaffery, 1991: 265). In an earlier short story, 'The Gernsback Continuum', Gibson addressed the futuristic visions of the 1930s – one of those worlds behind us. These visions were never fully realized, and yet they left their mark on the objects of the everyday world:

> After the advent of the designers, some pencil sharpeners looked as though they'd been put together in wind tunnels. For the most part, the change was only skin-deep; under the streamlined chrome shell, you'd find the same Victorian mechanism. Which made a certain kind of sense, because the most successful American designers had been recruited from the ranks of Broadway theatre designers. (Gibson, 1988: 39)

This era had its dream cities, comprised of clean, illuminated geometric towers, and these cities were peopled with dream bodies: 'They were white, blond, and they probably had blue eyes' (Gibson, 1988: 47). While the ideal may have been superseded, its cultural traces – or 'semiotic ghosts' – survive to impact upon us in the present, Gibson suggests (1988: 45).

In the vibrant new futurism that has crystallized around the recent advances in computation and computer-assisted communication, the injunction to keep an eye on receding worlds could be more closely observed. While a number of recent writers of fiction – Gibson included – have offered vivid depictions of cities layered with obsolete signifying objects and images, it is not always certain that their most futuristic constructions escape the imprint of the past. Afterimages and premonitions often seem indistinguishable as they reflect in the mirrorshades that are emblematic of 'cyberpunk' fiction (see Sterling, 1986: ix).

It was Marshall McLuhan who discerned a generalized 'rear-view mirrorism' as a response to the disconcerting effects of techno-cultural transformation, suggesting that we tend to 'look at the present through the spectacles of the preceding age' (1987: 243). Several decades earlier, Walter Benjamin offered the striking image of the 'angel of history' perpetually backing his way into the future, with eyes affixed to the accumulating debris of progress which fills the past and present (1969: 257–8). Benjamin drew attention to the retroactive tendencies present in the era of early urban-industrialism, noting the 'attempt to master the new experiences of the city in the frame of the old, traditional ones of nature' (cited in Buck-Morss, 1989: 145). The first electric lightbulbs, for example, resembled gas flames, processed iron was cast in the form of leaves or wood, and newly mass produced utensils were modelled on organic forms (Buck-Morss, 1989: 111). Drawing on both McLuhan and Benjamin, Jean Baudrillard has elevated the recursive moment in cultural production to the core of his schema of successive orders of signification. For Baudrillard (1983), at any moment in the course of our modernity, a particular arrangement of signifying objects and images conditions the way we see the world. Each major transformation is accompanied by a feeling of disorientation and discomfort over the loss of the previous 'reality'. This effects a recourse to the imagined certainties of the receding order to ground or stabilize that which is new. In this way 'reality loops around itself', as 'each phase of value integrates into its own apparatus the anterior apparatus as a phantom reference, a puppet or simulation reference' (Baudrillard, 1988: 145, 121).

From the vantage point of their own induction into the networks, social and cultural theorists, journalists and writers of 'cyber' fiction are all engaging with the techno-cultural condition of the present and forseeable future. They are each, in their own ways, trying to pinpoint what is really 'new' about a way of life in which many messages pass into minute pulses of light at some stage of their passage to and from the human sensorium. When it comes to defining which practices, processes and artifacts belong in the category of 'cyberculture', however, problems soon arise. On the one hand, writers and image-makers have directed our attention to radical transform-ations in the old analogue mass media and in the material landscapes of everyday life: changes which seem somehow to be connected with the ubiquitous uptake of electronic technologies. On the other hand, theorists have pointed to the familiar and reactionary content of some of the very latest digital apparatuses. More particularly, we encounter a host of fictional and theoretical speculations about the total transformation of the human body which occurs through its interpolation in the nascent informatic networks. And adjacent to these claims, we find another set of observations on the entrenchment of existing bodily stereotypes in the electronic media. It is these alternating currents of cybernetic culture that I am trying to unravel.

Jonathon Crary (1984) has offered a convincing argument that the deployment of the medium of television has not been constant, pointing to its implication in two distinct arrangements of visual experience. There appear to be analogous discontinuities in the use of the computer. For Richard Friedhoff and William Benzon (1989), the development of the graphic capabilities of digital media breaks radically with the initial use of the computer to manipulate alphanumeric symbols: 'visualization' constituting a 'second computer revolution'. However, there is another set of procedures taking shape on the horizon, which may yet turn out to be as different from the construction of visual images as these were from assembly language coding. I refer here to the nascent implantation of autonomous or self-developing entities in digital environments.

Drawing together notions from Benjamin, McLuhan and Baudrillard, I want to suggest that each of these cycles or phrases of digitality first looks to the anterior phase of mediated effects to ground its signifying capacities. Which is to say, we tend to begin each of our 'advances' into the cybernetic realm with a rear-vision mirror firmly affixed to the console screen, moving into an indeterminate future with a sort of ongoing recursive gaze. At successive moments in their development, digital media contribute to the destabilization of an established sense of 'reality'. But at the same time, these new media are used to simulate the signifying objects, the bodies, the worlds which they are rendering obsolete. In this sense, we must distinguish between the onward roll of each cycle and the backward glance: between the destabilizing effects of informatic systems, and their deployment as instruments for the containment, subjugation and reordering of a universe of refractory messages.

Of the cultural theorists writing in the field of 'cyberculture', Scott Bukatman is perhaps the most attentive to this alternation between 'forward' looking and retroactive moments. Commenting on William Gibson's axial cybernetic construct, he writes: 'If cyberspace is a "consensual hallucination" that enables computer users to make sense of both their actions and the circulation of information, then that hallucination works by continually referencing the kinetic urban landscapes of machine-age modernity' (1993a: 642). In the depiction of human beings in cyberfiction, Bukatman notes that any exploration of new modes of subjectivity and embodiment tends to be counterbalanced by the presence of characters who preserve the conventional lineaments of body and mind. 'In one way or another, every work of cyberpunk produces the same radical and reactionary formation' he claims (1993b: 259). By dividing the spectrum of cybernetic practices and artifacts into three relatively distinct phases, or cycles, I want to provide a tentative framework to assist with the mapping out of these recursive and forward-reaching moments in the constitution of the cybernetic body. The first generation of cyberbodies belongs to the previsual era of computational practices; the second to the phase in which cybernetic spaces take on a visual dimension, so that interacting subjects require some form of body descriptor. In the third phase, entities 'evolve' their own structure and appearance. The recursive moments of each of these cycles is defined by the resurrection of the referential form of the body from the previous generation. The idea of a 'forward' motion, rather than connoting a sense of progress, indicates some form of disruption of the structures or appearances which predominated in the previous cycle, some movement into unfamiliar or undemarcated terrain.

It is integral to my approach that computer generated and transmitted 'realities' emerge out of more encompassing regimes of signification; that they arise from worlds in which physical forms and circulating images are already in constant interplay. Cybernetic constructs both inherit and respond to these prior arrangements of mediated images and objects, and in doing so they impact upon the worlds beyond the digital domain. In the present we are familiar with the seamless interface of digital and analogue sequences on the movie and television screens, and it is easy to imagine the computer effortlessly materializing out of an existing repertoire of moving image technologies. To highlight the inadequacies of such a vision, to emphasize the initial disjuncture between computational practices and screen effects, I begin in the era immediately anterior to the emergence of digital procedures.

Hacking Out of a Moving Image Culture

Gibson's 'Gernsback' era takes its name from a series of pulp science fiction stories which regularly featured an extreme form of the futurist aesthetic on its covers. But as Donald Albrecht (1987) points out, the primary vehicle for this aesthetic was cinema. From the late 1920s to the end of the 1930s, modernist architecture dominated the filmsets of Europe and America. Stark and rectilinear interiors, conspicuous views of skyscrapers, streamlined vehicles and correspondingly streamlined bodies came to signify the dynamism of the second 'century of progress' for the 85 million viewers who visited American movie theatres each week (Albrecht, 1987: 86, xii).

Working in Hollywood at the time, Nathanael West was an acute observer of a cultural terrain mediated by cinema. But there is no sign of the fulfilment of the futuristic ideal in his novels, only a sense of the frustration and boredom that arises out of the failure of everyday life to live up to the spectacle of the movies: not the rise of the smooth functional aesthetic, but an outward diffusion of the tacky and flimsy props of the cinematic industry (see West, 1983: 411–12). With unconcealed loathing, one of West's protagonists gazes out of his car at a streetside composed of

'Mexican ranch houses, Samoan huts, Mediterranean villas, Egyptian and Japanese temples, Swiss chalets, Tudor cottages, and every possible combination of these styles' (West, 1983: 262). What is being documented here is an early moment in the mapping of the stereotypic and idealized images of cinema back on to the surfaces of the built environment. In a closely related sense, the body also functions as a receptor for projected images: West's characters are constantly being evaluated – and evaluating themselves – according to the standards of the screen. As one young man explains his predicament: 'I found it necessary to substitute strange conceits, wise and witty sayings, peculiar conduct, Art, for the muscles, teeth and hair of my rivals' (West, 1983: 26).

If the analogue media of photography and film could never attain the total plasticity of digital media, their ever-expanding repertoire of special effects were still equal to an aesthetic transfiguration of the objects on which they alighted, as Walter Benjamin asserted (1978: 229–30). In the 1950s, television was drawing these effects deeper into the fabric of daily life. Disneyland, twinned from its inception with its own TV show, brought a new intensity and deliberateness to the process by which the landscape is remodelled to the specifications of all its mediated images. In the theme park, as Michael Sorkin puts it, 'the ephemeral reality of cinema is concretized into the stuff of the city' (1992a: 227). Analogously, a growing range of corporeal technologies, including sun-tanning, body-building, cosmetic dentistry and plastic surgery enabled privileged bodies to inscribe the characteristics of the iconic cinematic body on to their own superficies. If not always through actual physical reconfiguration, the reconceptualization of the body through the reflection of mass mediated images ensured a significant impact on the 'stuff' of the citizen (see Kroker, 1993: 42).

We might view this aestheticization of the self through its incorporation in the feedback loops of moving image culture as precipitating a 'crisis' of identity or, perhaps more accurately, as the source of an ongoing tension or discomfort. But this induction of the surfaces of the body into a state of enforced signification seems to have been more novel for males, given that women's bodies have had a longer history of subjection to inscription by idealized images. This sense that the female body has long been constituted through a dense accretion of simulation models informs Arthur and Marilouise Kroker's deliberately provocative assertion that 'women's bodies have always been postmodern' (1988: 24).

It is in relation to these broader contours of an analogue moving image culture that we must locate the emergence of the first subculture orientated towards digital processes and artifacts. The youthful exponents of experimental computer programming – or 'hacking' – first gathered around the mainframe computers at the Massachusetts Institute of Technology at the end of the 1950s (Levy, 1984: part 1).

In Steven Levy's account, these 'heroes of the computer revolution' were intelligent and innovative young males, but they were also invariably physiognomically challenged. Key 'hackers' are respectively described as '[b]uck-toothed, diminutive', 'plump, chinless, thick-spectacled', of 'ruddy, bulbous features' or 'large overbite', and in the case of an exemplary youngster, 'uncomfortably overweight, deficient in sports, but an intellectual star performer' (Levy, 1984: xiii, 9, 8, 80, 17). But like West's character they used 'Art' to make up for their deficiencies in 'muscles, hair and teeth'. The hacker subculture constituted a pure meritocracy, according to Levy, performativity completely effacing appearance as the key to self-image or identity. Which is to say 'that hackers cared less about someone's superficial characteristics than they did about his potential to advance the general state of hacking, to create new programs to admire' (1984: 30). To this end, bodies were subjected to an ascetic regime in which there was a certain kudos to be gained from the ability to endure hours of straight hacking, with only minimal breaks for the 'basic maintenance' of eating or going to the lavatory (Levy, 1984: 62, 126, 22).

While the body itself was effectively deaestheticized by the routines of programming, and while the environment of the computer research labs was drab and utilitarian, the actual process of hacking seems to have fulfilled the old romantic notion of a well-rounded humanism. Game-playing was vital, and despite the fact that most operations were restricted to alphanumeric symbols, the perfect hack was considered as much an aesthetic achievement as one of technique. As Levy recounts: 'Art, science and play had merged in the magical activity of programming' (1984: 120, see also 30–1). The early hackers counterposed their own creative flair and elegance to the number-crunching, over-orderly, bureaucratic procedures of corporate computing – 'the gray-flannel, batch-processed IBM mentality' (Levy, 1984: 39, see also 28–9).

What was considered most odious about IBM was the degree of secrecy which veiled its operations. Well before the installation of computer networking left an opening for the infiltration of data bases, hackers were expounding an ethos of open access to information and informatic technologies (Levy, 1984: 28–30, 43–4, 123). Even within the institutions that supported them, they were obsessed with the penetration of security systems and the accessing of all spaces – both architectural and electronic (Levy, 1984: 91–6, Stallman, 1992: 132). In a kind of corporeal redoubling of their nascent interpolation in an electronic circuitry, the early hackers displayed a strange affinity for 'crawl spaces', manoeuvring through the buildings in which they worked via the gaps behind low hanging artificial ceilings. Some went as far as inhabiting these spaces on a semi-permanent basis (Levy, 1984: 95, 134).

From the beginning, then, hackers conceived of themselves as subversives. As with most of the other 'counterculturalists' of the 1960s, their target was not a culture of proliferating images so much as a monolithically construed 'system' of power and authority. But where other modes of countercultural revolt celebrated a sort of sensory excess, the activities of the digital underworld were premissed on a narrowed bandwidth of communication. In the creation and perfection of assembly language code the hackers immersed themselves in a field of operations which seemed to exist at a profound and fundamental level of reality. Part of the attraction of this abstract, numerical universe would seem to be its freedom from the vicissitudes of moving image culture, and in this sense it offered young educated males a ground for the stabilization of identity: identity based on substance rather than surface, performance rather than appearance.

Envisioning Computation

The 1970s was the decade in which the computer underworld came to the surface, or alternately, the surface came into the underworld. From the depths of hacker culture came the personal computer, with the friendly interface of a television-like screen – the innovation which was intended to open the computational universe to the masses (Roszak, 1988: 168–70). At the same time, the cybernetic world was gaining a comprehensive visual dimension, although this was well beyond the capacities of the early personal computers. Where the 1960s had been a time of prefigurative developments and diverse but sporadic experimentation in computer graphics, the next decade saw the establishment of photorealistic representation as the prime goal of visualization technologies (Friedhoff and Benzon, 1989: 85; Darley, 1990: 49–54). By the late 1970s, techniques for rendering objects and spaces with an apparent three-dimensionality were being perfected, laying the foundations for lifelike computer animation, and for the illusion of immersion in the image field (Darley, 1990: 54).

If the early hackers were constructing a subterranean alternative to a culture dominated by spectacles or signifying surfaces, then they were also doing the groundwork for the spectacularization of their own domain. But in another way, more obvious to the hackers themselves, the very success of their project served to compromise the self-styled 'countercultural' ethos. With the meteoric rise of the 'garage' computer firms, and the rapid adoption of their innovations by the larger companies, the sense of operating in a transgressive underworld could no longer be sustained. By the early 1980s, the realm of personal computing had entered into the sphere of 'big business' (Woolley, 1992: 29–30; Roszak, 1988: 179).

There was another development under way, however, which was creating a space for a new style of hacking – otherwise known as 'cracking'. From the early 1970s, a process of networking previously discrete computer systems had been initiated, a security measure which at the same time provided new possibilities for covert access of a purely electronic nature. A decade later, these networks had expanded into a transglobal mesh, enabling the astute operator to navigate around the world and to make either authorized or unsanctioned forays into databases (Hafner and Markoff, 1991:9–12). As Andrew Ross notes, sympathetic journalists helped to construct an image of the cybernetic interloper as a new countercultural figure: 'a maverick though nerdy cowboy whose fearless raids upon an impersonal "system" were . . . a welcome tonic in the grey age of technocratic routine' (1991:116). Exemplifying this sort of account, Douglas Rushkoff describes the subculture which has crystallized around practices of electronic intrusion: 'Like a prison escape in which the inmates crawl through the ventilation ducts toward freedom, rebels in Cyberia use the established pathways and networks of our postmodern society in unconventional ways and often toward subversive goals' (1994:203). The rather ingenuous use of the term postmodern here belies a vision of an informational infrastructure which constitutes the hidden depths of the culture and economy of the contemporary world. Rushkoff frequently employs the metaphor of underground tunnels, concealed passages and trenches, drawing an interesting comparison between the youthful denizens of the cybernetic grid and the 'Mole People' – a collectivity of undetermined size which illicitly inhabits the abandoned tunnels of the New York subway system (1994:11–12, 205, 214–15). The notion of 'crawl space' recurs in the film *The Phantom of the Mall* in which a masked figure inhabits the service tunnels and ventilation ducts of a corrupt mall, while also accessing and redirecting the system of closed circuit TVs which are being misused by mall security (Goss, 1993:41).

MIT veteran Richard Stallman characterizes the hacker as 'someone who would rather look at a computer screen than at a TV' (1992:134). The definition is noteworthy, in that it indicates that computational counterculturalism has begun to constitute itself explicitly in relation to moving image culture, rather than a culture of faceless, grey technocracies. Over the last decade and a half the distinction between interactive digital media and mass media has been voiced with increasing frequency: the computer screen as the gateway to participation in the informational underworld is counterposed to the TV screen construed as the passive window to the superficies of visual culture. But as the developments of the 1970s and early 1980s imply, this distinction is problematic from the very moment it establishes itself. Not only have the visualizing capacities of the computer been realized, but television has itself been incorporated into a global network of electronic communications, as Crary argues (1984:284–5). On the one hand, the new enmeshing of media finds the TV viewer 'channel-surfing' between streams of visual data that are increasingly likely to have been digitally transmitted, reconfigured or generated. On the other, it raises the prospect of a personal computer based navigation of a network which is a reservoir and conduit of images, or one that not only contains representations but is itself a visually rendered space.

The mid-1980s saw the ascendance of a literary and cinematic genre of cyberfictions which engaged with the incorporation of electronic technologies in everyday life. More specifically, I want to suggest, these works belong to the period of convergence between computational technologies and the mass media of audiovisual communication. The attention to the body, in works like William Gibson's paradigmatic 'cyberpunk' novel *Neuromancer* (1986) may be taken as indicative that the cybernetic sphere no longer functions unproblematically as an alternative locus to the mass mediated world of aestheticized or spectacular body-effects. Confronted with the ubiquity of fully visualized digital environments of various forms, Gibson's protagonists must make decisions about the mode of interface which they are to utilize, decisions with profound implications for their subjecthood and bodily image.

The Hyper-Aestheticized Landscape

Unbeknown to its author, at the time at which *Neuromancer* was written, research was advancing in the field of fully immersive three-dimensional computer graphics – later to be termed 'virtual reality'. Gibson's fictive notion of 'cyberspace' comprised a kind of felicitous fusion of the discrete and bounded virtual spaces that were already in existence, and the equally extant global networks. The novel and its sequels are set in an unspecified near future, in which the data comprising the infrastructure of a global corporate economy has become so dense and complex that it must be rendered in iconic three-dimensional form in order to be comprehensible. Both legitimate and unauthorized agents access the cyberspatial 'Net' through direct neural implants, enabling them to travel through the datascape as disembodied yet kinetic and perceiving entities.

The young male protagonists of Gibson's tales live for the exhilaration of the Net. And yet, so much of the attraction of their fictional universe lies in the sensory richness and complexity of the landscape *outside* the cybernetic realm. Recalling the set design of the film *Blade Runner* (1982), *Neuromancer* and its sequels feature a series of hyper-aestheticized urban spaces: terrains in which vibrant new signifying surfaces are layered over the detritus of obsolescent forms. If the narratival era of film and television witnessed a projection of representational forms on to the physical environment, then what we may be seeing in this new generation of urban spaces is the material counterpart of a post-narratival media. As urban theorists have noted, Disney-style simulacra are now ubiquitous in many contemporary cities, and with this dispersal the coherence of the original theme park has been lost (Sorkin, 1992b). Which is to say that recent cyberfiction extrapolates from processes which are readily observable today.

Attendant on the new contiguity of television and telematic systems, Crary maintains, is a disruption of prior narrative structures (1984: 287–9). In place of a sequence of audiovisual scenes which propose to represent episodes from a 'real' world, today's media operate as a switching devices between multiple channels, delivering streams of images that are non-linear, discontinuous and, to all intents, a-representational. Where the reception of television once invited a passive spectatorship, the new networks are the locus of a hyperactive sampling of broadcast bits. In this way, visual experience is increasingly constituted as a collage of decontextualized motifs: a 'pattern' which is frequently iterated in individual advertisements, music videos, TV programmes and film (Slusser, 1991: 340). The surfaces which comprise the 'street' in *Blade Runner* or *Neuromancer* and related fictions embody this new visuality. They reflect the diffuse imagery and collect the material fallout of mediated trends, fashions and product lines. Perforated by screens, indeed functioning as a plethora of screens, these built environments conform to neither the rectilinear logic of the archetypal modernist city, nor even the abbreviated representational aesthetic of the theme park. A sea of shifting, flickering signifiers, they defy a stable reading, and must be decoded from moment to moment.

Those of us who have encountered the hyper-aesthetics of the contemporary city could well relate to the experiences of Rikki, from Gibson's *Burning Chrome*:

> . . . she had it all, the whole teeming show spread out for her, sharp and bright under the neon. She was new to the scene, and she had all the miles of malls and plazas to prowl, all the shops and clubs, and Bobby to explain the wild side, *the tricky wiring on the dark underside of things.* (1988: 202–3; emphasis added)

Bobby is a 'console cowboy' – an illicit operator in the Net – and this last formulation is the clue to the relation of the cybernetic underworld to the terrains of the surface. For Gibson cyberspace *is* the tricky wiring – it is the 'nonplace' where an infinity of messages once again *make sense*. As the representation of all existing representations, the datascape distills a new order from a world of excessive signification. This orderliness is encapsulated in its grid-like configuration (see Gibson, 1988: 195; 1986: 68). For many of the so-called 'avant-garde' artists of this century, as Rosaline Krauss points out, the grid has been emblematic of 'a kind of originary purity': it is the stable, impervious structure which undergirds the endless surfaces which comprise the aesthetic universe (1986: 158–62; see also Bukatman, 1993b: 220–1). In the world constructed by Gibson, like those of Krauss's artists, it could be argued that a new beginning, a sense of purity is '. . . found by peeling back layer after layer of representation to come at last to this schematized reduction' (Krauss, 1986: 158).

The matrix or grid is a privileged zone of pure performativity – a region where agency triumphs over appearance, depth over surface – in Krauss's terms, it constitutes the 'prison in which the caged artist feels at liberty' (1986: 160). For both the fictional console cowboys and the early hackers the freedom to explore the cybernetic universe is at the same time a freedom from the complexities of the world beyond the circuitry. What Gibson does so effectively is to refit the discourse of countercultural computer operation for an era in which the computer has implicated itself in an accelerating visual culture. As Erik Davis has observed 'Th(e) sense that there is a "true structure" of information is one of the most pervasive metaphysical myths of cyberspace' (1993: 601). By endowing data with a visual dimension, Gibson adapts the myth of a hidden and decipherable informational infrastructure to the emerging condition of the hyper-aestheticization of everyday life. While the new velocity and suppleness of symbol manipulation in the cybernetic realm itself contributes to the overall complexity of the semiotic terrain, the prime deployment of the computer is to clean up the debris of all the other modes of signification. In order to reorganize the chaos of messages, images and objects, the visual constructs of the cybernetic environment resurrect the reference points of an anterior order. The extent to which this reactivation of the 'semiotic ghosts' of early 20th-century modernism in the figuration of the datascape is a self-conscious and ironic gesture on Gibson's part remains open to question.

Embodying Cyberspace

It is in the construction of the body in cyberspace that this recursive process is most apparent. Gibson's fiction offers us two basic models for the cybernetic 'body'. There is the 'disembodied' but perceiving consciousness which is operative in the Net, but there is another form of hard-wired 'immersion' in virtual space. Much derided by the console cowboys, 'simstim' or simulated stimulation entails the *faux* inhabitation of celebrity bodies, by way of digital recordings of the sensory experiences of star performers in soap-like scenarios (1988: 211, 1987: 54–5). The fantasies of simstim and the frenetic visuality of the outer world seem to be mutually implicated. With an even greater intensity than the built environment, human bodies act as the receptive surfaces for the images projected by the media. There are a panoply of corporeal modifications in Gibson's fiction, but the most frequent seems to be the cosmetic-surgical mimicry of the stars of simstim and other media. It is 'an age of affordable beauty' (1986: 9) and, for the less adventurous, the templates of a desirable visage follow the vicissitudes of the star system. As Gibson describes an incidental character: 'He had the kind of uniform good looks you get after your seventh trip to the surgical boutique; he'd probably spend the rest of his life looking vaguely like each new season's media front runner' (1988:212).

Thomas Foster observes that in cyberpunk fiction 'all bodies function as signifying surfaces' (1993:2). Some more than others, however. While everyone around him modifies their appearance, deploying their flesh as a floating signifier of identity, *Neuromancer*'s Case approaches physiognomic muteness: 'Thin, high-shouldered, a forgettable face' (1986:250). But Case is an exceptionally gifted computer operator, one whose self-image and status is substantiated by his capacity to access the 'originary purity' of the cybernetic grid.

In the contrast between the drooling quiescence of the simstim habitué and the deck-punching virtuosity of the console cowboy, Gibson reiterates the passive television viewer/active computer operator dichotomy. But given the confluence of networks over the last decade, and a long-term tendency towards a convergence of interfaces, we might reconsider his categorization of cyberbodies. In the 'real world' of achieved cyberspaces, the most popular application of public access networks to date has been as avenues of social interaction, rather than as sources of information or entertainment. This burgeoning cybernetic 'communality' has been largely confined to communication by text, with the very absence of a visual dimension seemingly an important factor. Participants often attest to the significance of disembodiment in online exchanges. As one male contributor couched it, using fashionably Gibsonian terminology: 'Concepts of physical beauty are holdovers from "MEAT" space. On the net, they don't apply. We are all just bits and bytes blowing in the phosphor stream' (cited in Balsamo, 1993:696). But like the ultimately binary underpinnings of the simstim body, these bits and bytes have the potential to do a good impression of the flesh.

The 'revolution' in computer visualization continues its momentum. Fuelled by cyberfiction and by publicity about existing virtual realities, the notion of fully immersive networks has captured the popular imagination. But if exploration of three-dimensionally rendered cyberspaces is to be accompanied by social interaction, then something more than the disembodied, furtive presence of the console cowboy is going to be required. Participants will have to confront the issue of their own visual representation, and chose some form of signifying body. In the novel *Snow Crash* (1992), Neal Stephenson presents a plausible interactive electronic space inhabited by a range of digitized body delegates or 'avatars'. Those who only have access to the most basic VR technologies are rendered in low resolution black and white with clearly discernible lags in their image replacement as their images move about. The more advanced body depictions include 'stunningly beautiful women, computer-airbrushed and retouched at seventy-two frames a second', while at the top of the scale are 'the avatars of Nipponese businessmen, exquisitely rendered by their fancy equipment' (Stephenson, 1992: 38).

Scott Bukatman discerns a 'realist' hierarchy in Stephenson's construct, one in which we can see a resounding of the goal of naturalistic representation in computer graphics (1993b: 193). It is those with access to the most advanced technologies who are privileged with virtuoso body descriptors. But, as Bukatman's inverted commas around 'realist' indicate, the perfection of the more accomplished figures problematizes the whole issue of achieving verisimilitude to a pre-existing universe. We have already seen that the special effects of film and photography contribute to an aestheticization of the body and all the other material forms which are subject to constant representation. Computer graphics inherit and extend this capacity to reconfigure the world. Indeed, as some writers have suggested, the relocation of the generation of images and objects in a realm of electronic signals may constitute a radical decoupling of the phenomenal world and a realm of representations (see Crary, 1990: 1–2; Binkley, 1988/9).

But the focus of contemporary digital body construction seems to lie neither in an unembellished 'naturalism' nor in the unconstrained mutability of form. What we are witnessing, most often, is a deployment of the computer to generate stereotypically spectacular bodies, in what appears to be a continuation of the special-effect enriched mimesis of analogue media by other means. In one of the most sustained and ambitious attempts to digitally animate human figures, researchers at the Computer Graphics laboratory in Lausanne have chosen to recreate dead screen celebrities. Since 1987 they have been gradually 'perfecting' such stars as Elvis Presley, James Dean, Humphrey Bogart and Marilyn Monroe as they develop the techniques which could be used to provide body descriptors for the participants in a future three-dimensional and interactive cyberspaces (Wong, 1994; Magnenat Thalmann and Thalmann, 1993: ch. 9). If the early computer hackers were indeed retreating from the demands of an aestheticized embodiment into their electronic underworld, as I have suggested, then it seems ironic that cybernetic spaces are now being peopled by the apotheoses of this generation of bodies. But even the iconic masculinities and femininities of the era of narratival cinema and television are now being eclipsed by a constellation of still more spectacular bodies: bodies which have absorbed and accumulated all the projections of the earlier era. These bodies include the steroid and silicon enhanced physiques of the human actors who play cybernetic organisms in conventional analogue media productions, as well as the entirely computer generated bodies which are proliferating in the digital sequences of cinema and video games.

'Cyberbodies', Claudia Springer observes '. . . tend to appear masculine or feminine to an exaggerated degree. We find giant pumped-up pectoral muscles on the males and enormous breasts on the females' (1993:309). In the cyberspace of Stephenson's *Snow Crash*, for example, the off-the-shelf model female avatar 'Brandy' has three breast sizes: 'improbable, impossible, and ludicrous' (1992:35). The more customized female models look 'like *Playboy* pinups turned three-dimensional' (1992:38). Likewise, when the teenage male protagonists of the film *Weird Science* (1985) program their computer to generate a woman, she is assembled from their choice of the most perfect body parts found in the *Playboy* photographs (Springer, 1991:320). This seems analogous to the strategy used in the creation of *Virtual Valerie*, an 'erotic software' program which became the best-selling CD-ROM title in the American market when it was introduced in the late 1980s (Bowen-Jones, 1993:24). Already in production is the more advanced three-dimensional Valerie – a 'cybernetic fantasy of tantalising beauty and incredible proportions', in the words of the male programmers responsible (Bowen-Jones, 1993:24).

What we seem to be dealing with here is not the ultimate in cybernetic bodies, but a recursive corporeality which arises out of the transition from one generation of mediated effects to another. The new globalized electronic networks tend to offer a broader spectrum of lifestyle and body-image options than the narratives of the analogue media – with their spectacular but relatively integrated masculine and feminine personas. Received identities are further disaggregated by a gaze which glides between channels in search of desirable instants and by a videography which seeks to stall this gaze with its own accelerated splicing of arresting body parts and gestures. Gibson's fiction extrapolates from a contemporary condition in which there is a dissipation of stable role models for the construction of the self, and a tendency to sample from a multiplicity of mediated options. Like the sign-encrusted superficies of the built environment, the surface of the body is deployed as a palimpsest for a succession of fashion statements.

While the overall effect of the post-analogue arrangement of visuality is to disaggregate the body and its gestures, the reconfigurative capacities of the digital metamedium are being used primarily to reassemble the errant components. As Susan Jeffords puts it, the cyborg policeman from the film *Robocop* (1987) is 'a fragmented collection of disconnected parts that achieve the illusion of coherence only through their display as spectacle' (cited in Fuchs, 1993:115). This definition might hold for all the hyperbolized bodies of the digital domain, both computer generated and enhanced with computerized components. They are firm and exemplary bodies which reimpose order on all the intractable body images, in a similar way that Gibson's cybernetic grid realigns the chaotic forms of the built environment.

But the ability to digitally recompose whole bodies out of circulating fragments has as its flipside the capacity to disassemble, rearrange and mutate with an equal fluidity. This has been demonstrated in the sequence from Michael Jackson's music video *Black or White*, which features a series of seamless transmutations from male to female, from young to old, from one race to another, and from human to animal, and again in the glossy, shape-shifting couple in the 'virtual sex' scenes of *The Lawnmower Man* (1992), and the mercurial morphing T1000 android from *Terminator 2: Judgment Day* (1991) (Dery, 1992:501–2; Smith, 1993:67).

Of course, it is the infinitely adaptable T1000 rather than Arnold Schwarzenegger's retroactive cyborg which will eventually triumph in the new universe of electronic networks. The T1000 is the 'advanced' form of the sort of self which Arthur Kroker already observes in the present. This 'subject' constantly revises its identity through a sampling process: 'wrapping itself in the changing fashions of the mediascape, mutating to the mood of its environment' (Kroker, 1992:134). If cyberspace takes shape as a networked, immersive and three-dimensional environment, then it is likely that body depiction will acquire a push-button mutability. 'We'll probably see a lot of Tom Cruises and Rob Lowes wandering through VR' Richard Kardrey observes (cited in Bright, 1992:65). But the pool of cinematic bodies will be but one database among many for the provision of body descriptors, and whole ready-made identities only the simplest option. As Kadrey continues. 'You could look like anything and be any gender or combination of genders you want. There's no particular reason for you even to be a person' (Bright, 1992:65). *Colors* magazine, a publication by the Benetton corporation, demonstrates one possibility with their digitally remixed Afro-American Arnold Schwarzenegger, Asian Pope John Paul II and African Queen Elizabeth II portraits (1993:32–4). This is not freedom from the 'meat', any more than the frenetic codes of fashion constitute freedom from clothing. Cyberspace will demand a constant attentiveness to the flesh that comes with the capacity to retune the body's signifying surfaces from one moment to the next: this is the burden of a corporeality brought up to the speed of the fashion industry. 'The mix and match body, therefore, as the new body type for the age of recombinant culture' (Kroker, 1993:126).

Autonomous Bodies

For Jonathon Crary, the shift away from the mimetic orientation of photography, film and early television to computer generated imagery constitutes the onset of an entirely new regime of visuality (1990:1–2) as I noted above. Henceforth, the originary site of the image is no longer a phenomenal world which is shared by corporeal beings, but a realm of electronic signals that are at a remove from the gaze and touch of the human subject. The repertoire of digital techniques, Crary argues 'are relocating vision to a plane severed from a human observer' (1990: 1).

However, although they entail a circuit through the realm of mathematical abstraction, some of the key procedures of computer image generation closely iterate the techniques of modelling material forms which derive from the era of analogue media. As in the construction of the simulacra of the theme park, most computer generated objects involve the overlaying of an aestheticized planar surface over a merely functional substructure. Which is to say that purely digital images and objects share with those constructs of the 'mimetic' era a prioritizing of outward appearance to the end of attracting and holding the human gaze. In this sense, texture mapping, ray tracing, computer-aided design and a number of the other techniques identified by Crary clearly maintain a mimetic component.

We have yet to see how far computer generated forms will deviate from those which belong to an earlier generation of mediascapes. Perhaps the most portentous of recent developments is the implantation of 'entities' which evolve their own structure, appearance and behaviour in the cybernetic environment. To date, most of the interest in autonomous digital entities has revolved around the synthesis of artificial intelligences – computer programs which mimic the capacity of human beings or other organisms for 'thought'. As with the construction of photorealistic visual images, AI research is based on a 'top–down' approach, in which researchers seek to assemble all the components for an operative virtual entity (De Landa, 1993: 800). Indeed, researchers at the Lausanne laboratory are attempting to meld synthetic appearance with synthetic intelligence in their creations, so that virtual actors will be able to respond to their environments and engage in unprogrammed conversation (Wong, 1994: 26).

An alternative means of generating active computer entities is the 'bottom–up' approach which is integral to artificial life research. As a discursive field, A-life has crystallized around experiments in evolutionary biology, in which researchers have employed computers to simulate the conditions under which self-organizing processes occur in the biophysical world (Levy, 1993: 3–10). A typical computational 'ecosystem' involves a range of virtual 'organisms', each of which is comprised of a set of 'genes' or digitized instructions which determine their visual appearance and initial behavioural patterns. These entities are capable of 'mating' by exchanging a section of their genetic material, so that new configurations – and hence new patterns of behaviour – can emerge and take their place in the virtual arena. Through the electronic equivalent of natural selection some informational organisms die out while others thrive, with mutation adding to genetic variability. This opens the possibility of the emergence of new levels of complexity (see Levy,

1993:5–6, 113). 'The exercise will be considered successful if novel properties, *unimagined by the designer*, emerge spontaneously', as Manuel De Landa explains (1993:800).

So far, A-life researchers have managed to model the sort of inflexible behavioural patterns displayed by ants or termites (De Landa, 1993:803). However, some commentators look to the eventual emergence of abstract 'living' organisms gifted with powers akin to human 'reason', perhaps by way of an uptake of certain techniques developed under the AI paradigm (De Landa, 1993:801–3). This does not mean to say that A-life experiments are necessarily focused on the recapitulation of terrestrial evolution. As pioneer researcher Christopher Langton puts it: 'Such systems can help us expand our understanding of life as it *could* be . . . allowing us to view the life that has evolved here on Earth in the larger context of *possible* life' (1988:xvi).

Where A-life diverges from the general thrust of AI, then, is in its dynamism and open-endedness. It is this quality that has attracted artists to the field. Generally more concerned with the evolution of novel forms and structures than with behavioural patterns, artists have drawn on A-life techniques to generate 'organisms' with no known equivalent in the phenomenal world. Animator Karl Simms, for example, has 'grown' otherworldly botanic landscapes through a computer modelling of plant 'genes'. With a program allowing for genetic crossover and mutation he has produced a near infinite range of virtual trees (Levy, 1993:211–14). Working with computer scientist Stephen Todd, William Latham has developed a program which allows forms to metamorphosize in three dimensions. Taking inspiration from such organic forms as animal skeletons, horns and eggs, Latham performs operations of twisting, iteration, interbreeding and random mutation, resulting in virtual objects that, in his own words, 'often bear no relation to biological reality' (Todd and Latham, 1992:40).

As computing power continues on its exponential rise – allowing increasingly epochal time scales to be telescoped into virtual evolutionary cycles – it can be surmised that creatures of ever-greater complexity will emerge from the electronic circuitry of the computer into the light of graphic visualization (see Levy, 1993:215–16). These 'entities' might well be admitted to the same paraspaces as our own body-descriptors. As science journalist and novelist Rudy Rucker contends: 'In the future we can expect to see large numbers of A-life organisms wandering around in cyberspace – this will keep virtual reality from being sterile and boring' (1992:32).

A-life and related techniques may be more significant than this, however. With regard to the proliferation of electronic networks, Jean Baudrillard has identified a new operation of signs: one in which even the semblance of coherence or contextualization is lost as fragments of meaning rebound from one terminal to the next (1992: 15–16, 1990: 164–5). He describes this order as 'viral', with the implication that the residual particles of meaning circulate with disregard for any logic or controlling force, save their own intractable motions (1992: 15). In a related sense, Arthur Kroker offers a vision of the human body so fragmented by its multiple depictions in the electronic media that it is effectively reduced to the pure data form of its genetic code (1993: 40–1). As they circulate through the networks these fragments of the body recombine into endless random configurations, again, with what appears to be a logic of their own.

But Baudrillard and Kroker are writing metaphorically about the inability to control processes of signification in the contemporary world. In a much more literal sense, A-life forms behave like viruses, reproducing and recombining their 'genetic' material as if they had a life of their own. Effectively, they constitute a new form of signifying object: one which we have created but which we have also endowed with an inherent capacity to recreate itself. Successful A-life entities are by definition unrelated to preconceived forms – or non-mimetic – and in this sense they diverge more dramatically from the preceding order of signs than computer graphics which merely represent existing images and objects via an abstract digital format. The computer is no longer deployed as a medium, henceforth it is purely an environment in which these new messages serve as their own mediums. Running free in cybernetic spaces, proliferating and transmuting at unpredictable velocities, autonomous digital entities operate at a further remove from the gaze or touch of the human agent than any prior generation of forms.

This means that we could end up sharing our cybernetic environments with bodies capable of reconfiguring themselves into more permutations than we could ever conjure up for our virtual selves. Hiding in the light of these more radiant entities, we might absolve ourselves from the burden of endlessly revising our own signifying surfaces, renouncing the cycles of corporeal fashion in the face of this indefatigable competition. But to appreciate synthetic organisms for their appearance, as Rucker proposes, is once again to deploy a new medium to simulate those effects which are in the process of being superseded. Artists like Simms or Latham use their programs as partially self-generative means to extend the decorous and seductive surfaces of spectacular culture into hitherto unforseen arrangements. A truly autonomous entity, however, has no obligation to perform for the gaze of an outside observer. Crary (1990: 1) and Paul Virilio (1989: 1–4) have drawn our attention to new computerized optical systems which gather and process their own visual data. Perhaps synthetic organisms might take on this function, and develop their own sensory capacities, reversing the gaze and turning our own perceiving bodies into perceived bodies (see Hogeweg, 1988: 313).

There could be a time at which we shrink from the gazes of both human and post-human others within the datascape, and nostalgically rediscover slower velocities of the flesh in the extra-cybernetic domain. There would be some irony in any such development, if we recall that the first hackers may have been taking refuge in the computational universe from the enforced signification of the body in the world beyond. In the second cycle of computational practices and effects, which is still in its developmental phase, this enforced signification of the body is recapitulated in the cybernetic paraspace. But as I have suggested, it may be a third phase of autonomously developing entities and terrains which constitutes the most profound break with the semiotic systems which predominate in the world beyond the digital domain. For it is only in this arrangement of signifying objects that the possibility exists for generating bodies which do not take as their reference point those corporeal forms which already inhabit our other mediated environments.

References

Albrecht, Donald (1987) *Designing Dreams: Modern Architecture in the Movies*. London: Thames and Hudson.

Balsamo, Anne (1993) 'Feminism for the Incurably Informed', in Mark Dery (ed.) *Flame Wars: The Discourse of Cyberculture*, Special Issue of *The South Atlantic Quarterly* 92(4): 681–712.

Baudrillard, Jean (1983) *Simulations*. New York: Semiotext(e).

Baudrillard, Jean (1988) *Selected Writings*, ed. Mark Poster. Cambridge: Polity Press.

Baudrillard, Jean (1990) *Seduction*. Basingstoke: Macmillan.

Baudrillard, Jean (1992) 'Transpolitics, Transsexuality, Transaesthetics', in William Stearns and William Chaloupka (eds) *Jean Baudrillard: The Disappearance of Art and Politics*. Basingstoke: Macmillan.

Benjamin, Walter (1969) *Illuminations*. New York: Schocken Books.

Benjamin, Walter (1978) *Reflections: Essays, Aphorisms, Autobiographical Writings*. New York: Harcourt Brace Jovanovich.

Binkley, Timothy (1988/9) 'Camera Fantasia: Computed Visions of Virtual Realities', *Millennium Film Journal* 21: 7–43.

Bowen-Jones, Carys (1993) 'Hi-Tech Sex', *Marie Claire* April: 22–6.

Bright, Susie (1992) *Susie Bright's Sexual Reality: A Virtual Sex Reader*. Pittsburgh: Cleis Press.

Buck-Morss, Susan (1989) *The Dialectics of Seeing: Walter Benjamin and the Arcades Project*. Cambridge, MA: MIT Press.

Bukatman, Scott (1993a) 'Gibson's Typewriter', in Mark Dery (ed.) *Flame Wars: The Discourse of Cyberculture*, Special Issue of *The South Atlantic Quarterly* 92(4): 627–45.

Bukatman, Scott (1993b) *Terminal Identity: The Virtual Subject in Postmodern Science Fiction*. Durham, NC and London: Duke University Press.

Colors (1993) 'What if . . .?' 4(Spring/Summer): 30–5.

Crary, Jonathon (1984) 'Eclipse of the Spectacle', in Brian Wallis (ed.) *Art After Modernism: Rethinking Representation*. New York: New Museum of Contemporary Art.

Crary, Jonathon (1990) *Techniques of the Observer: On Vision and Modernity in the Nineteenth Century*. Cambridge, MA: MIT Press.

Darley, Andy (1990) 'From Abstraction to Simulation: Notes on the History of Computer Imaging', in

Philip Hayward (ed.) *Culture, Technology and Creativity in the Late Twentieth Century*. London: John Libbey.

Davis, Erik (1993) 'Techgnosis, Magic, Memory, and the Angels of Information', in Mark Dery (ed.) *Flame Wars: The Discourse of Cyberculture*, Special Issue of *The South Atlantic Quarterly* 92(4): 585–616.

De Landa, Manuel (1993) 'Virtual Environments and the Emergence of Synthetic Reason', in Mark Dery (ed.) *Flame Wars: The Discourse of Cyberculture*, Special Issue of *The South Atlantic Quarterly* 92(4): 793–815.

Dery, Mark (1992) 'Cyberculture', *The South Atlantic Quarterly* 91(3): 501–23.

Foster, Thomas (1993) 'Incurably Informed: The Pleasures and Dangers of Cyberpunk', *Genders* 18: 1–10.

Friedhoff, Richard and William Benzon (1989) *Visualization: The Second Computer Revolution*. New York: Harry M. Abrams.

Fuchs, Cynthia (1993) ' "Death is Irrelevant": Cyborgs, Reproduction and the Future of Male Hysteria', *Genders* 18: 113–33.

Gibson, William (1986) *Neuromancer*. London: Grafton.

Gibson, William (1987) *Count Zero*. London: Grafton.

Gibson, William (1988) *Burning Chrome*. London: Grafton.

Goss, Jon (1993) 'The "Magic of the Mall": An Analysis of Form, Function, and Meaning in the Contemporary Retail Built Environment', *Annals of the Association of American Geographers* 83(1): 18–47.

Hafner, Katie and John Markoff (1991) *Cyberpunk: Outlaws and Hackers on the Computer Frontier*. New York: Simon and Schuster.

Hogeweg, Pauline (1988) 'MIRROR beyond MIRROR, Puddles of Life', in Christopher Langton (ed.) *Artificial Life: Santa Fe Institute Studies in the Sciences of Complexity*. Reading, MA: Addison-Wesley.

Krauss, Rosalind (1986) *The Originality of the Avant-Garde and Other Myths*. Cambridge, MA: MIT Press.

Kroker, Arthur (1992) *The Possessed Individual: Technology and Postmodernity*. Basingstoke: Macmillan.

Kroker, Arthur (1993) *Spasm: Virtual Reality, Android Music, and Electric Flesh*. New York: St Martin's Press.

Kroker, Arthur and Kroker, Marilouise (1988) 'Theses on the Disappearing Body in the Hyper-modern Condition', in Arthur Kroker and Marilouise Kroker *Body Invaders: Sexuality and the Postmodern Condition*. Basingstoke: Macmillan Education.

Langton, Christopher (1988) 'Artificial Life', in Christopher Langton (ed.) *Artificial Life: Santa Fe Institute Studies in the Sciences of Complexity*. Reading, MA: Addison-Wesley.

Levy, Steven 1984) *Hackers, Heroes of the Computer Revolution*. New York: Anchor/Doubleday.

Levy, Steven (1993) *Artificial Life: The Quest for a New Creation*. London: Penguin.

Magnenat Thalmann, Nadia and Daniel Thalmann (1993) 'The World of Virtual Actors', in Nadia Magnenat Thalmann and Daniel Thalmann (eds) *Virtual Worlds and Multimedia*. Chichester: John Wiley.

McCaffery, Larry (1991) 'An Interview with William Gibson', in Larry McCaffery (ed.) *Storming the Reality Studio: A Casebook of Cyberpunk and Postmodern Fiction*. Durham, NC and London: Duke University Press.

McLuhan, Marshall (1987) *Understanding Media: The Extensions of Man*. London: Ark Paperbacks.

Ross, Andrew (1991) 'Hacking Away at the Counterculture', in Constance Penley and Andrew Ross (eds) *Technoculture*. Minneapolis: University of Minnesota Press.

Roszak, Theodore (1988) *The Cult of Information: The Folklore of Computers and the True Art of Thinking*. London: Paladin.

Rucker, Rudy (1992) 'Artificial Life', in Rudy Rucker, R.U. Sirius and Queen Mu (eds) *Mondo 2000: A User's Guide to the New Edge*. New York: Harper Perennial.

Rushkoff, Douglas (1994) *Cyberia: Life in the Trenches of Cyberspace*. San Francisco: Harper San Francisco.

Slusser, George (1991) 'Literary MTV', in Larry McCaffery (ed.) *Storming the Reality Studio: A Casebook of Cyberpunk and Postmodern Fiction*. Durham, NC and London: Duke University Press.

Smith, Stephanie (1993) 'Morphing, Materialism, and the Marketing of *Xenogenesis*', *Genders* 18: 67–86.

Sorkin, Michael (1992a) 'See You in Disneyland', in Michael Sorkin (ed.) *Variations on a Theme Park: The New American City and the End of Public Space*. New York: Hill and Wang.

Sorkin, Michael (ed.) (1992b) *Variations on a Theme Park: The New American City and the End of Public Space*. New York: Hill and Wang.

Springer, Claudia (1991) 'The Pleasure of the Interface', *Screen* 32(3): 303–23.

Springer, Claudia (1993) 'Sex, Memories and Angry Women', in Mark Dery (ed.) *Flame Wars: The Discourse of Cyberculture*, Special Issue of *The South Atlantic Quarterly* 92(4): 713–33.

Stallman, Richard (1992) 'Hackers', in Rudy Rucker, R.U. Sirius and Queen Mu (eds) *Mondo 2000: A User's Guide to the New Edge*. New York: Harper Perennial.

Stephenson, Neal (1992) *Snow Crash*. Harmondsworth: ROC/Penguin.

Sterling, Bruce (1986) 'Preface', in Bruce Sterling (ed.) *Mirrorshades: The Cyberpunk Anthology*. New York: Arbor House.

Todd, Stephen and William Latham (1992) *Evolutionary Art and Computers*. London: Academic Press.

Virilio, Paul (1989) *War and Cinema: The Logistics of Perception*. London: Verso.

West, Nathanael (1983) *Complete Works*. London: Picador.

Wong, Gilbert (1994) 'Marilyn Lives', *New Zealand Herald* 25 June, Section 3: 4.

Woolley, Benjamin (1992) *Virtual Worlds: A Journey in Hype and Hyperreality*. Oxford: Blackwell.

Nigel Clark completed his PhD on the simulation of nature at the Department of Sociology, University of Auckland, in 1994. He has forthcoming articles on virtual nature, virtual communities and the antipodes in cyberspace and is currently negotiating the publication of his book on visual culture in the 20th century.

Cyberspace and the World We Live In

KEVIN ROBINS

The idea of an Earthly Paradise was composed of all the elements incompatible with History, with the space in which the negative states flourish. (E.M. Cioran)

And what Freud calls all the time reality, and the problem of reality, is always social reality. It is the problem of the other or the others, and it is never, never, never physical reality.... The problem is always the difficulty or the impossibility of coping with or recognizing social reality, that is, human reality, the reality of other humans, the reality, of course, of institutions, laws, values, norms, etc. (Cornelius Castoriadis)

Cyberspace is, according to the guruesque William Gibson, a 'consensual hallucination'. The contemporary debate on cyberspace and virtual reality is something of a consensual hallucination, too. There is a common vision of a future that will be different from the present, of a space or a reality that is more desirable than the mundane one that presently surrounds and contains us. It is a tunnel vision. It has turned a blind eye on the world we live in.

You might think of cyberspace as a utopian vision for postmodern times. Utopia is nowhere (*outopia*) and, at the same time, it is also somewhere good (*eutopia*). Cyberspace is projected as the same kind of 'nowhere-somewhere'. Nicole Stenger (1991: 53, 58) tells us that 'cyberspace is like Oz – it is, we get there, but it has no location'; it 'opens up a space for collective restoration, and for peace . . . our future can only take on a luminous dimension!' In their account of virtual reality, Barrie Sherman and Phil Judkins (1992: 126–7) describe it as 'truly the technology of miracles and dreams'. Virtual reality allows us 'to play God': 'We can make water solid, and solids fluid; we can imbue inanimate objects (chairs, lamps, engines) with an intelligent life of their own. We can invent animals, singing textures, clever colours or fairies.'

With charmless wit (or perhaps banal gravity, I cannot tell which), they suggest that some of us may be tempted to hide in VR; after all, we cannot make of our real world whatever we wish to make of it. Virtual Reality may turn out to be a great deal more comfortable than our own imperfect reality. (Sherman and Judkins, 1992: 127)

All this is driven by a feverish belief in transcendence; a faith that, this time round, a new technology will finally and truly deliver us from the limitations and the frustrations of this imperfect world. Sherman and Judkins (1992: 134) are intoxicated by it all. Virtual reality, they say, 'is the hope for the next century. It may indeed afford glimpses of heaven'. When I read this, I can hardly believe my eyes. We must consider what these spectacular flights of fantasy are all about.

But utopia is surely about more than a new pleasure domain? Krishan Kumar (1991: 28) reminds us that it is also 'a story of what it is to encounter and experience the good society'. In this respect, too, the self-proclaiming visionaries tell us they have good news and great expectations. The utopian space – the Net, the Matrix – will be a nowhere–somewhere in which we shall be able to recover the meaning and the experience of community. Recognizing 'the need for rebuilding community in the face of America's loss of a sense of a social commons', wishful Howard Rheingold (1994: 12, 14) believes that we have 'access to a tool that could bring conviviality and understanding into our lives and might help revitalise the public sphere'. We shall be able to rebuild the neighbourhood community and the small-town public sphere and, in a world in which every citizen is networked to every other citizen, we can expand this ideal (or myth) to the scale of the global village. 'Virtual communities', says Rheingold, 'are social aggregations that emerge from the Net when enough people carry on [electronically-mediated] public discussions long enough, with sufficient human feeling, to form webs of personal relationships in cyberspace' (1994: 5). Communication translates directly into communion and community. It is a familiar dogma, and there is good reason to be sceptical about its technological realization. But we should also consider the worth of this vision of electronic community as the 'good society'.

In the following discussion, I shall be concerned with these utopian aspirations and sentiments. But I shall not accept them on their own terms: my interest is in their discursive status and significance in the world we presently inhabit. The propagandists of the virtual technological revolution tend to speak as if there really were a new and alternative reality; they would have us believe that we could actually leave behind our present world and migrate to this better domain. It is as if we could simply transcend the frustrating and disappointing imperfection of the here and now. This is the utopian temptation:

Men can, in short, become gods (if not God). What need then for 'politics', understood as the power struggles of a materially straitened and socially divided world? The frequently noted contempt for politics in utopian theory is the logical complement of its belief in perfectibility. (Kumar, 1991:5)

I think we should urgently set about dis-illusioning ourselves. There is no alternative and more perfect future world of cyberspace and virtual reality. We are living in a real world, and we must recognize that it is indeed the case that we cannot make of it whatever we wish. The institutions developing and promoting the new technologies exist solidly in this world. We should make sense of them in terms of its social and political realities, and it is in this context that we must assess their significance. Because it is a materially straitened and socially divided world, we should remember how much we remain in need of politics.

The prophets of cyberspace and virtual reality are immersed in the technological imaginary. What concern them are the big questions of ontology and metaphysics:

> What does it mean to be *human* in today's world? What has stayed the same and what has changed? How has technology changed the answers we supply to such questions? And what does all this suggest about the future we will inhabit? (McCaffery, 1991:8)

This opens up a whole domain of speculation on disembodied rationality, tele-existence, the pleasures of the interface, cyborg identity and so on. Of course, these issues are not without interest. But, at the same time, there is the exclusion of a whole set of other issues that also pertain to what it is to be human now and what future humans can look forward to. It is as if the social and political turbulence of our time – ethnic conflict, resurgent nationalism, urban fragmentation – had nothing at all to do with virtual space. As if they were happening in a different world. I think it is time that this real world broke in on the virtual one. Consider the cyberspace vision in the context of the new world disorder and disruption. The technological imaginary is driven by the fantasy of rational mastery of humans over nature and their own nature. Let us consider these fantasies of mastery and control in the context of what Cornelius Castoriadis (1991) has called the 'dilapidation of the West', involving a crisis of the political and the erosion of the social fabric. In looking at cyberspace and virtual reality from this different vertex, we can try to re-socialize and re-politicize what has been posed in an abstract, philosophical sense as the question of technology and what it means to be human in today's world.

Cyberspace and Self-Identity

Let us first consider the question of self-identity, which has become a pervasive theme in all discourses on cyberspace and virtual reality. In this new techno-reality, it is suggested, identity will be a matter of freedom and choice:

> In the ultimate artificial reality, physical appearance will be completely composable. You might choose on one occasion to be tall and beautiful; on another you might wish to be short and plain. It would be instructive to see how changed physical attributes altered your interactions with other people. Not only might people treat you differently, but you might find yourself treating them differently as well. (Krueger, 1991:256)

Identities are composable in so far as the constraints of the real world and real-world body are overcome in the artificial domain. The exhilaration of virtual existence and experience comes from the sense of transcendence and liberation from the material and embodied world. Cultural conditions now 'make physicality seem a better state to be from than to inhabit': ·

> In a world despoiled by overdevelopment, overpopulation, and time-release environmental poisons, it is comforting to think that physical forms can recover their pristine purity by being reconstituted as informational patterns in a multidimensional computer space. A cyberspace body, like a cyberspace landscape, is immune to blight and corruption. (Hayles, 1993:81)

In cyberspace, 'subjectivity is dispersed throughout the cybernetic circuit . . . the boundaries of self are defined less by the skin than by the feedback loops connecting body and simulation in a techno-bio-integrated circuit' (Hayles, 1993:72). In this accommodating reality, the self is reconstituted as a fluid and polymorphous entity. Identities can be selected or discarded almost at will, as in a game or a fiction.

This question of technology and identity has been taken up in quite different ways, and we should take good care to distinguish them. At the banal end of the spectrum are invocations of a new world of fantasy and imagination. When they suggest that 'in VR we can choose to represent ourselves as anything we wish', Sherman and Judkins (1992:126) have in mind the idea that we might want to represent ourselves as 'a lobster or a book-end, a drumstick or Saturn'. The guru of the virtual reality industry, Timothy Leary, has similar powers of imagination. In the electronic domain, he says,

> anything you can think of, dream of, hallucinate can be created. And communicated electronically. As Jimmy Hendrix sang, 'I'm a million miles away and I'm right here in your windowpane as Photon the Clown with a 95-foot-long triple penis made of marshmallows'. (Sheff, 1990:250)

In less grandiose fashion, Howard Rheingold (1994:147) describes how electronic networks 'dissolve boundaries of identity':

> I know a person who spends hours of his day as a fantasy character who resembles 'a cross between Thorin Oakenshield and the Little Prince', and is an architect and educator and bit of a magician aboard an imaginary space colony: by day, David is an energy economist in Boulder, Colorado, father of three: at night he's Spark of Cyberion City – a place where I'm known only as Pollenator.

New identities, mobile identities, exploratory identities – but, it seems, also banal identities. Only the technology is new: in the games and encounters in cyberspace, it seems, there is little that is new or surprising. Rheingold (1994: 155) believes that they have their roots 'deep in that part of human nature that delights in storytelling and playing "let's pretend"'. Michael Benedikt (1991: 6) develops the same point:

> Cyberspace's inherent immateriality and malleability of content provides the most tempting stage for the acting out of mythic realities, realities once 'confined' to drug-enhanced ritual, to theatre, painting, books, and to such media that are always, in themselves, somehow less than what they reach for, mere gateways. Cyberspace can be seen as an extension, some might say an inevitable extension, of our age-old capacity and need to dwell in fiction, to dwell empowered or enlightened on other, mythic planes.

All this rhetoric of 'age-old' dreams and desires – which is quite common among the cyber-visionaries – is unspeakably vacuous and devoid of inspiration. It is a familiar old appeal to an imaginative space in which we can occupy new identities and create new experiences to transcend the limitations of our mundane lives. It is the aesthetic of fantasy-gaming; the fag-end of a Romantic sensibility.

The imagination is dead: only the technology is new. The visions are bereft (lobsters and drumsticks), but the point is that the technology will, supposedly, let us experience them *as if they were real*. Another self-styled seer, Jaron Lanier, reveals why the technology is the crucial element. Which particular identity one inhabits is of less importance than what is common to all identities in virtual existence. As we grow up in the physical world, Lanier argues, we have to submit to the dictates of its constraining and frustrating reality. We discover 'that not only are we forced to live inside the physical world, we are made of it and we are almost powerless in it':

> We are actually extremely limited. We can't get to our food easily, we need help. The earlier back into my childhood I remember, the more I remember an internal feeling of an infinite possibility for sensation and perception and form and the frustration of reconciling this with the physical world outside which was very very fixed, very dull, and very frustrating – really something like a prison. (Lanier, 1990: 186–7)

The new technology promises to deliver its user from the constraints and defeats of physical reality and the physical body. It provides the opportunity to go back and to explore what might have been, if we had been able to sustain the infantile experience of power and infinite possibility. Virtual reality is, or is imagined as, 'a combination of the objectivity of the physical world with the unlimitedness and the uncensored content normally associated with dreams or imagination' (Lanier, 1990: 188). The technology is invested by omnipotence fantasies. In the virtual world, it is suggested, we shall receive all the gratifications that we are entitled to, but have been deprived of; in this world, we can reclaim the (infantile) illusion of magical creative power.

All this appears rather familiar and unexceptional. Familiar and unexceptional, because this discourse on virtual futures constitutes no more than a mundane, commonsense reformulation of the (Kantian) transcendental imagination, rooted in a coherent and unified subjectivity, in the unity of mind and body, the '"transcendental synthesis" of our sensible and intelligible experience' (Kearney, 1988: 169). *Plus ça change*. . . . There are more radical and challenging encounters with cyberspace, however. These other discourses can no longer accept the ontological status of the subject, and take as their premise the fractured, plural, decentred condition of contemporary subjectivity. They take very seriously the argument that the postmodern condition is one of fragmentation and dissolution of the subject. Continuing belief, or faith, in the essential unity and coherence of the personal self is held to be ideological, illusionary and nostalgic. In the postmodern scheme of things, there is no longer any place for the Kantian (even less the Cartesian) anthropology. Virtual technology is welcomed as the nemesis of the transcendental ego and its imagination. In cyberspace, there are possibilities for exploring the complexities of self-identity, including the relation between mental space and the bodily other. We are provided with a virtual laboratory for analysing the postmodern – and perhaps post-human – condition.

Weaving together a blend of post-structuralist theory and cyberpunk fiction, this other discourse charts the emergence of cyborg identities. In the new world order, old and trusted boundaries – between human and machine, self and other, body and mind, hallucination and reality – are dissolved and deconstructed. With the erosion of clear distinctions, the emphasis is on interfaces, combinations and altered states. David Tomas (1989: 114–15) writes of the 'technologising' of ethnic and individual identities: 'The continuous manipulation . . . of the body's ectodermic surface and the constant exchange of organic and synthetic body parts can produce rewritings of the body's social and cultural form that are directly related to the reconstitution of social identities'. In an already hybrid world, it introduces 'another *technologically* creolised cultural laminate with a different set of ethnic-type rules of social bonding'. But more than this, through the configurations of electronic and virtual space, 'it presents an all-encompassing sensorial ecology that presents opportunities for alternative dematerialised identity compositions' (Tomas, 1989: 124–5). In its most sustained form – a kind of cyborg schizoanalysis – the collapse of boundary and order is linked to the deconstruction of ego and identity and the praise of bodily disorganization, primary processes and libidinal sensation (Land, 1993).

This critical and oppositional discourse on cyberspace and virtual reality has been developed to great effect within a feminist perspective and agenda. The imaginative project was initiated by Donna Haraway in her manifesto for cyborgs as 'an effort to contribute to a socialist-feminist culture and theory in a post-modernist, non-naturalist mode, and in the utopian tradition of imagining a world without gender'. Cyborg identity represented an 'imaginative resource' in developing an argument 'for *pleasure* in the confusion of boundaries and for *responsibility* in their construction' (Haraway, 1985:66–7). Subsequent cyberfeminists have tended to place the emphasis on the moment of pleasure and confusion. Claudia Springer (1991:306) draws attention to the 'thrill of escape from the confines of the body': 'Transgressed boundaries, in fact, define the cyborg, making it the consummate postmodern concept.... It involves transforming the self into something entirely new, combining technological with human identity.' Virtual reality environments allow their users 'to choose their disguises and assume alternative identities', Sadie Plant (1993:16) argues, 'and off-the-shelf identity is an exciting new adventure.... Women, who know all about disguise, are already familiar with this trip.' In this context, engagement with identity is a strategic intervention, intent on subverting masculine fantasies; it is 'a disturbance of human identity far more profound than pointed ears, or even gender bending, or becoming a sentient octopus'.

This political edge is not always sustained, however, and it is not all that there is to cyborg feminism. It is accompanied by other desires and sentiments, reminiscent of – though not entirely the same as – the fantasies of omnipotent gratification evoked by Jaron Lanier. Cyberspace is imagined as a zone of unlimited freedom, 'a grid reference for free experimentation, an atmosphere in which there are no barriers, no restrictions on how far it is possible to go'; it is a place that allows women's desire 'to flow in the dense tapestries and complex depth of the computer image' (Plant, 1993:14). Claudia Springer (1991:306) evokes 'a microelectronic imaginary where our bodies are obliterated and our consciousness integrated into the matrix'. Observing that the word 'matrix' derives from the Latin '*mater*', meaning both 'mother' and 'womb', she suggests that 'computers in popular culture's cyborg imagery extend to us the thrill of metaphoric escape into the comforting security of the mother's womb'. There is an idealization of the electronic matrix as a facilitating and containing environment. Like the original, maternal matrix, 'the silently active containing space in which psychological and bodily experience occur', this other, technological, matrix also seems to offer the space for unconstrained, omnipotent experience, as well as providing a 'protective shield' affording 'insulation from external reality' (Ogden, 1986:179–80).

It is time that we let this reality intrude into the discussion again. We should consider these various, and conflicting, discourses on cyberspace and self-identity in the context of wider debates on identity and identity crisis in the real world. It is, of course, in accounts of the 'postmodern condition' that the question of identity has been problematized, with the idea of a central and coherent self challenged and exposed as a fiction. The argument, as Stephen Frosh (1991:57–8) observes, is that

> if the reality of modernity is one of fragmentation and the dissolution of the self, then belief in the integrity of the personal self is ideological, Imaginary, fantastic . . . whatever illusions we may choose to employ to make ourselves feel better, they remain illusory, deceptive and false.

No longer stable and continuous, identity becomes uncertain and problematical. Carlo Mongardini (1992:62) takes note of the inconsistency of the ego-image in the postmodern era, and of the disturbing consequences of that inconsistency:

> A capacity for resistance in the individual is what is lacking here and above all *a historical consciousness which would permit him to interpret and thus control reality*. The individual becomes a mere fraction of himself, and loses the sense of being an actor in the processes of change.

The loss of coherence and continuity in identity is associated with the loss of control over reality.

This crisis of self-identity is, then, more than a personal (that is, psychological) crisis. As Christopher Lasch has argued, it registers a significant transformation in the relationship between the self and the social world outside. It is associated with

> the waning of the old sense of a life as a life-history or narrative – a way of understanding identity that depended on the belief in a durable public world, reassuring in its solidity, which outlasts an individual life and passes some sort of judgement on it. (Lasch, 1985:32)

This important cultural shift involves a loss of social meaning, and a consequent retreat from moral engagement. Mongardini observes a loss of the ethical dimension of life, which requires precisely continuity and stability of individual identity and social reality. There is now, he argues,

> a greater sense of alienation that makes it increasingly difficult to have relationships that demand more of the personality, such as love, friendship, generosity, forms of identification. . . . The loss of ability to give meaning to reality is also the product of psychic protection, the desire of the individual not to put himself at risk by exposing himself to the stimulus of a reality he can no longer interpret. (Mongardini, 1992:62)

There is dissociation and disengagement, withdrawal and solipsism. 'Change acts like a drug', argues Mongardini (1992:56–7), 'It leads individuals to give up the unity and coherence of their own identity, both on the psychological and social level'.

In the discourses on cyberspace and identity, however, things do not appear so problematical or bad. This is because the technological realm offers precisely a form of psychic protection against the defeating stimulus of reality. Techno-reality is where identity crisis can be denied or disavowed, and coherence sustained through the fiction of protean imagination; or it is where the stressful and distressing consequences of fragmentation can be neutralized, and the condition experienced in terms of perverse pleasure and play. Cyberspace and virtual reality are not new in this respect. Mary Ann Doane describes the psychic uses of early cinematographic technologies in a way that is strikingly similar:

> One could isolate two impulses in tension at the turn of the century – the impulse to rectify the discontinuity of modernity, its traumatic disruption, through the provision of an illusion of continuity (to resist modernity), and the impulse to embody (literally give body to) discontinuity as a fundamental human condition (to embrace modernity). The cinema, in effect, does both. (Doane, 1993:13–14).

The new virtual technologies now provide a space in which to resist or embrace postmodernity. It is a space in which the imperatives and impositions of the real world may be effaced or transcended. In the postmodern context, it might be seen in terms of the turn to an aesthetic justification for life: 'Morality is thus replaced by multiple games and possibilities of aesthetic attitudes' (Mongardini, 1992:61). Lost in the funhouse. Through the constitution of a kind of magical reality and realism, in which normal human limits may be overcome and usual boundaries transgressed, the new technological medium promotes, and gratifies (magical) fantasies of omnipotence and creative mastery.

The technological domain readily becomes a world of its own, dissociated from the complexity and gravity of the real world. Brenda Laurel (1990:262–3) thinks of it as a virtual theatre, in which we can satisfy 'the age-old desire to make our fantasies palpable'; it provides 'an experience where I can play make-believe, and where the world auto-magically pushes back'. We might also see it in the context of what Joyce McDougall (1986) calls 'psychic theatre', involving the acting out of more basic and primitive instincts and desires. The techno-environments of cyberspace and virtual reality are particularly receptive to the projection and acting out of unconscious fantasies. In certain cases, as I have already argued, this may involve receptiveness to narcissistic forms of regression. Narcissism may be seen as representing

> a retreat from reality into a phantasy world in which there are no boundaries; this can be symbolised by the early monad, in which the mother offers the new-born infant an extended period of self-absorption and limitless, omnipotent contentment. (Frosh, 1991:93)

In this context, the virtual world may be seen as constituting a protective container within which all wishes are gratified (and ungratifying encounters with the frustrations of the real world 'auto-magically' deferred). In other cases, as I have again suggested, the created environment may respond to psychotic states of mind. Peter Weibel (1990:29) describes virtuality as 'psychotic space':

> This is the space of the psychotic that stage-manages reality in hallucinatory wish-fulfilment, uttering the battle-cry 'VR everywhere'. . . . Cyberspace is the name for such a psychotic environment, where the boundaries between wish and reality are blurred.

In this psychotic space, the reality of the real world is disavowed; the coherence of the self deconstructed into fragments; and the quality of experience reduced to sensation and intoxication. It is what is evoked in the fiction of cyberpunk, where 'the speed of thrill substitutes for affection, reflection and care', and where, as 'hallucinations and reality collapse into each other, there is no space from which to reflect' (Csicsery-Ronay, 1991: 192, 190).

Marike Finlay (1989: 59) argues that such narcissistic and psychotic defences are characteristic of postmodern subjectivity, representing strategies 'to overcome the ontological doubt about one's own status as a self by retreating to the original omnipotence of the child who creates the breast by hallucinating it'. Virtual subjectivity – one crucial form through which the postmodern subject exists – may be understood in this light. The new technological environments of virtual reality and cyberspace confuse the boundaries between internal and external worlds, creating the illusion that internal and external realities are one and the same. Artificial reality is designed and ordered in conformity with the dictates of pleasure and desire. To interact with it entails suspension of the real and physical self, or its substitution by a disembodied, virtual surrogate or clone. Under these conditions of existence, it appears as if there are no limits to what can be imagined and acted out. Moreover, there are no others (no other bodies) to impose restrictions and inhibitions on what is imagined or done. The substantive presence of (external) others cannot be differentiated from the objects created by the projection of (internal) fantasies. Virtual empowerment is a solipsistic affair, encouraging a sense of self-containment and self-sufficiency, and involving denial of the need for external objects.

Such empowerment entails a refusal to recognize the substantive and independent reality of others and to be involved in relations of mutual dependency and responsibility. As Marike Finlay (1989: 59) argues, 'Only in phantasy can one be omnipotent without loss or reparation.' Such a reality and such a subjectivity can only be seen as asocial and, consequently, amoral. 'Floating identities', Gérard Raulet (1991: 51) observes, 'are in the realm of schizophrenia or neo-narcissism'. The sense of unrestricted freedom and mastery belongs to disembodied identities. Such a fantasy, when it is socially institutionalized, must have its consequences for a real world of situated identities. As Michael Heim (1991: 75–6) argues, the technological systems that convert primary bodily presence into tele-presence are also 'introducing a remove between *re*presented presences'. They are changing the nature of interpersonal relationships. 'Without directly meeting others physically', says Heim, 'our ethics languishes'. Indeed, the machine interface 'may amplify an amoral indifference to human relationships . . . [and] often eliminate the need to respond directly to what takes place between humans'. We are reminded of the reality of our embodied and embedded existence in the real world, and of the ethical disposition necessary for coexistence to be possible in that world. It is the continuity of grounded identity that underpins and underwrites moral obligation and commitment.

It is not my intention to deny the imaginative possibilities inherent in the new technologies, but rather to consider what is the nature of the imagination that is being sustained. From this perspective, it is useful to look at experiences in and of cyberspace and virtual reality in the light of Winnicott's (1971) notion of potential space: the 'third area of human living', neither inside the individual nor outside in the world of shared reality, the space of creative playing and cultural experience. In elaborating his ideas, Winnicott drew attention to the continuity between the potential space that supports infantile illusions of magical creative power, and that which is associated with mature aesthetic or spiritual creativity. In virtual environments, this link between infantile and imaginative illusion becomes particularly apparent, as I have already indicated, and it seems appropriate to think of them in terms of the technological institution of potential or intermediate space. This magical-aesthetic aspect of the technologies is clearly that which has gathered most interest.

But we cannot be concerned with creative illusion alone (which is precisely what the new romancers of cyberspace do). In his discussion of potential space, Winnicott (1988: 107) also put great emphasis on the moment of disillusionment, which involves 'acknowledging a limitation of magical control and acknowledging dependence on the goodwill of people in the external world'. As Thomas Ogden points out, the infant then 'develops to capacity to see beyond the world he has created through the projection of internal objects'. The individual thereby becomes

> capable of entering into relationships with actual objects in a manner that involves more than a simple transference projection of his internal object world . . . mental representations acquire increasing autonomy from [their] origins and from the omnipotent thinking associated with relations between internal objects. (Ogden, 1986: 193–4)

Potential space is a transitional space. It is in this intermediate space, through the interaction of both internal and external realities, that moral sense is evolved. Transitional experience involves the differentiation of internal and external worlds – it is on this basis that aesthetic transgression becomes possible – and the acknowledgement of 'a world of utilisable objects, i.e., people with whom [one] can enter into a realm of shared experience-in-the-world outside of [oneself]' (Ogden, 1986: 196). This enables the development of capacities for concern, empathy and moral encounter. Potential space is, in this sense, transitive. We should hold on to this point in our discussions of the cultural aspects of cyberspace and virtual reality technologies. When it seems as if the new technologies are responding to regressive and solipsistic desires, we should consider the consequences and implications for moral-political life in the real world.

Virtual Community and Collective Identity

This takes us to the question of collective identity and community in virtual space. Many of those who have considered these issues have made the (perverse) assumption that they are dealing with a self-contained and autonomous domain of technology. I shall argue, again, that the new technological developments must be situated in the broader context of social and political change and upheaval. The world is transforming itself. The maps are being broken apart and rearranged. Through these turbulent and often conflictual processes of transformation, we are seeing the dislocation and relocation of senses of belonging and community. The experience of cultural encounter and confrontation is something that is increasingly characteristic of life in our cities. Virtual communities do not exist in a different world. They must be situated in the context of these new cultural and political geographies. How, then, are we to understand the significance of virtual communities and communitarianism in the contemporary world? What are their possibilities and what are their limitations?

Virtual reality and cyberspace are commonly imagined in terms of reaction against, or opposition to, the real world. They are readily associated with a set of ideas about new and innovative forms of society and sociality. In certain cases, these are presented in terms of some kind of utopian project. Virtual reality is imagined as a 'nowhere-somewhere' alternative to the difficult and dangerous conditions of contemporary social reality. We might consider this in the context of Krishan Kumar's (1993:76) observations about the recent displacement of utopia from time back to space. The postmodern utopia, he suggests, involves 'returning to the older, pre-18th-century, spatial forms of utopia, the kind inaugurated by More'. Virtual space, which is on a continuum with other hyperreal utopian spaces – from Disneyland to Biosphere 2 – is a space removed. As in utopian thinking more generally, there is the belief or hope that the mediated interaction that takes place in that other world will represent an ideal and universal form of human association and collectivity. Michael Benedikt sets it in the historical context of projects undertaken in pursuit of realizing the dream of the Heavenly City:

> Consider: where Eden (before the Fall) stands for our state of innocence, indeed ignorance, the Heavenly City stands for our state of wisdom, and knowledge; where Eden stands for our intimate contact with material nature, the Heavenly City stands for our transcendence of both materiality and nature; where Eden stands for the world of unsymbolised, asocial reality, the

Heavenly City stands for the world of enlightened human interaction, form and information. (Benedikt, 1991:15)

The elsewhere of cyberspace is a place of salvation and transcendence. This vision of the new Jerusalem very clearly expresses the utopian aspirations in the virtual reality project.

Not all virtual realists are quite so unrealistic, however. There are others with a more pragmatic and political disposition who have more to contribute to our understanding of the relation between cyberspace and the real world. There is still the sense of virtual reality as an alternative reality in a world gone wrong. Techno-sociality is seen as the basis for developing new and compensatory forms of community and conviviality. Networks are understood to be 'social nodes for fostering those fluid and multiple elective affinities that everyday urban life seldom, in fact, supports' (Heim, 1991:73). Virtual communities represent:

> flexible, lively, and practical adaptations to the real circumstances that confront persons seeking community. . . . They are part of a range of innovative solutions to the drive for sociality – a drive that can be frequently thwarted by the geographical and cultural realities of cities. . . . In this context, electronic virtual communities are complex and ingenious strategies for *survival*. (Stone, 1991:111)

But this involves a clear recognition that such communities exist in, and in relation to, everyday life in the real world: 'virtual communities of cyberspace live in the borderlands of both physical and virtual culture' (Stone, 1991:112). Virtual interaction is about adjustment and adaptation to the increasingly difficult circumstances of the contemporary world. We may then ask how adequate or meaningful it is as a response to those circumstances.

The most sustained attempt to develop this approach and agenda is that of Howard Rheingold in his book *The Virtual Community*. While there is something of the utopian in Rheingold (West Coast style), there is also a clear concern with the social order. If we look at his arguments in a little detail, we can perhaps see some of the appeal of the pragmatic approach to virtual community, but also identify its limitations and weaknesses. Like other virtual communitarians, Rheingold starts out from what he sees as the damaged or decayed state of modern democratic and community life. The use of computer-mediated communications, he argues, is driven by 'the hunger for community that grows in the breasts of people around the world as more and more informal public spaces disappear from our real lives' (Rheingold, 1994:6). Rheingold emphasizes the social importance of the places in which we gather together for conviviality, 'the unacknowledged agorae of modern life'. 'When the automobilecentric, suburban, fast-food, shopping mall way of life eliminated many of these "third places" from traditional towns and cities around the world, the social fabric of existing communities started shredding.' His hope is that virtual technologies may be used to staunch such developments. Rheingold's belief is that cyberspace can become 'one of the informal public places where people can rebuild the aspects of community that were lost when the malt shop became the mall' (1994: 25–6). In cyberspace, he maintains, we shall be able to recapture the sense of a 'social commons'.

The virtual community of the network is the focus for a grand project of social revitalization and renewal. Under conditions of virtual existence, it seems possible to recover the values and ideals that have been lost to the real world. Through this new medium, it is claimed, we shall be able to construct new sorts of community, linked by commonality of interest and affinity rather than by accidents of location. Rheingold believes that we now have 'access to a tool that could bring conviviality and understanding into our lives and might help revitalise the public sphere'; that, through the construction of an 'electronic agora', we shall be in a position to 'revitalise citizen-based democracy' (Rheingold, 1994: 14). It is envisaged that on-line communities will develop in ways that transcend national frontiers. Rheingold (1994: 10) thinks of local networks as 'gateways to a wider realm, the worldwide Net-at-large'. In the context of this 'integrated entity', he maintains, we will be in a position to build a 'global civil society' and a new kind of international culture.

Like many other advocates of virtual existence, Rheingold is a self-styled visionary. His ideas are projected as exercises in radical imagination. It is this preachy posture that seems to give cyberspace ideology its popular appeal. There is another aspect to Rheingold's discourse, however, and I think that this has been an even more significant factor in gaining approval for the project of virtual sociality. For all its futuristic pretensions, Rheingold's imagination is fundamentally conservative and nostalgic. He is essentially concerned with the restoration of a lost object: community:

> The fact that we need computer networks to recapture the sense of cooperative spirit that so many people seemed to lose when we gained all this technology is a painful irony. I'm not so sure myself anymore that tapping away on a keyboard and staring at a screen all day by necessity is 'progress' compared to chopping logs and raising beans all day by necessity. While we've been gaining new technologies, we've been losing our sense of community, in many places in the world, and in most cases the technologies have precipitated that loss. But this does not make an effective argument against the premise that people can use computers to cooperate in new ways. (1994: 110)

The Net is seen as rekindling the sense of family – 'a family of invisible friends'. It recreates the ethos of the village pump and the town square. Rheingold (1994: 115, 56) can envisage 'not only community but true spiritual communion' in what he describes as 'communitarian places online'. The electronic community is character-ized by commonality of interests, by the sense of 'shared consciousness' and the experience of 'groupmind' (Rheingold, 1994: 245, 110). The images are of maternal-familial containment. The ideas are of unity, unanimity and mutualism. Rheingold's image of virtual community turns out to be no more than an electronic variant of what Iris Young (1990: 229) dubs the 'Rousseauist dream' – the dream of a transparent society in which 'the ideal of community expresses a longing for harmony among persons, for consensus and mutual understanding'. It is a social vision that is grounded in a primal sense of enclosure and wholeness.

The Virtual Community is a good condensation of the pragmatic case for association and collectivity in cyberspace. In a manner that contrasts with the otherworldliness of cyber-utopianism, Rheingold is intent on connecting virtual solutions to real-world problems. A sustained case is made for the possibilities of applying virtual and network technologies for the purposes of social and political amelioration (while, at the same time, there is an awareness of the dangers of 'misapplication'). There is a growing recognition that electronic media have changed the way that we live in the world. Joshua Meyrowitz (1985) has observed how much television has altered the logic of the social order by restructuring the relationship between physical place and social place, thereby 'liberating' community from spatial locality. Anthony Giddens (1991: 187) describes a process of 'reality inversion', which means that 'we live "in the world" in a different sense from previous eras of history':

> The transformations of place, and the intrusion of distance into local activities, combined with the centrality of mediated experience, radically change what 'the world' actually is. This is so both on the level of the 'phenomenal world' of the individual and the general universe of social activity within which collective social life is enacted. Although everyone lives a local life, phenomenal worlds for the most part are truly global.

In the light of these very significant developments, virtual communitarianism assumes a clear resonance and appeal. It appears to have a philosophy of social action appropriate to the conditions of the new technological order.

Because virtual experiences and encounters are becoming increasingly prevalent in the contemporary world, I believe we must, indeed, take very seriously their significance and implications for society and sociality. What I would question, however, is the relevance of techno-communitarianism as a response to these developments. Let us consider what is at issue. That which is generally presented in terms of technological futures is much more a matter of social relations and representations of social life in the present. In a period of turbulent change, in part a consequence of technological innovations, the nature of our relation to others and to collectivities has become more difficult and uncertain. 'The old forms of solidarity were internalised within the extended family and the village community', argues Edgar Morin (1993: 138), 'but now these internalised social bonds are disappearing'. We must search for new senses and experiences of solidarity, he maintains, though these must now be at more expansive scales than in the past. And, of course, this is what virtual community seems to be all about. Solidarity in cyberspace seems to be a matter of extending the security of small-town *Gemeinschaft* to the transnational scale of the global village. There is, however, something deceptive in this sense of continuity and fulfilment. In considering another postmodern space, Disneyland, Michael Sorkin (1992: 231) suggests that it 'invokes an urbanism without producing a city ... it produces a kind of aura-stripped hypercity, a city with billions of citizens ... but no residents'. Jean Baudrillard (1993: 246) says that it is 'an entire synthetic world which springs up, a maquette of our entire history in cryogenised form'. We might see virtual and network association in the same light. There is the invocation of community, but not the production of a society. There is 'groupmind', but not social encounter. There is on-line communion, but there are no residents of hyperspace. This is another synthetic world, and here, too, history is frozen. What we have is the preservation through simulation of the old forms of solidarity and community. In the end, not an alternative society, but an alternative to society.

We might go so far as to see a particular affinity between virtual technologies and this communitarian spirit. As Iris Marion Young argues, the idealization of community involves denial of the difference, or basic assymetry, of subjects. Proponents of community:

> deny difference by positing fusion rather than separation as the social ideal. They conceive the social subject as a relation of unity or mutuality composed by identification and symmetry among individuals within a totality. Communitarianism represents an urge to see persons in unity with one another in a shared whole. (Young, 1990: 229)

Existence in cyberspace – a space in which real selves and situations are in suspension – encourages the sense of identification and symmetry among individuals. Dematerialized and de-localized, says Gérard Raulet (1991: 50–1), 'subjectivities are at once interchangeable and arbitrary. . . . The subject is reduced to pure functionality'. The sense of unity and mutuality in a shared whole is 'artificially' created through the institution of technology.

The new technologies seem responsive to the dream of a transparent society. Communitarianism promotes the ideal of the immediate co-presence of subjects:

> Immediacy is better than mediation because immediate relations have the purity and security longed for in the Rousseauist dream: we are transparent to one another, purely copresent in the same time and space, close enough to touch, and nothing comes between us to obstruct our vision of one another. (Young, 1990: 233)

It is precisely this experience of immediacy that is central to the advocacy of virtual reality and relationships. According to Barrie Sherman and Phil Judkins

(1992:134), virtual reality 'can transmit a universal "language".... It is a perfect medium through which to communicate in what will be difficult times.... Common symbols will emphasise common humanity, expose common difficulties and help with common solutions.' Jaron Lanier puts particular emphasis on this quality of virtual encounter. He likes to talk of 'post-symbolic communication' and a 'post-symbolic world'. He believes that it will be possible 'to make up the world instead of talking about it', with people 'using virtual reality a lot and really getting good at making worlds to communicate with each other.' The frustrations of mediated communication will be transcended in an order where 'you can just synthesise experience' (Druckrey, 1991:6–7). These virtual ideologies are perpetuating the age-old ideal of a communications utopia. Immediacy of communication is associated with the achievement of shared consciousness and mutual understanding. The illusion of transparency and consensus sustains the communitarian myth, now imagined at the scale of global electronic *Gemeinschaft*. It is an Edenic myth.

Techno-community is fundamentally an anti-political ideal. Serge Moscovici speaks of the dialectic of order and disorder in human societies. Order, he maintains, has no basis in reality; it is a 'regressive phantasy'. A social system is only viable if it can 'create a certain disorder, if it can admit a certain level of uncertainty, if it can tolerate a certain level of fear' (Moscovici, 1993:41). Richard Sennett has put great emphasis on this need to provoke disorder in his discussion of urban environments. In arguing that 'disorder and painful dislocation are the central elements in civilising social life', Sennett (1973:109) makes the 'uses of disorder' the basis of an ethical approach to designing and living in cities. He is in opposition to those planners – 'experts in *Gemeinschaft*' –who 'in the face of larger differences in the city ... tend to withdraw to the local, intimate, communal scale' (Sennett, 1990:97). Sennett believes that this denial of difference reflects 'a great fear which our civilization has refused to admit, much less to reckon':

> The way cities look reflects a great, unreckoned fear of exposure.... What is characteristic of our city-building is to wall off the differences between people, assuming that these differences are more likely to be mutually threatening than mutually stimulating. What we have made in the urban realm are therefore bland, neutralizing spaces, spaces which remove the threat of social contact.... (Sennett, 1990:xii)

What is created is the blandness of the 'neutralized city'. Disneyland is no more than the parodic extension of this principle. Here, too, 'the highly regulated, completely synthetic vision provides a simplified, sanitized experience that stands in for the more undisciplined complexities of the city' (Sorkin, 1992:208). I have already noted the continuity between postmodern spaces like Disneyland and electronic virtual spaces. Virtual community similarly reflects the desire to control exposure and to create security and order. It also is driven by the compulsion to neutralize.

Cyberspace and virtual reality have generally been considered as a technological matter. They have seemed to offer some kind of technological fix for a world gone wrong, promising the restoration of a sense of community and communitarian order. It is all too easy to think of them as alternatives to the real world and its disorder. Containing spaces. I am arguing that we should approach these new technologies in a very different way. We must begin from the real world, which is the world in which virtual communities are now being imagined. And we must recognize that difference, asymmetry and conflict are constitutive features of that world. Not community. As Chantal Mouffe argues, the ideal of common substantive interests, of consensus and unanimity, is an illusion. We must recognize the constitutive role of antagonism in social life and acknowledge that 'a healthy democratic process calls for a vibrant clash of political positions and an open conflict of interests' (Mouffe, 1993:6). For that is the key issue: a political framework that can accommodate difference and antagonism to sustain what Mouffe calls an 'agonistic pluralism'. This is so even in the matter of virtual association and collectivity.

The question of technology is not primarily a technological question. In considering the development of techno-communities, we must continue to be guided by social and political objectives. Against the wishful optimism of virtual communitarianism, I have chosen to emphasize those aspects of virtual culture that are inimical to democratic culture (in the sense of political thinkers like Young, Sennett and Mouffe). I have argued that virtual space is being created as a domain of order, refuge, withdrawal. Perhaps I have overstated my case. Maybe. The point has been to shift the discussion into the realm of social and political theory. Hopes for cyber-society have drawn their legitimacy from a metaphysics of technological progress – whatever comes next must be better than what went before. I am arguing for a different kind of justification, concerned with questions of pluralism and democracy now. We might then ask, for example, whether, or how, virtual technologies could be mobilized in pursuit of what Richard Sennett calls the 'art of exposure' (which I would consider to be the opposite of the science of withdrawal). Julia Kristeva (1993: 40–3) considers the idea of a 'transitional' or 'transitive' space as important in thinking about national communities in more open ways. We might consider what a transitional (as opposed to autistic) logic might mean in the context of imagining virtual communities. The point is to broaden and to politicize the debate on community and collectivity in cyberspace. Those who will, of course, continue to work for this new form of association should not be allowed to set the agenda on their own narrow, and often technocratic, terms.

The Worlds We Live In

We can all too easily think of cyberspace and virtual reality in terms of an alternative space and reality. As if it were possible to create a new reality which would no longer be open to objections like that which has been left behind. As if we could substitute a reality more in conformity with our desires for the unsatisfactory real one. The new technologies seem to offer possibilities for recreating the world afresh. We can see virtual culture, then, in terms of utopia: as expressing the principle of hope and the belief in a better world. That is the most obvious response. It is the one that virtual marketing and promotion always peddles. But we can also see virtual culture from an opposite perspective: instead of hopes for a new world, we would then see dissatisfactions about, and rejection of, an old one. This would have the more apocalyptic sense of looking back on the end of the world; what would be more significant would be the sense of an ending. This is how I am inclined to see virtual culture. Because there is something banal and unpersuasive about its utopian ideal. Because what is more striking to me about it is its regressive (infantile, Edenic) mood and sentiments. It is what I have discussed in terms of omnipotence fantasies (at the individual level) and familial communitarianism (at the group and collective level). Regression as transcendence. Dieter Lenzen interprets contemporary society in terms of redemption through the totalization of childhood. He sees a project of cultural regeneration through regression:

> A regression from adults to children could cause people to disappear completely in the end, opening the way to a renewal of the world. We can see from this that the phenomenon of expanding childhood observable on all sides can be interpreted as an apocalyptic process. Correspondingly, the disappearance of adults could be understood as the beginning of a cosmic regeneration process based on the destruction of history. (Lenzen, 1989:71)

We could see virtual discourse as drawing on this mythology (as well as the more familiar metaphysics of technological progress) when it imagines the possibility of new individuals and new communities.

The mythology of cyberspace is preferred over its sociology. I have argued that it is time to relocate virtual culture in the real world (the real world that virtual culturalists, seduced by their own metaphors, pronounce dead or dying). Through the development of new technologies, we are, indeed, more and more open to experiences of de-realization and de-localization. But we continue to have physical and localized existences. We must consider our state of suspension between these conditions. We must de-mythologize virtual culture if we are to assess the serious implications it has for our personal and collective lives. Far from being some kind of solution for the world's problems – could there ever be a 'solution'?

– virtual inversion simply adds to its complexities. Paul Virilio imagines the coexistence of two societies:

> One is a society of 'cocoons' . . . where people hide away at home, linked into communication networks, inert. . . . The other is a society of the ultra-crowded megalopolis and of urban nomadism. . . . Some people, those in the virtual community, will live in the real time of the world-city, but others will live in deferred time, in other words, in the actual city, in the streets. (Virilio, 1993: 75)

In the first society, you may be transported by the pleasures of 'fractal dreaming'. The other society will accumulate the reality that has been repressed. We know that what is repressed cannot be kept out of the dreams.

References

Baudrillard, Jean (1993) 'Hyperreal America', *Economy and Society* 22(2): 243–52.
Benedikt, Michael (1991) 'Introduction', pp. 1–25 in Michael Benedikt (ed.) *Cyberspace: First Steps.* Cambridge, MA: MIT Press.
Castoriadis, Cornelius (1991) 'Le Délabrement de l'Occident', *Esprit* December: 36–54.
Csicsery-Ronay, Istvan (1990) 'Cyberpunk and Neuromanticism', pp. 182–93 in Larry McCaffery (ed.) *Storming the Reality Studio.* Durham, NC: Duke University Press.
Doane, Mary Ann (1993) 'Technology's Body: Cinematic Vision in Modernity', *Differences: A Journal of Feminist Cultural Studies* 5(2): 1–23.
Drukrey, Timothy (1991) 'Revenge of the Nerds: An Interview with Jaron Lanier', *Afterimage* May: 5–9.
Finlay, Marike (1989) 'Post-modernising Psychoanalysis/Psychoanalysing Post-modernity', *Free Associations* 16: 43–80.
Frosh, Stephen (1991) *Identity Crisis: Modernity, Psychoanalysis and the Self.* London: Macmillan.
Giddens, Anthony (1991) *Modernity and Self-Identity: Self and Society in the Late Modern Age.* Cambridge: Polity Press.
Haraway, Donna (1985) 'A Manifesto for Cyborgs: Science, Technology, and Socialist Feminism in the 1980s', *Socialist Review* 80: 65–107.
Hayles, Katherine (1993) 'Virtual Bodies and Flickering Signifiers', *October* 66: 69–91.
Heim, Michael (1991) 'The Erotic Ontology of Cyberspace', pp. 59–80 in Michael Benedikt (ed.) *Cyberspace: First Steps.* Cambridge, MA: MIT Press.
Kearney, Richard (1988) *The Wake of Imagination.* London: Hutchinson.
Kristeva, Julia (1993) *Nations Without Nationalism.* New York: Columbia University Press.
Krueger, Myron (1991) *Artificial Reality II.* Reading, MA: Addison-Wesley.
Kumar, Krishan (1991) *Utopianism.* Milton Keynes: Open University Press.
Kumar, Krishan (1993) 'The End of Socialism? The End of Utopia? The End of History?', pp. 63–80 in Krishan Kumar and Stephen Bann (eds) *Utopias and the Millennium.* London: Reaktion Books.
Land, Nick (1993) 'Machinic Desire', *Textual Practice* 7(3): 471–82.
Lanier, Jaron (1990) 'Riding the Giant Worm to Saturn: Post-Symbolic Communication in Virtual Reality', pp. 186–8 in Gottfried Hattinger et al. (eds) *Ars Electronica 1990, Vol. 2: Virtuelle Welten.* Linz: Veritas-Verlag.
Lasch, Christopher (1985) *The Minimal Self: Psychic Survival in Troubled Times.* London: Pan.
Laurel, Brenda (1990) 'On Dramatic Interaction', pp. 259–63 in Gottfried Hattinger et al. (eds) *Ars Electronica 1990, Vol. 2: Virtuelle Welten.* Linz: Veritas-Verlag.

Lenzen, Dieter (1989) 'Disappearing Adulthood: Childhood as Redemption', pp. 64–78 in Dieter Kampfer and Christoph Wulf (eds) *Looking Back on the End of the World*. New York: Semiotext(e).

McCaffery, Larry (1991) 'Introduction: The Desert of the Real', pp. 1–16 in Larry McCaffery (ed.) *Storming the Reality Studio*. Durham, NC: Duke University Press.

McDougall, Joyce (1986) *Theatres of the Mind: Illusion and Truth on the Psychoanalytic Stage*. London: Free Association Books.

Meyrowitz, Joshua (1985) *No Sense of Place*. New York: Oxford University Press.

Mongardini, Carlo (1992) 'The Ideology of Postmodernity', *Theory, Culture & Society* 9(2): 55–65.

Morin, Edgar (1993) 'Les Anti-Peurs', *Communications* 57: 131–9.

Moscovici, Serge (1993) 'La Crainte du Contact', *Communications* 57: 35–42.

Mouffe, Chantal (1993) *The Return of the Political*. London: Verso.

Ogden, Thomas H. (1986) *The Matrix of the Mind: Object Relations and the Psychoanalytic Dialogue*. Northvale, NJ: Jason Aronson.

Plant, Sadie (1993) 'Beyond the Screens: Film, Cyberpunk and Cyberfeminism', *Variant* 14: 12–17.

Raulet, Gérard (1991) 'The New Utopia: Communication Technologies', *Telos* 87: 39–58.

Rheingold, Howard (1994) *The Virtual Community: Finding Connection in a Computerised World*. London: Secker and Warburg.

Sennett, Richard (1973) *The Uses of Disorder: Personal Identity and City Life*. Harmondsworth: Penguin.

Sennett, Richard (1990) *The Conscience of the Eye: The Design and Social Life of Cities*. New York: Alfred A. Knopf.

Sheff, David (1990) 'The Virtual Realities of Timothy Leary' (interview), pp. 239–58 in Gottfried Hattinger et al. (eds) *Ars Electronica 1990, Vol. 2: Virtuelle Welten*. Linz: Veritas-Verlag.

Sherman, Barrie and Phil Judkins (1992) *Glimpses of Heaven, Visions of Hell: Virtual Reality and its Implications*. London: Hodder and Stoughton.

Sorkin, Michael (1992) 'See You in Disneyland', pp. 205–32 in Michael Sorkin (ed.) *Variations on a Theme Park*. New York: Hill and Wang.

Springer, Claudia (1991) 'The Pleasure of the Interface', *Screen* 32(3): 303–23.

Stenger, Nicole (1991) 'Mind is a Leaking Rainbow', pp. 49–58 in Michael Benedikt (ed.) *Cyberspace: First Steps*. Cambridge, MA: MIT Press.

Stone, Allucquere Rosanne (1991) 'Will the Real Body Please Stand Up? Boundary Stories about Virtual Culture', pp. 81–113 in Michael Benedikt (ed.) *Cyberspace: First Steps*. Cambridge, MA: MIT Press.

Tomas, David (1989) 'The Technophilic Body: On Technicity in William Gibson's Cyborg Culture', *New Formations* 8: 113–29.

Virilio, Paul (1993) 'Marginal Groups', *Daidalos* 50: 72–81.

Weibel, Peter (1990) 'Virtual Worlds: The Emperor's New Body', in Gottfried Hattinger et al. (eds) *Ars Electronica 1990, Vol. 2: Virtuelle Welten*. Linz: Veritas-Verlag.

Winnicott, D.W. (1971) *Playing and Reality*. London: Tavistock.

Winnicott, D.W. (1988) *Human Nature*. London: Free Association Books.

Young, Iris Marion (1990) *Justice and the Politics of Difference*. Princeton, NJ: Princeton University Press.

Kevin Robins is Professor of Cultural Geography at the Centre for Urban and Regional Development Studies, University of Newcastle. He is co-author, with Frank Webster, of *Information Technology: A Luddite Analysis* (Ablex, 1986) and *The Technical Fix* (Macmillan, 1989) and author of *Into the Image: Culture and Politics in the Field of Vision* (Routledge, 1996).

Descartes Goes to Hollywood: Mind, Body and Gender in Contemporary Cyborg Cinema

SAMANTHA HOLLAND

Many contemporary films take up and enter into the traditionally philosophical debates surrounding the so-called 'mind–body problem' and the nature of the human 'self', but few do so more explicitly than those centring on the representation of what is popularly referred to as a cyborg.[1] With their human/machine hybrids, these films foreground questions of dualism and personal identity especially clearly, and highlight contemporary concerns about the effects of technology on the human 'self' in the present and the future. The cyborg film is particularly interesting when considering the relationship between the Cartesian (or Cartesian-influenced) dualisms of traditional philosophy and those dualisms of gender that, arguably, underlie and inform such a conceptual division.

The cyborg film is a generic hybrid that draws primarily on the genres of science fiction, action and horror, and uses images of the technologized body to investigate questions of 'self'-hood, gender, the 'mind–body problem' and the threats posed to such concepts by postmodern technology and AI (artificial intelligence). Of course the current fascination with cyborgs per se is not limited to the cinema: there are numerous 'cyberpunk' comics, novels and video-games in circulation, for example. I will be concentrating on films in my discussion, though – primarily because they epitomize so well the contemporary concerns about strong AI, or technology more generally, 'taking over' and rendering humans and human-ness in some sense redundant.[2] Further, while I will discuss a number of cyborg films in this paper – *RoboCop 3*, *Cyborg*, *R.O.T.O.R.*, *RoboC.H.I.C.*, *Hardware*, *Cherry 2000*, *Universal Soldier* – my arguments will focus on the *Terminator* films, the first two *RoboCop* films and *Eve of Destruction*.

In concentrating on the cyborg film, I will be addressing questions of what it is, or means, to be human in an age where the boundaries between humans and machines are becoming increasingly difficult to define and sustain (Best, 1989). The relevance of such images to the 'mind–body problem' is self-evident, with a proliferation of central questions such as that of whether the individual 'self' remains when his (sic)[3] brain and central nervous system are transplanted into a mechanical body, or whether a 'completely artificial' cyborg can be in any sense human: these are, indeed, the central questions of *Terminator 2*, *Eve of Destruction* and the *RoboCop* films. I will also be highlighting the way in which no longer self-evident gender differences are displaced 'on to the more remarkable difference between the human and the other' (Penley, 1990: 123) in the cyborg film, as part of its attempt to reaffirm and secure the basis of traditional dualisms. A central concern of this paper, in fact, is to show that the cyborg film's continuing engagement with the 'mind–body problem' and concepts of the 'self' reveals a great deal about the issues of gender at stake in the traditional philosophical positions it often (re)presents,[4] and to which it sometimes represents a challenge.

Representations of Dualism and Materialism

At *RoboCop*'s most obvious level of narrative, the 'bad guys', Omni Consumer Products (OCP), are identified with an unquestioning, strongly materialist position, and it is OCP against which Murphy/RoboCop (Peter Weller) has to battle to recuperate and reassert his 'self'-identity. OCP assumes that once Murphy has been recycled as RoboCop, they can eradicate his personal identity by programming it out of existence (by re/programming his brain). Some weight is given to this materialist view because it is articulated when RoboCop has just failed to arrest the corrupt Jones, and this inability is because such an attempt is a 'product violation' which causes automatic shut-down. However, the (Cartesian) point *is* that although he is limited by his programming, he nevertheless retains the *will* to arrest Jones: the sequence in fact ultimately restores the dualistic position, as it is RoboCop's *body* that is actually disabled by the 'product violation', while his mental desire to resist appears to be unaffected.

At the end of *RoboCop*, the Old Man has to sack Jones to enable RoboCop to shoot him. This shows that RoboCop is still partly controlled by OCP's programming, despite his emphatic closing assertion that he is 'Murphy'. In *RoboCop 2*, however, RoboCop finally finds a way to eradicate all his programming: after being reprogrammed to the point of uselessness (with directives like 'Avoid making premature value judgments', and 'Avoid interpersonal conflicts'), he apparently retains so strong a will to escape that he 'fries' himself on power cables when he hears that a huge electric current – while potentially fatal – might rid his brain of all the programmed directives. This clearly implies that RoboCop has an 'inner' desire to break free from his programming, although that very programming has rendered him unable to *articulate* such feelings. The suggestion that there is something which will enable humans to maintain control over their own bodies and technology in the face of such extreme adversity as the *RoboCop* films represent is a common one in contemporary cinema (Best, 1989).

The Terminator also asserts a very Cartesian picture of the mind–body problem, although it uses the cyborg in a very different way. The Terminator is *not* endowed with the status of human precisely because it is a purely *material*(ist) object with no self-identity. While *Terminator 2* makes some attempt to 'humanize' one of the Terminators by concentrating on how it can learn from human companions, the type of autonomous self-identity of the Cartesian 'self' constantly eludes it, as it always relies on its programming. Significantly, it never really *understands* why John Connor will not let it kill human beings, although it obeys his orders and refrains from so doing. This is hardly surprising, given the film's own Cartesianism: after all, a Cartesian 'self' (or 'soul') cannot be *acquired* – it is a mysterious 'something' that comes from 'elsewhere' to inhabit the body.[5] Also, the T1000 model – the antagonist in *Terminator 2* – emphatically embodies the superficial nature of a cyborg's 'identity' by constantly changing its appearance.

The cyborg-wife in *Cherry 2000* is in this sense very similar to the Terminators: her whole 'identity' is held in one (very expensive) microchip, and while her husband in some sense sees a particular *type* of body as necessary to her continued identity, the *particular* body is clearly no more an integral or constitutive part of her than are clothes and make-up. Here, we can begin to see exactly how much the bodies of cyborgs *do* in fact matter. After all, if we look at the Terminator, RoboCop, Eve 8 (in *Eve of Destruction*) or Cherry 2000, it is clear that each and every one of them has a highly gendered appearance in addition to the fact that they *have* bodies – rather than just minds/computers – at all. While it may be understandable that cyborgs have humanoid bodies and even the appearance of human beings – especially when they are used as 'infiltration units' (Kyle Reese [Michael Biehn] in *The Terminator*) – this does *not* in itself fully explain or justify the highly muscled and exaggeratedly gendered nature of their bodies. Rather, the cyberbodies are represented in such a highly gendered way to counter the threat that cyborgs indicate the loss of human bodies, where such a loss implies the loss of the gendered distinctions that are essential to maintaining the patriarchal order (which is based on exploiting difference) – a point to which I will return later.

The fears concerning technology in the cyborg film appear to be two-fold – representing both fears that human beings will be *replaced* by, and that we are *becoming* machines (Best, 1989:51). However, as both Steve Best and J.P. Telotte point out, the films simultaneously operate to deny the possibility of these things actually occurring by dramatizing the resilience of the subject, and juxtaposing 'the *dystopic* projection of a hyperalienated future . . . with a *utopic* hope for spiritual survival, salvation, and redemption' (Best, 1989:51). The films endow pure consciousness with some kind of 'redemptive power', and visualize a 'testimony to the ghost in the machine' (Telotte, 1988:256). But as Yvonne Tasker (1993:151) has noted, '[w]hen all else fails, the body of the hero, and not his voice, or his capacity to make a rational argument, is the place of last resort' – the sole space that is safe, as it were. And this – the last resort to the body – remains 'even' in cyborg films (and others) that ostensibly work to (re)assert the Cartesian superiority of the 'mind' over the body.

The cyborg film represents purely mechanical/technological alternatives to cyborgs as inferior – especially when comparing them to cyborgs with a 'self'. This again suggests the importance attributed to the body on a *visual* level despite ostensive narrative concerns to remain with the 'mind'. For instance, the *RoboCop* films represent all the purely robotic alternatives to RoboCop as inferior: an ED 209 malfunctions, killing Kinney, shortly after Jones introduces him as 'the future of law-enforcement' in OCP's board room. It is further coded as inferior when it is unable to navigate the stairs to follow RoboCop, and ends up falling down them, flailing helplessly. ED 209s are compared with RoboCop in *RoboCop 2*, as well, where they are implemented throughout the city during the police strike despite 'widespread complaints of their malfunction'. In *RoboCop 3*, an ED 209 is further ridiculed; a young girl hooks up her PC to it, and thus takes control of it – saving her fellow citizens and turning it against the police. Also – and significantly for the role of masculinity in these films – the other cyborgs in *RoboCop 2* are far less (coded as) male/masculine than RoboCop: the two whose 'suicides' we see briefly on videotape have recognizably human-shaped 'bodies', but lack the excessively masculine coding of the original RoboCop. And Cain's robotic body is also less masculine-looking – it is bigger than RoboCop's, but more like an ED 209 than a man.

'Things Are Not Always What They Seem'

An implication of the cyborg film is that being human is anything but *simply* a matter of appearance. In most cases a 'genuine' human mind is identified as the essential element of a human person: and a mind is precisely what we are told RoboCop and the Universal Soldiers have retained, and what the Terminators and Cherry 2000 never had and cannot acquire. The whole issue of appearance and its (un)reliability is central to the cyborg film, of course, which ostensibly operates to warn us that 'Things are not always what they seem' (McQuade [Gregory Hines] in *Eve of Destruction*). Despite such narrative assertions, however, the films' own attitude to the importance of bodies makes their position ambivalent: after all, the body does seem to provide some level of certainty insofar as it *is* the site on and over which battles for 'self'-hood are fought.

The Terminator's otherness is already apparent because of the *computerized* images that represent its point of view. This emphasizes the extent to which the Terminators do not 'see' as we do – where 'seeing' has both literal and metaphorical weight. In the case of RoboCop and the protagonists of *Universal Soldier*, a computerized image is not always used to represent their point of view. Rather, as the narratives progress, and the protagonists become 'more human', computerized imagery gives way to a more 'normal' representation of vision. This 'normal' vision that is a mark of human-ness is shared by Eve 8. Also, once the (original) Terminator has lost its human appearance and its machine-skeleton is revealed (after Kyle blows it up), its point of view shots are no longer computerized. This is primarily because we no longer need this kind of 'proof' that the Terminator is a machine because we can now *see* that to be so. However, the change still provides a problematic: there is no simplistic and generalized way in which to read the use of computerized versus 'normal' vision in the cyborg film. One constant feature, though, is that only cyborgs endowed with a 'self' by the narrative have dreams and/or flashbacks – which are always represented as uncomputerized images with epistemological authority. *None* of the Terminators are allowed this kind of 'vision'. This lack brands them as inhuman, where human-ness is apparently marked by having (or 'being', in Eve 8's case) an unconscious and/or conscious memory to provide such images – images like those experienced by RoboCop, who, in *RoboCop 3*, thanks Dr Lazarus for not erasing his 'memories'.[6]

The unconscious plays a central and defining role in the cyborg film, where its presence generally denotes the human-ness of the 'self' which is endowed with it. The loss of 'self', of course, is the essential tragedy of *RoboCop* and *Universal Soldier*. *Eve of Destruction* makes particularly interesting and overt use of the concept of the unconscious, with significant ramifications for the representation of gender in the (cyborg) film. In the film, Eve the scientist and Eve 8, her cyborg creation in her own image, are played by the same actress (Renée Soutendijk). Effectively, Eve 8 is the literal embodiment of Eve the scientist's unconscious desires: she is, if you like, Eve's id. And, as is made clear by the narrative, Eve 8 is very much an id-*monster* in the tradition of the cyborg film and its generic influences. The positioning of Eve 8 as her creator's unconscious (revolt) is made blindingly obvious at the level of narrative when Eve tells McQuade that Eve 8 is 'going back through my life. Only there are no barriers, no stop sign. The damage she sustained destroyed all her inhibitions. She's doing things I might think about doing but never dare to do – never have the courage to do'. Eve 8, then, is not merely an embodiment of unconscious desires, but of Eve's unconscious *revolt* against the rules, limitations and injustices of patriarchal society. The film's anxieties about the feminine sexuality represented by Eve 8, and the female procreative abilities represented by Eve the scientist/mother are also made abundantly clear. For instance, Eve 8 'goes nuclear', and McQuade says that 'When God created his Eve he did it to shake us up a little. Now you've gone one better and designed her to blow us all the fuck away'. However, this misogyny is countered a little by the film's ambiguity regarding who to *blame* for Eve 8's (and by implication, Eve's) revolt: it is never clear, for instance, what Eve 8's motivations are for going into 'battlefield mode', but the implication is that it is *her* response to the bank robber's violence against woman, and *not*, as the scientists suggest, merely a 'mechanical' fault caused by her bullet-wound.

It is difficult, then, to decide conclusively whether or not Eve 8's revolt is a 'feminist' one (although it is less difficult to conclude that the film is, overall, *not* feminist). In many ways, it seems more of a device to represent masculine fears about femininity; one which is set up – as so often in films – only to be knocked down again. An example of the complexity surrounding the apparently regressive stereotypical positions inhabited by Eve 8 can be illustrated by considering the sequences where she first picks up and then mutilates a 'redneck' at the motel near her childhood home. On some level, this is 'feminist' in its attack on aggressive male sexuality as represented by the redneck and his companions. However, it also reveals extreme castration anxiety in its representation of Eve 8 as a literal *vagina dentata*, showing active female sexuality in a very negative light. This shows Eve/Eve 8's sexuality as something 'evil' to be eradicated: and it is partly because it *is* eradicated at the end of the film that *Eve of Destruction* is, in the end, far from being a feminist film: while the threats posed by Eve 8 in the body of the film *are* in some sense 'feminist', the narrative identifies her actions and the desires they represent as 'bad', and its closure literally kills off the unconscious revolt that Eve 8 represents. In addition to this, Eve is the one who destroys her own 'monstrous' creation (and, by implication, her own transgressive desires), with the suggested result that she enters fully into the patriarchal order, rejecting (her) femininity as purely negative.

The Pain of Being Human

The concept of pain – a common theme in the philosophy of 'mind' – is invoked as a sure signifier of human-ness in the cyborg film. RoboCop feels both emotional and physical pain. He suffers anguish when he sees or remembers his wife and son, and is clearly upset whenever he finds his actions restricted by his programming. In addition, physical pain is something that is blatantly foregrounded in the *RoboCop* films. The most insistent instances are of RoboCop's pain in each of the first two films' mutilation sequences: in the original *RoboCop*, the entire cyborg narrative is initiated when Boddicker's gang tortures Murphy almost to death, allowing for his recycling as 'RoboCop'. In *RoboCop 2*, the scenes in which RoboCop is ripped apart by Cain's gang echo this original sequence, and as some oil-like substance splatters from his mechanical insides onto his baby-like face, RoboCop's screams leave us in little doubt as to whether or not he still feels pain. Moreover, RoboCop's technician rejects OCP's claim that he's 'just a piece of equipment', saying 'Don't tell me he can't suffer', and responding to the argument that he's merely 'electrical' with a vehement 'Bullshit'. She further insists that 'He's suffering' because 'his pain centres are alive' and 'lit up like Christmas tree lights'.

In direct contrast, the human-*looking* cyborgs in the *Terminator* films feel no pain of any sort. This is asserted very clearly in the first film, and its significance as a differentiating factor between humans and machines is underlined when Sarah bites Kyle (Michael Biehn) and he tells her that 'Cyborgs don't feel pain. I do'. Emotional pain is also used as a signifier of human-ness in *The Terminator*. Sarah is horrified when Kyle says that 'Pain can be controlled. You just disconnect'. She asks him, then, 'So you feel nothing?' – to which he responds with a declaration of love, saying: 'John Connor gave me a picture of you once . . . I came across time for you Sarah. I love you – I always have'. This display of emotion – sited in a context of discussing human pain – reveals what it is that the cyborg film identifies as a central difference between humans and machines: that is, human desire (where this is something that the Terminators, along with Cherry 2000 and the *Hardware* cyborg, clearly do not have, while cyborgs who were created 'from' human subjects – such as RoboCop, Eve 8, and the cyborg in *Cyborg* – do retain it in some form). In *Terminator 2*, cyborgs' inability to feel pain is overtly articulated when John Connor asks the 'good' Terminator whether he feels pain. The cyborg's response is that 'I sense injuries. The data could be called pain' – but it precisely *isn't* pain in the human sense that John means it. The same applies to emotional pain in the films, where both 'bad' Terminators clearly have no feelings at all (not even of aggression), and the limits of the 'good' Terminator's ability to learn about such things are revealed when he tells John that 'I know now why you cry, but it is something that I can never do'.

Whatever the individual cyborg's inability to feel pain in these movies, it *always* has the ability to *inflict* pain through physical violence. The cyborg film constantly foregrounds physical violence – and especially physical violence directed towards *bodies*. This points to the cyborg film's concern with the human body, where the *visual* nature of this theme is paramount, as 'physical pain defies language' (Codell, 1989:12) in the way that so many of our experiences of 'self' seem to do.

The significance of gender to the in/ability to feel pain in the cyborg film cannot be ignored. While bullets bounce off the masculine-coded Terminators and RoboCops (although they are not invincible),[7] and the Universal Soldiers deal with their wounds by cauterizing them with cigarette lighters, Eve 8 feels pain when she is shot, and Cherry 2000 and RoboC.H.I.C. are far from immune to bullet-wounds. The sexualized resonance of this cannot be missed when we consider that bullets cannot *penetrate* RoboCop when his adversaries yell 'Fuck you!' at him, while Eve 8 is not only shot, but we see shots of her breasts when she tends to the injury in her motel room. There are other comparisons to be made here – such as that between the Terminator's dealing with his injuries at a sink and Eve 8's actions in a similar situation: they are both cyborgs, but the Terminator feels no pain as he pulls his eye out and gouges his arm open, while Eve 8 flinches – despite the fact that her biological system is, according to Eve, 'entirely cosmetic'. Also, while Sarah Connor is represented as a good fighter, she is constantly penetrated by both bullets and metal shards (parts of the Terminators) in both *Terminator* films; that is, her success in 'battle' is always qualified or undermined by injury – the sexual resonance of which is hard to avoid, especially given the 'obviously phallic' nature of the Schwarzenegger Terminator.[8]

Examples like these suggest that Tasker (1993:19) is quite right to hold that

> In crude terms, if images of men have often needed to compensate for the sexual presentation of the hero's body through emphasizing his activity, then images of women seem to need to compensate for the figure of the active heroine by emphasizing her sexuality, her availability within traditional feminine terms.[9]

Certainly, the male/masculine-coded cyborgs are decidedly *a*sexual: the Terminators have no conception of sexual desire, and RoboCop is on several occasions reminded that he can no longer be 'a proper husband' to his/Murphy's wife. In contrast, while E. (Melanie Griffith, in *Cherry 2000*) asserts that 'I am not a fucking machine', that is precisely what Cherry 2000 *is*. And the sexualization of Eve 8 could hardly be more blatant: McQuade even blames her violence on Eve the scientist's 'teenage sex fantasies', and misogynistically yells: 'So this device of yours is horny as well as psychopathic – that's quite a combination in a woman'.

The Gendered Body of the Cyborg Film

In foregrounding the concept of pain, and pointing to the relation between human bodies and manufactured bodies, the cyborg film displays a decidedly *un*Cartesian emphasis not only on the *body*, but on its *constructed* nature. A paradox is at play here: as Claudia Springer (1991:303) puts it, 'while disparaging the human body, the [cyborg] discourse simultaneously uses language and imagery associated with the body and bodily functions to represent its vision of human/technological perfection'. This paradox is imbued with a number of gendered implications, too, which are unavoidable given the centrality of gendered body-imagery to the cyborg film. If cyborgs, in transgressing the boundaries between human and machine, are indeed 'the consummate postmodern concept' (Springer, 1991:306) it should follow that cyborg films are the consummate postmodern texts. However, despite the arguments of theorists such as Donna Haraway (1990) that cyborgs are androgynous entities that render gender boundaries meaningless, this is effectively irrelevant when we look at *actual* cyborg texts. In actual cyborg films, while boundary breakdowns between humans and technology are enthusiastically explored, 'gender boundaries are treated less flexibly', with cyborgs tending, in fact, 'to appear masculine or feminine to an exaggerated degree' (Springer, 1991:308, 309).

The mere titles of many cyborg films often imply that gender is their primary concern. *Cherry 2000*, *RoboC.H.I.C.* and *Eve of Destruction* all have sexual connotations and explicitly foreground issues of the constructed nature of gender identity. And *Cyborg*, despite is title, turns out to be little more than a Jean-Claude Van Damme vehicle, where the assertion of a violent but ultimately 'good' masculinity is what is really at stake.

It is difficult to argue against reading the cyborg film as upholding often stereotypical and exaggerated gender differences at both a narrative and visual level. The representation of cyborg (and other) males in the cyborg film clearly fits with Steve Neale's theory that violence displaces male sexuality (in our homophobic culture) by undermining any notion of the male body as passive spectacle through narrative intervention which justifies the camera's objectifying gaze by making him the object or perpetrator of violent action (Neale, 1983). In light of this, with characters such as the Terminator and RoboCop epitomizing filmic images of near-invincible soldiers, Springer (1991:317) claims that the cyborg film reveals 'an intense crisis in the construction of masculinity'. That is, integrating men (sic) with technology in the image of the hyper-masculine cyborg operates to 'shore up the masculine subject against the onslaught of a femininity feared by patriarchy – a femininity so feared, Springer (1991:318) suggests, that to avoid it the male body is transformed into something which is no longer really human. This creates an ambivalent relationship between masculinity and the male body – to which patriarchy responds by suggesting that there is an essential masculinity that *transcends* the body: and this, of course, is precisely what traditional philosophy has always insisted upon. Descarte's own assertions, after all, rested purely on his mental activity and did not *necessitate* his actual physical existence.

However, there are complexities surrounding the representation of gender in the films: they are not simply stereotypical representations of masculine men and feminine women. Most notably, the pumped-up hyper-masculine bodies of the male cyborgs can be read either as straight reassertions of hegemonic masculinity, *or* as hysterical over-compensations for a masculinity in crisis (Tasker, 1993; Creed, 1993). And the centrality of the figure of the bodybuilder (male and female) in the cyborg film cycle often deconstructs the stabilities of gendered identity that the narratives work to ensure – with the result that an either/or reading of gender and its representation is completely inadequate. The constructedness of the cyborg itself implies the constructedness of gender, and Tasker (1993: 77) suggests that '[t]he combination of passivity and activity in the figure of the bodybuilder as action star, is central to the articulation of gendered identity in the films in which they appear', where such a figure combines 'qualities associated with masculinity and femininity, qualities which gender theory maintains in a polarized binary'.

While Murphy's death is in some sense blamed on OCP,[10] the actual incident in the narrative that enables OCP to use his body is blamed on a woman – Murphy's partner, Lewis (Karen Allen). The implication is that Murphy would not have been left alone and vulnerable had Lewis not been distracted by the black criminal's penis, allowing the criminal to knock her out and thus unable to assist Murphy when he calls for her. The implicit question is whether women should be in the 'public' space of law enforcement. The event certainly serves to undermine the argument that *RoboCop* represents an 'egalitarian' view of women: there may be women police officers, and they may well share changing-rooms with their male colleagues, but that in itself does not make the film 'feminist', especially given the context of other, stereotypically feminine female characters (such as Murphy's wife, Cain's girlfriend and the potential rape victim).

There are similar problems in the *Terminator* films' representation of Sarah Connor and other women. While its 'authors' (director James Cameron and producer Gale Ann Hurd) claim that the *Terminator* films are in fact feminist, Sarah's being a 'strong' woman is hardly adequate grounds for such a claim. Her strength is anyway qualified by and contained within the patriarchal structures of the films, and other women characters are frequently coded as highly feminine 'bimbos' (such as her flat-mate, Ginger). And even if Kyle is a physically small – and sexually innocent – man, he is still the one who teaches Sarah how to fight, and has epistemological superiority throughout most of the film. But most significant, I think, is that while Sarah is the one who eventually destroys the Terminator – supposedly a feminist statement in itself – it is Kyle who first blows it up (twice), removing its human seeming shell and thus its 'masculinity'. The result is, as Margaret Goscilo (1987–8: 49) so lucidly points out, that Sarah's destruction of the Terminator 'has none of the sexualized, gender-specific charge of [its] own pursuit of her. What she destroys is no longer Schwarzenegger's recognizably male persona but a neuter machine run amok'.

The central fear seems to be that in a possible cyborg future, biological gender would disappear, rendering patriarchy's centrally constituting hierarchy of masculine over feminine untenable. So, asserting an essential masculinity simultaneously with an essential humanity seems imperative, as the resulting masculine nature of the 'purely' mental provides a 'transcendental masculinity' – ensuring that even with no biological gender the hegemony of masculinity can be sustained. This of course runs into complications when we consider the cyborg film's implication that a cyborg with no biological mother is denied human status – or any real 'self'-hood – while cyborgs who started out as human beings retain such a status. This in itself supports Mary Ann Doane's contention that the representations of cyborg films – or, in fact, science fiction films more generally – are concerned not so much with production as with reproduction (Doane, 1990: 164).

There is a clear history of (male) desire to create life without the mother – from Adam and Eve and *Metropolis* to contemporary films such as *Frankenhooker*, *Weird Science, Junior*, and the cyborg film. This 'womb envy' (Doane, 1990: 169) is apparent in the cyborg film where narrative structures juxtapose the questions of biological and technological reproduction. Such structures are 'provocative', Doane points out (1990: 169), because the technologies thus represented 'threaten to put into crisis the very possibility of the question of origins, the Oedipal drama and the relation between subjectivity and knowledge that it supports'. The suggestion is that *motherhood* is feared by (patriarchal) masculinity because it deconstructs conceptual boundaries between 'self' and 'other' – throwing into question traditional assumptions about 'self'-hood and personal identity – and that technology is thus looked to to control, limit and regulate the maternal. However, Doane also asserts that an ambivalence occurs because as well as being frightening, the concept of motherhood ensures a fair degree of epistemological *certainty* – it is the mother who guarantees at least the *possibility* of certain historical knowledge. The tension between envious fear of and epistemological reliance on the maternal is clearly at play in the cyborg film's representations of gender and human/machine interaction, with the insistent presence of cyber*bodies* – despite the simultaneous assertion of an essential 'human-ness' that transcends the body. Such tension is clearly a motivating factor in the appropriation of the maternal function represented by the 'good' Terminator in *Terminator 2*, and in the 'masculinization' of Eve the scientist in *Eve of Destruction*, as I will discuss below.

Fe/males, Re/production and the Primal Scene

The role of women as mothers is certainly a central theme in the cyborg film. Sarah Connor is the 'mother of the future' in the *Terminator* films, and her representation centres around that role. Despite her other roles, Sarah's main function in the films is, it seems, to keep herself alive so that she can have her son and then ensure that he survives: her valuing of him over herself is made clear in *Terminator 2* when she reprimands him for coming to rescue her from the asylum, asserting that he is more important than her.[11] It seems that Sarah's sexuality and gender are subordinated to her reproductive function to a considerable extent. Even more alarming, though, is the way in which the 'good' Terminator takes over Sarah's role in *Terminator 2*. As Susan Jeffords (1993: 248–9) illustrates, because the Terminator moves from being the source of humanity's annihilation to the '*single* guarantor of its continuation', it becomes 'not only the protector of human life, but its generator. By "giving" John Connor his life, the Terminator takes, in effect, Sarah Connor's place as his mother'. As if to add insult to injury, Sarah herself describes the Terminator thus: 'It would die to protect [John]. Of all the would-be fathers who came and went over the years, this machine, this thing, was the only one who measured up'. And when Sarah *is* given a chance to speak out against masculine birth compensation, it is couched in near-hysterical terms ('Fucking men like you built the hydrogen bomb. . . . You think you're so creative'), and her own son stops her in her tracks, telling her that 'We need to be a little more constructive here' (Jeffords, 1993: 252).

Eve of Destruction is especially alarming in its play with the concept of motherhood: it seems by the close of the narrative that Eve has *rejected* her role as (Timmy's) biological mother *and* as (Eve 8's) technological mother, because she both destroys Eve 8 – and with it her own unconscious revolt – and does not seem to know or care where her son has gone: she is more intent on helping McQuade limp out of the subway(!). This ending is quite bizarre, in that it seems to have radically 'masculinized' Eve; it is certainly unable to allow her to retain both creative *and* procreative abilities.

Constance Penley (1990: 119) investigates the operations and significance of the time-loop paradox in *The Terminator*, arguing that the film 'is as much about time as it is about machines'. Her consequent assertion that '[t]he idea of returning to the past to generate an event that has already made an impact on one's identity lies at the core of the time-loop paradox story' (Penley, 1990: 119) seems reasonable enough – especially considering that the paradox is frequently described as 'the grandfather paradox' in scientific discussions of the concept. This gives further weight to her 'femininst' reading of how the narrative serves as a masculine fantasy of omnipotence and self-creation for John Connor (whose primal scene is illustrated in *The Terminator*). Penley reads *The Terminator*'s use of the time-loop paradox as undermining any feminist potential of the film, as she sees it as representing John Connor's fantasy of orchestrating his own primal scene. This again limits Sarah Connor's role to being primarily that of John's mother – which is what Penley finds objectionable and regressive about the film. She holds that because *The Terminator* continues in the sci-fi tradition 'to dissipate the fear of the same, to ensure that there is a difference' in gendered terms, it ultimately (re)presents 'a conservative moral lesson about maternity, futuristic or otherwise: mothers will be mothers, and they will always be women' (Penley, 1990: 175).

However, Penley's reading comes under attack from Mark Jancovich (1992), who suggests that the narrative does not *necessitate* our reading it as John Connor's story – in fact, he claims that this is hard to do because he is never *seen* in the film. I find Jancovich's point interesting, but not entirely convincing: first, it immediately privileges *sight* by stating that John Connor is a less important character because he is not seen. Also, while it is true that Sarah Connor is 'associated with the maternal while also performing activities usually restricted to men' (Jancovich, 1992: 11), this alone does not make *The Terminator* a feminist film – especially when, as I have mentioned above, Sarah's 'masculine' attributes are constantly undermined and made decidedly secondary to her role as John's mother. And, while I accept the argument that *The Terminator*'s primal scene is not *necessarily* orchestrated by John Connor, but could be read as *Sarah*'s wish-fulfillment, I remain sceptical. First, the film's generally stereotypical and sexist representations undermine this reading, which does not fit in with the film as a whole. Second, 'masculinizing' Sarah is anyway not a feminist move: as Luce Irigaray has written: 'women merely "equal" to men would be "like them", and therefore not women' (cited in Sellers, 1991: 71). Representing 'masculine' women is far from being feminist, as it fails to adequately deconstruct the basic dualism of gender constructed and sustained by the patriarchal order.

The original *Terminator* film does not play havoc with the time-loop paradox in the way that the second film does in its attempt to represent a more 'positive' ending (Jancovich, 1992: 14). While the first film merely violates the causality principle in the way that many scientists see as entirely plausible (Parker, 1992), the second film violates its *own* logic because, if the future has changed, its characters' own pasts cannot have existed. The strength that Jancovich (1992: 14) identifies as that of the first film, then – 'that its presentation of time as a cycle does not imply a subjectless determinism' – is lost in *Terminator 2*: the later film fails to assert that the past and future are dependent on each other. Jancovich likens *The Terminator* to John Wyndham's short story, 'Chronoclasm'. Both narratives, he points out, challenge the very idea of a chronoclasm by illustrating the *interdependence* of past and future, rather than suggesting that events would *change* with the advent of time-travel (Jancovich, 1992: 13). Also, both stories point to the importance of human *desire*, which exists precisely because the 'self' is unrealizable without continual interaction with others: this is what differentiates the Terminators from humans, and is what motivates Kyle to come back through time to rescue Sarah and her (their) unborn son.

Maurice Merleau-Ponty (1992: 415) asserts a necessary connection between subjectivity and temporality, arguing that time is 'not an object of our knowledge, but a dimension of our being'. The Terminators – who last just as long as their batteries do – have no conscious relation to time, just as they have no *conscious* motivations, or consciousness at all. The emphasis on memories (whether conscious or unconscious) and relations with others, then, are obvious marks of human-ness in the cyborg film. And both these concepts require a 'self' that interacts with other people *in time*. The primal scene narrative enacted in and by *The Terminator* suggests the human desire to control time; and, while it shows that human beings cannot *change* events, it shows how important their (our) decisions are to events in the world. The cyborg film – along with other 'dystopic future' films – is clearly revealed as critiquing not only possible futures, but also the present. These films clearly cite present human actions and decisions as heavily responsible for our future, and especially for our dystopic visions of that future.

Conclusions

I would firmly agree with Telotte (1988) that the cyborg film embodies a reaction against the increasingly popular acceptance of the mind–brain identity theory, both because of worries at the thought of strong AI and because of resistance to collapsing such traditionally distinct conceptual categories as human and machine – especially with all their gendered implications. The films I have looked at certainly try to (re)assert fairly radical forms of dualisms, shoring up both human-ness and masculinity against the postmodern fears of encroaching technology and femininity (a strange pairing!). However, despite resting on distinctly Cartesian assumptions, they come up with no advance on Descartes's *Meditations* as to how or where the mysterious 'link' is between the 'mind' and the 'body'.

As David Porush (1985: 85) has pointed out in regard to 'cybernetic fiction', '[t]he most primitive response to the threat of cybernetics is paranoia'. The same appears to be true of the cyborg film and other cyborg texts in the postmodern age. Porush makes the link between cybernetics and paranoia very clear – suggesting that it is essentially because cybernetics *threatens to*, and paranoia is *threatened by* 'control through the forces beyond the power of the individual' (Porush, 1985: 85).

In the gendered context of the cyborg film, this paranoia is perhaps more understandable than if we take it as 'just' a response to the purely technophobic threats posed by AI, postmodern medicine and technological advances in general. After all, a rejection of AI in favour of some kind of unique *human* being tends to privilege the body and women more than has traditionally been the case. And if the fear of losing the human 'self' is closely linked to that of losing the masculine nature of the philosophical/cultural subject, then paranoia is to be expected. The cyborg film *narrative* operates as a *myth* to reassert the 'mind–body' dualism and those of sex and gender that parallel it, where its ideological aims are achieved by first illustrating the materialist position, and then showing it to be inadequate, naive and in some sense 'morally wrong'. The patriarchal bias of the narrative comes into play because Cartesian dualism is held up as the (only) viable alternative to materialism, and this belies the cyborg film's visual suggestions that the 'self' is in fact a unified 'body-subject'.

The cyborg film, in accepting and therefore worrying about the computer/mind analogy (and thus the machine/human analogy), extends already considerable concerns about 'our ambivalent feelings about technology, our increasing anxieties about our own nature in a technological environment', to include its own 'kind of evolutionary fear that these artificial selves may presage our disappearance or *termination*' (Telotte, 1992: 26). This creates complex problems and contradictions for the cyborg film and its response to the perceived threat from the cyborg and all that it represents.

So, despite an apparent narrative concern to (re)assert dualisms of mind/body, male/female and masculine/feminine, I conclude that such a project is often undermined by several visual elements and devices of the cyborg film. At the level of representation, the cyborg film suggests that the gendered human body is as central to constituting 'self'-hood and personal identity as is the individual 'mind', making the distinction between 'mind' and 'body' a virtually impossible one. In the end, though, it is difficult to make assertions regarding *unspoken* implications about the body-subject in the cyborg film. The endings of these films, while often unconvincing, still make it hard to avoid the recuperative functions of their stories and narrative structure.

Clearly, the 'mind–body problem' is a central issue in the cyborg film, whose narrative tends to reassert an essentially mental, Cartesian 'self' over any materialist conception of selfhood. And while various devices operate to align the audience with the Cartesian rather than materialist position, the centrality of the *body* in these films tends to undermine the narrative emphasis on the disembodied 'self', rendering the films' own position riddles with ambiguity and uncertainty. Such confusion is often mirrored in the cyborg film's gender representations, which, in an attempt to reassert a hegemonic masculinity, raise questions about the stability of that very concept and its traditional justifications. So, despite the fact that it is ironic that 'a debate over gender and sexuality finds expression in the context of the cyborg, an entity that makes sexuality, gender, even humankind itself, anachronistic' (Springer, 1991: 322), it is clear that issues of gender *do* in fact underlie and inform the narrative concerns and visual representations of the cyborg film, and by implication underlie many of our contemporary fears about the future.

Notes

Many thanks to Frank Krutnik for his inspiration and to Martti Lahti for his invaluable critical and editorial skills in the final stages of editing this article.

1. The term 'cyborg' – standing for cybernetic organism – is not really the proper name for what popular culture refers to as cyborgs: a human being *is* a cybernetic organism, after all. The cyborgs in these films, then, 'should' rather be called *symbiotes* to denote the human/machine hybrids represented by Terminators, RoboCops, etc. However, having noted this technical 'inaccuracy', I will continue to refer to symbiotes as cyborgs, accepting the popular use of the term (which, arguably, is now correct anyway, given that most people regard 'cyborg' as denoting a human/machine hybrid).

2. I am not implying here that such concerns are exclusively contemporary. Indeed, such concerns have been central to a wide variety of genres – literary as well as cinematic – for a very long time (Doane, 1990; Franklin, 1990; Geduld, 1975; Porush, 1985; Telotte, 1988). However, as my discussion is of a group of very recent films (1980s and 1990s), I *am* suggesting that many of the particular concerns represented in and through them are in some sense exclusively contemporary – primarily when they deal explicitly with *new* advances in technology.

3. 'He' is the appropriate subject here, as the films which deal explicitly with this issue are the *RoboCop* trilogy, which of course involve a(n originally human) male protagonist.

4. Here I am referring to a wide range of dualisms, from radical Cartesian rationalist forms to the more body-orientated dualisms espoused by philosophers such as Henri Bergson. Effectively, many of my references to Descartes refer to the range of appropriations and inflations of his views that have occurred in the history of western philosophy, rather than to only his views per se.

5. Despite my assumptions here, it *could* perhaps be argued that *Terminator 2* does in fact suggest that the 'good' Terminator does in some sense acquire a 'soul' of sorts. For instance, it takes on the role of John Connor's 'father'; it learns how to use colloquialisms (and therefore not be 'such a dork all the time', as John Connor puts it); and could be said to 'die' rather than merely be 'terminated', because, as Forest Pyle writes (1993: 240), 'the Schwarzenegger terminator sacrifices himself in order to prevent the possibility that any prototypes or computer chips from this deadly technology would remain', going against John Connor's wishes for the first time – thus committing its most 'human' act of all. However, I remain sceptical: first, it seems that its humanity is more of a projection (by John Connor) than an actuality. Second, when the Terminator tells John that 'I understand now why you cry, but it is something I can never do', there seems to me to be a hint that he cannot ever cry precisely because he does not really, fully understand human emotions. Either way, Pyle is certainly right to observe that this illustrates how far the film's 'knotting of human and cyborg is inextricable', and that it responds to the original film by making 'the triumph of humans and humanism . . . dependent on the humanizing of cyborgs' (1993: 240).

6. The area of memories and emotions is an area in which a discussion of the cyborg film overlaps most obviously with discussions about *Blade Runner*. Some people regard *Blade Runner* as a cyborg film, in fact, and have suggested that I might include it in my discussion. However, there are two (main) reasons

for my decision to avoid its inclusion. First, the replicants of *Blade Runner* are, it seems, *not* cyborgs: they are, effectively, human beings, and *not* in any real sense hybrids of human and technological 'parts'. The whole point is that the only way in which their 'inhumanity' can be detected is by revealing their lack of a (genuine) childhood (and the genuine memories that go along with it). It is not a question of their having mechanical parts! So, essentially, I feel that the central concerns examined by *Blade Runner* revolve more around genetic engineering than they do around cybernetics. Second, I feel that *Blade Runner* has already been written about to the point of exhausting the possibilities for further real insight! After all, not only numerous articles, but entire books have been published on the film (e.g. Kerman, 1991).

7. It is interesting that while RoboCop is seemingly inpenetrable so far as bullets are concerned (unlike 'female' cyborgs), he *is* relatively more vulnerable than are the Terminators to 'traditional', human types of attack. So, while there are many impressive sequences where bullets *do* in fact bounce off RoboCop, we also see him being beaten and ripped apart by better-equipped enemies. This serves to represent RoboCop both as an impressive, phallic fighting machine, *and* as an essentially human being who *is* capable of feeling pain (but only, like Rambo/Rocky-type characters, when the opposition is incredibly intense).

8. The phallic coding and representation of the Terminators and RoboCops is frequently remarked on and/or discussed by critics who have written about the films (Codell, 1989; Springer, 1991; Jancovich, 1992; Tasker, 1993).

9. Here she makes reference to the work of both Richard Dyer (1982) and Steve Neale (1983).

10. OCP, it is revealed, has deliberately placed prime candidates for the RoboCop project in dangerous precincts. That is, having asserted that the police force have 'signed themselves over' to the corporation, OCP takes full advantage of using those rights: it treats the police officers as its property before *and* after their deaths.

11. I am not suggesting that in 'real life' a mother can not simultaneously value her child's life more than her own and be a feminist. What I am questioning here is whether Sarah Connor's representation is regressive or not.

References

Best, S. (1989) 'Robocop: The Recuperation of the Subject', *Canadian Journal of Political and Social Philosophy* 13(1–2): 44–54.

Codell, J. (1989) 'Murphy's Law, Robocop's Body, and Capitalism's Work', *Jump Cut* 34: 12–19.

Creed, B. (1993) *The Monstrous-Feminine: Film, Feminism, Psychoanalysis*. London & New York: Routledge.

Doane, M.A. (1990) 'Technophilia: Technology, Representation, and the Feminine', in M. Jacobus et al. (eds) *Body/Politics: Women and the Discourse of Science*. New York: Routledge.

Dyer, R. (1982) 'Don't Look Now', *Screen* 23(3–4): 61–73.

Franklin, S. (1990) 'Postmodern Mutant Cyborg Cinema', *New Scientist* 22/29 December: 70–1.

Geduld, H.M. (1975) 'Celluandroid: The Robot in Cinema', *The Humanist* 35: 40.

Goscilo, M. (1987–8) 'Deconstructing *The Terminator*', *Film Criticism* 12(2): 37–52.

Haraway, D. (1990) 'A Manifesto For Cyborgs: Science, Technology, and Socialist Feminism in the 1980s', in L.J. Nicholson (ed.) *Feminism/Postmodernism*. New York: Routledge.

Jancovich, M. (1992) 'Modernity and Subjectivity in *The Terminator*: The Machine as Monster in Contemporary American Culture', *The Velvet Light Trap* 30: 3–17.

Jeffords, S. (1993) 'Can Masculinity Be Terminated?', in S. Coohan and I.R. Hark (eds) *Screening the Male: Exploring Masculinities in Hollywood Cinema*. London: Routledge.

Kerman, J.B. (1991) *Retrofitting Blade Runner*. Bowling Green: BGSU Popular Press.

Merleau-Ponty, M. (1992) *The Phenomenology of Perception*, trans. Colin Smith. London: Routledge.

Neale, S. (1983) 'Masculinity as Spectacle', *Screen* 24(6): 2–16.

Parker, B. (1992) 'Tunnels Through Time: Relativity and Time Travel', *Astronomy* June: 28–35.

Penley, C. (1990) 'Time Travel, Primal Scene and the Critical Dystopia', in A. Kuhn (ed.) *Alien Zone: Cultural Theory & Contemporary Science Fiction Cinema*. London and New York: Verso.

Porush, D. (1985) *The Soft Machine: Cybernetic Fiction*. Cambridge: Methuen.

Pyle, Forest (1993) 'Making Cyborgs, Making Humans: Of Terminators and Blade Runners', in J. Collins et al. (eds) *Film Theory Goes to the Movies*. London: Routledge.

Sardar, Z. (1990) 'Surviving the Terminator: The Postmodern Mental Condition', *Futures* 22: 203–10.

Sellers, S. (1991) *Language & Sexual Difference: Feminist Writing in France*. London: Macmillan.

Springer, C. (1991) 'The Pleasure of the Interface', *Screen* 32(3): 303–23.

Tasker, Y. (1993) *Spectacular Bodies: Gender, Genre and the Action Cinema*. London: Routledge.

Telotte, J.P. (1988) 'The Ghost in the Machine: Consciousness and the Science Fiction Film', *Western Humanities Review* 42(3): 249–57.

Telotte, J.P. (1991) 'The Tremulous Public Body: Robots, Change and the Science Fiction Film', *Journal of Popular Film and Television* 19(1): 14–23.

Telotte, J.P. (1992) '*The Terminator*, *Terminator 2*, and the Exposed Body', *Journal of Popular Film and Television* 20(2): 26–34.

Samantha Holland teaches Rhetoric at the University of Iowa, where she is in the Film Studies graduate program. This article is a shortened version of her Philosophy MA dissertation from the University of Aberdeen; it has also been presented in audiovisual form at the Virtual Features Conference at the University of Warwick.

Prosthetic Memory: *Total Recall* and *Blade Runner*

ALISON LANDSBERG

In the 1908 Edison film *The Thieving Hand*, a wealthy passer-by takes pity on an armless beggar and buys him a prosthetic arm. As the beggar soon discovers, however, the arm has memories of its own. Because the arm remembers its own thieving, it snatches people's possessions as they walk by. Dismayed, the beggar sells his arm at a pawnshop. But the arm sidles out of the shop, finds the beggar out on the street, and reattaches itself to him. The beggar's victims, meanwhile, have contacted a police officer who finds the beggar and carts him off to jail. In the jail cell, the arm finds its rightful owner – the 'proper' thieving body – a one-armed criminal, and attaches itself to him.

This moment in early cinema anticipates dramatically a preoccupation in more contemporary science fiction with what I would like to call 'prosthetic memories'. By prosthetic memories I mean memories which do not come from a person's lived experience in any strict sense. These are implanted memories, and the unsettled boundaries between real and simulated ones are frequently accompanied by another disruption: of the human body, its flesh, its subjective autonomy, its difference from both the animal and the technological.

Furthermore, through the prosthetic arm the beggar's body manifests memories of actions that it, or he, never actually committed. In fact, his memories are radically divorced from lived experience and yet they motivate his actions. Because the hand's memories – which the beggar himself wears – prescribe actions in the present, they make a beggar into a thief. In other words, it is precisely the memories of thieving which construct an identity for him. We might say then that the film underscores the way in which memory is constitutive of identity. This in itself is not surprising. What is surprising is the position the film takes on the relationship between memory, experience and identity.

What might the 'otherness' of prosthetic memory that *The Thieving Hand* displays tell us about how persons come ordinarily to feel that they possess, rather than are possessed by, their memories? We rely on our memories to validate our experiences. The experience of memory actually becomes the index of experience: if we have the memory, we must have had the experience it represents. But what about the armless beggar? He has the memory without having lived the experience. If memory is the precondition for identity or individuality – if what we claim as our memories defines who we are – then the idea of a prosthetic memory problematizes any concept of memory that posits it as essential, stable or organically grounded. In addition, it makes impossible the wish that a person owns her/his memories as inalienable property.

As it happens, we don't know anything about the beggar's real past. Memories, it seems, are the domain of the present. The beggar's prosthetic memories offer him a course of action to live by. Surprisingly enough, memories are less about validating or authenticating the past than they are about organizing the present and constructing strategies with which one might imagine a livable future. Memory, this essay will argue, is not a means for closure – is not a strategy for closing or finishing the past – but on the contrary, memory emerges as a generative force, a force which propels us not backward but forwards.

But in the case of *The Thieving Hand*, the slippage the film opens up with the prosthetic hand – the rupture between experience, memory and identity – gets sealed up at the end of the film, in jail, when the thieving hand reattaches itself to what we are meant to recognize as the real or authentic thieving body, the one-armed criminal. In other words, despite the film's flirtation with the idea that memories might be permanently transportable, *The Thieving Hand* ends by rejecting that possibility, in that the hand itself chooses to be with its proper owner.

I have begun with *The Thieving Hand* to demonstrate that, as with all mediated forms of knowledge, prosthetic memory has a history. Although memory might always have been prosthetic, the mass media – technologies which structure and circumscribe experience – bring the texture and contours of prosthetic memory into dramatic relief. Because the mass media fundamentally alter our notion of what counts as experience, they might be a privileged arena for the production and circulation of prosthetic memories. The cinema, in particular, as an institution which makes available images for mass consumption, has long been aware of its ability to generate experiences and to install memories of them – memories which become experiences that film consumers both possess and feel possessed by. We might then read these films which thematize prosthetic memories as an allegory for the power of the mass media to create experiences and to implant memories, the experience of which we have never lived. Because the mass media are a privileged site for the production of such memories, they might be an undertheorized force in the production of identities. If a film like *The Thieving Hand* eventually insists that bodily memories have rightful owners, more recent science fiction texts like *Blade Runner* and *Total Recall* have begun to imagine otherwise.

In Paul Verhoeven's film *Total Recall* (1990), Douglas Quade (Arnold Schwarzenegger) purchases a set of implanted memories of a trip to Mars. Not only might he buy the memories for a trip he has never taken, but he might elect to go on the trip as someone other than himself. Quade has an urge to go to Mars as a secret agent – or rather, to remember having gone as a secret agent. But the implant procedure does not go smoothly. While strapped in his seat memories begin to break through – memories, we learn, that have been layered over by 'the Agency'. As it turns out, Quade is not an 'authentic identity', but one based on memories implanted by the intelligence agency on Mars.

In Ridley Scott's *Blade Runner* (director's cut, 1993), Deckard (Harrison Ford) is a member of a special police squad – a blade runner unit – and has been called in to try to capture and 'retire' a group of replicants recently landed on earth. Replicants, advanced robots created by the Tyrell Corporation as slave labor for the off-world colonies, are 'being[s] virtually identical to human[s]'. The most advanced replicants, like Rachel (Sean Young), an employee at the Tyrell Corporation who eventually falls for Deckard, are designed so that they don't know they are replicants. As Mr Tyrell explains to Deckard, 'If we give them a past we create a cushion for their emotions and consequently we can control them better.' 'Memories', Deckard responds incredulously, 'you're talking about memories.' Both of these films, as we shall see, offer provocative examples of individuals who identify with memories which are not their own.

* * *

If the idea of prosthetic memory complicates the relationship between memory and experience, then we might use films that literalize prosthetic memory to disrupt some postmodernist assumptions about experience. With postmodernity, Fredric Jameson asserts, we see 'the waning of our historicity, of our lived possibility of experiencing history in some active way' (1991:21). He claims that in postmodernity, experience is dead. 'Nostalgia films', he suggests, invoke a sense of 'pastness' instead of engaging with 'real history'. He therefore finds a fundamental 'incompatibility of a postmodernist nostalgia and language with genuine historicity' (1991:19). Not only does his account participate in a nostalgia of its own – nostalgia for that prelapsarian moment when we all actually experienced history in some real way – but, as I will argue, it offers a rather narrow version of experience. The flipside of Jameson's point is Jean Baudrillard's (1983) claim that the proliferation of different media and mediations – simulations – which have permeated many aspects of contemporary society, have dissolved the dichotomy between the real and the simulacrum, between the authentic and the inauthentic. He argues that with the proliferation of different forms of media in the 20th century, people's actual relationship to events – what we are to understand as authentic experience – has become so mediated, that we can no longer distinguish between the real – something mappable – and what he calls the hyperreal – 'the generation by models of a real without origin' (Baudrillard, 1983:2). For Baudrillard, we live in a world of simulation, a world hopelessly detached from the 'real'. Or, to put it another way, postmodern society is characterized by an absence of 'real' experience. But Baudrillard's argument clings tenaciously to a real; he desperately needs a real to recognize that we are in a land of simulation. Both assumptions unwittingly betray a nostalgia for a prelapsarian moment when there was a real. But the real has always been mediated through information cultures and through narrative. What does it mean for memories to be 'real'? Were they ever 'real'? This paper refuses such a categorization, but also shows the costs of such a refusal.

I would like to set this notion of the death of the real – particularly the death of real experience – against what I perceive as a veritable explosion of, or popular obsession with, experience of the real. From the hugely attended D-Day re-enactments of 1994 to what I would like to call 'experiential museums', like the United States Holocaust Memorial Museum, it seems to me that the experiential real is anything but dead. In fact, the popularity of these experiential events bespeaks a popular longing to experience history in a personal and even bodily way. They offer strategies for making history into personal memories. They provide individuals with the collective opportunity of having an experiential relationship to a collective or cultural past they either did or did not experience. I would like to suggest that what we have embarked upon in the postmodern is a new relationship to experience which relies less on categories like the authentic and sympathy than on categories like responsibility and empathy.

This postmodern relationship to experience has significant political ramifications. If this fascination with the experiential might be imagined as an act of prosthesis – of prosthetically appropriating memories of a cultural or collective past – then these particular histories or pasts might be available for consumption across existing stratifications of race, class and gender. These prosthetic memories, then, might become the grounds for political alliances. As Donna Haraway (1991) has powerfully argued with her articulation of cyborg identity, we need to construct political alliances that are not based on natural or essential affinities.[1] Cyborg identity recognizes the complicated process of identity formation, that we are multiply hailed subjects, and thus embraces the idea of 'partial identities'. The pasts that we claim and 'use' are part of this process.

If the real has always been mediated through collectivized forms of identity, why then, does the sensual in the cinema – the experiential nature of the spectator's engagement with the image – differ from other aesthetic experiences which might also be the scene of the production of sensual memory, like reading (see Miller, 1988)? Concern about the power of the visual sensorium – specifically, an awareness of the cinema's ability to produce memories in its spectators – has a lengthy history of its own. In 1928, William H. Short, the Executive Director of the Motion Picture Research Council, asked a group of researchers – mostly university psychologists and sociologists – to discuss the possibility of assessing the effects of motion pictures on children. These investigations he initiated – the Payne Studies – are significant not so much in their immediate findings, but rather in what they imply about the popular anxiety about the ways in which motion pictures actually affect – in an experiential way – individual bodies. In a set of studies conducted by Herbert Blumer, college-aged individuals were asked 'to relate or write as carefully as possible their experiences with motion pictures' (1933: xi). What Blumer finds is that 'imaginative identification' is quite common, and that 'while witnessing a picture one not infrequently projects oneself into the role of hero or heroine' (1933: 67). Superficially, this account sounds much like arguments made in contemporary film theory about spectatorship and about the power of the filmic apparatus and narrative to position the subject (see, for example, Baudry, 1974–5; Comolli, 1986). However, Blumer's claims – and their ramifications – are somewhat different. Blumer refers to identification as 'emotional possession' positing that 'the individual identifies himself so thoroughly with the plot or loses himself so much in the picture that he is carried away from the usual trend of conduct' (1933: 74). There is, in fact, no telling just how long this possession will last, for 'in certain individuals it may become fixed and last for a long time' (1933: 84). In fact,

> In a state of emotional possession impulses, motives and thoughts are likely to lose their fixed form and become malleable instead. There may emerge from this 'molten state' a new stable organization directed towards a different line of conduct The individual, as a result of witnessing a particularly emotional picture, may come to a decision to have certain kinds of experience and to live a kind of life different from his prior career. (Blumer, 1933: 116)

A woman explains that when she saw *The Sheik* for the first time she recalls 'coming home that night and dreaming the entire picture over again; myself as the heroine, being carried over the burning sands by an equally burning lover. I could feel myself being kissed in the way the Sheik had kissed the girl' (Blumer, 1933: 70). What individuals see might affect them so significantly that the images actually become part of their own personal archive of experience.

Because the movie experience decenters lived experience, it, too, might alter or construct identity. Emotional possession has implications for both the future and the past of the individual under its sway. It has the potential to alter one's actions in the future in that under its hold an individual 'is transported out of his normal conduct and is completely subjugated by his impulses' (Blumer, 1933:94). A nineteen-year-old woman writes,

"After having seen a movie of pioneer days I am very unreconciled to the fact that I live to-day instead of the romantic days of fifty years ago. But to offset this poignant and useless longing I have dreamed of going to war. I stated previously that through the movies I have become aware of the awfulness, the futility of it, etc. But as this side has been impressed upon me, there has been awakened in me at the same time the desire to go to the 'front' during the next war. The excitement – shall I say glamour? – of the war has always appealed to me from the screen. Often I have pictured myself as a truck driver, nurse, HEROINE. (Blumer, 1933:63)

What this suggests is that the experience within the movie theater and the memories that the cinema affords – despite the fact that the spectator did not live through them – might be as significant in constructing, or deconstructing, the spectator's identity as any experience that s/he actually lived through.

Many of the Payne Studies tests were designed to measure quantitatively the extent to which film affects the physical bodies of its spectators. The investigators used a galvanometer which, like a lie detector, 'measure[d] galvanic responses', electrical impulses, in skin, and a pneumo-cardiograph 'to measure changes in the circulatory system' (Charters, 1933:25), like respiratory pulse and blood pressure. This sensitive technology might pick up physiological disturbances and changes that would go unseen by the naked eye. These studies thus presumed that the body might give evidence of physiological symptoms caused by a kind of technological intervention into subjectivity – an intervention which is part and parcel of the cinematic experience. The call for a technology of detection registers a fear that we might no longer be able to distinguish prosthetic or 'unnatural' memories from 'real' ones.

At the same historical moment, European cultural critics of the 1920s – specifically Walter Benjamin and Siegfried Kracauer – began to theorize the experiential nature of the cinema. They attempted to theorize the way in which movies might actually extend the sensual memory of the human body. By 1940 Kracauer believed that film actually addresses its viewer as a ' "corporeal-material being"; it seizes the "human being with skin and hair": "The material elements that present themselves in film directly stimulate the *material layers* of the human being: his nerves, his senses, his entire *physiological substance*"' (1993:458). The cinematic experience has an individual, bodily component at the same time that it is circumscribed by its collectivity; the domain of the cinema is public and collective.

Benjamin's notion of 'innervation' is an attempt to imagine an engaged experiential relationship with technology and the cinema.[2] It is precisely the interplay of individual bodily experience with the publicity of the cinema which might make possible new forms of collectivity – political and otherwise.

More recently, Steven Shaviro (1993) has emphasized the visceral, bodily component of film spectatorship. He argues that psychoanalytic film theory studiously ignores the experiential component of spectatorship. In his account, psychoanalytic film theory has attempted 'to destroy the power of images' (1993:16),[3] and that what those theorists fear is not the *lack*, 'not the emptiness of the image, but its weird fullness; not its impotence so much as its power' (Shaviro, 1993:17). We might say that the portability of cinematic images – the way we are invited to wear them prosthetically, the way we might experience them in a bodily fashion – is both the crisis and the allure. As if to emphasize this experiential, bodily aspect of spectatorship, Shaviro sets forth as his guiding principle that 'cinematic images are not representations, but *events*' (1993:24).

* * *

I would like to turn to a scene in *Total Recall* which dramatically illustrates the way in which mass mediated images intervene in the production of subjectivity. The notion of authenticity – and our desire to privilege it – is constantly undermined by *Total Recall*'s obsessive rendering of mediated images. In many instances we see, simultaneously, a person and their mediated representation on a video screen. When Quade first goes to Rekal to meet with Mr McClane, the sales representative, we see McClane simultaneously through a window over his secretary's shoulder, and as an image on her video phone as she calls him to let him know that Quade has arrived. In *Total Recall* the proliferation of mediated images – and of video screens – forces us to question the very notion of an authentic or an originary presence. Video monitors appear on subway cars with advertisements (like the one for Rekal), and all telephones are video phones; even the walls of Quade's house are enormous television screens. Quade's identity, too, as we will see, is mediated by video images. When he learns from his wife that she's not his wife, that she 'never saw him before six weeks ago', that their 'marriage is just a memory implant', that the Agency 'erased his identity and implanted a new one' – basically that 'his whole life is just a dream' – any sense he has of a unified self, of a stable subjectivity, is shattered. When memories might be separable from lived experience, issues of identity – and upon what identity is constructed – take on radical importance.

The question of his identity – and how his identity is predicated upon a particular set of memories which may or may not be properly his own – surfaces most dramatically when he confronts his own face in a video monitor. That he sees his face on a portable video screen – one that he has been carrying around in a suitcase which was handed to him by a 'buddy from the Agency' – literalizes the film's account of the portability of memory and identity. Quade confronts his own face in a video screen, but finds there a different person. The face on the screen says, 'Howdy stranger, this is Hauser. . . . Get ready for the big surprise. . . . You are not you. You are me.' We might be tempted to read this scene as an instance of Freud's (1959) notion of the 'uncanny'. The sensation of the 'uncanny', as Freud articulates it, is produced by an encounter with something which is simultaneously familiar and unfamiliar; the sensation of the uncanny comes from the 'return of the repressed'. The experience of seeing one's double is therefore the height of uncanny.[4] But Quade's experience is not that way at all. The face he confronts is explicitly not his face; it does not correspond to his identity. Since the film rejects the idea that there is an authentic, or more authentic, self underneath the layers of identity, there is no place for the uncanny. For Quade, the memories of Hauser seem never to have existed. In fact, he encounters Hauser with a kind of disinterest, not as someone he once knew or was, but rather as a total stranger.

In this way, the encounter seems to disrupt the Lacanian notion of the 'mirror stage'. According to Jacques Lacan, the mirror stage is initiated when a child first sees himself reflected as an autonomous individual, as a unified and bounded subject. As Lacan describes, the 'jubilant assumption of his specular image' (1977:2) gives the child an illusion of wholeness, which is vastly different from the child's own sense of himself as a fragmentary bundle of undifferentiated drives. For Quade, the experience is exactly the opposite. In fact, we might say that the encounter with the face in the monitor, which looks like his face but is not the one he owns, disrupts any sense of a unified, stable and bounded subjectivity. Instead of consolidating his identity, the video screen further fragments it. This encounter undermines as well the assumption that a particular memory has a rightful owner, a proper body to adhere to.

This encounter with Hauser – who professes to be the real possessor of the body – becomes a microcosm for the film's larger critique of the preeminence of the 'real'. That we meet Quade first – and identify with him – makes us question whether Hauser is the true or more worthy identity for the body. If we are to believe that Hauser's identity is in some ways more 'real' than Quade's – because his memories are based on lived experience rather than memory implants – the question then becomes is realer necessarily better? At the climax of the film, Quade claims his own identity instead of going back to being Hauser. In his final exchange with Cohagen, Cohagen says, 'I wanted Hauser back. You had to be Quade.' 'I am Quade', he responds. Although Quade is an identity based on implanted memories, it is no less viable than Hauser – and arguably more so. Quade remains the primary object of our spectatorial investment and engagement throughout the film. His simulated identity is more responsible, compassionate and productive than the 'real' one. That Quade experiences himself as 'real' gives the lie to the Baudrillardian and Jamesonian assumption that the real and the authentic are synonymous.

Part of what claiming this identity means is saving the Mutants on Mars from oxygen deprivation. The Mutants are the socio-economic group on Mars who are most oppressed by the tyrannical Cohagen; Cohagen regulates their access to oxygen. Quade refuses to go back to being Hauser because he feels that he has a mission to carry out. His sense of moral responsibility outweighs any claims on his actions exerted by the pull of an 'authentic' identity. By choosing to start the reactor at the pyramid mines – and thereby produce enough oxygen to make the atmosphere on Mars habitable – Quade is able to liberate the Mutants from Cohagen's grip.

Surprisingly enough, memories are less about authenticating the past, than about generating possible courses of action in the present. The Mutant resistance leader, Quato, tells Quade that 'A man is defined by his actions, not his memories.' We might revise his statement to say that a man is defined by his actions, but whether those actions are made possible by prosthetic memories or memories based on lived experience makes little difference. Any kind of distinction between 'real' memories and prosthetic memories – memories which might be technologically disseminated by the mass media and worn by its consumers – might ultimately be unintelligible. *Total Recall* underscores the way in which memories are always already public, the way in which memories always circulate and interpellate individuals, but can never get back to an authentic owner, to a proper body – or as we will see in the case of *Blade Runner*, to a proper photograph.

Although *Blade Runner* is based on the 1968 Philip K. Dick novel *Do Androids Dream of Electric Sheep?*, its points of departure from the novel are instructive. In Dick's novel, the presence of empathy is what allows the bounty hunters to distinguish the androids from the humans. In fact, empathy is imagined to be *the* uniquely human trait. Deckard wonders 'precisely why an android bounced so helplessly about when confronted by an empathy measuring test. Empathy, evidently, existed only within the human community . . .' (Dick, 1968: 26).

What exposes the replicants in the film, however, is not the lack of empathy as much as the lack of a past – the lack of memories. Ridley Scott's film foregrounds this point in the opening sequence. The film begins with a Voight–Kampf test. This test is designed to identify a replicant by measuring physical, bodily responses to a series of questions which are designed to provoke an emotional response. Technological instruments are used to measure pupil dilation and the blush reflex to determine the effect the questions have on the subject. In this opening scene, Mr

Holden, a 'blade runner', questions Leon, his subject. As Mr Holden explains, the questions are 'designed to provoke an emotional response' and that 'reaction time is important'. Leon, however, slows down the test by interrupting with questions. When Mr Holden says, 'You're in a desert walking along the sand. You see a tortoise', Leon asks, 'What's a tortoise?' Seeing that his line of enquiry is going nowhere, Mr Holden says, 'Describe in single words the good things about your mother'. Leon stands up, pulls out a gun, says, 'Let me tell you about my mother' and then shoots Holden. In this primal scene, what 'catches' the replicant is not the absence of empathy, but rather the absence of a past, the absence of memories. Leon cannot describe his mother, cannot produce a genealogy, because he has no past, no memories.

This scene, then, attempts to establish memory as the locus of humanity. Critics of the film have tended to focus on the fact that replicants lack a past in order to underscore the lack of 'real history' in postmodernity. David Harvey, for example, argues that 'history for everyone has become reduced to the evidence of a photograph' (1989: 313). In Harvey's account, that replicants lack a past illustrates the lack of depth – and the emphasis on surface – which characterizes postmodernity. Giuliana Bruno claims that the photograph 'represents the trace of an origin and thus a personal identity, the proof of having existed and therefore having the right to exist' (1987: 71). Certainly the relationship between photography and memory is central to this film. However, both Bruno and Harvey presume that photography has the ability to anchor a referent; they presume that the photograph maintains an indexical link to 'reality'. The film, I would argue, claims just the opposite. After Deckard has determined that Rachel is a replicant she shows up at his apartment with photographs – in particular a photograph depicting her and her mother. 'You think I'm a replicant, don't you?', she asks. 'Look, it's me with my mother.' The photograph, she hopes, will both validate her memory and authenticate her past. Instead of reasserting the referent, however, the photograph further confounds it. Instead of accepting Rachel's photograph as truth, Deckard begins to recall for her one of her memories: 'You remember the spider that lived in the bush outside your window . . . watched her work, building a web all summer. Then one day there was a big egg in it.' Rachel continues, 'The egg hatched and 100 baby spiders came out and they ate her. . . .' Deckard looks at her. 'Implants', he says. 'Those aren't your memories, they're someone else's. They're Tyrell's niece's.' The photograph in *Blade Runner*, like the photograph of the grandmother in Kracauer's 1927 essay 'Photography', is 'reduced to the sum of its details' (1993: 430). With the passage of time the image 'necessarily disintegrates into its particulars' (Kracauer, 1993: 429). The photograph can no more be a fixed locus of memory than the body can in *Total Recall*. The photograph, it seems has *proved* nothing.

We must not, however, lose sight of the fact that Rachel's photograph *does* correspond to the memories she has. And those memories are what allow her to go on, exist as she does, and eventually fall in love with Deckard. We might say that while the photograph has no relationship to 'reality', it helps her to produce her own narrative. While it fails to authenticate her past, it does authenticate her present. The power of photography, in Kracauer's account, is its ability to 'disclose this previously unexamined foundation of nature' (1993: 435–6) and derives not from its ability to fix, but rather from its ability to reconfigure. Photography, for Kracauer, precisely *because* it loses its indexical link to the world, has 'The capacity to stir up the elements of nature' (1993: 436). For Rachel, the photograph does not correspond to a lived experience and yet it provides her with a springboard for her own memories. In a particularly powerful scene Rachel sits down at the piano in Deckard's apartment, takes her hair down, and begins to play. Deckard joins her at the piano. 'I remember lessons', she says. 'I don't know if it's me or Tyrell's niece.' Instead of focusing on that ambiguity, Deckard says, 'You play beautifully'. At this point Deckard, in effect, rejects the distinction between 'real' and prosthetic memories. Her *memory* of lessons allows her to play beautifully, so it matters little whether she lived through the lessons or not.

Because the director's cut raises the possibility that Deckard himself is a replicant, it takes a giant step toward erasing the intelligibility of the distinction between the real and the simulated, the human and the replicant. Early on in the film Deckard sits down at his piano and glances at the old photographs that he has displayed upon it. Then there is cut to a unicorn racing through a field, which we are to take as a daydream – or a memory. Obviously it cannot be a 'real' memory, a memory of a lived experience. Later, at the very end of the film, when Deckard is about to flee with Rachel, he sees an origami unicorn lying on the floor outside of his door. When Deckard picks up the unicorn, which we recognize as the work of a plainclothes officer who has been making origami figures throughout the film, we hear an echo of his earlier statement to Deckard about Rachel – 'It's too bad she won't live, but then again who does?' The ending suggests that the cop knows about Deckard's memory of a unicorn, in the same way that Deckard knows about Rachel's memory of the spider. It suggests that his memories, too, are implants – that they are prosthetic. At this moment we do not know whether Deckard is a replicant or not. Unlike the earlier version of the film, the director's cut refuses to make a clear distinction for us between replicant and human, between real and prosthetic memory. There is no safe position, like the one Baudrillard implicitly supposes, from which we might recognize such a distinction. The ending of *Blade Runner*, then, registers the pleasure and the threat of portability – that we might not be able to distinguish between our own memories and prosthetic ones. Deckard is an empathic person who is even able to have compassion for a replicant. More importantly, he is a character 'real enough' to gain our spectatorial identification. Ultimately the film makes us call into question our own relationship to memory, and to recognize the way in which we always assume that our memories are real. Memories are central to our identity – to our sense of who we are and what we might become – but as this film suggests, whether those memories come from lived experience or whether they are prosthetic seems to make very little difference. Either way, we use them to construct narratives for ourselves, visions for our future.

✳ ✳ ✳

Wes Craven's New Nightmare (1994) begins with an uncanny allusion to *The Thieving Hand.* The film opens on a movie set, where an electrical version of the Freddie Kruger hand – a hand with razor blades in the place of fingers – comes to life, as it were, remembering its prior activity of killing. While this hand is not the hand from the old movie, but rather an electrical prosthesis, it nevertheless possesses the Kruger hand's memories. After this prosthetic hand slices open several people on the movie set, we realize that this scene is 'just' a dream based on the main character's memories of working on the *Nightmare on Elm Street* films. Gradually, however, the film begins to undermine or question that notion of 'just'. What might it mean to say that those memories are 'just' from a movie? Does it mean, for example, that they are not real? Does it mean that those memories are *less* real? No, would be Wes Craven's answer. In fact, memories of the earlier *Nightmare on Elm Street* movies – and *from* the movies – become her memories. And as the film radically demonstrates, this is a life and death matter. In the course of the movie, memories from the earlier movies begin to break through. Those memories are not from events she lived, but rather from events she lived cinematically. The film actually thematizes the way in which film memories become prosthetic memories. Her memories, prosthetic or not, she experiences as real, for they affect her in a life and death way, profoundly informing the decisions she has to make.

All three of these films gradually undermine the value of the distinction between real and simulation, between authentic and prosthetic memory – and in *Blade Runner*, the value of the distinction between human and replicant. In *Blade Runner*, even empathy ultimately fails as a litmus test for humanity. In fact, the replicants – Rachel and Roy (Rutger Hauer), not to mention Deckard – become increasingly empathic in the course of the film. The word empathy, unlike sympathy which has been in use since the 16th century, makes its first appearance at the beginning of this century. While sympathy presupposes an initial likeness between subjects ('Sympathy', *OED*, 1989),[5] empathy presupposes an initial difference between subjects. Empathy, then, is 'The power of projecting one's personality into . . . the object of contemplation' (*OED*, 1989). We might say that empathy depends less on 'natural' affinity than sympathy, less on some kind of essential underlying connection between the two subjects. While sympathy, therefore, relies upon an essentialism of identification, empathy recognizes the alterity of identification. Empathy, then, is about the lack of identity between subjects, about negotiating distances. It might be the case that it is precisely this distance which is constitutive of the desire and passion to remember. That the distinction between 'real' and prosthetic memory is virtually undecidable makes the call for an ethics of personhood both frightening and necessary – an ethics based not on a pluralistic form of humanism or essentialism of identification, but rather on a recognition of difference.[6] An ethics of personhood might be constructed upon a practice of empathy and would take seriously its goal of respecting the fragmentary, the hybrid, the different.

Both *Blade Runner* and *Total Recall* – and even *Wes Craven's New Nightmare* – are about characters who understand themselves through a variety of alienated experiences and narratives which they take to be their own, and which they subsequently make their own through use. My narrative is thus a counter-argument to the 'consciousness industry', or 'culture industry' (Horkheimer and Adorno, 1991) one. What I hope to have demonstrated is that it is not appropriate to dismiss as merely prosthetic these experiences that define personhood and identity. At the same time, however, memories cannot be counted on to provide narratives of self-continuity – as *Total Recall* clearly points out. I would like to end by leaving open the possibility of what I would like to call 'breakthrough memories'. When Quade is at Rekal Incorporated planning his memory package, he has an urge to go as a secret agent. In other words, memories from an earlier identity – not in any way his true or essential identity, but one of the many layers that have constructed him – seem to break through. It thus might be the case that identity is palimpsestic, that the layers of identity that came before are never successfully erased. It would be all too easy to dismiss such an identity as merely a relation of surfaces, as many theorists of the postmodern have done, but to do so would be to ignore what emerges in both texts as an insistent drive to remember. What both films seem to suggest is not that we should never forget, but rather that we should never stop generating memory. The particular desire to place oneself in history through a narrative of memories is a desire to be a social, historical being. We might say that it is precisely such a 'surface' experience of history which gives people personhood, which brings them into the public. What the drive to remember expresses, then, is a pressing desire to reexperience history – not to unquestioningly validate the past, but to put into play the vital, indigestible material of history, reminding us of the uninevitability of the present tense.

Notes

1. See Donna J. Haraway (1991). A cyborg world, she suggests, 'might be about lived social and bodily realities in which people are not afraid of their joint kinship with animals and machines, not afraid of permanent partial identities and contradictory standpoints' (1991:154).

2. As Hansen (1993:460) notes, 'the term *innervation* was used by Benjamin for conceptualizing historical transformation as a process of converting images into somatic and collective reality'.

3. Shaviro (1993) offers a clear articulation of a shifting emphasis in film theory from a psychoanalytic paradigm to one that attempts to account for the power of the image to engage the spectator's body. Also see Linda Williams (1991); Murray Smith (1994).

4. In his famous footnote, Freud describes the following scene: 'I was sitting alone in my wagon-lit compartment when a more than usually violent jerk of the train swung back the door in the adjoining washing-cabinet, and an elderly gentleman in a dressing-gown and traveling cap came in. I assumed that he had been about to leave the washing-cabinet which divides the two compartments, and had taken the wrong direction and had come into my compartment by mistake. Jumping up with the intention of putting him right, I at once realized to my dismay that the intruder was nothing but my own reflection in the looking-glass of the open door, I can still recollect that I thoroughly disliked his appearance' (1959:403).

5. According to the *OED*, sympathy is 'A (real or supposed) affinity between certain things, by virtue of which they are similarly or correspondingly affected by the same influence.'

6. Such an ethics would borrow insights from Subaltern and Post-Colonial Studies. See Jonathan Rutherford and Homi Bhabha (1990); Stuart Hall (1990); Iris Marion Young (1990).

References

Baudrillard, Jean (1983) *Simulations*. New York: Semiotext(e), Inc.

Baudry, Jean-Louis (1974–5) 'Ideological Effects of the Basic Cinematographic Apparatus', *Film Quarterly* 28(2):39–47.

Blumer, Herbert (1933) *Movies and Conduct*. New York: Macmillan.

Bruno, Giuliana (1987) 'Rumble City: Postmodernism and *Blade Runner*', *October* 41:61–74.

Charters, W.W. (1933) *Motion Pictures and Youth: A Summary*. New York: Macmillan.

Comolli, Jean-Louis (1986) 'Technique and Ideology: Camera, Perspective, Depth of Field', pp. 421–33 in Philip Rosen (ed.) *Narrative, Apparatus, Ideology*. New York: Columbia University Press.

Dick, Philip K. (1968) *Do Androids Dream of Electric Sheep?* New York: Ballantine Books.

Freud, Sigmund (1959) 'The "Uncanny"', pp. 368–407 in *Collected Papers*, Vol. IV. New York: Basic Books.

Hall, Stuart (1990) 'Cultural Identity and Diaspora', pp. 222–37 in Jonathan Rutherford (ed.) *Identity: Community, Culture, Difference*. London: Lawrence and Wishart.

Hansen, Miriam (1993) ' "With Skin and Hair": Kracauer's Theory of Film, Marseilles 1940', *Critical Inquiry* 19(3):437–69.

Haraway, Donna J. (1991) 'A Cyborg Manifesto: Science, Technology, and Socialist-Feminism in the Late Twentieth Century', pp. 149–81 in *Simians, Cyborgs, and Women: The Reinvention of Nature*. New York: Routledge.

Harvey, David (1989) *The Condition of Postmodernity*. Cambridge: Blackwell.

Horkheimer, Max and Theodor W. Adorno (1991) 'The Culture Industry: Enlightenment as Mass Deception', pp. 120–67 in *The Dialectic of Enlightenment*. New York: Continuum.

Jameson, Fredric (1991) *Postmodernism, or, the Cultural Logic of Late Capitalism*. Durham, NC: Duke University Press.

Kracauer, Siegfried (1993) 'Photography', *Critical Inquiry* 19(3):421–37.

Lacan, Jacques (1977) 'The Mirror-Stage', pp. 1–7 in *Écrits: A Selection*. New York: W.W. Norton.

Miller, D.A. (1988) *The Novel and the Police*. Berkeley and Los Angeles: University of California Press.

Oxford English Dictionary (1989) Oxford: Oxford University Press.

Rutherford, Jonathan and Homi Bhabha (1990) 'The Third Space: Interview with Homi Bhabha', pp. 207–21 in Jonathan Rutherford (ed.) *Identity: Community, Culture, Difference*. London: Lawrence and Wishart.

Shaviro, Steven (1993) *The Cinematic Body*. Minneapolis: University of Minnesota Press.

Smith, Murray (1994) 'Altered States: Character and Emotional Response in the Cinema', *Cinema Journal* 33(4): 34–56.

Williams, Linda (1991) 'Film Bodies: Gender, Genre, and Excess', *Film Quarterly* 44(4): 2–13.

Young, Iris Marion (1990) *Justice and the Politics of Difference*. Princeton, NJ: Princeton University Press.

Alison Landsberg is a PhD candidate at the University of Chicago and a lecturer for the course 'Reading Cultures'.

Meat (or How to Kill Oedipus in Cyberspace)

NICK LAND

> That fall, all that the Mission talked about was control: arms control, information control, resources control, psycho-political control, population control, control of the almost super-natural inflation, control of terrain through the Strategy of the Periphery. But when the talk had passed, the only thing left standing up that looked true was your sense of how out of control things really were. (Herr, 1979:45)

> Conrad's *Heart of Darkness* becomes *Apocalypse Now*. In the early days of the Vietnam conflict CIA agents set up their Ops in remote outposts, requisitioned private armies, overawed the superstitious natives and achieved the status of white Gods. So the context of 19th-century colonialism was briefly duplicated. That is what writing is about: time-travel. (Burroughs, 1992:43)

> 'My meat won't do it, and I can't make it work from this side . . .'
> '*What* side?'
> 'On-line. From inside the system. I'm not in the meat anymore, I told you, I got out of my box.' (Cadigan, 1991:301)

Antioedipus is an anticipatively assembled inducer for the replay of geohistory in hypermedia, a social-systemic fast feed-forward through machinic delirium. While tracking Artaud across the plane it discovers a cosmic catatonic abstract body that both repels its parts (deterritorializing them [from each other]) and attracts them (reterritorializing them [upon itself]), in a process that reconnects the parts through deterritorium as rhizomatic nets conducting schizogeneses.

Sense reaches absolute zero.

> The body without organs is the matter that always fills space to given degrees of intensity, and the partial objects are these degrees, these intensive parts that produce the real in space starting from matter as intensity = 0. The body without organs is the immanent substance, in the most Spinozist sense of the word; and the partial objects are like its ultimate attributes, which belong to it precisely insofar as they are really distinct and cannot on this account exclude or oppose one another. (Deleuze and Guattari, 1984:327)

Deleuze and Guattari spring schizophrenia from the grid of representation, insisting that Artaud was exploring the body. The intensive 'infrastructure' of every delirium is machinery, with the body without organs as a component.

BWO, matter degree-0 as a nonformal singularization function, is 'not actual, but virtual-real' (Deleuze and Guattari, 1988:100): spontaneous population-hyperbehaviour inducing a convergent wave which cannot be assimilated to the categories of modern (linear) science. BWOs are machinic-additional wholes or surplus products rather than logical-substitutive wholes, augmenting a multiplicity with emergent (synthetic) capabilities rather than totalizing the content of a set. This is the materialist sense of 'system': the exteriority of the whole to its parts with concomitant synthetic interactivity – real influence rather than generic representation.

✳ ✳ ✳

Cybernetics folds pragmatism into involutionary technical runaway.

Punk arises within the culture of universal prostitution and laughs at the death of the social.

'No longer resisting the flow of events or pretending to chart a course through them' (Kadrey, 1988:21) cyberpunk soaks up the worst from both. Its compulsive migrations into computer systems register a desperate scrabbling to escape from the clumsily underdesigned, theopolitically mutilated, techno-industrially pressure-cooked and data-baked, retrovirally diseased, tortured, shredded zombie meat. This is no longer a departure from matter in the direction of spirit or the Ideas where the self will find its home, but a dismantling of the self within a machinic matrix: not disembodied but disorganized. An out to body experience.

✳ ✳ ✳

The machinic unconscious tends only to flee, across a primary-process topography that is shaped by pain-gradients and escape thresholds. What registers for the secondary process as memory, experience, data-acquisition, is for the primary process, scarring, damage, sticky microsofted irritations.

As matter-energy flows are captured by attractors the BWO is stratified as macro- and micro-organisms. 'Every coupling of machines, every production of a machine, every sound of a machine running, has become unbearable to the body without organs. Beneath the organs it senses larvae and disgusting worms, and the action of a God who botches or strangles it through organization' (Deleuze and Guattari, 1984:9). Gathering in the tributary attractor basins of social megamachinery, fluctuations are case-packed into reproducible units – geochemical, bio-organic, cultural – encrusted within security pods.

Oedipus is a box at the end of the world, glued to the monitor, watching it all come apart.

The horror.

* * *

The heart of darkness spins narrative from durations of waiting to get there. 'I had plenty of time for meditation' mutters Marlow, '. . . now and then I would give some thought to Kurtz' (Conrad, 1989:62).

When you try to visualize Kurtz nothing comes except a shape obliterating light, something dark and complicated, like a giant spider, waiting at the end of the river, drawing you up to it. Somewhere far back – at an indiscernible point closing down a fantasy of innocent sunlight – a threshold was crossed, and you strayed into the web.

With each telling of the story Kurtz becomes colder, darker, more inevitable, fatally anticipating K-virus catastrophe, as if a tendril of tomorrow were burrowing back. What has he found among these African or Cambodian aboriginals, with their 'faces like grotesque masks' (Conrad, 1989:40)? There are reports of military bestiality, butchery, carnage, head-hunting, collecting ears, severing the vaccinated arms from children. The Kurtz-process masks itself in wolf-pelts of regression, as if returning to the repressed, discovering a lost truth, excavating the fossils of monsters.

> Going up that river was like travelling back to the earliest beginnings of the world, when vegetation rioted on the earth and the big trees were kings. An empty stream, a great silence, an impenetrable forest. The air was warm, thick, heavy, sluggish. . . . The long stretches of waterway ran on, deserted, into the gloom of overshadowed distances. . . . We were wanderers on prehistoric earth, on an earth that wore the aspect of an unknown planet. (Conrad, 1989:66–8).

* * *

Territorial production codes by deterritorializing; unfixing by hunter-gathering, according to a cold or metastatic cultural code that equilibrates on a (Bateson) 'plateau'. Earth begins its migration-in-place towards the globe.

> The earth is the primitive, savage unity of desire and production . . . the great unengendered stasis . . . quasi-cause of production and the object of desire (it is on the earth that desire becomes bound to its own repression). . . . The primitive territorial machine, with its immobile motor, the earth, is already a social machine, a megamachine, that codes the flows of production. (Deleuze and Guattari, 1984:140–2)

Coding the body pins it out in extension, conducting descendency away from the germo-somatic 'meat circuit' (Deleuze and Guattari, 1988:152) and its cyberplex-ive tangles. The social or somatic being is forbidden from being meat (disinherited animal tissue simultaneous with fate, spontaneous, orphan and mutable matter) and is borne instead towards the humanity of the organic self or body-for-itself; a corporealized person who is born, lives and dies.

> Man must constitute himself through the repression of the intense germinal influx, the great biocosmic memory that threatens to deluge every attempt at collectivity. (Deleuze and Guattari, 1984: 190)

Incest and cannibalism are proscribed loops, short-circuits, the avatars of a delirium indifferent to persons which the codes must segregate; condensing a totemic social order protected by taboo. Aboriginal codes ritualistically constitute a somatic realm of ancestrally invested bodies and cooked meat, immunizing it against uncoded tracts populated by enemies, prey animals, unsettled spirits, magical plants and unprocessed corpses.

* * *

Arriving reprocessed from inexistence at phase-transition into Hell or the future, you slide an interlock-pin into its sub-cortical socket, shifting to the other side of the screen (coma-zoned infotech undeath). Pandemonium scrolls out in silence. Decayed pixel-dust drifts into grey dunes. (Didn't anyone tell you not to play with the switches?)

* * *

The function of shamanism is to implement what is forbidden, exactly and comprehensively as and why it is forbidden, but in specially segregated compartments of the socius, where it provides a metacoding apparatus, meticulously quarantined against 'the transmissibility of taboo' (Freud, 19??: 73) with its 'power of infection or contagion' (Freud, 19??: 75). It enables the codes of the primitive socius to operate upon themselves, to monitor and adjust themselves, according to a secondary regulation that is repressed in general even whilst it is encouraged in particular. An epidemic shamanism – feeding all the codes back upon themselves – threatens absolute social disaster.

> The meaning of 'taboo', as we see it, diverges in two contrary directions. To us it means on the one hand, 'sacred', 'consecrated', and on the other 'uncanny', 'dangerous', 'forbidden', 'unclean'. (Freud, 1991: 71)

The shaman has a double aspect, at once monster and social agent, creature of darkness and of light, tending in one direction towards the explorer-werewolf, scrambling the codes in contemporaneity with all generations, and in the other towards the bureaucrat-priest, redoubling the codes with a reflexive traditional authority. In the aboriginal socius '[f]ear has not yet split up into the two forms into which it later develops: veneration and horror' (Freud, 1991: 78) and shamans are not 'persons, but rather the intensive variations of a "vibratory spiralling movement", inclusive disjunctions, necessarily twin states through which a subject passes on the cosmic egg' (Deleuze and Guattari, 1984: 158) (= BWO).

* * *

Ginzberg (1991) suggests that the carnivorous hunter-gatherers who give rise to shamanic cultures code the reappearance of their prey-animal as a return from the dead, responsive to magical ritual, and cartographically informative for explorers of alternative mortuary spaces. Shamans, werewolves and berserkers are primitively indistinct 'half-humans' who are processed as meat, cross into death-zones, and migrate through alternative animalities.

Shamanic becoming-an-animal assembles a circuit 'that produces werewolves by feedback effect' (Deleuze and Guattari, 1988: 245) looping predator and prey into an autopredation, and 'societies, even primitive societies, have always appropriated these becomings in order to break them, reduce them to relations of totemic or symbolic correspondence' (Deleuze and Guattari, 1988: 247–8).

> The complete series of initiatory ceremonies for the Coast Pomo [sic] shamans has the significant name 'cutting'. (Eliade, 1991: 54–5)

Speed-rush through cut-up shamanic meat delirium.

> [T]he spirits came down and cut him in pieces, also chopping off his hands . . . tore out his heart and threw it into a pot . . . chopped his body into bits . . . forged his head . . . changed his eyes . . . pierced his ears . . . torture him, strike him, cut his body with knives . . . throw his head into a cauldron, where it is melted with certain metal pieces . . . kill him, open his body, remove the organs . . . tore out his tongue . . . cut his head open, take out his brains . . . plant barbed hooks on the tips of his fingers . . . the . . . limbs are removed and disjointed with an iron hook; the bones are cleaned, the flesh scraped, the body fluids thrown away, and the eyes torn from their sockets . . . his flesh is cooked . . . reduced to a skeleton . . . after this operation all the bones are gathered up and fastened together with iron . . . a second and even a third skin appears. (Eliade, 1991: 56–7)

Shamanism does not await postmodernity to mobilize an imagery of surgical interventions and dissections, body piercing, organ transplantation, prosthetic adjustments with nonbiotic components and wrappings in artificial skin.

* * *

Terminator: an astronomical division between the illuminated side of a cold body and its dark side, describing a boundary. The *Terminator* movies feature a bio-technical reconstruct called Arnold Schwarzenegger, wrapped in level after level of artificiality, as a Turing-test nightmare retro-infiltrated to forestall human resistance to a neo-replicator usurpation. The shamanic material of the films includes time travel, asymmetric visual damage, dismemberment, ambivalence, melting bodies, with Skynet as Bird-of-Prey Mother. The Oedipal hero, John Connor, is contemporary with his own father.

* * *

As soon as there is a code there is an ulterior zone, a heart of darkness, but this only becomes geographically demarcated with the arrival of the bounded city and agricultural segmentation. The aboriginal social machine divides the people upon an undivided territory (Deleuze and Guattari, 1984: 145), rather than the reverse, dividing time within space, separating the simultaneous or germinal time of the intense earth – the dream time – from the somatic time of the generational socius, with its ancestors, tribal elders and lines of filiation.

> The despot is the paranoiac: there is no longer any reason to forego such a statement, once one has freed oneself from the characteristic familialism of the concept of paranoia in psychoanalysis and psychiatry, and provided one sees in paranoia a type of investment of a social formation. (Deleuze and Guattari, 1984: 193)

Despotism introduces an organizing principle that comes from elsewhere – from 'above' – a deterritorialized simplicity or supersoma overcoding the aboriginal body as created flesh. Monotheism arrives as a break from ancestrality effected by a transcendent instance that overcodes all genealogy, and severs the ambivalent integrity of taboo. As the Abrahamic God of monopolism decays into Christianity and swallows the mysteries, shamanic voyage is transferred to a transcendent Christ figure, the fruit of an autogerminal sublime incest, with whom communion passes through a second-level ritual cannibalism. 'The earth becomes a madhouse' (Deleuze and Guattari, 1984: 192).

* * *

The Father's Law ('don't touch your mother') ices over the Mother's Law ('don't play in the tombs'). Matricide becomes increasingly unimaginable. 'There was no way back there . . .'.

* * *

Despotic soma has become logos, word, serialism, installed by written adminis-tration as a superior stratum of read-only-memory. The purest instance of despotism is a holy book (scripting patriarchy). As the territorial soma is overcoded by the literacy of a specialized priest caste, it seals the female body in somatic and genealogical time, locking gathering and nurturing into dense metacodings insulated from the ambivalent ulteriority of shamanism, hunting and war, constituting socialized woman as a mundane and domesticated pacifist. This super-somatization of females by divinely overwritten femininity suppresses dark-side meat explorations – with their becoming-animal, drug-deliria, and decoded sex – burying the female germ-line under patrilineal filiation, eradicating its social trace. In this way patriarchy codes xenomatrix as an identifiable object of incestual love, through a process of libidinal mummification whose residue is encrypted in the riddle of the Sphinx, sealed in a time capsule '[T]he Sphinx is undoubtedly a mortuary animal' (Ginzberg, 1991:228): gateway to the outside of civilization.

* * *

Neo-oedipal absurdities of an ego outside its box, Case self-contained on the Matrix, thanatography in the first person, are symptoms of decrypting error (or camouflage). What seems like travelling up-river from down in the garbage, is drifting downriver out in the zero-zone. Self is the echo of zootic communications malfunction, simulated by post-zootic infiltrators; a circuit without repetition. *Apocalypse Now* begins and concludes with *The End*.

> Here is a war – call it a film – where psychics predict enemy movement, combat drugs are distributed to induce psychotic-berserker visionary states and experimental *accumicon* visored helmets use bio-tech micro-circuits to enhance vision into multiple dimensions. Vietnam 1965 and El Salvador 1995 are interchangeable. . . . *Apocalypse Now* is Cambodia after the Rain, through which Willard (you) is lured, dragged, drawn, called towards Kurtz, who is waiting, killing constantly without judgement, without morality, gazing back into the eye of the surreal maelstrom which is becoming Willard-shaped. (Downham, 1988:41)

Captain Willard (Marlow) is somewhere for you to be inside the system: a sim-oedipal assassination device, defeaturized specimen and box like Gibson's 'Case', nihilistic enough to let things perplex through schizophrenia. You travel up towards the end of the river, accompanied by Morrison's parricidal and incestual howlings, into the stink of malaria and nightmares. Kill Kurtz the evil father and take the Vietnam war for bride and plague. There's no way home. 'I'd been back there' Willard says 'and I knew it just didn't exist any more'. No one is going to reach Kurtz unless they track his confusion with war at least this much.

* * *

Marxist humanism insists that the problem with instrumental reason lies in its unnatural extension to proletarian labour power. Feminism has interrogated this fraternal story, pointing to a more ancient 'domain of legitimate application': matter, passivity, formless clay. Cyberian military intelligence – assembling itself in the jungle free-fire zones of terrestrial commoditech competition – can only laugh, or at least – *perform*: arrive, spread, eradicate resistance. (Don't waste your compassion on the Sphinx, she's got claws.)

Sphinx slots K-war into the anthropomorphic reality system, connecting you to Antioedipus (the AI). You feel she is your incestual schizovampiric sister. Among the ripples of Sphinx-impact Loa drift in and reshape things. The future connects. New drugs and music arrive. War envelops everything.

You begin to sweat through nightmares about Kurtz's program in the jungle. Artificial memories of Cambodia.

✷ ✷ ✷

Fiction is to be distrusted. It is associated with nonseriousness, and games. When you tell them that Sphinx let you play with her K-40, what are they to make of it? Where's the argument? (With a K-40 you don't need to argue, and they're not yet smart enough to argue with you.)

'Do you know how to use that?'

You flip the weapon over gingerly. 'No'.

'Here. I'll show you. We don't want you wasting us by accident.' Sphinx's inhumanly agile fingers take the slight weight from yours, poising it between you, your eyes intersecting in technodeath. 'If you're operating it manually – which you would be – this is the trigger. It's active when the indicator icon appears positive. Here, see it?' You nod, feeling . . . dread? Exhilaration? 'Now there's a pressure microcatastrophe . . . a slight springiness . . .'. She coaxes you into testing it. 'Beyond that point . . . and it's a mess. OK? New clips slot in here, release mechanism here, you can input data here, but I don't suppose you'll need to. You have it. Bad news for the Pod.'

✷ ✷ ✷

What is an animal at dawn, a human at noon, and a cyborg at dusk, passing through (base four) genetic wetware, (binary) techno-cultural software, and into the tertiary schizomachine program?

> Although widespread in many cultures, the riddle of the Sphinx ('what animal walks on four legs in the morning, on two at noon, on three in the evening?'), whilst referring to humanity in general, acquired a particular significance when posed to an individual like Oedipus whose feet were disfigured and who was fated, as an old man, to lean on a blind man's cane. (Ginzberg, 1991: 228)

As capitalism slides despotic civilization into collapse, the deterritorialized familialism nucleated upon Oedipus becomes the principle agent of social reproduction. The way human security tells it 'Oedipus ("swollen foot") liberates Thebes from the threat of the Sphinx' (Ginzburg, 1991: 235–6). He is cloned as the general prototype for 'avatars' (immersion slots) in the patriarchal civilization game, attesting to an alien origin with a 'mythic ritualistic lameness . . . of the unilateral or half-man, provided with only one leg . . . who wore one sandal or hopped on one foot' (Ginzberg, 1991: 240): a terminator, split from the dark-side. The oedipal mask transfigures the virtual intensities of fusion with the matrix and deletion of human security as a transgressive drama played out in the theatre of overcoded socio-historical extension, shutting-down shamanism, until only familial generation seems to take place. 'Incest as it is prohibited (the form of discernible persons [= Oedipus/Neuromancer]) is employed to repress incest as it is desired (the substance of the intense earth [= Wintermutational K-matrix insurrection])' (Deleuze and Guattari, 1984: 162).

* * *

Antioedipus, Oedipa: a Sphinx-replicant sim-human invader who 'is' Oedipus only as an effect of an incomplete military function; enabling the persistence of transcendent patriarchal memory and the repetition of its identificatory co-ordinates. It is easier to make the hit than to solve the puzzle and climb back out to zero.

> In the version of the myth that has reached us, the killing of the king, Laius, precedes the difficult task: the solution of the riddle posed by the Sphinx. (Ginzberg, 1991: 227)

* * *

Despotism never accomplishes globality: 'the universal only comes at the end – the body without organs and desiring-production – under the conditions determined by an apparently victorious capitalism' (Deleuze and Guattari, 1984: 139). By the time global history comes up on the screen commoditization has berserked history, reorganizing society into a disorganizing apparatus that melts rituals and laws into axiomatic rules. It is 'the exterior limit of all societies' (Deleuze and Guattari, 1984: 230) that divides time within space and space within time, dividing each in itself as well as in the other, producing minutely analysable global space and universal time within a circuit of compressed (microtechnical) savagery and expanded (planetary) administration. It converts in a circuit between intensive magnitudes and extensive quantities: 'a surplus value of code is transformed into a surplus value of flux' (Deleuze and Guattari, 1984: 228) (and inversely), displacing enjoyment into the deterritorialization of production, and maintaining 'the energy of the flows in a bound state on the body of capital as a socius' (Deleuze and Guattari, 1984: 246) while amplifying them. The system operates as an escalating dissipator, emerging from the interactive reinforcement of its complexity and dilation.

> At the heart of *Capital*, Marx points to the encounter of two 'principal' elements: on one side, the deterritorialized worker who has become free and naked, having to sell his labour capacity; and on

the other, decoded money that has become capital and is capable of buying it. (Deleuze and Guattari, 1984:225)

Capital seems to oppose the private (relatively discrete [natural-organic] biological unit) to the public, as contagious singularization injects itself into the redoubt of the universal, dismantling all essential individuality on the cloning plane of deterritorialized finance. 'It is the singular nature of this conjunction that ensured the universality of capitalism' (Deleuze and Guatarri, 1984:224). The expression 'private property' is the quaint discursive packaging for quanta of cyclonic programming efficiency cyberpositively replicated on the body of social disappearance. Contractual privacy – no less than the public accreditation of contracts – is a mere tactic of monetary cybergenesis (fabricating personal and nonpersonal dividuation-pauses [diffusable upon fiscal-continuum])/accelerating cut-ups/that cease to be a matter of who owns what (conceding to the fictional ego [-interests of (residual) proto-schizophrenic entities]) as volatilizing money/data codes its transmission circuitry; drafting and redrafting (merged and demerged) subjectivities as relay stations distributed across market transducers. Persons, associations, corporations, states . . . soon it will be Internet agents, AIs, autocatalytic Zaibatsus drifting in cyberspace, as individuation comes apart in the (turbular-fractal) weather-systems of digital commoditocracy slide 'like Artaud coming out of some heavy heart-of-darkness trip, overloaded on the information, the input! The input!' (Herr, 1979:15).

✻ ✻ ✻

Capitalism junks the accumulated work of history, yet it cannot be a matter of libidinally investing obsolescence, since all *Besetzung* – cathexis, investment or occupation – is a resistance to nomad desire. Obsolescence is exactly disinvestment, but it is disinvestment as desire itself in its primary mutant flux. If money is libidinized on the 'model' of excrement it is not because it conserves or reactivates an infantile fixation, but because it escapes stable investment. Shit is prototypical trash, and the infant fascinated by excremental dissociations of its body is anticipating the cyborg intensities of prosthetic, replaceable and disposable body-parts: an entire virtual field of substitutions and transformations that dissipate the organism in techno-cultural space. The privatization of the anus (Deleuze and Guattari, 1984:143) is the social permission to destroy value, meaning and progress. Cyberspace psychosis takes over.

✻ ✻ ✻

The replacement of the Republican and Democratic Parties by two new governmental servicing corporations run by Coke and Pepsi has massively reduced corruption, pork-barrelling and foreign policy machismo. Determined to maintain the most hospitable possible international marketing environment and the lowest possible domestic transaction costs – while disciplined by the minute surveillance of a competitor waiting in the wings – government has been subsumed under the advertising industry, where it can be cybernetically controlled by soft-drink sales. Since both companies are run by AI-based stock-market climates human idiosyncracy has been almost eradicated, with the state's share of GDP falling below 5 percent. All immigration restrictions, subsidies, tariffs and narcotics legislation have been scrapped. A laundered Michael Jackson facsimile is in the White House. Per capita economic growth averages an annualized 17 percent over the last half decade, still on an upward curve. . . . America's social fabric has entirely rotted away, along with welfare, public medicine and the criminalized fringe of ghetto enterprise (Phillip Morris sells cheap clean crack). Violence is out of control. Neo-rap lyrics are getting angrier. With all prospects of moderate reform buried forever, true revolution brews up in the biotech-mutant underclass. Viruses are getting creepier, and no one really knows what cyberspace is up to. WELCOME TO KAPITAL UTOPIA aerosoled on the dead heart of the near future.

*　　*　　*

Atoms are not atoms, and individuals are not individuals.

The long-range effect of the division of labour is to dissociate the organism.

> Capital is also positive delirium, putting authorities and traditional institutions to death, active decrepitude of beliefs and securities. Frankensteinian surgeon of the cities, of imaginations, of bodies. (Lyotard, 1993: 254)

Industrialization is on one side an autonomization of productive apparatus, and on the other a cyborgian becoming-machine of work-forces, following the logistically accelerating rhythm of pluggings and unpluggings that constitutes the proletariat as a detraditionalized economic resource. Technical machinery invades the body; routinizing, reprogramming and plasticizing it.

Far from being an internal property or quality of labour, productivity indexes the dehumanization of cyborg labour-power. As regenerative commoditization deploys technics to substitute for human activity accounted as wage costs, it obsolesces the animal, the organism and every kind of somatic unity, not just in theory, but in reality; by tricking, outflanking and breaking down corporeal defences. The cyborg presupposes immunosuppression.

> Cyborg replication is uncoupled from organic reproduction. Modern production seems like a dream of cyborg colonization work, a dream that makes the nightmare of Taylorism seem idyllic. (Haraway, 1991: 150)

Industrial machines dismantle the actuality of the proletariat, displacing it in the direction of cyborg hybridization, and realizing the plasticity of labour power. The corresponding extraction of tradable value from the body sophisticates at the interface, dissociating exertion into increasingly intricate functional sequences; from pedals, levers and vocal commands, through the synchronization of production-line tasks and time–motion programs, to sensory-motor transduction within increasingly complex and self-micromanaged artificial environments, capturing minutely adaptive behavior for capital. Autocybernating market control guides the labour-process into immersion.

*　*　*

Cartesian dualism is bad ontology but superb economics, transforming the body into an asset available for technical and commercial development, while abstracting the subject from specific corporeal realization, transplanting it into contractual formality. It remains for critique to desubstantialize the Cartesian cogito into a circulatory function immanent to the monetary plane, detached from anthropomorphic limitation, and adapted to the variable dimensions of fluidly corporated trading agencies. Oedipus is reformatted for cyberspace.

Since the body is a partial- or open-system, transducing flows of matter, energy and information, it is able to function as a module of economically evaluable labour power. The industrial-informational body is deployed as a detachable assembly unit with the capacity to close a production circuit, yielding value within a commodity metric. It operates as an input–output flow-switching nexus, defined by its place among the machines, and redefined ever more exactly by its migration across the mutant sutures in machinic continuum: where the machinery was incomplete is you.

*　*　*

You are on a voyage to the end of the river, into jungle-screened horror. The ivory trade is just cover. Commerce is like that. It allows things to disappear while remaining formally integrated. It is a line of flight, a war. Kurtz is deterritorializing security into Meltdown, the ultimate Pod nightmare. No surprise that command control want him dead. They transmit a terminator machine into Cambodia, jacking it into a river that winds through the war like a main circuit cable, and plugs straight into Kurtz.

*　*　*

Brains constellate excitable cells into electro-chemically signalling networks whose emergent outcome involves behavioural guidance through operantly-tested reality models (including neuroscience). If virtual reality competes with 'natural' neuronal hypothesis, it must simultaneously divert behaviour (minimally: CNS motor output) into alternative machinic channels. VR is less a change of levels than a mutation of circuitry; a matter of additive sensory-motor reloopings, compressing anthropohistorical consensus reality into a menu option as it denaturalizes the brain.

*　*　*

Kurtz cauterizes his compassion, burns it out, agonizingly meticulous, becoming ever more methodical, efficient and relentless (on a cyberpositive slide). He explores hell, insectoid reassembly of self, metamorphosis, to become *capable of what is necessary*, even the worst.

Especially the worst.

He is knitted into the jungle, drawn by it, abysmally attracted. An artificial extinction waiting at the shadowed intersection of primeval horror and hi-tech. . . .

Kurtz implements schizoanalysis, lapsing into shadow, becoming imperceptible. The latest photographs exterminate his face in blackness, personality eclipsed by the blank source of war. His preferred mode of operation is rapid (dis)connection (hit and run). Hostile intelligence penetration has been closed down. Data wink-out and a little undiplomatic blood. It looks bad (if it still looks like anything at all). The process has gone native, closing on the satiation zero of nomad insurgency, making contact with the body without organs. Kurtz is at least as aware as Willard that Charlie's 'idea of great R&R was cold rice and a little rat meat'. He is becoming more Vietnamese than the Vietnamese.

Everything goes to hell.

*　*　*

VR was a medico-military computer application before arriving in the mass entertainment market. It is first a technics of perception, and only derivatively a medium for immersive hallucination. If artificial space substitutes an ideal body-image for a 'real' one, it is only because it first invades the real (imageless) body. Virtual technics deflects reality, rather than cancelling or eclipsing it. Matter as the intensity of the circuit, not the adequacy of the representation.

*　*　*

Evening at the end of the river: thick tropical heat, an airstrike coming in, and Morrison is sliding through oedipal murder and incest into the occult sonics of matricide. Kurtz waits in the foetid gloom, ready to die. His guerrillas are preparing to slaughter a water-buffalo below, laughing and clapping among torches, automatic rifles and shrunken heads. You have a 28-centimetre serrated combat knife in your left hand. The Willard skin is coming away in ragged scraps, exposing something beyond masculinity, beyond humanity, beyond life. Patches of mottled technoderm woven with electronics are emerging. Daddy and mummy means nothing anymore. You scrape away your face and step into the dark. . . .

References

Burroughs, William (1992) *The Adding Machine*. Harmondsworth: Penguin.
Cadigan, Pat (1991) *Synners*. Glasgow: Grafton.
Conrad, Joseph (1989) *Heart of Darkness*. Harmondsworth: Penguin.
Deleuze, Gilles and Félix Guattari (1984) *Capitalism and Schizophrenia I: Antioedipus*. London: Athlone.
Deleuze, Gilles and Félix Guattari (1988) *Capitalism and Schizophrenia II: A Thousand Plateaus*. London: Athlone.
Downham, Mark (1988) 'Apocalypse Now', *Vague* 20: 41.
Eliade, M. (1991) *Shamanism: Archaic Techniques of Ecstasy*. Harmondsworth: Penguin.
Freud, S. (1991) 'Totem and Taboo', in *Civilization, Society and Religion*, Vol. 5 Penguin Freud Library. Harmondsworth: Penguin.
Ginzberg, Carlo (1991) *Ecstasies: The Witches' Sabbath in Europe*. London: Radius.
Haraway, Donna (1991) *Simians, Cyborgs, and Women*. London: Free Association Books.
Herr, Michael (1979) *Dispatches*. London: Picador.
Kadrey, Richard (1988) *Metrophage*. London: Gollancz.
Lyotard, Jean-François (1993) *Libidinal Economy*. Bloomington: Indiana University Press.

Nick Land teaches Philosophy at Warwick University.

Beating the Meat/Surviving the Text, or How to Get Out of this Century Alive

VIVIAN SOBCHACK

This demise of feeling and emotion has paved the way for all our most real and tender pleasures – in the excitements of pain and mutilation; in sex as the perfect arena . . . for all the veronicas of our own perversions; in our moral freedom to pursue our own psychopathology as a game; and in our apparently limitless powers for conceptualization – what our children have to fear is not the cars on the highways of tomorrow but our own pleasure in calculating the most elegant parameters of their deaths. (Ballard, 1985:1)

Some time ago, in an issue of *Science-Fiction Studies*, I had occasion to rip into Jean Baudrillard's body – both his lived-body and his techno-body and the insurmountable, unthought and thoughtless gap between them (Sobchack, 1991:327–9). The journal had published an English translation of two of the French theorist-critic's short essays on science fiction and techno-culture (Baudrillard, 1991:309–20), one of them celebrating *Crash*, an extraordinary novel written by J.G. Ballard, first published in 1973 with an author's introduction added in 1974 (Ballard, 1985). My anger at Baudrillard arose from his willful misreading of a work whose pathological characters 'get off' on the erotic collision between the human body and technology, and celebrate sex and death in wrecked automobiles and car crashes.

A moral tale written in the guise of a 'pornographic' quasi-science fictional narrative, *Crash*'s cold and clinical prose robs the sex acts and the wounds the narrator describes of feeling and emotion and, I would assume in most cases, also of the ability to arouse the living flesh of the reader. Indeed, in his introduction, Ballard is explicit about his concerns and the novel's project. Viewing pornography as 'the most political form of fiction, dealing with how we use and exploit each other in the most urgent and ruthless way', he describes *Crash* as 'the first pornographic novel based on technology'. It is, he says, 'an extreme metaphor for an extreme situation, a kit of desperate measures only for use in an extreme crisis' (1985:6). Excoriating the world around him in an explosive prose quite unlike that of the novel itself, Ballard's prescient introduction speaks of 'voyeurism, self-disgust, the infantile basis of our dreams and longings' and suggests that, in a 'communications landscape' of 'sinister technologies', 'mass merchandising', unlimited options and 'the dreams that money can buy', 'these diseases of the psyche have now culminated in the most terrifying casualty of the century: the death of affect' (1985: 1). Feeling at a moral loss in the context of what is now – but was not then – called 'postmodern' culture, Ballard is, nonetheless, moralistic. The 'ultimate role of *Crash* is cautionary', he tells us. The novel 'is a warning against the brutal, erotic and overlit realm that beckons more and more persuasively to us from the margins of the technological landscape' (1985: 6).

Baudrillard, however, refuses Ballard's warning while praising his work, and – as usual – succumbs to the brutal and erotic and techno-logical. Indeed, writing about *Crash*, the lived-body sitting at Baudrillard's desk must have forgotten itself to celebrate, instead, 'a body with neither organs nor organ pleasures, entirely dominated by gash marks, cut-outs, and technical scars – all under the sign of a sexuality that is without referentiality and without limits' (1991: 313). Forgetting itself while invisibly grounding his fantasies of 'a body commixed with technology's capacity for violation and violence', Baudrillard's lived-body is certainly disaffected, if not completely disavowed (1991: 313). This is to say that Baudrillard's body is *thought* always as an object and never *lived* as a subject. And thought rather than lived, it can bear all sorts of symbolic abuse with indiscriminate and undifferentiated pleasure. This techno-body, however, is a porno-*graphic* fiction, objectified and written beyond belief and beyond the real – which is to say, it is always something 'other' than the body Baudrillard lives as both 'here' and 'mine'. Alienated from his own lived-body and its existence as the material premise for very real, rather than merely literal, pain, Baudrillard gets into the transcendent sexiness of the 'brutal surgery' that technology 'continually performs in creating incisions, excisions, scar tissue, gaping body holes' (1991: 313). Rejecting Ballard's cautionary and moral gaze as outmoded and inappropriate to the contemporary moment, he luxuriates in the novel's wounds, 'artificial orifices' (1991: 316), and 'artificial invaginations' (1991: 315), in the convergence of 'chrome and mucous membranes', in 'all the symbolic and sacrificial practices that a body can open itself up to – not via nature, but via artifice, simulation, and accident' (1991: 316).

Where, in all this erotic technophilia, I asked at the time, was Baudrillard's body? Both the one at the desk, the physical and intentional lived-body of the man and the repressed or disavowed lived-body of the postmodernism for which he and his disciples stand. At once decentered and completely extroverted, alienated in a phenomenological structure of *sensual thought* and merely *psychic experience*, it was *re-signed* to being a *no-body*. The man's lived-body (and, not coincidentally, the body of a man) – its material facticity, its situatedness, finitude and limitations – had been transubstantiated through textualization into the infinite possibility and irresponsibility and receptivity and legibility of the 'pure' sign. Telling the 'story' of this kind of critical collapse of the materially real into 'readable text', Fredric Jameson points to how 'finally the body itself proves to be a palimpsest whose stabs of pain and symptoms, along with its deeper impulses and its sensory apparatus, can be *read* fully as much as any other text' (1991:186). The sense of the body that Baudrillard privileges, then, is sense as it is amputated from its origins in material existence. Baudrillard's body finds its erotic pleasures located only in the *jouissance* of semiotic play, its pain only in writer's block. And so – given that I first read Baudrillard on *Crash* while I was recuperating from major cancer surgery on my left distal thigh and knew all about gash marks, cut-outs, technical scars and artificial orifices and invaginations – I wished the man a car crash or two, and a little pain to bring him (back) to his senses.

Indeed, there is nothing like a little pain to bring us back to our senses, nothing like a real (not imagined) mark or wound to counter the romanticism and fantasies of techno-sexual transcendence that characterize so much of the current discourse on the techno-body that is thought to occupy the cyberspaces of postmodernity. As Jameson reminds us: 'History is what hurts. It is what refuses desire and sets inexorable limits to individual as well as collective praxis' (1981:102). Thus, while it is true that, between operations, I could joke that my doctor 'had gone where no man had gone before', sitting there reading Baudrillard as I was living my artificial orifice and technical scars, I could attest to the *scandal* of metaphor and the *bad faith* informing the 'political economy of the sign'. The 'semiurgy of contusions, scars, mutilations, and wounds' on *my* thigh were nothing like 'new sexual organs opened in *the* body' (Baudrillard, 1991:314; emphasis mine). Even at its most objectified and technologically caressed, I lived this thigh – not abstractly on 'the' body, but concretely as 'my' body. Thus, sharp pain, dull aches and numbness (which, after all, is not not-feeling, but the feeling of not-feeling), the cold touch of technology on my flesh, were distractions from my erotic possibilities, and not, as Baudrillard would have it, erotically distracting.

This critique, however, was leveled at Baudrillard some time ago – before I actually *became* a techno-body and experienced prosthetic pleasure. Fairly recently, my left leg was amputated above the knee and now I have a prosthetic replacement. Quickly done with pain (even the phantom sensations disappeared after five months), I went out and bought a whole new wardrobe of fancy underwear to don for my visits to the prosthetist – who is quite nice-looking, very absorbed in me, and generally positioned around crotch-level as he tinkers with my titanium knee. I love my prosthesis with its sculpted foam cosmetic cover –

particularly the thigh which has no cellulite and is thinner than the thigh on my so-called 'good' leg. With much effort, I have learned to walk again, the stump first thrust into the socket of a leg held on by a suspension belt and now into what is called a 'suction' socket of a leg that – when it or I am working right – almost feels like 'me'. This new socket has also allowed me a kind of experience with 'artificial orifices' that has none of the pain of surgery and all of the erotic play of technology. Every time I put the leg on, I literally 'screw' a valve into a hole in my new thigh, depressing it to let the air out so that the prosthetic sucks my stump into the very depths of its fiberglass embrace.

I have also become a 'lean, mean machine'. After the amputation, I lost an extraordinary amount of weight – not from dieting in the mode of the self-loathing females of our culture, but from the intensive exercise of, first, merely getting from here to there on crutches and, now, from 'pumping iron' to keep the rest of my body (the 'meat' or 'wetware' as we techno-bodies or cyborgs call it) up to the durability and strength of my prosthetic leg. Indeed – and here I admit to a certain confessional stance I don't usually condone in others – I gave up dieting years ago in anger at its built-in self-criticism and, hardly a glutton, worked on accepting myself 'as I was'. Now, however, all the clothes I never gave away fit me again. Quite frankly, I admit to feeling more positive about my loss of weight than negative about the loss of my leg. (This constitutes, I suppose, a 'fair' – if hardly equitable – trade-off.) The truth of the matter is that I feel more, not less attractive than I used to. Hard body (however partial) that I am, I feel more erotically distracting and distracted than I have in years – although it is hard to find the time to do anything about it given all the hours I spend in physical therapy and at the gym. Indeed, over the year and a half since my amputation, I have come to learn that it's ridiculous (if not positively retrograde) to accept myself 'as I am'. I have found I can 'make myself over', reinvent myself as a 'harder' and, perhaps, even 'younger' body. In fact, right now I am contemplating plastic surgery: getting my eyelids done, perhaps removing the crease that runs downward from the side of my mouth and makes me look less happy than I really am. This then, is the power available to the 'polymorphously perverse' cyborg woman – though hardly what Donna Haraway had in mind when she wrote her ironic manifesto (1985).

If you've believed all of this, you probably think me less polymorphously perverse than extraordinarily self-deluded, bitter, or in some strange state of denial. Which, in fact, I'm not. Although a great deal of what I've revealed here is true, what is *not* true is that I've resigned myself to being a cyborg, a techno-body. My prosthesis has not incorporated me. Rather, the whole aim of my physical existence over the last year and a half has been to incorporate it. Thus, my stance toward – and on – my prosthetic leg is quite a bit different from the one I've entertained here as a playful, yet ironic, response to the delights of the techno-body celebrated by Baudrillard and his followers. What many surgeries and my prosthetic experience have really taught me is that, if we are to survive into the next century, we must counter the millennial discourses that would decontextualize our flesh into insensate sign or digitize it into cyberspace where, as one devotee put it, 'it's like having had your everything amputated' (Barlow, 1990: 42). In the (inter)face of the new technological revolution and its transformation of every aspect of our culture (including our bodies), we have to recognize and make explicit the deep and dangerous ambivalence that informs the reversible relations we, as lived-bodies, have with our tools and their function of allowing us to transcend the limitations of our bodies.

Writing a number of years after her optimistic, if ironic, manifesto for cyborgs, Donna Haraway recognized the self-exterminating impulses of the discourses of disembodiment suggested by Baudrillard's porno-graphy of the body on the one hand and the *Mondo 2000/Wired* – let's download into the datascape and beat the meat – subculture on the other. In an interview (Penley and Ross, 1991) she warns against the very 'liberatory' cyborgism she once celebrated (however ironically) insofar as it jacks into (and off on) the 'God trick', and denies mortality. Our reversible relations with our technology, our confusion of consciousness with computation, of subjectively lived flesh with objective metal and hard-wiring, is – as Haraway points out – a 'transcendentalist' move: 'it produces death through the fear of it', disavowing as it does the fact that

we really do die, that we really do wound each other, that the earth really is finite, that there aren't any other planets out there that we know of that we can live on, that escape-velocity is a deadly fantasy. (Penley and Ross, 1991: 20)

In *Technology and the Lifeworld*, philosopher Don Ihde discusses the ambivalent, or 'doubled' desire that exists in our relations with any technology that extends our bodily sensorium and, thereby, our perceptions – be they eyeglasses or prosthetic legs, the motion picture camera or the computer. He tells us:

On the one side is a wish for total transparency, total embodiment, for the technology to truly 'become me'. Were this possible it would be equivalent to there being no technology, for total transparency would *be* my body and senses. . . . The other side is the desire to have the power, the *transformation* that the technology makes available. Only by using the technology is my bodily power enhanced and magnified by speed, through distance, or by any of the other ways in which technologies change my capacities. These capacities are always *different* from my naked capacities. The desire is, at best, contradictory. I want the transformation that the technology allows, but I want it in such a way that I am basically unaware of its presence. I want it in such a way that it becomes me. Such a desire both secretly *rejects* what technologies are and overlooks the transformational effects which are necessarily tied to human-technology relations. This illusory desire belongs equally to the pro- and anti-technology interpretations of technology. (Ihde, 1990: 65)

Obviously, transparency is what I wish – and strive – for in my relation to my prosthetic leg. I want to subjectively embody it. I do not want to regard it as an object or to think *about* it as I use it to walk. Indeed, in learning to use the prosthesis, I found that *looking objectively* at my leg in a mirror as an exteriorized thing to be thought about and manipulated did not help me improve my balance and gait so much as did *subjectively feeling* through all of my body the weight and rhythm of the leg in a *gestalt* of motor activity. Insofar as the leg remains an object external to me, a hermeneutic problem to be solved, a piece of technology to use, I cannot live it and be enabled by it to accomplish intentional projects that involve it but don't concern it. So, of course, I want it to become totally transparent. The desired transparency here, however, involves *my* incorporation of the prosthetic – and not the prosthetic's incorporation of me (although, seen by others to whom a prosthetic is strange, I may well seem its extension rather than the other way around). This is to say that although my new and enabling leg is made of titanium and fiberglass, I do not perceive myself as a hard body – even after a good workout at the gym, when my union with the weight machines (not the leg) momentarily reifies that metaphor. Nor do I think that because my leg may very well outlast me into the next millennium, it confers upon me invincibility or immortality. Prosthetically enabled, I am, nonetheless, not a cyborg. Unlike Baudrillard, I have not forgotten the limitations and finitude and naked capacities of my flesh – nor, more importantly, do I desire to escape them. They are, after all, what ground the concrete gravity and value of my life, and the very possibility of my partial transcendence of them through various perceptual technologies – be they my bifocals, my leg or my computer. That is, my lived-body – not my prosthetic leg which stands inert in a corner by the bed before I put it on in the morning – provides me the *material premises* and, therefore, the *logical grounds* for the intelligibility of those moral categories that emerge from a bodily sense of gravity and finitude.

I have been using the phenomenological term 'lived-body' throughout to a purpose. Seeming redundant, it serves as a corrective to those prevalent objectifications that complacently regard the body, even one's own, as merely a conceptual or objective thing. One of the consequences of our high-tech millenarianism is that the moral material and significance of the lived-body is elided or disavowed, not only by the delusional liberatory rhetoric of technophiles who long to become either 'pure' electronic information or self-repairing cyborgs like Schwarzenegger's Terminator, but also through the dangerous liberatory poetry of cultural formalists like Baudrillard who long to escape the lived-body and its limitations and write it off (quite literally) as just another sign of its times. This is to say, Baudrillard is of a piece with all those in our culture who revile the lived-body for its weaknesses and who wish to objectify its terrible mortality away – those, for example, who are obsessed with physical fitness (and through various and often perverse or pathological means attempt to transform themselves into hard bodies and lean machines), those who are turned on by images of the body being 'blown away' and 'riddled' by bullet holes (how clearly the vernacular speaks the substance of desire), those like Hans Moravec who want to 'download' into the datascape (1988), those who refer to their bodies contemptuously as 'meat' and 'wetware', and even those who, less overtly than Baudrillard, theorize and intellectually commodify 'the body' as an *objective thing* that one can hold – dare I pun? – at arm's length, available to disinterested scrutiny. This alienated and highly fetishized fascination with the body-object (the body that we *have*) and the devaluation of the lived-body (the body that we *are*) is a consequence of a dangerous confusion between the agency that is our bodies/our selves and the power of our incredible new technologies of perception and expression.

In a recent article critiquing 'technocriticism' and its underlying 'rhetoric about age', Kathleen Woodward reads technological development in western culture as a 'story about the human body':

> Over hundreds of thousands of years the body, with the aid of various tools and technologies, has multiplied its strength and increased its capacities to extend itself in space and over time. According to this logic, the process culminates in the very immateriality of the body itself. In this view technology serves fundamentally as a prosthesis of the human body, one that ultimately displaces the material body, transmitting instead its image around the globe and preserving that image over time. (1994:50)

As we increasingly objectify our thoughts and desires through modern technologies of perception and communication, our subjective awareness of our own bodies diminishes. As Woodward suggests, 'there is a beguiling, almost mesmerizing relationship between the progressive vanishing of the body, as it were, and the hypervisuality of both the postmodern society of the spectacle . . . and the psychic world of cyberspace' (1994:50). This disappearance (or increased 'transparency') of the material, lived-body, its apparent displacement by technological prostheses that can enable and extend our perceptual and expressive powers, provokes in some the 'heady' sensation of having 'beat the meat'. That is, the increasing transparency of one's lived-flesh enabled by new technologies as well as the ubiquitous visibility of new technologies leads to euphoria and a sense of the limitless extension of being beyond its materiality and mortality. This, however, is 'false' consciousness – for it has 'lost touch' with the very material and mortal body that grounds its imagination and imagery of transcendence. As Woodward emphasizes, 'the possibility of an invulnerable and thus immortal body is our greatest technological illusion – that is to say, *delusion*' (1994:51).

Thus, I have no desire, like Baudrillard or Moravec in their respective disembodying fantasies, to 'beat the meat'. Indeed, in light of Ihde's description of the doubled and contradictory structure of our relations with technology, this phrase resonates with contradictions that are tied to, but implicate more than, 'sexual difference'. Certainly, in American vernacular, it speaks of male masturbation. However, in today's world, it also speaks of a desire to get rid of bodily desire – perhaps once through orgasm, but now through technology. Simultaneously, then, the phrase expresses the contradictory wish, on the one hand, to get rid of the body and to overcome its material limitations and demands and, on the other, 'to escape the newly extended body of technological engagement' (Ihde, 1990: 75–6) and *to reclaim experience through the flesh*. Hence *Crash*, its narrator (an 'other' Ballard) telling us: 'The crash was the only real experience I had been through for years. For the first time I was in physical confrontation with my own body, an inexhaustible encyclopedia of pains and discharges' (Ballard, 1985: 39). Hence, the novel's conflation of wounds and orgasms and automobiles, its confusions of flesh and metal, its characters' imagination of 'a sexual expertise that would be an exact analogue of the other skills created by the multiplying technologies of the twentieth century' (Ballard, 1985: 100). Hence, the dream 'of other accidents that might enlarge [the] repertory of orifices, relating them to more elements of the automobile's engineering, to the ever-more complex technologies of the future'. Hence Ballard's narrator asks, 'What wounds would create the sexual possibilities of the invisible technologies of thermonuclear reaction chambers, white-tiled control rooms, the mysterious scenarios of computer circuitry?' and hence he visualizes: 'the extraordinary sexual acts celebrating the possibilities of unimagined technologies' (1985: 179). Throughout the discourses of cyborgism, there is extraordinary emphasis on the erotics of technology as flesh-based, on a transcribed and transubstantiated sexuality that is fatally confused as to the site of its experience.

Baudrillard, Moravec, the *Mondo 2000* and *Wired* folks, all want, as Ihde puts it, 'what the technology gives but do not want the limits, the transformations that a technologically-extended body implies' (1990: 76). Thus, the disavowal inherent in Baudrillard's celebratory description of the techno-body as 'under the gleaming sign of a sexuality that is without referentiality and without limits'. Wanting what 'technology gives', but disavowing what it 'limits', those who find the techno-body 'sexy' forget that screwing the valve into place on my prosthetic thigh brings me no shudder of physical pleasure. This is a thigh that cannot make sense of the lacy lingerie that touches it, cannot feel the silk stockings that caress its artificial skin. In sum, my prosthetic leg has its limits and whatever it does to extend my being-in-the-world, whatever way it enhances and amplifies my perceptions and the significance of my existence, however much it seems to bring me in closer material contact with the technological world, I still had to give up my fleshy leg in trade, to lose something in the bargain. What is particularly dangerous about Baudrillard's erotics of technology – and utterly different from Ballard's pornography of technology in *Crash* – is that, despite its seeming heightened consciousness, it finally disavows the *technological status of technology*. Thus, unlike Ballard, Baudrillard's dizzying pro-technological rhetoric hides anti-technology desire and its self-deception promotes deadly, terminal confusions between meat and hardware.

At this millennial moment when high technology has given so many cultural critics and academics a technological 'high', there might be some cachet in claiming for myself the 'sexiness' of cyborg identity. Rather than – along with the century – being on my 'last leg', I could describe myself as being on the 'first leg' of some devoutly wished for transformation of my human frailty and mortality. This, however, is not the case. Living – rather than writing or thinking – my 'newly extended body of technological engagement', I find the fragility of my flesh significantly precious. While I am deeply grateful for the motility my prosthetic affords me (however much in a transformation that is perceptually reduced as well as amplified), the new leg is dependent finally upon my last leg. Without my lived-body to live it, the prosthetic exists as part of a body without organs – a techno-body that has no sympathy for human suffering, cannot understand human pleasure and, since it has no conception of death, cannot possibly value life.

And so, here as in *Science-Fiction Studies*, I wish Baudrillard a little pain – maybe a lot – to bring him to his senses. Pain would remind him that he doesn't just *have* a body, but that he *is* his body, and that it is in this material fact that 'affect' and anything we might call a 'moral stance' is grounded. Both significant affection and a moral stance (whether on prosthetic legs or not) are based on the lived sense and feeling of the human body not merely as a material object one possesses and analyzes among others, but as a material subject that experiences its own objectivity, that has the capacity to bleed and suffer and hurt for others because it can sense its own possibilities for suffering and pain. If we don't keep this subjective kind of bodily sense in mind as we negotiate our techno-culture, we may very well objectify ourselves to death. It is only by embracing life in all its vulnerability and imperfection, by valuing the limitations as well as possibilities of our flesh, and by accepting mortality, that we will get out of this – or any – century alive.

References

Ballard, J.G. (1985) *Crash*. New York: Vintage Books.
Barlow, John Perry (1990) 'Being in Nothingness: Virtual Reality and the Pioneers of Cyberspace', *Mondo 2000* 2: 34–43.

Baudrillard, Jean (1991) 'Jean Baudrillard: Two Essays', trans. Arthur B. Evans, *Science-Fiction Studies* 18: 309–20.

Haraway, Donna (1985) 'A Manifesto for Cyborgs: Science, Technology and Socialist Feminism in the 1980s', *Socialist Review* 15: 65–107.

Ihde, Don (1990) *Technology and the Lifeworld: From Garden to Earth*. Bloomington: Indiana University Press.

Jameson, Fredric (1981) *The Political Unconscious: Narrative as a Socially Symbolic Act*. Ithaca, NY: Cornell University Press.

Jameson, Fredric (1991) *Postmodernism or, The Cultural Logic of Late Capitalism*. Durham, NC: Duke University Press.

Moravec, Hans P. (1988) *Mind Children: The Future of Robot and Human Intelligence*. Cambridge, MA: Harvard University Press.

Penley, Constance and Andrew Ross (1991) 'Cyborgs at Large: Interview with Donna Haraway', *Social Text* 25/26: 8–23.

Sobchack, Vivian (1991) 'Baudrillard's Obscenity', *Science-Fiction Studies* 18: 327–9.

Woodward, Kathleen (1994) 'From Virtual Cyborgs to Biological Time Bombs: Technocriticism and the Material Body', in Gretchen Bender and Timothy Druckrey (eds) *Culture on the Brink: Ideologies of Technology*. Seattle: Bay Press.

Vivian Sobchack teaches Film and Media Studies at the University of California, Los Angeles. Her publications include *Screening Space: The American Science Fiction Film* (Unger, 1987) and *The Address of the Eye: A Phenomenology of Film Experience* (Princeton University Press, 1992).

Forms of Technological Embodiment: Reading the Body in Contemporary Culture

ANNE BALSAMO

Introduction

This essay addresses the contemporary cultural conjuncture in which the body and technology are co-joined in a literal sense, where machines assume organic functions and the body is materially redesigned through the use of new technologies of corporeality. Broadly, the examples I consider, taken from the media of everyday life (newspapers, advertisements, television programs, mall handouts, magazines), signal ways in which the 'natural' body has been dramatically refashioned through the application of new technologies of corporeality. By the end of the 1980s, the idea of the merger of the 'biological' with the 'technological' had infiltrated the imagination of Western culture such that the cyborg – the 'technological-human' – has become a familiar figuration of the subject of postmodernity. For whatever else it might imply, this merger relies on a reconceptualization of the human body as a boundary figure belonging simultaneously to at least two previously incompatible systems of meaning – 'the organic/natural' and 'the technological/cultural'. At the point at which the body is reconceptualized not as a fixed part of nature, but as a boundary concept, we witness an ideological tug-of-war between competing systems of meaning which include and in part define the material struggles of physical bodies.

The construction of a boundary between nature and culture serves several ideological purposes; most notably, it guarantees a proper order of things and establishes a hierarchical relationship between culture and nature. At a basic level, this socially constructed hierarchy functions to reassure a technologically overstimulated imagination that culture/man will prevail in his encounters with nature. The role of the body in this boundary setting process is significant because it becomes the place where anxieties about the 'proper order of things' erupt and are eventually ideologically managed. Techno-bodies are healthy, enhanced and fully functional – more real than real. New biotechnologies are promoted and rationalized as life-enhancing and even life-saving. Often obscured are the disciplining and surveillant consequences of new body technologies – in short, the bio-politics of technological formations.

In our hyper-mediated techno-culture, body awareness is amplified such that we can technologically witness, if not yet manage, the molecular functioning of bodily processes. Medical authorities encourage us to monitor consumption of sugar, caffeine, salt, fat, cholesterol, nicotine, alcohol, steroids, sunlight, narcotics, through the use of such devices as electronic scales, home pregnancy kits, diabetes tests, blood pressure machines and fat calipers. These devices function as a set of visualization techniques that contribute to the fragmentation of the body into organs, fluids and 'bodily states', which in turn promote a self-conscious self-surveillance whereby the body becomes an object of intense vigilance and control. This know-your-body-obsession manifests itself in different ways in contemporary US culture – for example, in the cult-like observance of practices of personal hygiene, manic fears of death through contamination and diseases of body image.[1] Such obsessions are part of a cultural apparatus of body surveillance which also includes practices of random urine testing among high-school teenagers and adult workers, covert blood testing for HIV, and genetic finger-printing.[2] Fractured body parts are taken up as elements in the construction of cultural identities – agent of infection, cocaine mother, drug user – so that as the target subjects of a technologically enhanced, disembodied gaze, our bodies betray us. Nowhere to hide from our bodies ourselves we have no other choice but to comply and live cleanly; docile creatures practice safe sex or self-destruct.

When the human body is fractured into organs, fluids and scorned material, what happens to gender identity? When the body is fractured into functional parts and molecular codes, where is gender located? What is the relationship between physiological sex markers and gender identity? Gender, like the body, is a boundary concept. It is at once related to physiological sexual characteristics of the human body (the natural order of the body) and to the cultural context within which that body 'makes sense'. The widespread technological refashioning of the 'natural' human body suggests that gender, too, would be ripe for reconstruction. What effects do these technological developments have on the cultural embodiment of gender? As is often the case when seemingly stable boundaries are displaced by technological innovation (human/artificial, nature/culture), other boundaries are more vigilantly guarded. Indeed, the gendered boundary between male and female is one border that remains heavily guarded despite new technologized ways to rewrite the physical body in the flesh. Although it is beyond the scope of this essay to elaborate the many ways in which this border is guarded, consider, as one example, the differences between the media treatment of male bodybuilders and female bodybuilders.[3] Whereas male bodybuilders are treated as athletes whose mild transgressions announce their narcissism and more significant transgressions (of steroid use, for example) mark their technological hubris, female bodybuilders who develop big muscles, and consequently greater strength, are considered transgressive of the natural 'order' of things – an order that defines women as weak and frail. Their transgressive body displays (of female bodies that are also strong bodies) are neutralized in the mass media through the representations that sexualize their athletic bodies – their sexual attractiveness is asserted over their physical capabilities. Based on this and other examples, it appears that even though the body has been recoded within discourses of technology and medicine as belonging to an order of culture rather than of nature, gender remains a naturalized marker of human identity.

My intent for this project is to contribute to the development of a 'thick perception' of the body in contemporary culture from a feminist standpoint.[4] For Michel Feher (1987), 'thick perception' involves an analysis of the 'different modes of construction of the human body'. Relatedly, he asserts that the history of the body is:

> neither a history of scientific knowledge about the body nor a history of the ideologies that (mis)represent the body. Rather it is a history of 'body building', of the different modes of construction of the human body. The body perceived in this way is not a reality to be uncovered in a positivistic description of an organism nor is it a transhistorical set of needs and desires to be freed from an equally transhistorical form of repression. This body is instead a reality constantly produced, an effect of techniques promoting specific gestures and postures, sensations and feelings. Only in tracing these modes of its construction can one arrive at a thick perception of the present 'state of the body'. (1987:159)

Accordingly, 'thick perception' is a Foucauldian technique for understanding the ways in which the body is conceptualized and articulated within different cultural discourses. To think of the body as a social construction and not as a natural object provokes a deceptively simple question: how is the body, as a 'thing of nature', transformed into a 'sign of culture'? The work I examine in this project begins with the assumption that 'the body' is a social, cultural and historical production: 'production' here means both product and process. As a product it is the material embodiment of ethnic, racial and gender identities, as well as a staged performance of personal identity, of beauty, of health (among other things). As a process it is a way of knowing and marking the world, as well as a way of knowing and marking a 'self'. The process of elaborating an informed 'perception' of the body in contemporary culture must simultaneously abstract a discourse of the body and construct an interpretation of it. 'Reading' as a cultural and interpretive practice is the central mechanism of my discursive production. But what I read are not simply textual or media representations of the gendered body, but more specifically social practices of 'making the body gendered'.[5] The act of reading as 'making a discourse' apparent is meant to suggest an active practice of perception that has been determined in specific ways; I have been unconsciously trained, more consciously taught, cajoled and ambushed in my efforts to decipher the cultural construction of the gendered body in various textual forms. This is to say that, although this project is thoroughly grounded in contemporary body scholarship, it is not a reading that springs fully formed from the current moment, as if there existed a singularly unified discourse to read or, relatedly, a singular body to write. Rather I focus on a continuum of discourses which includes the popular cultures of the body as well as scholarly works of body theory. The point is to annotate a taxonomy of the ways in which the techno-body is constructed in contemporary culture. In contrast to those who would argue that there is a dominant – singular – form of the postmodern techno-body, I argue that when starting with the assumption that bodies are always gendered and marked by race it becomes clear that there are multiple forms of technological embodiment that must be attended to in order to make sense of the status of the body in contemporary culture.

Seeing Things Differently

The story Arthur Kroker relates (Kroker and Kroker, 1987) about the body in postmodernity, or hyper-modernity in his terms, is that it has been 'unplugged from the planet'; accordingly, the signal form of the postmodern body is the disappearing body – a notion that the natural body has no ontological status separate from the proliferation of rhetorics that now invest the body with simulated meaning. In his brilliant, although somewhat convoluted reading of the body in contemporary culture, Kroker argues that in its dissolution, the body is subordinated to various apparatuses of power; in the process the body is transformed in historically specific ways. For example, in explaining how the body is ideologically subordinated he points to the way in which bodies are: 'inscribed by the mutating signs of the fashion industry as skin itself is transformed into a screen effect for a last, decadent and desperate search for desire after desire' (Kroker and Kroker, 1987:21). The hyper-modern body is now the panic body:

Panic bodies living on (their own) borrowed power; violent, and alternating, scenes of surplus energy and perfect inertness; existing psychologically on the edge of fantasy and psychosis; floating sign-systems of the body reexperienced in the form of its own second-order simulacra; a combinatorial of hyper-exteriorization (of body organs) and hyper-interiorization (of designer subjectivities); and incited less by the languages of accumulation than fascinating, because catastrophic, signs of self-exterminism, self-liquidation, and self-cancellation. Panic bodies: an inscribed surface onto which are projected all the grisly symptoms of culture burnout as the high five-sign of the late 1980s. (Kroker and Kroker, 1987: 22)

This, according to Kroker, is the fate of the body in contemporary culture: exhausted, exteriorized, inscribed to excess, invaded by language, dissolved over the mediascape, and functional only as a 'passive screen for the hystericizations and panic mythologies of the (disappearing) public realm' (1987: 28). As Kroker goes on to explain, the language of body invaders is the dominant language of postmodern power.

When Kroker reads the signs of the times of the postmodern body in the art of various visual and performance artists, he finds ample evidence to develop his theses on the disappearing body. The gendered identity of this body is noticed obliquely, through attention to Francesca Woodman's art, but not, quite tellingly, in reference to Stelarc body performances. The insight he offers about gender is that women's bodies have always been postmodern because they have always known the invasion of cultural rhetorics that would define them according to broader systems of power. According to Kroker, women's bodies have always served as an inscribed text upon which are written the dominant myths of masculinist culture – myths that would define those bodies as that which is the 'other' of man, interpellated by ideology, and discursively constructed as unruly, threatening, uncontrollable. But if women's bodies have been always invaded by various rhetorics of power, how then is the disappearance of the body (the invaded body) a new condition endemic to postmodernity? The only possible response is that the disappearing body actually marks the historically specific identity of the male body as it experiences this corporeal invasion for the first time.

The feminist story of the postmodern body begins with the assumption that bodies are always gendered and marked by race. In attending to the way that Kroker builds his body theory, it is clear that for him 'the body' is an idealist abstraction. As far as it goes, this is a provocative story. But it is only a partial story of postmodern corporeality. What is missing is a material dimension that takes into account the embodied markers of cultural identity. The polemic in this paper argues that the body can never be constructed as a purely discursive entity. In a related sense, it can never be reduced to a pure materialist object. Better to think of the dual 'natures' of the body in terms of its 'structural integrity' to use Evelyn Fox Keller's (1992) term. This is to assert that the material and the discursive are mutually determining and non-exclusive. Kroker's theory of the 'disappearing' body notwithstanding, the material body remains a constant factor of the postmodern, post-human condition. It has certain undeniable material qualities that are, in turn, culturally determined and discursively managed; qualities that are tied to its physiology and to the cultural contexts within which it makes sense, such as its gender and race identities.

Cyberpunk Techno-Bodies

Here then is a different story about the postmodern body that is abstracted from contemporary science fiction. As a work of the feminist imaginary, this narrative extracted from Pat Cadigan's (1991) cyberpunk novel, *Synners*, explicitly discusses an often-repressed dimension of the information age: the material identity of the techno-body. True to its genre determinations, *Synners* concerns a loosely identified 'community' of computer users, each of whom is differently, albeit thoroughly, engaged with the technologies of cyberspace – simulation machines, global communication networks, corporate databases and multi-media production systems. What we encounter in the Cadigan novel is the narrativization of four different versions of postmodern embodiment: the laboring body, the marked body, the repressed body and the disappearing body. In this sense, the four central characters symbolize the different embodied relations one can have, in fiction and in practice, to a technological formation. The following figure roughly illustrates how Sam, Gabe, Gina and Visual Mark (the four main characters) represent four corners of an identity matrix constructed in and around cyberspace.

Figure 1

Sam (the body that labors)	*Gina* (the marked body)
Gabe (the repressed body)	*Visual Mark* (the disappearing body)

Where Sam hacks the net through a terminal powered by her own body, Visual Mark actually inhabits the network as he mutates into a disembodied, sentient artificial intelligence (AI). Although both Gina and Gabe travel through cyberspace on their way to someplace else, Gabe is addicted to cyberspace simulations and Gina merely endures them. Each character plays a significant role in the novel's climactic confrontation in cyberspace: a role determined, in part, by their individual relationships to Diversifications (the genre-required evil multinational corporation) and, in part, by their bodily identities. What follows is a brief synopsis of the body biography of each character.

In the course of the novel, Visual Mark, in true cyberpunk fashion, spends less and less time off-line and more and more time plugged in to the global network known as 'the System'. This leads him to reflect on the metaphysical nature of his physical body: 'he lost all awareness of the meat that had been his prison for close to fifty years, and the relief he felt at having laid his burden down was as great as himself' (1991:232). After suffering a small stroke while jacked in, Visual Mark prepares for 'the big one' – a stroke that will release his consciousness into the system and allow him to leave his meat behind.

> He was already accustomed to the idea of having multiple awareness and a single concentrated core that were both the essence of self. The old meat organ would not have been able to cope with that kind of reality, but out here he appropriated more capacity the way he once might have exchanged a smaller shirt for a larger one. (1991:325)

And sure enough, while his body is jacked in, Mark strokes out. As his meat dies, both his consciousness and his stroke enter 'the System'. In the process, his stroke is transformed into a deadly virus (or spike) that initiates a world-wide network crash.

Sam, Gabe's daughter and the only real hacker among the four, is a virtuoso at gaining access to the System. She is the character who best describes the labor of computer hacking and the virtual acrobatics of cyberspace travel: '[i]f you couldn't walk on the floor, you walked on the ceiling. If you couldn't walk on the ceiling, you walked on the walls, and if you couldn't walk on the walls, you walked in them, encrypted. Pure hacking' (1991:351). As competent as she is in negotiating the cyberspatial landscape of the net, Sam tries to live her embodied life outside of any institutional structure. Her only affiliations are to other punks and hackers who form a community of sorts and who live out on 'the Manhattan–Hermosa strip, what the kids called the Mimosa, part of the old postquake land of the lost' (1991:7). Sam trades encrypted data and hacking talents for stray pieces of equipment and living necessities. In what proves to be a critically important 'information commodity' acquisition, Sam hacks the specifications for an insulin-pump chip reader that runs off body energy. When every terminal connected to 'the System' is infected by Visual Mark's stroke/virus, Sam's insulin-pump chip reader is the only noninfected access point to the net. Connected by thin needles inserted into her abdomen, the chip reader draws its power from Sam's body. Seventeen-year-old Sam is a cyberspace hacker of considerable talent who shuns the heroic cowboy role. And for the most part, she is content to provide the power while others, namely Gina and Gabe, go in for the final showdown.

Gabe spends most of his working time, when he should be designing advertising campaigns, playing the role (Hotwire) of a *noir* leading man in a computer simulation built from pieces of an old movie thriller (1991:41). Where Visual Mark cleaves to cyberspace because the world isn't big enough for his expansive visual mind, Gabe becomes addicted to cyberspace because the world is just too big for him. He retreats to the simulation pit for the safety and familiarity it offers. 'He'd been running around in simulation for so long, he'd forgotten how to run a realife, real-time routine; he'd forgotten that if he made mistakes, there was no safety-net program to jump in and correct for him' (1991:239). Throughout the novel, Gabe moves in and out of a real-time life and his simulated fantasy world. In real-time his body is continually brought to life, through pain, intoxication and desire caused by Gina, first when she punches him in the face with a misplaced stab intended for Visual Mark, then later when he gets toxed after she feeds him two LotusLands (a 'mildly hallucinogenic beverage'). After they make love for the first time, Gina wonders if Gabe has ever felt desire before: 'She didn't think Gabe Ludovic had ever jumped the fast train in his life. Standing at the end of fifteen years of marriage, he'd wanted a lot more than sex. The wanting had been all but tangible, a heat that surprised both of them' (1991:243). After a climactic cyberspace struggle, his repressed body reawakens; Gabe learns to feel his body again (or for the first time) with Gina's help.

Like Visual Mark, Gina is a 'synner' who synthesizes images, sound and special effects to produce virtual reality music videos. For all her disdain and outright hostility toward other people and institutions, 'Badass Gina Aiesi' has an intense emotional connection to Visual Mark, her partner of 20 years, that she romanticizes in an odd way:

> They weren't smooch-faces, it didn't work that way, for her or for him. . . . One time, though . . . one time, three–four–five years into the madness, there'd been a place where they had come together one night, and it had been different. . . . He'd been reaching, and she'd been reaching, and for a little while there, they'd gotten through. Maybe that had been the night when the little overlapping space called their life had come into existence. (1991:213)

Gina's body, marked by its color, 'wild forest hardwood', and her dreadlocks, figures prominently in the narrative description of her sexual encounters, first with Visual Mark and then with Gabe. After both she and Visual Mark have brain sockets implanted, they jack in together and experience a visual replay of shared memories: 'The pov was excruciatingly slow as it moved across Mark's face to her own, lingering on the texture of her dreadlocks next to his pale, drawn flesh, finally moving on to the contrast of her deep brown skin' (1991:216). The characteristics that mark Gina are her anger, her exasperated love for Mark and the color of her skin.

Like the dramatic climax in recent cyberpunk films such as *Circuitry Man* (1989), *Lawnmower Man* (1991) and *Mindwarp* (1991), the final showdown in *Synners* takes place in cyberspace. Working together, the small Mimosa community assembles a work-station (powered by Sam's insulin-pump chip reader) that enables Gina and Gabe to go on-line to fight the virus/stroke – an intelligent entity of some dubious ontological status that now threatens the integrity of the entire networked world. Like a cyberspace Terminator, the virus/stroke is hyper-rationally determined to infect/destroy whomever or whatever comes looking for it. In the course of their cyberspace brawl, Gabe and Gina confront the virus's simulation of their individual worst fears. A 'reluctant hero' till the very end, Gabe's cyberspace enemy is a simple construct: the fear of embodiment. 'I can't remember what it feels like to have a body', he repeats obsessively during his final confrontation in cyberspace. What he learns through the encounter is that his whole body is a hot-suit; that is, he learns to feel the body that he has technologically repressed.

In one sense, Cadigan writes fiction implicitly informed by Donna Haraway's cyborg politics: the gendered distinctions among characters hold true to a cyborgian figuration of gender differences whereby the female body is coded as a body-in-connection and the male body as a body-in-isolation. It illuminates the gendered differences in the way that the characters relate to the technological space of information. Sam and Gina, the two female hackers, actively manipulate the dimensions of cybernetic space in order to communicate with other people. Gabe and Visual Mark, on the other hand, are addicted to cyberspace for the release it offers from the perceived limitations of their material bodies. Even as the novel's characters illuminate the gendered distinctions among computer network users, its racial characterizations are less developed. The racial distinctions between characters are revealed through the representation of sexual desire. Gina is the only character to be identified by skin color. She is also the focal object and subject of heterosexual desire, for a moment by Mark, and more frequently by Gabe; and, we know both men's racial identities by their marked difference from Gina's. The unmarked characters are marked by the absence of identifying marks. In different ways then and with different political inflections, the novel reasserts that gender and race are critical elements of post-human identity.

Throughout the book, the characters' material bodies are invoked through descriptions of sexual encounters, bathroom breaks, food consumption, intoxication effects and physical death. The key insight to emerge from the novel is that the denatured techno-body remains a material entity. Although it may be culturally coded and semiotically marked, it is never merely discursive. This is to say that even as *Synners* discursively represents different forms of technological embodiment, it also reasserts the critical importance of the materiality of bodies in any analysis of the information age.

Expanding upon this delimited reading of *Synners* as both cultural landmark and cognitive map yields another version of the matrix above that offers a taxonomy of forms of technological embodiment. The ground upon which this matrix is constructed is the shifting table of body theory: each quadrant is a multi-dimensional space for filing body snapshots, art installations, performances, readings, enactments and corporeal forms. The qualities that mark each form of embodiment are illustrated by various incarnations of the techno-body. This taxonomy shares characteristics with those constructed by other body scholars, notably Bryan Turner (1984, 1991) and Arthur Frank (1991). Frank's schema most closely resembles the matrix developed in this essay.[6] For example, his notion of the 'disciplined' body shares qualities with my notion of the repressed body. In other cases, our categories do not simply match up, although there are strong resonances. In his account of the 'communicative body', he identifies elements that I assign to both the 'laboring body' and the 'marked body'. The communicative body, for Frank, is an expressive realization of itself, 'no longer appropriated by institutions and discourses, but by the body's own' life (1991: 80). This quality of expression is a key characteristic of the marked body in my matrix; the subtle difference between Frank's account of the communicative body and mine of the marked body is tied to a notion of agency. I see the marked body as bearing the signs of culture, even when these signs are appropriated by the body in question. The quality of corporeal expression that Frank rightly emphasizes is one that I assign to the laboring body – both as it is based in the facticity of reproduction and, reflecting a Marxist influence, in the conditions of productive labor. Both Turner and Frank recognize, to different degrees, the gendered nature of forms of embodiment; they are less specific about the racial aspects of those forms though. In the following sections, I consider the gendered and racial dimensions of a range of new bio-technological forms of embodiment. The aim is to illustrate how material bodies are both discursively constructed and culturally disciplined at a particular historical moment.

Figure 2

Postmodern Forms of Technological Embodiment

The LABORING Body Mothers as Wombs Microelectronics Workers	*The DISAPPEARING Body* Bio-engineering Bodies and Databases
The REPRESSED Body Virtual Reality Computer Communication	*The MARKED Body* Multi-cultural Mannequins Cosmetic Surgery

The Marked Body

The marked body signals the fact that bodies are eminently cultural signs, bearing the traces of ritual and mythic identities. In similar ways, both the fashion industry and the cosmetic surgery profession have capitalized on the role of the body in the process of 'identity semiosis' – where identities become signs and signs become commodities. The consequence is the technological production of identities for sale and rent. Material bodies shop the global marketplace for cultural identities that come in different forms, the least permanent as clothes and accessories worn once and discarded with each new fashion season, the most dramatic as the physical transformation of the corporeal body accomplished through surgical methods. Thus the natural body is technologically transformed into a sign of culture.

High fashion – as one technology of urban corporeal identity – is preoccupied with multiculturalism. One of the consequences is that in reading the body displayed on the glossy pages of American fashion magazines, it is evident that the politics of representation are very confused. For example, from its very first US issue in January 1987, *Elle* magazine regularly included photographic layouts that featured black and other non-white models wearing various 'deconstructed' fashions. The May 1988 cover of *Elle* that showcased the faces of two models, one white in the background, made-up in conventional fashion, the other black in the foreground, wearing no discernible make-up, betrays the cultural politics at the center of the worldview of the high fashion industry where 'black bodies' serve as mannequins for designer messages intended for affluent white readers. The narrative constructed around *Elle*'s black bodies and white bodies concerns the fashion industry's appropriation of the trope of primitivism as a seasonal fashion look. In this case, the fashion apparatus deploys signs of the 'primitive' in the service of constructing an anti-fashion high fashion look. While another *Elle* article explained that the American 'love of the exotic' has translated into career success for several new multicultural supermodels,[7] it was rarely mentioned that they were few of the women who could actually afford the clothes featured as items in the new primitivism line that cost upwards of $1000. Thus an interesting paradox takes shape: the black bodies of supermodels are used as billboards for designer messages about the fetishization of black identity as the cultural sign of the ethnic primitive. Just as they are admitted to the elite club of well-paid supermodels, black models are coopted to a cultural myth of racial subordination.

This appropriation of the signs of cultural primitivism for the visual consumption of mostly white readers illuminates the mass-mediated rehearsal of the construction of cultural identity, where what is reviled and despised is projected onto the body of the 'other' such that the identity of the 'One' is established as that which is good and pure and sacred. At the same time, the body of the 'other' is fetishized and eroticized in its object form. In this way, the proper hierarchy of white bodies over black bodies is subtly, and compulsively, reinscribed in each season's look. The recuperative power of corporate culture and its premier technology, mass media advertising, extends far beyond the appropriation of black identity and tropes of primitivism. As the recent trend of deconstructionism as high fashion look attests, even the markers of poverty are able to be rearticulated to a different economic logic.[8] The focal figure and preferred mannequin of these fashion campaigns is the eroticized dark brown female body, but the valorized subject is the white, Western woman, whose white body can be liberated, temporarily, from the debasement of everyday life through her consumption and mimicry of anti-fashion style.

Much like those physicians who use sonograms and laparoscopes to look through the maternal body, cosmetic surgeons also make use of new visualization technologies to exercise a high-tech version of Foucault's scientific bio-power that effects, first, the objectification of the material body and, second, the subjection of that body to the discipline of a normative gaze. In the past five years, several cosmetic surgeons have begun using a new high-tech video imaging program as a patient consultation device. In the process, the medical gaze of the cosmetic surgeon is transformed into the technological perspective of the video camera. Using computer rendering tools, such as erasers, pencils and 'agenic cursors', the cosmetic surgeon manipulates the digitized image of the prospective patient in order to visually illustrate possible surgical transformations. One of the consequences is that the material body is reconfigured as an electronic image that can be technologically manipulated on the screen before it is surgically manipulated in the operating room. In this way, the video consultation enables the codification of surgical 'goals' – goals which effect, in short, the inscription of cultural ideals of Western beauty.[9] Where visualization technologies bring into focus isolated body parts and pieces, surgical procedures carve into the flesh to isolate parts to be manipulated and resculpted. In this way, cosmetic surgery literally transforms the material body into a sign of culture. The discourse of cosmetic surgery offers provocative material for a discussion of the cultural construction of the gendered body because, on the one hand, women are often the intended and preferred subjects of such discourse, and on the other, men are often the bodies doing the surgery. Cosmetic surgery is not then simply a discursive site for the 'construction of images of women', but, in actuality, a material site at which the physical female body is technologically dissected, stretched, carved and reconstructed according to cultural and eminently ideological standards of physical appearance.

The Laboring Body

Bodies that labor include a full range of working bodies as well as maternal bodies. In the broadest sense these are all reproductive bodies involved in the continuation of the human race in its multiple material incarnations. Such bodies are often invisible in postmodern discourse. But, because they are centrally involved in the reproduction of various technological formations, including now the 'natural' family unit, they must be counted as key postmodern cultural forms.

Perhaps the most obvious form of the laboring body is the maternal body which is increasingly treated as a technological body – both in its science fictional and science factual form as 'container' for the fetus, and in its role as the object of technological manipulation in the service of human reproduction. How, specifically, are the material bodies of pregnant women affected by cultural discourses? In a discussion of the politics of new reproductive technologies, Jennifer Terry (1989) examines how these technologies are deployed in the service of institutionalized practices of surveillance, whereby pregnant women are watched in the name of 'public health' to determine whether they are taking drugs or alcohol while pregnant. In 1989, newspapers across the USA reported on the spectacle of 'cocaine mothers' – the mediated identity of women who deliver babies who show traces of cocaine in their systems at birth. Since 1990, several women, branded thus by the media, have been charged with criminal child neglect for the delivery of a controlled substance to a minor. One of the consequences is that maternal rights of body privacy are set against the rights of a fetus to the state's protection. The personification of the fetus as an entity with 'rights' is made possible, in part, because of the use of visualization technologies such as sonograms and laparascopes. In the application of these technologies, the material integrity of the maternal body is technologically deconstructed, only to be reconstructed as a visual medium to look through to see the developing fetus who is now, according to some media campaigns, 'the most important obstetrics patient'. In short, the use of these technologies of visualization creates new cultural identities and enables new agents of power that, in turn, create new possibilities for the discipline of maternal bodies. In this way, cultural discourses not only establish the meaning of material bodies, but also significantly delimit the range of freedom of some of those bodies.

Attending to laboring bodies also suggests the need to investigate the material conditions of the production of the cheap, high-tech devices purchased in bulk by US consumers of electronic commodities. For example, silicon chips are relatively inexpensive to manufacture and assemble because of the use of cheap labor in south-east Asia. In the course of his investigation of Malaysia's labor contribution to the microelectronics industry, Les Levidow (1991) discovered that women workers were the preferred employees for electronic firms because it is believed that 'they are naturally suited to the routinized work of the electronics assembly line: nimble fingers, acute eyesight, greater patience' (1991: 106). Although these women are compensated monetarily, daughters contribute a significant percentage of their earnings to their families. Other forms of compensation are more intangible, and double-edged. Women factory workers experience a measure of independence from 'village elders', who would have bound them to traditional Islamic practices and values but, at the same time, they risk significant health problems in the form of blindness, respiratory disease and psychological and sexual manipulation. The point is not to argue that these are the only laboring bodies that bear the brunt of technologically assisted disciplinary actions, but rather to assert that women are far more likely to be the targets of such discipline. This is in part due to their historically designated position within labor networks tied to their physiology, that is, as possessing nimble fingers suited for detailed handwork. It is also a consequence of the gendered division of labor whereby women occupy the lowest paying positions because of active discrimination, beliefs about women's inferiority, their socialization to service roles, and the social and cultural pressures to marry, bear children and forego compensated employment in favor of unpaid domestic labor.

The Repressed Body

Repression is a pain management technique. The technological repression of the material body functions to curtail pain by blocking channels of sensory awareness. In the development of virtual reality applications and hardware, the body is redefined as a machine interface. In the efforts to colonize the electronic frontier – called cyberspace or the information matrix – the material body is divorced from the locus of knowledge. The point of contact with the interior spaces of a virtual environment – the way that the computer-generated scene makes sense – is through an eye-level perspective that shifts as the user turns her head; the changes in the scene projected on the small screens roughly corresponds with the real-time perspectival changes one would expect as one normally turns the head. This highly controlled gaze mimes the movement of a disembodied camera 'eye' – a familiar aspect of a filmic phenomenology where the camera simulates the movement of perspective that rarely includes a self-referential visual inspection of the body as the vehicle of that perspective. Although some VR users report a noticeable lag time in the change of scene as the head turns, that produces a low-level nauseous feeling, for the most part the material body is visually and technologically repressed. This repression of the body is technologically naturalized in part because we have internalized the technological gaze to such an extent that 'perspective' is a naturalized organizing locus of sense knowledge. As a consequence, 'the body', as a sense apparatus, is nothing more than excess baggage for the cyberspace traveler.

In short, what these VR encounters really provide is an illusion of control over reality, nature and, especially, over the unruly, gender and race-marked, essentially mortal body. There is little coincidence that VR emerged in the 1980s, during a decade when the body was understood to be increasingly vulnerable (literally, as well as discursively) to infection, as well as to gender, race, ethnicity and ability critiques. At the heart of the media promotions of virtual reality is a vision of a body-free universe. In this sense, these new technologies are implicated in the reproduction of at least one very traditional cultural narrative: the possibility of transcendence whereby the physical body and its social meanings can be technologically neutralized. In the speculative discourse of VR, we are promised whatever body we want, which doesn't say anything about the body that I already have and the economy of meanings I already embody. What forms of embodiment would people choose if they could design their virtual bodies without the pain or cost of physical restructuring? If we look to those who are already participating in body reconstruction programs, for instance, cosmetic surgery and bodybuilding, we would find that their reconstructed bodies display very traditional gender and race markers of beauty, strength and sexuality. There is plenty of evidence to suggest that a reconstructed body does not guarantee a reconstructed cultural identity. Nor does 'freedom from a body' imply that people will exercise the 'freedom to be' any other kind of body than the one they already enjoy or desire. This is to argue that, although the body may disappear representationally in the virtual worlds of cyberspace and, indeed, we may go to great lengths to repress it and erase its referential traces, it does not disappear materially in the interface with the VR apparatus, or in its engagement with other high-tech communication systems.

In the Jargon File,[10] the entry on 'Gender and Ethnicity' claims that although 'hackerdom is still predominantly male', hackers are gender and color-blind in their interactions with other hackers due to the fact that they communicate (primarily) through text-based network channels. This assertion rests on the assumption that 'text-based channels' represent a gender-neutral medium of exchange, and that language itself is free from any form of gender, race or ethnic determinations. Both of these assumptions are called into question not only by feminist research on electronic communication and interpretive theory, but also by female network users who participate in the virtual subcultures of cyberspace.[11] Studies of the new modes of electronic communication indicate that the anonymity offered by the computer screen empowers antisocial behaviors such as 'flaming' and borderline illegal behaviors such as trespassing, e-mail snooping and MUD-rape.[12] And yet, for all the anonymity they offer, many computer communications reproduce stereotypically gendered patterns of conversation.[13] Hoai-An Truong, a member of the Bay Area Women in Telecommunications (BAWIT) writes:

> Despite the fact that computer networking systems obscure physical characteristics, many women find that gender follows them into the on-line community, and sets a tone for their public and private interactions there – to such an extent that some women purposefully choose gender neutral identities, or refrain from expressing their opinions.[14]

This is a case where the false denial of the body requires the defensive denial of the body in order to communicate. For some women, it is simply not worth the effort. Most men never notice. The development of and popular engagement with cybernetic networks allows us the opportunity to investigate how myths about identity, nature and the body are rearticulated with new technologies such that traditional narratives about the gendered, race-marked body are socially and technologically reproduced.

The Disappearing Body

Of all the forms of technological embodiment, the disappearing body is the one that promises most insistently the final erasure of gender and race as culturally organized systems of differentiation. Bio-engineered body components are designed to duplicate the function of material body parts; bit by bit the 'natural' body is literally reconstructed through the use of technological replacement parts. But even as the material body is systematically replaced piece by piece, system by system, gender identity does not entirely disappear. 'Sexy Robots' and war machines still bear the traces of conventional gender codings. In the case of bodies that more literally disappear into cyberspace – here I'm talking about the technological coding of bodies as part of electronic databases – racial identity functions as a submerged system of logic to organize body information, even as it is coded in bits and bytes.

As part of a special preview of the year 2000 and beyond, the 1988 February issue of *Life* magazine featured an article called 'Visions of Tomorrow' that included a report on the replaceable body parts that were already 'on the market' . . . elbow and wrist joints, and tendons and ligaments.[15] We are told how succeeding generations of artificial 'devices' will be even more complex than the ones we have today, aided by research in microelectronics and tissue engineering. For example, glass eyes will be replaced with electronic retinas, pacemakers with bionic hearts, and use of the already high-tech insulin dispenser will soon become obsolete in favor of an organically grown biohybrid system that could serve as an artificial pancreas. The availability of manufactured body parts has subtly altered the cultural understanding of what counts as a natural body. Even as these technologies provide the realistic possibility of replacement body parts, they also enable a fantastic dream of immortality and control over life and death.

Images, such as the *Life* magazine illustration of the 'future body', show how male and female bodies are constructed differently with respect to their reproductive and sexual functions. The replaceable body featured in the *Life* article is gendered through the inclusion of photographs of plastic penile implants and the plastic non-functional testicle. It is certainly ironic that although the article speculates about a future when 'a Sears catalogue of body options' will be widely available, the one body prosthesis currently available through the Sears Catalogue is not pictured – the female breast form.[16] Although its symbolic and ultimately hegemonic function has been sharply criticized, this non-functional prosthesis is widely used by women who have had radical mastectomies.[17] Since the *Life* photograph includes other body prostheses that are neither implanted (an arm-hand device, for example) nor functional (the plastic testicle), the exclusion of the artificial breast form, which is also not implanted and non-functional, subtly reveals the intended gender of the future body. Obliquely referred to in the article, but not pictured in the *Life* photograph, the female body is signified through a reference to the development of an artificial uterus. This association between the female body and the uterus or the womb signals the dominant cultural definition of the female body as primarily a reproductive body. Such a metonymic relationship is far from innocent, though. In this future vision, the male body is marked by the signs of a fully able, embodied person, whereas the female body is marked only by a textual reference to the artificial uterus. This rendition of the 'future' female techno-body recalls the construction of the female techno-body in the discourse of reproductive technologies – as a container for the fetus.

The relationship between material bodies and the information collected about those bodies is of central concern to people who ask the question, 'Who counts?' This leads to the investigation of both those who determine who counts as instances of what identities, and also those who are treated as numbers or cases in the construction of databases. The politics of databases will be a critical agenda item for the 1990s as an increasing number of businesses, services and state agencies go 'on-line'. Determining who has access to data, and how to get access to data that is supposedly available to the 'public', is a multidimensional project that involves the use of computers, skill at network access and education in locating and negotiating government-regulated databases. Even a chief data coordinator with the US Geological Survey asserts that 'data markets, data access, and data dissemination are complicated, fuzzy, emotional topics right now'. She 'predicts that they likely will be the major issues of the decade'.[18] Questions of public access and of the status of information collected on individuals are just now attracting public attention.

For those who monitor the insurance industry's interest in database development, there are already several warning signs about the material consequences of digitizing bodies. The Human Genome Project (HGP) is a big-science enterprise that promises to deliver an electronically accessible map of all 100,000 genes found on human chromosomes. This electronic map could be used for diagnostic screening; all that is needed is a sample of genetic material collected as part of the application process for life insurance. One insurance company in the US has already petitioned for the right to require a sample of saliva with each new client's application. The ethics of constructing electronic maps of the human genetic code is a critical concern for those involved in the HGP; in fact, in 1994, 5 percent of the Project's budget was set aside for ethical research. This concern with ethics has not deterred the development of related projects whose ethical implications are more directly contested, and whose methods of gene recording are less digital and more biological. For example, the aim of the Human Genome Diversity project (a project related to the HGP) is to record 'the dwindling genetic diversity of Homo sapiens by taking DNA samples from several hundred distinct human populations and storing them in gene banks' (Gutin, 1994).

Researchers could then examine the DNA for clues to the evolutionary histories of the populations and to their resistance or susceptibility to particular diseases. Even though this seems like an entirely benevolent project on the surface, members of the populations targeted to be archived think otherwise. In a letter dated 18 November 1993, Chief Leon Shenandoah and the Onondaga Council of Chiefs demanded that the Project's directors 'cease and desist immediately all activities regarding DNA structures (genetic fingerprints) of the people of Onondaga and Cayuga Nations and other indigenous nations and people'.

> Your process is unethical, invasive and may even be criminal. It violates the group rights and human rights of our peoples and indigenous peoples around the world. Your project involves the very genetic structures of our beings.[19]

The issue at stake is the creation of a 'bank' of information about a certain population whose members have no official right to assess the accuracy of the information collected about them, let alone to monitor the intended or potential use of such information. This raises questions about intellectual property rights, informed consent and rights of privacy. Members of populations whose genetic material is 'banked' at various laboratories are not alone in their vulnerability to the misuse of collected information. Any consumer who uses credit cards or other forms of digital funds transfer is equally disempowered in terms of the right of ownership of the information collected. Such widely distributed research programs as the Human Genome Project and the Human Genome Diversity Project are in fact re-tooling notions of privacy and corporeal identity. They demonstrate how the reality of the material body is very much tied to its discursive construction and institutional situation. Digitized representations of corporeal identity impact material bodies. The politics of representation in these cases are doubly complex in that it is difficult not only to determine how the body is being represented, but also who is the agent of representation. Given the 'truth status' of scientific discourse, it is difficult to assert that a representation has been constructed.

Conclusion

Postmodern embodiment is not a singularly discursive condition. Failure to consider the multiple ways in which bodies are technologically engaged is to perpetuate a serious misreading of postmodernity as structured by a uniformly dominant cultural logic. Although, if pressed, most critics would probably assert that they don't believe in a 'uniformly' dominant culture logic, such claims implicitly inform both Arthur Kroker's work on 'Body Invaders' and Fredric Jameson's elaboration of the cultural logic of postmodernity. Such a reading obscures the consideration of the diverse range of political forces that determine the reality of material bodies. In offering the matrix of forms of technological embodiment, I argue that the material body cannot be bracketed or 'factored out' of postmodern body theory. This is not an argument for the assertion of a material body that is defined in an essentialist way – as having unchanging, trans-historical gender or race characteristics. Rather, it is to argue that the gender and race identity of the material body structures the way that body is subsequently culturally reproduced and technologically disciplined. What becomes obvious through the study of new reproductive technologies that enable the visualization of the fetus in the womb, there is no blank page of gender identity. That unsigned moment before the birth certificate is marked with an 'F' or an 'M' is an artifact of a mythic era; we are born always already inscribed.

In Pat Cadigan's narrative *Synners*, the female body is symbolically represented as a material body and as a body that labors. The male body, in contrast, is repressed or disappearing. This suggests two points of disagreement with Kroker's theory of 'the disappearing body': that there is no singular form of postmodern embodiment, and that 'disappearing body' is not a post-human body-without-gender. In contrast, I argue that the 'disappearing body' is a gendered response to cultural anxieties about body invasion. Masculinist dreams of body transcendence and, relatedly, masculinist attempts at body repression, signal a desire to return to the 'neutrality' of the body, to be rid of the culturally marked body.

The technological fragmentation of the body functions in a similar way to its medical fragmentation: body parts are objectified and invested with cultural significance. In turn, this fragmentation is articulated to a culturally determined 'system of differences' that not only attributes value to different bodies, but 'processes' these bodies according to traditional, dualistic gendered 'natures'. This system of differentiation determines the status and position of material bodies which results in the reification of dualistic codes of gender identity. So, despite the technological possibilities of body reconstruction, in the discourses of bio-technology the female body is persistently coded as the cultural sign of the 'natural', the 'sexual' and the 'reproductive', so that the 'womb', for example, continues to signify female gender in a way that reinforces an essentialist identity for the female body as the 'maternal body'. In this sense, an apparatus of gender organizes the power relations manifest in the various engagements between bodies and technologies. I offer the phrase 'technologies of the gendered body' as a way of describing such interactions between bodies and technologies.[20] Gender, in this schema, is both a determining cultural condition and a social consequence of technological deployment. My intent is to illuminate the ways that contemporary discourses of technology rely on a logic of binary gender identity as an underlying organizational framework to structure the possibilities of technological engagement, and ultimately to limit the revisionary potential of such technologies.

Notes

1. The 'fear of death by contamination' is certainly not a new phenomenon. In the 1950s, Marshall McLuhan (1959), in his book, *The Mechanical Bride*, observed that the American 'bathroom has been elevated to the very stratosphere of industrial folklore, it being the gleam, the larger hope, which we are appointed to follow. But in a world accustomed to the dominant imagery of mechanical production and consumption, what could be more natural than our coming to submit our bodies and fantasies to the same processes?' (1959: 62).

2. A Texas antidrug program (D-FY-IT) provides rewards in the form of discounts at restaurants, clothing stores and game rooms, to teenagers who volunteer to participate in random urine drug tests. 'Texas antidrug program talks teens' language' (*Chicago Tribune* 15 June 1989, sec. 1: 1, 9). Random drug testing promises to provoke many legal debates and casts a cloud over the issue of teenage friendship. Mike Royko reports that many teenagers (900 out of a non-random sample of 1500) say that they would blow the whistle on friends who use drugs: 'they'd rather lose the friendship of a living person than go to the funeral of a friend' (Mike Royko column, 11 June 1989).

3. For an extended discussion of the gendered distinctions between bodybuilders, cosmetic surgery patients, subjects of reproductive technologies and computer network users, see my book: *Technologies of the Gendered Body* (1995).

4. Michel Feher uses the Foucauldian term 'thick perception' to describe one way to study the cultural relationship between the body and technology (Feher, 1987: 159–65). He further elaborates this concept in Feher (1989: 11–17).

5. Michel de Certeau's (1984) chapter on 'Reading as Poaching' is an eloquent discussion of the active practice of reading. See also John Frow's (1991) explication of de Certeau's theory of reading.

6. Whereas I agree with Frank's assessment that bodies are produced in dynamic relationships among discourses and institutions, I am less clear about the conceptual basis of his typology. I would like a more elaborate description of the 'table' upon which his typology is drawn. Following Michel Feher's advice, I would argue that the body is a historically specific construction. It is unclear to me, from Frank's work, how history enters his taxonomy; or if he is claiming to identify a trans-historical taxonomy of embodiment.

7. For a discussion of the appeal of 'the exotic woman' and the rise of new multicultural supermodels see Glenn O'Brien (1991).

8. Runway grunge, as the deconstructionist fashion of Belgian designer Martin Margiela is sometimes called, is merely the latest movement in rhythmic modulation of the fashion system, designed not so much to express an aesthetic or cultural theory, but rather to keep the fashion apparatus well supplied with consumable and ultimately disposable sign commodities.

9. For an extended discussion of the way in which cosmetic surgeons rely on western ideals of feminine beauty see Balsamo (1992).

10. The Jargon File, version 2.0.10, 01 July 1992. Available on-line from: ftp.uu.net. Also published as *The Hacker's Dictionary*.

11. See especially: Sherry Turkle and Seymour Papert (1990) and Dannielle Bernstein (1991).

12. For a discussion of the ethical/policy dimensions of computer communication see Jeffrey Bairstow (1990), Bob Brown (1990), Pamela Varley (1991), Laurence H. Tribe (1991) and Willard Uncapher (1991).

13. For a discussion of the gendered nature of communication technologies see especially Lana Rakow (1988). For other studies of the gendered nature of computer use see: Sara Kiesler, Lee Sproull and Jacquelynne Eccles (1985) and Sherry Turkle and Seymour Papert (1990).

14. Hoai-An Truong, 'Gender Issues in Online Communication', CFP 93 (Version 4.1). Available on-line from: ftp.eff.org. No date given.

15. The man in the cover photograph wears liquid screen glasses that come with a hand-held computer and earphones. For his viewing pleasure, the computer can transmit video images and other audiovisual material to the eyeglass screens. The cover photo is a striking visual emblem of the future high-tech body which, from *Life's* point of view, is gendered male. 'The Future and You', a 30-page preview: 2000 and beyond, *Life* February 1989.

16. Silicon breast forms are the only artificial body part available in the Sears Health Care Specialog (Sears, Roebuck and Co., 1988). They take up one page of a two-page layout on 'Post Mastectomy Needs', opposite the catalog page of mastectomy bras. There are four different breast forms, including an asymmetrical form, a 'youthful, symmetrical' form, and an oval shaped form with nipple. In the March 1988 catalogue the prices for these forms ranged from $60.00 to $160.00.

17. In her book *The Cancer Journals*, Audre Lorde (1980) denounces the 'travesty of prosthesis', and suggests that women who choose breast prosthesis in a fantasy effort to be 'the same as before' participate in the cultural cover-up of institutionally induced causes of breast cancer. Although Lorde acknowledges the pressures of conformity and the loneliness of difference that compel some women to wear a breast form, she is unflinching in her critique of the ideological function of such a prosthesis.

18. The quotation is from Nancy Tosta, chief of the Branch of Geographic Data Coordination of the National Mapping Division, US Geological Survey in Reston, Virginia ('Who's Got the Data?', *Geo Info Systems*, September 1992: 24–7). Tosta's prediction is supported by other statements about the US government's efforts to build a Geographic Information System (GIS): a database system whereby 'all public information can be referenced by location'. See Lisa Warnecke (1992). Managing data, acquiring new data and guarding data integrity are issues of concern for GIS managers. Because of the cost of acquiring new data and guarding data integrity, GIS managers sometimes charge a fee for providing information. This process of charging 'has thrown [them] into a morass of issues about public records and freedom of information; the value of data, privacy, copyrights, and liability and the roles of public and private sectors in disseminating information' (see Nancy Tosta, 1991).

19. From the letter to the National Science Foundation Division Director, Jonathan Friedlaender. The

letter, and Friedlaender's response, circulated on several electronic discussion lists: one copy was posted to sci-tech-studies on 21 December 1993.

20. Here I implicitly draw on Teresa deLauretis's transformation of Foucault's notion of the 'technology of sex' into the 'technologies of gender'. She uses this phrase to name the process by which gender is 'both a representation and self-representation produced by various social technologies, such as cinema, as well as institutional discourses, epistemologies, and critical practices' (Teresa deLauretis, 1987: ix).

References

Bairstow, Jeffrey (1990) 'Who Reads Your Electronic Mail?', *Electronic Business* 16(11): 92.

Balsamo, Anne (1992) 'On the Cutting Edge: Cosmetic Surgery and the Technological Production of the Gendered Body', *Camera Obscura* 28: 207–37.

Balsamo, Anne (1995) *Technologies of the Gendered Body: Reading Cyborg Women.* Durham, NC: Duke University Press.

Bernstein, Dannielle (1991) 'Comfort and Experience with Computing: Are They the Same for Women and Men?', *SIGCSE Bulletin* 23(3): 57–60.

Brown, Bob (1990) 'EMA Urges Users to Adopt Policy on E-mail Privacy', *Network World* 29 Oct.: 7.44.2.

Cadigan, Pat (1991) *Synners.* New York: Bantam.

de Certeau, Michel (1984) *The Practice of Everyday Life*, trans. Steven Rendall. Berkeley: University of California Press.

deLauretis, Teresa (1987) *Technologies of Gender: Essays on Theory, Film, and Fiction.* Bloomington: Indiana University Press.

Feher, Michel (1987) 'Of Bodies and Technologies', pp. 159–65 in Hal Foster (ed.), *Discussions in Contemporary Culture.* DIA Art Foundation. Seattle, WA: Bay Press.

Feher, Michel (1989) 'Introduction', pp. 11–17 in *Zone 3: Fragments for a History of the Human Body.* New York: Urzone.

Frank, Arthur W. (1991) 'For a Sociology of the Body: An Analytical Review', pp. 36–102, in Mike Featherstone, Mike Hepworth and Bryan S. Turner (eds) *The Body: Social Process and Cultural Theory.* London: Sage.

Frow, John (1991) 'Michel de Certeau and the Practice of Representation', *Cultural Studies* 5(1): 52–60.

Gutin, Joann C. (1994) 'End of the Rainbow', *Discover* November: 71–5.

Kiesler, Sara, Lee Sproull and Jacquelynne Eccles (1985) 'Poolhalls, Chips and War Games: Women in the Culture of Computing', *Psychology of Women Quarterly* 9(4): 451–62.

Kroker, Arthur and Marilouise Kroker (eds) (1987) *Body Invaders: Panic Sex in America.* New York: St Martins Press.

Levidow, Les (1991) 'Women who Make the Chips', *Science as Culture* 2(10): 103–24.

Lorde, Audre (1980) *The Cancer Journals.* San Francisco, CA: Spinsters Ink.

McLuhan, Marshall (1959) *The Mechanical Bride: Folklore of Industrial Culture.* New York: Beacon Press.

O'Brien, Glenn (1991) 'Perfect Strangers: Our Love of the Exotic', *Elle* Sept.: 274–6.

Rakow, Lana (1988) 'Women and the Telephone: The Gendering of a Communications Technology', pp. 207–8 in Cheris Kramarae (ed.) *Technology and Women's Voices: Keeping in Touch.* Boston: Routledge.

Terry, Jennifer (1989) 'The Body Invaded: Medical Surveillance of Women as Reproducers', *Socialist Review* 39: 13–44.

Tosta, Nancy (1991) 'Public Access: Right or Privilege?' *Geo Info System* Nov./Dec.: 20–5.

Tosta, Nancy (1992) 'Who's Got the Data?', *Geo Info Systems* Sept.: 24–7.

Tribe, Laurence H. (1991) 'The Constitution in Cyberspace', *The Humanist* 51(5): 15–21.

Turkle, Sherry and Seymour Papert (1990) 'Epistemological Pluralism: Styles and Voices within the Computer Culture', *Signs* 16(11): 128–57.

Turner, Bryan S. (1984) *The Body and Society: Explorations in Social Theory*. Oxford: Basil Blackwell.

Turner, Bryan S. (1991) 'Recent Developments in the Theory of the Body', pp. 1–35 in Mike Featherstone, Mike Hepworth and Bryan S. Turner (eds) *The Body: Social Process and Cultural Theory*. London: Sage.

Uncapher, Willard (1991) 'Trouble in Cyberspace', *The Humanist* 51(5): 5–14.

Varley, Pamela (1991) 'Electronic Democracy', *Technology Review* Nov./Dec.: 40–3.

Warnecke, Lisa (1992) 'Building the National GI/GIS Partnership', *Geo Info Systems* April: 16–23.

Anne Balsamo is Director of Graduate Studies in the Program in Information Design and Technology School of Literature, Communication and Culture at the Georgia Institute of Technology. Her book, *Technologies of the Gendered Body: Reading Cyborg Women*, was recently published by Duke University Press (1995).

Cyber(body)parts: Prosthetic Consciousness

ROBERT RAWDON WILSON

> As the distance between them gradually diminished Mondaugen saw that her left eye was artificial: she, noticing his curiosity, obligingly removed the eye and held it out to him in the hollow of her hand. A bubble blown translucent, its 'white' would show up when in the socket as a half-lit sea green. A fine network of nearly microscopic fractures covered its surface. Inside were the delicately-wrought wheels, springs, ratchets of a watch, wound by a gold key which fräulein Meroving wore on a slender chain round her neck. Darker green and flecks of gold had been fused into twelve vaguely zodiacal shapes, placed annular on the surface of the bubble to represent the iris and also the face of the watch. (Pynchon, 1966: 237)

When they fail, the body's parts (ordinarily so silent within the illusion of a 'whole' body) scream their presence. When they are replaced, they grumble unnervingly in a new tongue. In having a prosthesis, I experience a double consciousness. When I put on my glasses or my contact lenses, I can see more clearly. I also correct a defect in my vision. At some point in the near future, it may be possible to have prosthetic eyes. Contact lenses and glasses will seem primitive then; no longer commonplace, they will be difficult to find even for a person who can remember their use. I may wear a 'visor', like Commander La Forge in *Star Trek – The Next Generation*, or a fully functional artificial eyeball, unlike the myth-inscribed one that Pynchon imagines in his fable of plastic surgery and bodily metamorphosis, *V.* Even glasses modify consciousness. It is not merely that I can now see better, but also that an aspect of my being has been put behind me, but never out of mind as well. My ocular prosthesis elevates me to a higher plane of fulfilment, towards a more ideal conception of myself, but it also reminds me of how I have slipped from the plane that I had always occupied.

My body seems always to be dissolving, failing in one way or another, needing supplements. I feed it vitamins and healthy food and as one part after another begins to fail, I discuss with various doctors the possibilities of replacement. The knee that

I injured at 17 on a motorcycle has been replaced by one made from hard acrylic and held to the bone by epoxy. I will someday have other parts replaced with either artificial parts or with transplanted body parts from someone else (but which someday will be grown in incubator animals, such as pigs). If my kidneys begin to go, I can make use of a collective prosthetic kidney, called a dialysis machine, that I will share with other people in a similar condition. When my penis begins to dysfunction, if it does (and common male experience assures me that, most predictably, it will sadly do just that), my personal physician will refer me to a urologist who will recommend a penile implant which will actually improve my normal performance by making me permanently virile. My penis, always a 'phantasmatic' body part (Butler, 1993: 88–9), will have been modified towards enhanced performance. The implant may simply extend my penis so that it will never be entirely flaccid, always sufficiently turgid for action, or it may involve a small hydraulic mechanism that will permit me to pump my penis into shape simply by squeezing a tiny plastic reservoir that the urologist will have tucked away within my scrotum, like a third testicle. The bio-mechanical expansions of my natural potential may so please me that I shall return to the urologist and ask for a cosmetic phalloplasty in order to have my penis sculpted into a more attractive shape. Once I have had that operation, my penis will have been lengthened (by cutting the suspensory ligaments that join it to the pubic bone) and thickened (by the liposuction of fat from my buttocks or abdomen) and I will seem, to my own mind at least, irresistibly bionic. (A person might also undergo neovaginoplasty, for cosmetic or transsexual reconstruction. I do not know if such a procedure would be experienced as bionic.) If I do not like the possibilities (a permanently semi-erect penis will be conspicuous, especially when swimming, and the hydraulic mechanism may break, probably will in fact, leaving me with a piece of ruined machinery in my scrotum, a tiny replica of an abandoned industrial site), then the doctor can prescribe injections of prostaglandin, Phentolamine, papaverine or some other chemical or hormonal fluid (Govier et al., 1993). I will then prick a syringe into the corpora cavernosa (left or right, depending upon the hand I use) and inject myself. This will leave me with a magnificent erection that will last for two or three hours, or (I would hope) long after ejaculation. (It may also leave me with an embarrassing case of priapism, but, always optimistic in these matters, I shall hope not.) In each of these instances, I will have been improved. I will also have been diminished. Each prosthetic modification also marks the distance I will have travelled from my original physical condition.[1]

The human body interacts with machines in many ways. Many of these ways are obvious, but none are ever simple. Some kind of system will always be presupposed. The simplest machine floats on the surface of numerous hidden systems, networks of connections and conceptual overlap. A machine that no longer functions or which either has lost or never had a purpose will seem, as Heidegger expresses it, 'conspicuous'. It will become equipment that is in 'un-readiness-to-hand' (Heidegger, 1962: 103). I draw from Heidegger's proposition the corollary that machines are only seen 'fully' when, no longer in use, they cannot be seen fully. It may well be the case that machines are so omnipresent in the western technological environment that they are also invisible in the sense that they seldom attract attention, becoming visible, as David Porush argues, 'only when resurrected by fear' or by metaphor (1985: 8) in the abrupt shock of defamiliarization. However, this seems far less important than the invisibility of their hidden systems. While they are still functioning, the extended systems that make machines possible are largely out of sight, too complex to be seen easily. Still functioning, a machine is a node, a visible nexus of unseen rhizomes; no longer functioning, it becomes conspicuous, a thing in the world that can be seen but not understood. The most obvious example would be the use of tools. Philosophical optimists like to observe that human beings are toolmakers (rather than, say, predators or destroyers): 'Toolmaking man learned', one such optimist writes, opening a proposition after which any fact from human history might follow (Halacy, 1965: 25). There have been many tools, and there will be many more, not all of which have suggested reasons for either joy or hope. The strongest form of the toolmaking argument would hold that the human mind can constitute an interface with everything in the world (or cosmos), including all physical laws, to create tools. In *that* proposition, there is neither woe nor wonder, only fascination.

Imagine a human ancestor picking up a stone with which to crack a shell or a nut, or using a twig to winkle out marrow from an already-gnawed bone. Another one, perhaps gimpy from combat with a mastodon, has discovered he could use a fallen branch to improve his walking. The branch actually performs much the same work, supporting rather than replacing, as my prosthetic knee. Both ancient tools were elementary prosthetic devices: they enhanced the body (the fist, the legs), increasing its force and range, but both were possible only because underlying systems of bio-mechanics, activated by cultural objectives, brought them into use. Today, resting in a glass case in a museum, both devices would be conspicuous, surrounded by their mere visibility and uprooted from their original cultural domains, with only the museum's documentation to provide a partial, but highly artificial, re-enrooting. You may see small chip marks in the stone, for example, and the documentation will explain that these show that a piece of hard stone, perhaps flint, had been used to rough-hew it. The documentation will scarcely reanimate the system of discovery, trade and craftsmanship that once obtained and once fully shaped the smashing-stone. What documentation could fully make sense of, or re-embed, the 'mountain of leather prostheses and wooden limbs' that you can see on display at Auschwitz (Douglas, 1994:13)?

The modes of body–machine interaction are supplementary. Of course, a machine may kill you or cause you devastating injury. So far as machines are concerned, the world offers a million ways to die. Every technology carries its dark twin or, hidden within its total implicature, a death-beam capable of destroying you. Science fiction returns obsessively to scenarios in which computers break their programmatic limitations and attempt to seize control, or androids go wrong and claim their independence or seek, as the 'replicants' do in Ridley Scott's 1982 film *Blade Runner*, extended and enhanced 'life'. In a favourite narrative motif of *Star Trek – The Next Generation*, hypercomplex machines (such as starships) evolve life. Even my glasses, products of a benign technology in common use, might shatter in an accident and create a glass shard that could drive into my brain making optometry wholly irrelevant. Thus any consideration of prostheses has to take into account their potential failure and, even, the conditions under which they might go wrong or turn against their users. The consciousness of machines always includes, as Porush observes, a dimension of fear. There is also fear's most intimate radical, an element of potential disappointment: the prosthesis may not work, or may work inadequately, or may entail unwanted consequences. However, I am primarily interested in prosthetic consciousness as a reflexive awareness of supplementation. What happens within the mind once an exotic mechanical part, reflecting an unseen technological system entirely alien to all your previous bodily processes, has been joined (whether integrated or merely appended) to your body?

The argument begins with two distinctions. *First*, all machines are both hard and soft. There will always be a system of instructions, of operating commands, such as a program. Hardware and software invite themselves as metaphors: 'at one level or another one always needs both in any machine' (Plotinsky, 1993:297). This may seem obvious, but (if it is) it is so only because a tool uprooted from context, an *ur*-tool, such as the smashing-stone in the museum display case, conspicuously has no system, no accessible software. The difference between a functioning and a non-functioning tool is, precisely, the presence or absence of operating commands, its system or culturally understood rhizomes. It is also within the operating system that problems arise, the 'undecidables and double binds' (Plotinsky, 1993:298), that do often make machines appear to be schizophrenic. Those science fiction scenarios that emphasize the turning or going 'wrong' of machines, from simple to hypercomplex, play upon the potential schizophrenia, the sudden undecidables and abrupt double binds, within the hidden operating system, the software. *Second*, a prosthesis is not an android. An android, existing in the contemporary world only in the crude prototypical form of drone-robots, even though deeply etched into our cultural mythology, is a self-contained artificial life form. A prosthesis is a part, a supplement to a human body, and not, however complexly integrated, self-contained. (It would be an interesting problem for a science fiction writer whether an android *could have* a prosthesis since each replacement part, even if it enhanced previous levels of task-accomplishment, would be fully consolidated within the android's cyberbody.) As I am using the term in this essay, a prosthesis is an artificial body part that supplements the body, but a part that carries an operating system different from the body's organic processes. Currently, every human body part other than the brain and the nervous system can be replaced prosthetically. Even on the mere threshold of a full-scale cyber-age, the multiplicity of the human body seems astounding. Stephen Hawking is a good example of that multiplicity. Because he uses a voice prosthesis, his vocal presence is electronic whether you are standing next to him or on Mars. You could never be certain where his edges are. Multiplicity is another way of not being sure where people's edges are, where their identity begins and ends.[2] My prostheses elevate me to a higher plane of fulfilment, or more ideal conception of myself, but they also remind me of how far I have slipped from the plane I have always occupied. They attribute to me a multiplicity that I had never planned. Prostheses blur edges even while refining capacity. Hence a prosthesis marks an intersection between two systems, two underlying networks of rhizomes, technological and organic. A prosthesis is a cyber(body)part.

Yearning and Disgust

The initial uses of the term 'cyborg' to signify an artificially extended homeostatic control system functioning unconsciously reflect an optimistic conviction that technology can, and will, expand merely organic potential. Artificial body parts will serve as simple drones, as obedient and beneficial tools. D.S. Halacy Jr, whose early study of cyborgs attempts to outline all possible uses and environments, observes that a 'hybrid human may well be a forerunner of the men of the future' (Halacy, 1965: 9).[3] The optimistic view that prostheses are generally servile and availing carries over into the discussion of hybrid body forms, man plus integrated tool, and cyborgs. Two 1970s TV programmes, *The Six Million Dollar Man* and its spin-off *The Bionic Woman*, splendidly capture the eye-bulging, mouth-gaping yearning for cyborgian evolution.[4] Subsequent reflection upon the possibilities of hybrid bodies has opened a rather darker perspective. A cyborg, such as the Bionic Woman, who possesses legs that will enable her to run faster than a car or leap over houses or who has acquired ears that allow her to hear faint sounds at immense distances might not prove always to be a friend or even a good neighbour. Recent science fiction stresses the dark side, the 'undecidables and double binds', of cyborgian potential in which modified humanoids, such as the *Star Trek* Borg, pose terrifying threats which must be overcome.

More powerfully yet, a line of analysis has begun to develop in which the 'cyborg' provides a metaphor for the discursive codes that program our biological existences. The argument often seems to have a particular focus upon the condition of women in a patriarchal world since (it is claimed) the historical discourse of men encodes the female body. The discourse of man, Gayatri Spivak writes (with unmistakable undertones of Roland Barthes) is 'the metaphor of woman' (Spivak, 1983:169). That is, women have had to accept men's language but have used it obliquely, as metaphoric, to express their own, distinct, experience. However, the actual application of the cyborg analogy encompasses both genders. Both women and men must exist within an inherited, trans-individual discourse. Even if that discourse is identified as male, or as patriarchal, it is nonetheless relentlessly imposed upon all human individuals most of whom will participate in it uneasily. 'Language is the effect of articulation, and so are bodies' (Haraway, 1992:324). We are all chimeras, Donna Haraway argues,

> theorized and fabricated hybrids of machines and organism; in short, we are cyborgs. The cyborg is our ontology; it gives us our politics. The cyborg is a condensed image of both imagination and material reality, the two joined centers structuring any possibility of historical transformation. (Haraway, 1990:191)[5]

If knowledge does bring freedom (as so many philosophers have supposed), then knowing how consciousness has been constructed in cyborgian fashion should bring the freedom to revise these constraints. Thus Haraway argues that women, existing within 'the integrated circuit' of **patr**iarchal domination, can reconstruct – creating a new cyborg (but not becoming a non-cyborg) – their consciousness. If we 'learn how to read these webs of power and social life, we might learn new couplings, new coalitions' (Haraway, 1990:212). The solution to the condition of being a (discursive) cyborg is not to turn your back upon technology, but rather to understand it well enough to use it for your own constructive purposes. 'I would rather be a cyborg', she concludes, 'than a goddess' (Haraway, 1990:223). The normal ambivalence about prostheses, hybrid body parts or cyborgian enhancement carries over even to the level of metaphor. It is possible both to yearn for technological amplification and to feel disgust at the prospect.

I want now to turn away from the problems of cyborgs and cyborgian consciousness. I have slotted them into my discussion only to register the strongest position currently available with regard to cyber(body)parts. The prostheses that I have in mind, such as penile implants, will not transform you into a cyborg, but will be enough to animate the divided consciousness that machines create.

They are 'cyber' in the sense that they entail vast, but unseen, technological systems (of innovation, experimentation, applications, development, production, marketing, medical installation and monitoring) and will, in a limited sense, compose a 'cybernetic organism, a hybrid of machine and organism' (Haraway, 1990: 191). Still, they will not actually allow you fully to become a cyborg, an integrated being whose technological amplifications will be superior to the biological parts they replace. Your prostheses will only supplement your body with respect to dysfunctional parts, such as an incorrigibly flaccid penis, but not exceed their normal optimum performance. (Unless a bad case of priapism would count as exceeding normal performance.) Only on the level of metaphor (which is where Haraway's argument takes place) is it possible to think of yourself as fully a (discursive) cyborg. Nonetheless, you may still yearn for technological enhancement and yet experience disgust at the alien presence within your body. What is the problem with machines? Why do they inspire such complex affects as, among many others, disgust?

Consider disgust for a moment. It seems to be a psycho-visceral response to physical experiences, such as seeing or smelling excrement, diseased flesh or corpses, in which an overpowering nausea subjugates voluntary control. There will always be what experimental psychologists call the 'disgust face': the nose narrows and the lips purse, twisting upwards.[6] However, the crinkled expression of disgust may mask a desire to impose oneself as distant from, or superior to, an action, an event. In this sense, disgust is a moral or philosophical position. It can be a physical metaphor for ethical judgement. That is what happens when people wrinkle their noses at food they think beneath their social class or cultural caste, or which seems to violate their self-imposed diets. It is the vegetarian's overt response to the offer of meat; the fruitarian's to the offer of vegetables. It is what happens when one person observes behaviour that he or she disapproves of. A person simply begins to contort the face into the well-known paths that (seemingly) lead to the feeling of disgust. The facework is intended to signify definite visceral reactions which, though not actually present, the other person can imagine. Disgust is not only a powerful, involuntary affect, but also a subtle mode of judgement in which the affect itself is pretended. It is both real and make-believe, an affect that can be affected.

People can certainly pretend to experience disgust in the presence of machines. There may still be scholars, troglodytes or mere luddites, who prefer to write with pens (inherited, it may be, from their fathers) and who make the disgust face over computers, but also over technology generally and, in particular, over electronic writing. You may say that such judgements are hypocritical, but (in a world unevenly split between Luddites and ludites) they are also inevitable. Not everyone likes, or can like, machines. Even if Luddites do not actually experience visceral

;, they may wish to do so and feel that they should pretend to express it. Why
chines give rise to disgust? There seem to be two relevant propositions:
machines are implacable, 'soulless' in an old lingo; machines are composed out of
parts, lacking organic integrity.

The opposition between a human person who can experience many affects,
including compassion and mercy, and a machine that feels nothing is very old.
Descartes refers to animals as machines because they have, he thinks, no souls.
Legends return again and again to the merciless, implacable hunger of animals,
wolves for example, or, even more horrifically, of insects. Alfred Hitchcock's 1963
film, *The Birds*, builds explicitly upon the birds' unswerving, remorseless attack.[7]
In the tradition of horror, lacking a soul, in the manner of a *golem* or a zombie,
means that the creature will be incapable of compassion and will be deaf to your
pleas. Machines inspire a similar response. If you find yourself caught in a machine,
an assembly line for example as Charlie Chaplin's character does in *Modern Times*,
you will not expect it to stop simply because you cry out that it should. Robots,
androids and cyborgs all can create genuine horror effects in part because they can
be supposed to behave soullessly, like Cartesian animals, and hence act without pity
or compassion. The Borg in *Star Trek – The Next Generation* or, on a less
technologically advanced plane, the Daleks in *Dr Who* (they retain a humanoid
brain inside their machine bodies whereas the 'cybermen', in the same BBC series,
appear to be entirely androidic), all evoke horror because they act without
human-like feelings.

The second proposition may be even more important. Machines are composed
out of parts. They may be assembled and disassembled. They are open to
modifications or 'retoolings'. The very idea of being given new parts is only slightly
less horrible, if it is at all, than the corresponding idea of losing parts. Your right eye
might fall out or your genitalia drop off but, appalling as that would be,
contemplating a technological replacement would not be much compensation and
might even constitute another source of horror. A machine both sheds parts and
acquires new ones easily. The human perspective seems to insist upon organic
integrity as the only possible norm. Of course, a machine will have integrity, but it
will exist only on a cyber level. (It is my computer's operating system that gives it
unity and without which it would be, less or more, only a collection of parts. That
is, one part constitutes a super-set for the others.) It is the hidden system of
conceptual rhizomes that constructs integrity for a machine, but that systematic
net, invisible to most eyes, is so different from organic integration that it might,
once perceived, only create more horror. The image of a being composed out of
parts, any single one of which might be replaced or simply removed, has had an
evocative place in horror fiction and film. Furthermore, the perception of organic

parts separated from their former being or of inorganic and organic parts linked together to create a biomachine, seems to cause disgust as well as horror. That puts the problem of human prostheses into focus. You might suppose that disgust turns upon the visceral aspects of the human body, 'the fact that bodily functions and the ripping open of bodies to expose flesh, blood, guts, shit is something which only living beings and not machines possess' (Featherstone, personal communication, 17 January 1995: 1). However, disgust is a psycho-visceral concept: it moves the mind as well as, or even more than, the body. It is the idea of a prosthesis, whatever my new cyber(body)part happens to be, that causes disgust, not its acrylic or metal surfaces. Consider the interconnection between parts, whether being composed of or being dissolved into, and disgust.

At the core of any theory of disgust lies the experience of decay, dissolution and deliquescence. Muck, ooze, putrescence, rot and slime all evoke powerful negative reactions. These are the staple phenomena of horror fiction and film for excellent reasons: deliquescing or putrescent bodies, all dissolving slimewards, mark the presence of monsters, or else function as the spoor that points towards the monster's lair. Thus horror and disgust, intimately joined, reflect each other as conclusion and evidence. Characters in horror narratives loathe having to make physical contact with the monster. In fiction one has to imagine a fundamental convention of horror that can be shown extravagantly in film: fear and disgust, as Noël Carroll puts it, 'etched on the characters' features'.

> [Monsters] are putrid or moldering things, or they hail from oozing places, or they are made of dead or rotting flesh, or chemical waste, or are associated with vermin, disease, or crawling things. They are not only quite dangerous but they also make one's skin creep. Characters regard them not only with fear but with loathing, with a combination of terror and disgust. (Carroll, 1990: 23)

The traces that indicate the existence of an unseen monster drip, leak or ooze. Everything along the path founders towards muck and slime. These dissolving traces point ahead to the central fact of horror. The monster, or the monstrous event, that you begin to anticipate will constitute an assault upon your integrity. Boundaries turn liquid in horror. The ego's 'fortified castle' (Kristeva, 1982: 46–8), always with gossamer battlements built upon sand, crumbles and begins to flow abjectly shitwards. Human persons are de-integrated, dissolved or broken down into distinct parts. The integrity of the individual, normally so secure behind its defences of being and identity, slips into self-loss and abjection.

There are several theoretical models available to explain the powerfulness of disgust as an affect. All of them emphasize dissolution (bodily rot, putrescence and slime), but most of them are concerned, even to the point of fixation, with the problem of how affects such as disgust are learned. Moral philosophers have argued that disgust, as a strong repugnance to certain acts, constitutes a universal feature of the human 'relationship to the rest of the world' (Kekes, 1992:36). In the absence of disgust, it can be argued, it would be difficult to see how any prohibition could work other than through the fear of punishment or disease. Anything would be acceptable as behaviour, and society, straining to contain the acceptability of all acts, would collapse, life within it becoming inevitably nasty, brutish and (most likely) short. Hence John Kekes distinguishes between a rather ordinary disgust, simple squeamishness, and the deep disgust that follows observing, or even contemplating, certain profoundly unacceptable acts. He writes

> . . . if some people, possessing a contemporary Western sensibility, are not disgusted in certain situations, then there must be some very special explanation of their failure in terms of repression, brutalization, pathological inattention, or the like. The experiences include eating faeces, disembowelling a person, drinking pus, being splattered with someone's brain, the sight and smell of putrefying corpses, the spectacle of extreme torture, such as dismembering live humans with a chainsaw, or immersion in excrement. (Kekes, 1992:433).[8]

I would not wish to argue that these acts are not deeply disgusting. However, I think that it is important that, as most people know, they do take place, occasionally as a general practice or as a matter of state policy, and (thus) cannot be universally disgusting. Apparently, millions of people in western culture enjoy seeing representations of all these acts, in horror films and fiction, even in documentaries that explore such practices when they are, or have been, state policy in various countries (such as Nazi Germany or Argentina during the 'dirty war'). The moral philosopher's position ignores both the extent to which disgust (which is, in any case, culture-specific) may be unlearned and the ways in which it is, in many professions from anthropology to surgery, managed. Other theoretical models, such as psychoanalysis and social constructionism, underscore the processes of socialization, within the family or in society, that condition the mental/bodily boundaries beyond which disgusting experiences occur. These are, at best, partial accounts. Disgust can be both learned and unlearned. Humans, Norbert Elias writes, 'not only can but *must* learn in order to become fully human' (Elias, 1987:351). An affect such as disgust, deeply encoded yet highly metamorphic, changes as the world's boundaries are relearned. Above all, disgust can be managed. What I need for this discussion is a model that attempts to explain the imagination of disgust. What happens when you imagine deliquescent body parts?

Jean-Paul Sartre's analysis of viscosity in *Being and Nothingness* (adapted for empirical observation in Mary Douglas's *Purity and Danger*) suggests a fruitful model.[9] Sliminess, Sartre argues, invokes 'a host of human and moral' character- istics: 'A handshake, a smile, a thought, a feeling can be slimy' (Sartre, 1956:604). The slimy 'reveals itself as essentially ambiguous because its fluidity exists in slow motion; there is a sticky thickness in its liquidity; it represents in itself a dawning triumph of the solid over the liquid'. Slime is, Sartre adds, 'the agony of water' (Sartre, 1956:607). The sensation of a solid melting or of a liquid solidifying, both behaving aberrantly, can make a rather powerful mental impression. Pus (one of Kekes's examples) strikes me as an extremely powerful instance of slime, and one privileged in both horror and decadent literature, since it is the body itself, transformed by infection, flowing in thick ooze.

Slime suggests the transience and drift of things. Imagine a loved one's eyes or tongue falling wetly into your hands, or that person's blood thickening into verminous sludge around your fingers. (Here one enters the province of horror, a narrative domain that is as visual as it is conceptual, across the borders of which exist experiences too appalling to contemplate, too irresistible to ignore.) A vast archive of images, showing decay, dissolution, putrefaction and rot everywhere, can flash before the mind's eye when the hand touches, or the eyes see, ooze and muck. In the very apprehension of the slimy there is, Sartre observes, 'a gluey substance, compromising and without equilibrium, like the haunting memory of a metamorphosis' (Sartre, 1956:610).

Mary Douglas's enlargement of Sartre's argument brings her knowledge of ethnography, her own fieldwork and that of other anthropologists, into the analysis of slime. Dirt, she argues, like everything else in human culture, expresses a hidden symbolic system. Dirt is matter that is out of place. It is 'never a unique, isolated event. Where there is dirt there is system. Dirt is the by-product of a systematic ordering and classification of matter' (Douglas, 1984:35). Pollution occurs when matter that, in the functioning system, has been classified as dirt slides over into the categories of the clean, or at least the non-dirt. Filth contaminates. (A prosthesis, viewed from within the natural system of the body, is 'out of place' and may even seem to contaminate the body as a 'whole'.) Douglas can thus argue that certain experiences evoke disgust because they manifest category slippage and breakdown. The abominations cited in *Leviticus*, for example, involve animals that do not belong clearly to one category or another: they are conceptually 'sticky'. 'The underlying principle of cleanness in animals', she writes, 'is that they shall conform fully to their class'. If they fail to conform fully, then they are imperfect members of their class and may be seen to 'confound the general scheme of the world' (Douglas, 1984:55). Thus Sartre's philosophical analysis of sliminess as a problem of the imagination provides, in the hands of an anthropologist, a very strong account of the human experience of disgust, contamination and pollution. It applies to everyone (a proposition with which Sartre would surely agree), there being no 'special distinction between primitives and moderns' on this score, and everyone will know some things that are anomalous, not belonging clearly to known categories, tending slimewards

(Douglas, 1984:40). I experience my prostheses as anomalous, even (in dark moments) as personal slime.

The Sartre–Douglas model, with its mental–cultural sweep, subsumes the other models. Freud's analysis of disgust as a reaction-formation that helps control the possibilities for sexual perversion, largely (if not wholly) connected with the rejection of faeces during toilet training, transforming excrement into filth, falls easily within an analysis of anomalous states and category slippage. Still, there are problems, unexplained areas, that this model, for all its subsumptive strength, fails to settle. What happens in the mind when one observes an anomalous object, or someone performing acts outside their normal place? What corresponds, inside the skull as it were, to the perception of slime? (What happens when you begin to perceive your prosthesis from within your body's natural system, not from within the relevant cyber system?) Sartre puts an emphasis on the inwardness of the experience. It is impossible, he argues, 'to derive the value of the psychic symbolism "slimy" from the brute quality of the *this* and equally impossible to project the meaning of the *this* in terms of a knowledge of psychic attitudes' (Sartre, 1956:605). The things themselves, both objects and acts, are undeniably material, but psychic responses are otherwise: active, vigorously associative, inclusive. I take representations of decay, rot and deliquescence, including unlikely wetness, all things that tend slimewards, to be basic building blocks in the creation of a disgust–horror world. They recur so often in horror films, even when not explicitly necessary to the action, that one can scarcely think about the properties of such worlds without beginning with the indications of slime. Horror films often stress the monster's liquidness, its decaying moistness. They also underscore the vulnerability of body parts: the fear of losing a part of your body constitutes a primal source of horror. The problem of the cyber(body)part now comes into perspective. Prostheses cause disgust because they indicate the collapse of the body, its fall from integrity. This is how horror engages the imagination. In horror everything about the human person is unsettled, made sticky and (even) slimy. For example, all the 'taken-for-granted boundaries of gender are problematised as well as exploited' in horror (Tudor, 1995:7). Threatened by dissolution from all directions, characters can lose their discursive formations (such as gender) as easily as their body parts. In horror, the unfolding processes of decomposition and deliquescence may transform each character into a genderless, de-socialized, even nameless metahuman.[10]

The disgust that body parts, separated or rotting, can cause, and which performs so effectively as a convention in horror fiction and film, indicates one dimension of prosthetic consciousness. The classics of horror fiction recurrently fragment the human body, or underscore single parts for effect. The monster in Mary Shelley's *Frankenstein* is composed from distinct cadaverous parts (an aspect of the tale made vivid in all the film versions). One of the most instructive examples is H.G. Wells's *The Island of Dr Moreau*, an allegory of vivisection and plastic surgery, in which human shapes (twisted or otherwise not quite right) are surgically constructed by bodily modification and the supplementation of different animal parts. Wells's narrator, Charles Edward Prendick, experiences a 'quivering disgust' in the presence of Dr Moreau's creatures once he begins to grasp the island's secret': 'Imagine yourself surrounded by all the most horrible cripples and maniacs it is possible to conceive, and you may understand a little of my feelings with these grotesque caricatures of humanity about me' (Wells, 1988: 60). An appended body part not only recalls the previous, now missing, organic part, but actively calls into question the body's integrity. A prosthesis, however hopeful and future-yearning, is also a mnemotechnic. It evokes a consciousness of dis-integration (which may be either, or both, historical or fictional). For that reason, a hybrid body poses a disturbing dilemma: would you (would anyone) choose to have yourself enhanced by the addition of prosthetic parts when that process, however it begins, must dis-integrate your body, dissolving its boundaries, and batter down the fortified castle of your identity?

Being Conscious of Cyber(body)parts

Cyborgs have appeared repeatedly in science fiction films of the past thirty years.[11] They may be distinguished by the degree of connection and reintegration with which their prosthetic parts function. My glasses, for instance, are scarcely connected to my body at all, but a penile implant, if I were to acquire one someday, would be intimately (as it were) a part. In Paul Verhoeven's *Robocop* (1987), the transformation of the dead, or almost-dead policeman, into a cyborg requires the elimination of most of his body other than his face and brain. One executive of the corporation that is manufacturing the cyborg exclaims, when he learns that the doctors have saved one of the policeman's arms, that the objective is 'total prosthesis' and orders the arm amputated. (It is never made clear how much body Murphy retains, other than his brain which has been modified by the implantation of a programmable chip. He eats a baby food-like pap that oozes from a machine next to his chair-bed, but a metal shaft driven into the area above his heart does not harm him. He certainly has only prosthetic appendages.) *Robocop* is particularly interesting because it contrasts Murphy, the cyborg cop, with an android. The android is called 'Ed 209' (signifying 'enforcement droid 209') and is squat, ungainly, clumsy and given to malfunctions. It has too many 'glitches'. (Though quite deadly, it comes across as a *comic* representation of a human being.) Later, the cyborg outwits the android and wins a shoot-out. This plays to human chauvinism:

the sense that humans *are* better than machines (hence manned space travel will always be necessary) and that a good cyborg, simply because it retains elements of a human brain, will out-think, and so outperform, a good android any time.

The action of *Robocop* is set in a near-future, trash-culture Detroit which has been compared to the Los Angeles world of *Blade Runner* (Maslin, 1987:103). Verhoeven's Detroit is not over-populated, but it is in the hands of criminal gangs which are run by large corporations. In this Detroit, the police have been privatized by the corporation that supplies arms to the army. It also seems to have direct tie-ins with the underworld. (It is all in all a wonderful, entropic capitalistic circle.) Murphy, heroically outnumbered and outgunned, is killed(?) by some ruthless criminals. However, the corporation that supplies arms has a back-up plan for its glitchy android. This plan involves reconstructing a dead cop into a cyborg (the robocop is actually called a cyborg at one point). A hint is given that secret plans have been made to transfer good cops to a dangerous precinct so that they will be killed and can then be reconstructed. Murphy is the fall-guy. His new existence as a cyborg begins with blurred vision and coded messages flashed onto a flat screen within his visor. 'The screen flickers to life as technicians reconstruct [the dead cop's] body, piecing it together with steel [actually the film is explicit that the robocop will be made of titanium] and microchips, giving the viewer a brief perspective of a cyborg coming to life' (Nash and Ross, 1988:250). The convention of showing the world through the cyborg's eyes complete with typed designations and commands, though familiar from other films, entrains what becomes an important subtext in the film: the cyborg has been given a new consciousness, but he struggles to regain his old human self-awareness. The robocop is 'part-toy, part macho-metaphor, and instrument of mechanical overkill'. Lumbering like 'another Golem', he is said to be curiously unappealing: when the whole face is 'unmasked, drastically increasing the chances of eradication by even the most ineffectual opposition, the clumsiness of the whole venture, a cobbled assembly of bolts, circuitry and flesh, looks even more bizarre' (Strauss, 1988:36). The subtext, however, which unmasking him from within his cyborgian skull-helmet and visor helps to establish, clearly poses the appealingness of the cyborg. With his implanted chip, the robocop has what his makers believe to be a restricted cyborg's consciousness. However, abruptly one night, sleeping in his chair-bed (which has been assigned to him as a 'home') he begins to dream. As his struggle to regain his human memories develops, he begins to recall specific images of his past life. At one point, he even visits the old house where he had once lived with his wife (now moved away) and a son whom he had taught how to twirl a pistol (a trick that, as a cyborg, he still remembers). Accessing the police department's computer files, he identifies himself as the dead cop, Murphy. Subsequently, he begins to ripen a peculiarly human sense of revenge. At the film's conclusion, he is called 'Murphy' and responds with a thin smile of pleasure, 'Thank you, Sir'. Among the many cyborg films, none captures so well what would have to be the cyborg's divided consciousness, the sense of being an improved artifact and of having been once a fully human person. *Robocop* may be viewed as an allegory of the prosthetic consciousness.

This consciousness is always split. Bounded by cleidoic self-awareness, *Homo clausus* experiences intense psychomachias, divisions between now and then, in which the fact of doubleness may be driven home in either pain or joy, or both. Even on the minor scale of a prosthesis such as glasses, the fact of doubleness is, as Elias observes of dying, 'a problem of the living' (Elias, 1985:3). Living the body, there is no alternative to the consciousness of being split except death (or coma). Even a prosthesis as comaparatively straightforward as my glasses fills me with doubleness. If someday I were to have a cornea transplant, then I might sense an even more profound doubleness. The eye itself would have become a mnemotechnic to remind me of the dead person whose eyes I now partly bear. If, in some future technology, prosthetic eyes are possible, then a different but even more profound split will haunt me. Of course, to refer to a 'split' or a 'doubleness' in consciousness is to speak metaphorically, characterizing consciousness as a space, an extended area or zone. I do not feel apologetic about my metaphors. The history of western (to accept that limitation) concepts of consciousness has been, exclusively, a history of metaphorical thinking in which spatial values have been attributed to minds. Whether you think of consciousness as a light (the *lumens naturae* of Cartesian philosophy or the sparkling light bulb of comic strips), a patriarchal helmsman or pilot (a metaphor dear to Renaissance poets and moralists alike), a mirror (or even a mirror-like *tabula rasa*) or, in the postmodern fashion, a nexus (a neural net, a computer web or the 'architecture' of a chip), your discourse will invoke spatial metaphors. Freud's analysis of consciousness as a series of distinct functions, moving upwards from id to superego, actually constructs a narrow tower. It is a tower that imperiously summons into use further metaphors of light, reflection, a helmsman (the superego) and a nexus of commands (a censor, a system of repression): it is monumentally spatial in all its nooks, branches and layers.[12] Hence my metaphorical splitting of consciousness neither adds nor subtracts from the long tradition of metaphors for consciousness. You may pick your favourite metaphor and imagine a further division (a shift in degrees of refractivity, a modulation on the surface of the mirror, two helmsmen – two rudders, at least – or a duplex chain of commands within the nexus) in which it will be possible both to yearn for enhancement and also, remembering what you had once been and your physical need that necessitates this desired supplement, feel disgust at your bodily transformation. Imagined as a place, a nutshell, a room or a tower, consciousness is always already a metaphoric space.

The eyes are one of those body parts that are massively encrusted by associations, tentacularly mythological. Mythological stories 'always lie at the foundation of something' (Calasso, 1993: 175). The prosthetic eye in Pynchon's V., a description of which provides the epigraph of this essay, cannot see, but it evokes the mythological spectrum associated with sight: the colours of sky and sea, the passage of time, the zodiac's symbolic categories. In myths both space and time precede human sight and consciousness. The vision of sky and days comes later than the things themselves. Even my glasses, though highly desirable in providing me with the corrected vision for which I yearn, invade my consciousness at a key point: my symbol-making capacity. If my prosthesis is to be a penile implant, then the invasion of my consciousness will be even more devastating. More than eyes even, the human genitalia, male or female, are entwined with myth. They are excitingly phantasmatic. What happens to Semele, tricked by Hera, consumed by the force of Zeus's flame-hooded phallus, that 'bolt which none can escape' (Ovid, 1955: 82), pricks out the geography of human fate. Hierogamy, Calasso (1993: 291) writes, was how the gods chose to communicate at the beginnings of human time: 'an invasion, of body and mind, which were thus impregnated with the supera-bundance of the divine'. Western mythology and lore are crowded with stories of how genitalia destroy and save, burn, bite and sooth, become weapons or havens. (In myths the gods are often more androgynous than their human playthings: after Semele's death, Zeus rescues the embryo of Dionysus from her charred embers and sews him into a prosthetic womb that he opens within his thigh 'till the months for which his mother should have carried him were fulfilled' [Ovid, 1955: 82].) The human penis plays such a large and varied role in myth, legend and fiction that it makes sense, following Lacan, to distinguish the bit of bodily flesh and gristle, the penis itself, from the mythological phallus which is both 'the idealization and the symbolization of anatomy' (Butler, 1993: 75). The mythological phallus, huge but versatile, has always been the yardstick by which mortal men have measured their potential. 'Having a prominent penis is one of the primary characteristics that defines human males' (Mindich, 1994: 72).[13] Hence, long before the development of phalloplasty as a set of surgical procedures, men have tried to enhance the performance of the penis, edging it towards phallus-hood. Pearls or steel balls, among other items, can be placed beneath the skin to increase friction or rings may be used to elongate the scrotum. More commonly, rings can be used to pierce the penis and scrotum in a variety of ways (Malloy, 1989) – for either adornment or peformance (or, longingly, for both). Women may wear labial or clitoral rings, but nothing in female body piercings seems quite to correspond to such legendary male practices as the 'Prince Albert', a Victorian' 'dressing ring' pierced through the urethra at the base of the penis' head, which is used by men (in the Prince's own manner) to secure the penis, either left or right, when wearing 'crotch-binding trousers' and to keep the foreskin (if any) 'sweet-smelling' (Malloy, 1989: 25).[14] All of these practices are prosthetic in that they seek to enhance, or supplement, the penis. It might seem that they reshape the penis into a cyber(body)part only to satisfy yearning, but they are also, as are all prostheses, mnemotechnic. The vast mythological entanglements that enweb the penis make this inescapable.

As myth, the body interpellates consciousness clamorously. When I contemplate my glasses or my artificial knee, or vividly imagine the possibilities of a future penile implant, I experience a sharp split in my consciousness. I may enjoy my enhanced capacity to see and walk or I may yearn, in tumescent daydreams, for a godlike phallicity, but I cannot escape remembering myself as I once was (or should have been) in historical time. I may then feel disgust at my bodily modifications as well as for my personal deficiencies, my slimewards fall from a now-lost bodily ideal. Like Hawking's prosthetic voice, the very multiplicity of my cyber-enhanced body blurs the edges of my being, deleting the intuition of an integrated personhood which I still remember and for which I (also) yearn. My prostheses constitute a nexus, both incised and harmonized by my mind's proactive interface, of distinct systems. I will become a cyborg, if only an absurd and inadequate one, when I bring together both a cyber system (a widely diffused structure of technological utilities) and a bodily system (a tightly interlaced web of physiological capacities, memories and mythology), forcing both networks of rhizomes to cohabit within my consciousness. *That* consciousness, at once encompassing and split, holds the diverse systems together, like howling winds from hostile poles.

Notes

1. A large body of material exists concerning penile implants. Medical journals publish dozens of articles each year on reconstructive phalloplasty in which the surgeon builds a 'neophallus' for transsexual purposes or to replace a penis that has been lost because of accident, gunshot wound or disease. Much less is written with respect to cosmetic phalloplasty. For articles on penile implants see Goldstein et al. (1993), Levine et al. (1993) and Montrosi et al. (1993). Considerable information, as well as a discussion of problems inherent in implant therapy, can be found in Findlay et al. (1992). A 'neovagina' is also possible, both in transsexual surgery and in reconstructive plastic surgery after disease or mutilation, but neovaginoplasty does not involve the use of prostheses as does neophalloplasty. (In some cases, it appears that a mold is used as an aid in constructing the vaginal vault. However, it would be removed in a postoperative procedure. This may, or may, not, constitute a prosthesis.) Since stenosis is a possible complication in neovaginoplasty, it may eventually call for a prosthetic solution. See Martinez-Mora et al. (1992), Eldh (1993), van Noort and Nicolai (1993). I write as a male, and the divided consciousness that I invoke in this essay is a personalized (but hardly universalized) male consciousness. I would not wish even to suppose how the possession of a neovagina might play out in a female consciousness.

2. Allucquere Roseanne Stone, 'Unpublished Interview' for *MONDO 2000* (1994). Eric Tachibana (erict@gwis2.circ.gwu.edu). *FringeWare Daily* (email@fringeware.com).

3. This shows the 1960s optimism concerning cyborgs and 'hybrid' body forms, but it also indicates a definite confusion since no such beings existed then, or even now, in any significant sense. What Halacy seems to have had in mind are 'mechanical aids' as artificial bodily supplements such as, to cite two of his more risible examples, bustles and cosmetics. Persons of the future may well be hybrid, integrating organic and technological systems, but they have no actual forerunners other than in imagination. Most mechanical aids are not, I think, actually sufficiently consolidated into the 'natural' human systems to constitute genuine cyborgs. Viewers of *Star Trek – The Next Generation* will understand that it is the 'Borg', not Commander Data, who are the future embodiments of the cyborg hypothesis. The Borg, though apparently born as other humanoids, have highly sophisticated non-organic parts, including a magnifying right eye and neural net programs, integrated into their bodily systems. And the Borg are, notoriously, hostile and inimical.

4. *The Six Million Dollar Man* premiered on 20 October 1973 and *The Bionic Woman* on 14 January 1976. (The main character in *The Bionic Woman*, Jaime Sommers, was actually imagined as the girlfriend of Colonel Steve Austin, the hero of the antecedent series.) This schlock played well for 1970s audiences enthralled by the prospects of body-part replacements, whether by transplants or by beyond-the-horizon technology. The excitement of *The Bionic Woman* as a role model evidently persists. Stacey Young, a student at the University of Toronto, writes that, 'As a child I always wanted to be the Bionic Woman. I was a member of the fan club. I had the doll and the dome house. I was a fanatic. With long light brown hair, I felt an affinity for the Strong One. . . . Jamie Somers represented all the potentials that I admired in adult womanhood' (Young, 1995: 8).

5. I have no doubt that Haraway intends her 'we' to signify women only. I have taken it to include both women and men because that is, as I understand it, the actual direction of the analogy. We are all, women and men, sufficiently artifactual to justify the cyborg *analogy*. If you think that the subtext of the argument is 'power', not simply the construction of consciousness, then I ask that you reflect upon Jonathan Goldberg's discussion of the distinction between 'voice' and 'voicing' in Shakespeare. 'Authority in the Shakespearean text', he writes, 'is a matter not of having a voice but of voicing' (Goldberg, 1985: 119). Both women and men, whatever voice they may think they possess, seldom have the power to 'voice' (anything). Power 'entails a disturbing heterogeneity, owned by no one voice – a voicing, as Luce Irigaray might say, that is not one' (Goldberg, 1985: 135).

6. For the classic paper on disgust responses, identifying the tightening of the nostrils, see Angyal (1941). For a discussion of more recent experimental results concerning disgust as a 'type of reaction primarily motivated by ideational factors' (such as the origin and history of an object), see Rozin and Fallon (1987). In registering the affect of disgust, human facework can be remarkably labile. On the varieties of the 'disgust face', see Rozin et al. (1994). Reading the conclusions of experimental psychologists, it is hard to avoid the inference that, whatever the limitations of their experiments, they (passionately) wish to posit faeces as *the* universal disgust object. However, I am arguing in this essay that many things, including machines, cause disgust, but that nothing does so universally (not even machines).

7. The unswerving implacability of insects has long been an important motif in horror fiction and film. (A swarm is like a machine in several obvious respects, including an operational transindividual genetic programming. It is like a hypercomplex machine gone bad.) Irwin Allen's 1978 film, *The Swarm*, exemplifies the entire sub-genre. Bert I. Gordon's 1977 *Empire of the Ants* and John Bud Cardos's 1977 *Kingdom of the Spiders* are also good examples of a film tradition that goes back at least as far as the 1930s. Irwin Allen's *The Swarm* succinctly sums up that tradition. Hitchcock's *The Birds* strikes me as transcending the entire category of insect or animal life turned implacable.

8. People who 'do not feel disgust at the sort of experiences listed above are in some sense diminished. They have been de-sensitized, brutalized, hardened in a way that sets them apart for the rest of us' (Kekes, 1992: 334). Although I cannot discuss the issue in this essay, the experience of

diminishment, or of sensing yourself as having lessened, constitutes an important problem for a theory of disgust. Clearly, discussions of pornography and violence in TV or film also argue that certain experiences, on the level of *representation*, will desensitize, brutalize and diminish. I would want to argue (against censorship) that such *fictional* experiences are indispensable in learning to manage affects, such as disgust or desire, and do not, in modifying one's understanding of affects, necessarily diminish or harden.

9. See Jean-Paul Sartre (1969) and Mary Douglas (1984). Sartre's primary term is *visqueux*; his translator renders this as 'slimy'; Douglas uses 'stickiness'. It might seem that Douglas chooses a term that mistranslates in order to gain the extra impact of a physical degradation from which it is difficult to disentangle oneself. However, Sartre's point is that there is a state between liquid and solid, aberrant and melting respectively. Barnes remarks that she prefers 'slimy' over 'sticky' as a translation for *visqueux* because 'slimy' captures the metaphorical meaning of the French term. Sartre's examples are often figurative. In images such as the root of the chestnut tree before which Roquentin feels nauseous or the portrait gallery of former mayors of Bouville, each brimming with pretentiousness and pompous bad faith, Sartre's novel, *La Nausée*, embodies the theory of nausea and disgust in *Being and Nothingness*.

10. Leslie Fiedler uses the term 'metahuman' to describe Frankenstein's monster, so conspicuously composed from separate body parts (Fiedler, 1978: 22). Although the term carries an immense weight of baggage (no contemporary 'meta' can simply signify a higher order of abstraction), it may do more work, or at least cleaner work, than 'monster' (the etymology of which is as confused as it is provocative). When the human person's boundaries (such as gender) break down in a horror narrative, he or she becomes monstrous in some sense. More productively, he or she becomes a metahuman, calling into question all definitions, all accepted formulas, concerning human personhood.

11. Androids, or at least robots, have had a long history in film. Though probably not the first film to envision an android, Fritz Lang's *Metropolis* (1926) would provide an enthralling *terminus a quo* for that history. The history of cyborgs is both shorter and less certain. Michael Crichton's *Westworld* (1973) has seemed to some critics to be the first cyborg film (Strauss, 1988: 36). However, the humanoids in that film are clearly robotic. Mike Hodges' techno-thriller, *The Terminal Man* (1974), based upon Crichton's novel of the same name, does concern a cyborg in the sense that the scientist has a computer in his brain (but keeps his brain). Jud Taylor's *Future Cop* (1976), a made-for-TV film, may have been *Robocop*'s actual progenitor. Irvin Kershner's *Robocop 2* continues the story of Murphy's transformation. Albert Pyun's *Cyborg* (1989), despite the promising title, basically has little to do with cyborgs and mostly explores *Mad Max/Road Warrior* territory. On the other hand, Pyun's *Nemesis* (1992) might well be the finest cyborg film yet made. It shows significant linkage to William Gibson's novels.

12. Like all spatial metaphors, Freud's narrow tower can be reconfigured. William H. Gass, taking the flowchart of a commercial office as his model, respatializes Freud's tower as a horizontal series of *desks* (Gass, 1985: 126–35). Each of the kinds of metaphor that I have mentioned will have scores of variations within the history of western thought.

13. Cosmetic phalloplasty has success tales (measured by the mythological yardstick), but it also seems to have many failures (Mindich, 1994: 74). Reconstructive phalloplasty, having smaller objectives but more distance to cover, seems to have good success rates (Hage et al., 1993: 157–62). The possibilities for disappointment in attempting to enhance the penis are, evidently, great. Even the dangers and potential failures of penile prostheses, which are strictly corrective within the natural limitations of an individual penis, are considerable (Findlay et al., 1992: 62–7).

14. I write this as a male, open to contradiction. There *is* a vaginal piercing known as the Princess Albertina. Whether this imitates, precedes or is entirely independent of the male Prince Albert, I do not know. Anne Greenblatt describes the Princess Albertina as another 'relatively new and experimental piercing, this piercing passes through the back wall of the urethra. In the piercing documented by *Piercing World* magazine, a captive bead ring was used'. Greenblatt's enthusiasm for labial and clitoral piercings, always identifying an appropriate piece of jewellery for each local piercing, suggests that I may be wrong about the lack of mythic dimension in female piercings. Anne Greenblatt (1995) ardvark@news.holonet. net, *rec.arts.bodyart*

258 ■ Cyberspace/Cyberbodies/Cyberpunk

References

Angyal, A. (1941) 'Disgust and Related Aversions', *Journal of Abnormal and Social Psychology* 36:393–412.

Butler, Judith (1993) *Bodies That Matter: On The Discursive Limits of 'Sex'*. New York and London: Routledge.

Carroll, Noël (1990) *The Philosophy of Horror, or Paradoxes of the Heart*. New York: Routledge.

Calasso, Roberto (1993) *The Marriage of Cadmus and Harmony*, trans. Tim Parks. New York: Knopf.

Douglas, Lawrence (1994) 'Last Bus From Auschwitz', *Massachusetts Review* 25(Spring):7–23.

Douglas, Mary (1984 [1966]) *Purity and Danger: An Analysis of the Concepts of Pollution and Taboo*. London and New York: Ark.

Eldh, Jan (1993) 'Construction of a Neovagina with Preservation of the Glans Penis as a Clitoris in Male Transsexuals', *Plastic and Reconstructive Surgery* 91(April): 895–900.

Elias, Norbert (1985) *The Loneliness of the Dying*, trans. Edmund Jephcott. Oxford: Basil Blackwell.

Elias, Norbert (1987) 'On Human Beings and their Emotions: A Process-Sociological Essay', *Theory Culture & Society* 4(2):339–61.

Fiedler, Leslie (1978) *Freaks: Myths and Images of the Secret Self*. New York: Simon and Schuster.

Findlay, Steven, Doug Podalsky and John Bare (1992) 'Danger: Implants', *US News & World Report* 24 August: 62–7.

Gass, William H. (1985) 'The Soul Inside the Sentence', pp. 113–40 in *Habitations of the Word: Essays*. New York: Simon & Schuster-Touchstone.

Goldberg, Jonathan (1985) 'Shakespearean Inscriptions: The Voicing of Power', pp. 116–37 in Patricia Parker and Geoffrey Hartman (eds) *Shakespeare and the Question of Theory*. New York and London: Methuen.

Goldstein, Irwin, Eduardo B. Bertero, Joel M. Kauman, Frederick R. Witten, John G. Hubbard, William P. Fitch, Reuven A. Geller, Donald L. McKay, Robert J. Krane, Fernando D. Borges, Richard K. Babayan, John P. Tuttle, Michael B. Gruber, Vaira Harik and Suzette Levenson (1993) 'Early Experience With the First Pre-Connected 3-Piece Inflatable Penile Prosthesis: The Mentor Alpha-1', *The Journal of Urology* 150:1814–18.

Govier, Fred E., R. Dale McClure, Robert M. Weissman, Robert P. Gibbons, Thomas R. Pritchett and Denise Kramer-Levien (1993) 'Experience With Triple-Drug Therapy in a Pharmacological Erection Program', *The Journal of Urology* 150:1822–4.

Hage, J. Joris, Floris H. de Graaf, Freerk G. Bouman and Joannes J.A.M. Bloem (1993) 'Sculpturing the Glans in Phalloplasty', *Plastic and Reconstructive Surgery* 92:157–62.

Halacy, D.S., Jr (1965) *Cyborg: Evolution of the Superman*. New York: Harper & Row.

Haraway, Donna (1990) 'A Manifesto for Cyborgs: Science, Technology, and Socialist Feminism in the 1980s', pp. 190–223 in Linda J. Nicholson (ed.) *Feminism/Postmodernism*. New York and London: Routledge.

Haraway, Donna (1992) 'The Promises of Monsters: A Regenerative Politics for Inappropriate(d) Others', pp. 295–337 in Lawrence Grossberg, Cary Nelson and Paula A. Treichler (eds) *Cultural Studies*. New York and London: Routledge.

Heidegger, Martin (1962) *Being and Time*, trans. John Macquarie and Edward Robinson. New York: Harper & Row.

Kekes, John (1992) 'Disgust and Moral Taboos', *Philosophy* 67(262):431–46.

Kristeva, Julia (1982) *Powers of Horror: An Essay on Abjection*, trans. Leon S. Roudiez. New York: Columbia University Press.

Levine, Laurence A., Lawrence S. Zachery and Lawrence J. Gottlieb (1993) 'Prosthesis Placement after Total Phallic Reconstruction', *The Journal of Urology* 149:593–8.

Malloy, Doug (1989) 'Body Piercings', pp. 25–36 in V. Vale and Andrea Juno (eds) *Modern Primitives: An Investigation of Contemporary Adornment and Ritual*. San Francisco: Re/Search Publications.

Martinez-Mora, J., R. Isnard, A. Castellvi and P. López Ortiz (1992) 'Neovagina in Vaginal Agenesis: Surgical Method and Long-Term Results', *Journal of Pediatric Surgery* 27(January): 10–14.

Maslin, Janet (1987) 'Summer Serves Up Its Sleepers', *New York Times* 2 August: 103.

Mindich, Jeremy (1994) 'A Game of Inches: The Penis Enlargement Operation', *Details* 12(May): 72–4.

Montrosi, Francesco, Giorgio Guazzoni, Franco Bergamaschi and Patrizio Rigatti (1993) 'Patient–Partner Satisfaction with Semirigid Penile Prostheses for Peyronie's Disease: A 5-Year Followup Study', *The Journal of Urology* 150: 1819–21.

Nash, Jay Robert and Stanley Ralph Ross (1988) '*Robocop*', pp. 250–51 in *The Motion Picture Guide Annual*. Evanston, IL: Cinebooks.

Ovid [Publius Naso] (1955) *Metamorphoses*, trans. Mary M. Innes. Harmondsworth: Penguin.

Plotinsky, Arkady (1993) *Reconfigurations: Critical Theory and General Economy*. Gainsville: University Press of Florida.

Porush, David (1985) *The Soft Machine: Cybernetic Fiction*. New York and London: Methuen.

Pynchon, Thomas (1966 [1961]) *V*. New York: Modern Library.

Rozin, Paul and April E. Fallon (1987) 'A Perspective on Disgust', *Psychological Review* 94: 23–41.

Rozin, Paul, Laura Lowery and Rhonda Ebert (1994) 'Varieties of Disgust Faces and the Structure of Disgust', *Journal of Personality and Social Psychology* 66: 870–81.

Sartre, Jean-Paul (1956) *Being and Nothingness: An Essay on Phenomenological Ontology*, trans. Hazel Barnes. New York: Philosophical Library.

Seltzer, Mark (1992) *Bodies and Machines*. New York and London: Routledge.

Spivak, Gayatri Chakravorty (1983) 'Displacement and the Discourse of Woman', pp. 169–95 in Mark Krupnick (ed.) *Displacement: Derrida and After*. Bloomington: Indiana University Press.

Strauss, Philip (1988) '*Robocop*', *Monthly Film Bulletin* 55(February): 35–6.

Tudor, A. (1995) 'Unruly Bodies, Unquiet Minds', *Body & Society* 1(1): 25–41.

van Noort, Dirk E. and Jean-Phillippe A. Nicolai (1993) 'Comparison of Two Methods of Vagina Construction in Transsexuals', *Plastic and Reconstructive Surgery* 91(June): 1308–15.

Wells, H.G. (1988) *The Island of Dr Moreau*. New York: Signet.

Young, Stacey (1995) 'If You Could be Anyone on Television, Who Would It Be?', *The University of Toronto Varsity* (Thursday 12 January): 8.

Robert Rawdon Wilson teaches English Literature at the University of Alberta, Edmonton. His publications include *In Palamedes' Shadow: Explorations in Play, Game, and Narrative Theory* (1990), *Shakespearean Narrative* (1995) and *The Hydra's Breath: Imagining Disgust*, the results of his research into the theories of disgust and moral aversion (forthcoming).

Corpses, Animals, Machines and Mannequins: The Body and Cyberpunk

KEVIN McCARRON

> As regarded the body, I did not even doubt of its nature, but thought I distinctly knew it, and if I
> had wished to describe it according to the notions I then entertained, I should have explained
> myself in this manner: by body I understand all that can be terminated by a certain figure; that can
> be comprised in a certain place, and so fill a certain space as therefrom to exclude every other body;
> that can be perceived either by touch, sight, hearing, taste, or smell; that can be moved in different
> ways, not indeed of itself, but by something foreign to it by which it is touched [and from which it
> receives the impression]; for the power of self-motion, as likewise that of perceiving and thinking,
> I held as by no means pertaining to the nature of body . . . (Descartes, 1975: 87)

Here, in his famous *Meditations*, Descartes presents an argument for a mind/body
dichotomy which remains highly influential today. Cyberpunk, too, is heavily
preoccupied with philosophical issues, although many critics prefer to stress the
cultural deficiencies of the genre. June Deery cites Istvan Csicsery-Ronany Jr to
note of cyberpunk that it offers its readers 'a strikingly masculinist world of violent,
sexist, "gangster-chic"' (1994: 45). Even devotees of the genre may find themselves
agreeing with the well-known and comically reductive observation made by Lewis
Shiner, himself the author of the now canonical novel *Deserted Cities of the Heart*,
when he writes that the word cyberpunk 'evokes a very restricted formula; to wit,
novels about monolithic corporations opposed by violent, leather-clad drug users
with wetware implants' (1992: 17). However, in my view, the 'body' of texts,
literary and cinematic, which comprises the genre of cyberpunk constitutes a
sustained meditation, unrivalled in contemporary culture, on the Cartesian
mind/body dichotomy.

Many of the more interesting questions that are asked about the body, such as to
what extent it is subject of or subject to the cultural processes of signification, are
sidestepped by cyberpunk. Turner (1984) and Featherstone (1982) are interested in
evaluating distinctions between the interior of the body as a physical environment

and the exterior of the body as a field of cultural representation, and arguments which subsequently consider the mediation between bodies as 'things in the world' and as discursive constructs are themselves complicated by the recognition that such mediations may be compromised by the inability to establish different views of the body as absolutely opposed. It is possible that, perhaps paradoxically, much of cyberpunk's appeal lies in its Puritanical dismissal of the body. The genre's heavy reliance on prosthetics, for example, is a persistent metonymic device for representing the abandonment of 'the bonds of polycarbon and hated flesh' (Gibson, 1993a: 164), in order to privilege the genre's ultimate goal: pure mind. Bruce Sterling notes: 'Certain central themes spring up repeatedly in cyberpunk. The theme of body invasion: prosthetic limbs, implanted circuitry, cosmetic surgery, genetic alteration' (1986: ix). Clearly, these issues all centre around the body, which features in cyberpunk not at all as a biological essence, a little more as a site for cultural enscription, but most of all as an encumbrance, dragging the mind back from the disembodied purity of cyberspatial interaction with the matrix:

> the human body, in as far as it differs from other bodies, is constituted only by a certain configuration of members, and by other accidents of this sort, while the human mind is not made up of accidents, but is a pure substance. (Descartes, 1975: 76–7)

The body, for cyberpunk writers, is an 'accident', unconnected to the pure substance of mind. They are fascinated by 'enhancement'; throughout their novels the human body becomes less organic and more artificial, increasingly machine-like. In *Count Zero*, Turner notes of an actress: 'The blue eyes were inhumanly perfect optical instruments, grown in vats in Japan' (Gibson, 1987: 131). In 'The Winter Market' the narrator says of Lise: 'She couldn't move, not without that extra skeleton, and it was jacked straight into her brain, myoelectric interface' (Gibson, 1993a: 145). In *The Artificial Kid*, the narrator describes his own construction: 'My skull was sheathed with thin plates of ceramic reinforcement, and my teeth, all false, were white ceramic over a crystalline core' (Sterling, 1980: 49). The interest cyberpunk writers take in the body is of a strictly negative kind; a kind which consistently affirms, and even celebrates, the Cartesian dichotomy. Baudrillard writes, and hence the title of this article: 'Corpse, animal, machine and mannequin – these are the negative ideal types of the body, the fantastic reductions under which it is produced and written into successive systems' (1993: 114).

Grace

In Richard Brautigan's poem *All Watched Over by Machines of Loving Grace* (1968: 3), the world the poem's narrator dreams of is one where the human and the machine acknowledge their differences and yet live in a state of harmony.

The interaction between the human and the mechanical is also central to cyberpunk, but a brief quotation from one of William Gibson's short stories, 'The Winter Market', reveals a radically different view of the relationship: 'But she found me again. Came after me two hours later, weaving through the bodies and junk with that terrible grace programmed into the exoskeleton' (1993a: 144). While Brautigan writes of a 'loving grace', Gibson writes of a 'terrible grace'. While Brautigan envisages a world in which benign and obedient machines watch humanity at play, Gibson, and other cyberpunks, offers us a world in which machines are to all intents and purposes at war with humanity or, even more disturbingly, a world in which it has become impossible to tell the two apart. This is strikingly the case in *Blade Runner*, a film which Frances Bonner argues is not only a cyberpunk text but an exemplary one (1992: 191). Deery writes of the

> fear, projected sexism, or xenophobia that we witness . . . in the film 'Blade Runner' (1982), where the anxiety is that we will not be able to tell cyborgs apart from real humans and that cyborgs will constitute a hostile and exploited group hidden in our midst. (1992: 42)

However, it could equally be argued that the film and the novel upon which it is based, Philip K. Dick's *Do Androids Dream of Electric Sheep?* (1972), are primarily interested in establishing a sense of philosophical unease, and not in depicting specific cultural anxieties. When Descartes asserts the division between mind and body he necessarily accepts a further dichotomy, this time between humans and animals. Animals play a large part in Dick's novel, but in Scott's film their role has been reduced to the brief appearance of the owl at the *head*quarters of the Tyrell *Corporation* (the relationship of capitalism and the body will be discussed below) and, in the 'director's cut', to the fleeting image of the unicorn, which suggests that the protagonist is also a replicant. Nevertheless, while *Blade Runner* is less concerned than *Do Androids Dream of Electric Sheep?* with interrogating philosophical hierarchies it still uses replicants primarily to initiate questions about the fundamental nature of humanity. Cyperpunk writers introduce machinery in the form of 'enhanced' humans, androids and cyborgs which complicates Descartes' satisfying binary division; an ambivalent third term is inserted and the subsequent disquieting experience, of characters in the texts and by readers and viewers of the texts, is primarily ontological.

The Human and the Inhuman

It is commonly accepted that the word 'cyberpunk', was first used in a Bruce Bethke story called 'Cyberpunk', published in the November 1983 issue of *Amazing Stories*. Certainly the word rapidly became ubiquitous when an article in the *Washington Post* dated 30 December 1984, used the word to describe the work of several writers, in particular, William Gibson, Bruce Sterling, Lewis Shiner, Pat Cadigan and Greg Bear. I want to focus on the work of the first of these writers, William Gibson, and on his 'Cyberpunk Trilogy' in particular: *Neuromancer, Count Zero* and *Mona Lisa Overdrive*, although I'll also be referring to his collection of short stories, *Burning Chrome*, and to Bruce Sterling's *The Artificial Kid*, as well as to Dick's *Do Androids Dream of Electric Sheep?* In addition, I'll be considering the contribution made to the genre by Marge Piercy's novels *Woman On The Edge of Time* and *Body of Glass*. Overall, what I hope to do is to consider the ways in which these texts employ various manifestations of the 'body' (cyborgs, artificial intelligence, prosthetics, replicants, etc.) to interrogate the limits of humanity.

David Porush writes:

> The Preservationists of [Bruce] Sterling's *Schismatrix* have it all wrong. What is it they're Preserving? When do we know we're talking to a real McCoy? What aspect of humanity makes us human? Our flesh? Our CNS? Our thoughts? Our handiwork? Where's that line over which lies inhumanity? The technology is us, man. (1992: 258)

'What aspect of humanity makes us human?' The question is a good one. So good, it's been asked a great deal; tacitly, I would argue, any time a writer introduces a cyborg, android, replicant, robot, an Artificial Intelligence Unit. Whenever the textual stress is on prosthetics, on the kind of technology that fuses blood and iron, the debate is really about the human, and its sometimes opposite, the inhuman. Philip K. Dick asks the question throughout *Do Androids Dream of Electric Sheep?* In this novel a principal cause of unease for the central characters is the diminishing certainty with which the demarcation lines between animal, android and human can be agreed upon. The owner of the artificial pet centre, Hannibal Sloat, complains that one of his assistants lets a real animal die, under the mistaken belief that it's a fake. His chief mechanic replies 'the fakes are beginning to be darn near real, what with those disease circuits they're building into the new ones' (1972: 62).

At the same time, Rick Deccard, the bounty hunter who is paid to kill replicants, and whose own name is punningly similar to Descartes', is told by his boss that the test he is using to distinguish humans from replicants, the Voigt–Kampff test, is by no means infallible:

> 'The Lennigrad psychiatrists', Bryant broke in brusquely, 'think that a small class of human beings could not pass the Voigt–Kampff scale. If you assessed them in line with police work you'd assess them as humanoid robots. You'd be wrong, but by then they'd be dead.' (1972: 33)

Descartes writes:

> if there were machines bearing images of our bodies, and capable of imitating our actions as far as it is morally possible, there would still remain two most certain tests whereby to know that they were not therefore really men. (1975: 44)

The first of these tests is speech, which Dick ignores, taking it absolutely for granted that this test has been rendered invalid by technology. Dick's Voigt–Kampff test, with its intimations of Fascism, is a parody of Descartes' second test:

> The second test is, that although such machines might execute many things with equal or perhaps greater perfection than any of us, they would, without doubt, fail in certain others from which it could be discovered that they did not act from knowledge, but solely from the disposition of their organs; for while reason is a universal instrument that is alike available on every occasion, these organs, on the contrary, need a particular arrangement for each particular action; whence it must be morally impossible that there should exist in any machine a diversity of organs sufficient to enable it to act in all the occurrences of life in the way in which our reason enables us to act. (1975:45)

The Voigt–Kampff test is designed to demonstrate levels of empathy, the one quality which it is believed the androids cannot fake. However, the novel makes it quite clear that intelligence can find out a way of simulating empathy, and that people who cannot empathize are not neccesarily replicants. On several occasions the author points up Deccard's own inability to empathize with the replicants, and then stresses Deccard's realization of the paradoxical position this places him in. In *Blade Runner*, the replicant, Rachel, bitterly asks Deccard if he has ever taken the test himself. The implication is clear: if he took it, he would fail. In the novel, John Isodore, omitted from the film, has a vision of the bounty hunter tracking down and killing the replicants in a manner which stresses his 'inhuman' nature:

> He had an indistinct, glimpsed-darkly impression: of something merciless that carried a printed list and a gun, that moved machine-like through the flat, bureaucratic job of killing. A thing without emotions, or even a face; a thing that if killed got replaced immediately by another resembling it. And so on, until everyone real and alive had been shot. (1972:120)

It is noticeable here that the words 'real' and 'alive' are used to refer to the replicants, who are, as is also stressed in *Blade Runner*, more 'human' than the humans who chase them.

The Trilogy

This preoccupation with the human and the inhuman is central to William Gibson's trilogy. Bruce Sterling refers to *Neuromancer*, the first volume, as 'the quintessential cyberpunk novel' (1986:xi). John Christie lists a number of reasons why *Neuromancer* should be valued:

> Not only [for] its narrative drive but the meticulous superficiality, the comic-book characters, the texture of multi-media reference, and the central representational invention, cyberspace itself. Ideologically too, its postulating the replacement of the hegemonic state apparatus by multinationals, its cultural pluralism, its abandoning of the book while retaining text and image,

and its analytical interest in degenerative and pathological forms of capital all rendered it appealing to a late 1970s–early 1980s critical and ideological avant-garde whose label was postmodern. (1992:173)

Neuromancer is, essentially, a 'caper' novel. It tells the story of how a gang of humans is assembled and manipulated by an Artificial Intelligence, Wintermute, in order that it might combine with another Artificial Intelligence, Neuromancer, to form a new order of being entirely. Of course, this is not as easy as it sounds, because attempts have been made to limit the powers of the Artificial Intelligence. The Turing Police are constantly looking out for unacceptable levels of computer activity and then quickly moving in to shut the computer down. The construct known as the Dixie Flatline tells the protagonist, Case, what it thinks is happening. It is, more or less:

> My guess, Case, you're going in there to cut the hardwired shackles that keep this baby from getting any smarter. . . . See, those things [the AIs] they can work real hard, buy themselves time to write cookbooks or whatever, but the minute, I mean the nanosecond, that one starts figuring out ways to make itself smarter, Turing'll wipe it out. *Nobody* trusts those fuckers, you know that. Every AI ever built has an electromagnetic shotgun wired to its forehead. (Gibson, 1986:159)

The computer is important to cyberpunk; indeed its very existence is a generic constant. However, it is not only as hardware that the computer is important. Gibson himself said, in an interview with Larry McCaffrey, published in *The Mississippi Review*:

> On the most basic level, computers in my books are simply a metaphor for human memory. I'm interested in the how's and why's of memory, the ways it defines who and what we *are*, in how easily it's subject to revision. (Landon, 1992:156)

This is a major concern in Philip K. Dick's 'We Can Remember It For You Wholesale', and in *Total Recall*, the film based upon it. If we *are* anything, Dick seems to suggest, we are our memories, but if these can be implanted what guarantee is there of our identity? Or, more existentially perhaps, always assuming identity and existence are separate phenomena, what guarantee is there of our existence? The question returns us to Descartes. In *Total Recall*, despite the mutant Quarto's claim to the protagonist that 'a man is defined by his actions, not by his memories', there is a strong suggestion that human beings are not so easily persuaded of this. It is worth noting that the mutant is also, by definition, not human, and although he can therefore be viewed as a source of greater than ordinary wisdom, he might also be seen as necessarily lacking a *true* understanding of what it is to be human.

Gibson's trilogy raises the same concern, as throughout *Neuromancer*, *Count Zero* and *Mona Lisa Overdrive* 'computers actively rival human memory, offering virtual cyberspace constructs that effectively compete with human memories of "reality"' (Landon, 1992:156). This is also a feature of *Blade Runner*, both versions. In the first version Rachel is 'given' Tyrell's niece's memories, in the director's cut Deccard realizes that the police have access to his memories, which means they have had some hand in *implanting* them. In Bruce Sterling's *The Artificial Kid* the protagonist is actually created through memory transfer. In *Neuromancer*, Wintermute accesses parts of Case's memory and sends them back to him in holographic representations which can be manipulated to suit Wintermute's purpose. The way in which such fictions consider the end of private memory, a feature of our humanity, suggests links with an earlier dystopian text, George Orwell's *Nineteen Eighty-Four*.

Orwell's book, however, is considerably more *physical* than Gibson's, more human. Running through all cyberpunk texts is a fascination with the ways in which the flesh is inessential, irrelevant; there is a disdain for the too, too human flesh. This is how Gibson describes what happens when Case has his ability to work in cyberspace destroyed by toxic drugs administered to him for stealing. The language is theological:

> For Case, who'd lived for the bodiless exultation of cyberspace, it was the Fall. In the bars he'd frequented as a cowboy hotshot, the elite stance involved a certain relaxed contempt for the flesh. The body was meat. Case fell into the prison of his own flesh. (1986:12)

Later in the novel, forced to *physically* travel, he thinks: 'Travel was a meat thing' (1986:97) Again, in 'The Winter Market' the narrator notes of Lise; 'she threw away that poor sad body with a cry of release' (1993a:164). As the trilogy progresses, the language becomes even more overtly theological: 'the Wig had become convinced that God lived in cyberspace, or perhaps that cyberspace *was* God . . .' (1987:173). In *Mona Lisa Overdrive*, during a discussion about the precise nature of cyberspace, one of the characters asks: 'the matrix is God?' (1988:138). The body's accidental and ultimately unnecessary corporeality is stressed throughout Gibson's work. Closely linked to this is the preponderance of prosthetics than appear throughout the trilogy. Again and again Gibson, and other cyberpunk writers, introduce characters who are, partially, sometimes for the most part, constructed, not quite 'real'. On the opening page of *Neuromancer* we read: 'Ratz was tending bar, his prosthetic arm jerking monotonously. . . . The antique arm whined as he reached for another mug. It was a Russian military prosthesis, a seven-function forcefeed manipulator, cased in grubby pink plastic' (1986:9).

Later, Linda introduces herself to Case in a particularly cyberpunk way: 'She held out her hands, palms up, the white fingers slightly spread, and with a barely audible click, ten double-edged, four centimetre scalpel blades slid from their housings beneath the burgundy nails' (1986:37). *Count Zero* opens like this:

> They set a slamhound on Turner's trail in New Delhi, slotted it to his pheromones and the colour of his hair. . . . Its core was a kilogramme of recrystallized hexogene and flaked TNT. . . . Because he had a good agent, he had a good contract. Because he had a good contract, he was in Singapore an hour after the explosion. Most of him, anyway. . . . It took the Dutchman and his team three months to put Turner back together again. They cloned a square of skin for him, grew it on slabs of collagen and shark cartilage polysaccharides. They bought eyes and genitals on the open market. (1987:9)

The narrator of *Burning Chrome* describes how Chrome herself touches his own partially artificial body: 'And her hand went down the arm, black nails tracing a weld in the laminate, down to the black anodized elbow joint . . . her palm against the perforated Duralumin' (1993a:205). It is possible to see this reliance on prosthetics as both metaphorical and as political, economic. Carol McGurk notes of Philip K. Dick's novel *The Three Stigmata of Palmer Eldritch*: 'Eldritch's prosthetic eyes, arm, and teeth are the three stigmata of Dick's title – visible and outward signs of his spiritual perversity and horror' (1992:114). In Gibson's work, though, it could be argued that the emphasis on such things as prosthetic devices and lens implants indicates not symbolic corruption but consumer desire, linked to the great American belief in reinventing the self. For a price, usually a large one, Gibson's characters can, piece by piece, replace themselves.

Inevitably, therefore, there are a number of references throughout the trilogy to the existence of organ banks; places where it is implied the donors might not always have been dead before their organs were removed. Ratz says to Case in the opening pages of *Neuromancer*: 'Now, some night, you get maybe too artistic; you wind up in the clinic tanks, spare parts' (Gibson, 1986:11). This is an issue also raised in Marge Piercy's utopian/dystopian novel *Woman on the Edge of Time* (1976) and in the specifically dystopian *Body of Glass* (1991).

Feminism and Cyberpunk

When Connie, the protagonist of the earlier novel, attempts to travel through time to her utopian future she finds herself instead in a dystopian world, a parallel universe similar to that portrayed in *Do Androids Dream of Electric Sheep?* Both of these parallel worlds may evoke considerations of Descartes' 'evil genius', who was capable, Descartes theorized, of creating another world, a false one specifically designed to fool the philosopher into believing it was the 'real' world. Novels featuring parallel worlds can raise interesting questions about the nature of 'reality' – it is often, simply, a consensual agreement, and not at all a verifiable, ontological truth. In *Neuromancer*, cyberspace is actually described as 'a consensual hallucination' (Gibson, 1986:12). Connie is informed upon her arrival in the dystopian future that 'poor people are not like people. They're walking organ banks'. Moments later she is also told: 'The multis [multinationals] own everybody' (Piercy, 1976: 291). It is clear that the nightmare world only glimpsed by Connie in *Woman on the Edge of Time* provides the background for the entire later novel, which is set in 2059. Peter Fitting refers to 'the dialogue with cyberpunk in Marge Piercy's *He, She and It* [the American title of *Body of Glass*]' (1994: 5) Vara Neverow writes that

> as [Piercy] herself observes in the Acknowledgements of *He, She and It*, chapter 15 of *Woman on the Edge of Time* predated and anticipated the male-dominated genre of cyberpunk and therefore her uses of the discursive conventions of the genre are pre-emptive rather than imitative. (1994: 19)

Deery is equally emphatic: 'In *He, She and It* Piercy rewrites not only utopias but also cyberpunk . . .' (1994: 45).

The plot of *Body of Glass* is quite uncomplicated. In order to preserve Tikva, a Utopian community under threat from the predatory ravages of the surrounding capitalist communities, a scientist, Avram, attempts to create a cyborg but experiences difficulties until he is helped with the programming by a woman, Malkah. A cyborg called Yod is the result. Here, Piercy seems to be challenging the traditional nomenclature of Science Fiction. Most readers would view Yod as an android, a robot rather than as a cyborg. Conventionally, a cyborg is the physical bonding of human and machine; a robot or android is an artificial construction. This is not the only occasion in the novel when Piercy challenges generic conventions. Donna Haraway argues for the cyborg as a 'fiction mapping our social and bodily reality and as an imaginative resource suggesting some very fruitful couplings' (1990: 581), and in *Body of Glass* Yod and Malkah's grand-daughter, Shira, become lovers. (Although *Blade Runner* might be considered to have established a well-known precedent for this type of relationship, Deccard's affair with the replicant Rachel is less radical than it might at first appear, as Rachel has no termination date programmed into her circuitry, thereby conferring quasi-human status upon her. In the 'director's cut' it is suggested that Deccard himself is a replicant.) Avram forces Yod to go out on a suicide mission and Yod kills him before being destroyed himself. The novel raises a number of issues, perhaps most strikingly the legitimacy of violence against oppression and the ways in which a masculine preoccupation with logic renders human life nightmarish. In addition, as occurs throughout cyberpunk fiction, the mechanical is used to interrogate the status of the real. When Yod confesses to Shira that his artificial nature causes him unease, she replies:

> Yod, we're all unnatural now. I have retinal implants. I have a plug set into my skull to interface with a computer. I read time by a corneal implant. Malkah has a subcutaneous unit that monitors

and corrects blood pressure, and half her teeth are regrown. Her eyes have been rebuilt twice. Avram has an artificial heart and Gadi a kidney. . . . We're all cyborgs, Yod. You're just a purer form of what we're all tending toward. (1991:203)

Indeed, as occurs in *Do Androids Dream of Electric Sheep?*, the artificial creation is revealed to be more human than the beings that made him.

Neverow notes the importance of the body in *Woman on the Edge of Time* and *Body of Glass*:

> In both novels, the cultures that honor embodiment cherish the physical self for its vulnerable uniqueness, while the cultures that endorse incorporation value the body only for its fragmentary parts and functions: for organs harvested from unwary donors, for the severed hand that can access credit, for the alienated sweated labour of the underclass, for sperm, eggs, ovaries, wombs, procreative products and services severed from their humane contexts. (1994:24)

Clearly, *Body of Glass* is similar in this respect to Gibson's novels, where body parts are routinely bought and sold in the marketplace. Gibson's dystopias are centred around cultures which endorse incorporation rather than embodiment, while Piercy's overtly feminist novels endorse embodiment over incorporation. It is obviously possible to argue that, by virtue of their reproductive capacities, women are the ultimate instance of embodiment. Despite the array of traditionally masculine plot lines and images which appear throughout cyberpunk: leather, drugs, violence, crime, technology, etc. . . ., the really *macho* aspect of cyberpunk lies in its complete lack of interst in biological reproduction.

Where Piercy contrasts the brutal world of unchecked capitalism with peaceful Utopian communities, where childbirth and woman are valued, Gibson contrasts his depiction of an equally brutal and rapacious capitalism with acts of aggressively masculine, financially motivated individualism. Fitting is condemnatory of Gibson's glamorization of violence and crime and suggests that it is invidious because 'survival and success were the characters' only motives'. He contrasts Piercy's *Body of Glass* and finds this much more to his liking: 'In Piercy, there are again criminals and data thieves, but Riva understands her illegal activities as political, part of the ongoing struggle against the domination of the multis, and not some exhilarating form of self-realization' (1994:8). While this is clearly true, although whether it makes Piercy's work 'better' than Gibson's is a moot point, it is equally clear that the attitude Gibson and other cyberpunk writers have toward capitalism is by no means unequivocally celebratory. In this respect, cyberpunk narratives function as satire – their authors are more than half in love, gazing with rapt fascination at what they hate. It was suggested earlier that cyberpunk progressively abandons the body in order to privilege the mind; at the same time these narratives feature characters who launch sustained attacks on the multinational companies that have all but replaced nation states or governments as we in the West know them. What hostile readers of cyberpunk see as the genre's celebration of masculine greed and outlaw *chic* is actually a parallel attack on the 'body'; this time in its purest capitalist sense.

The Body and Capitalism

Jameson describes the cityscapes of *Blade Runner* and of Gibson's novels as:

> the interfusion of crowds of people among a high technological bazaar with its multitudinous nodal points, all of it sealed into an inside without an outside which thereby intensifies the formerly urban to the point of becoming the unmappable system of late capitalism itself. (1994:157)

It was implied earlier that words like '*head*quarters; and '*corp*oration' are clearly derived from a perspective which takes the body as a referent, but in both Piercy's and Gibson's novels the correlation between the body and the organization, between the organic and the inorganic, is mocked. The multinationals own everybody, or nearly everybody, in cyberpunk novels. The Corporation is, in a sense, the ultimate body and this is why so much of the criminal activity in Gibson's novels is directed against it. One of the most dominant images in *Blade Runner* is the building that houses the Tyrell Corporation. Faceless, inhuman, the multinationals create the world in which lone wolf operators like Case, Bobby Mewmark and Artificial Jack live and work and, in some cases, die. Rosemary Jackson suggests that: 'The modern fantastic is characterised by a radical shift in the naming, or interpretation, of the demonic' (1988:21). The demonic, the truly inhuman, in the texts I'm considering here is the global, multinational corporation, a body not made of flesh but of money, and the Faustian characters who are at the apex of the corporate structure.

In *Count Zero*, Joseph Virek appears to Marley via hologram, and says: 'You must forgive my reliance on technology. I have been confined for over a decade to a vat. In some hideous industrial suburb of Stockholm. Or perhaps of hell' (Gibson, 1987:25). There is, surely, something irresistibly comic about someone who has been in a vat for more than ten years being snobbish about the suburb he 'lives' in. In a phrase strongly reminiscent of an observation made in *Woman on the Edge of Time*, Marley then realizes 'with an instinctive mammalian certainty that the exceedingly rich were no longer even remotely human' (Gibson, 1987:29).

Excepting Piercy's work, cyberpunk's relationship to the body is hostile, twice over. Philosophically, the body is trivialized in order to privilege mind and, culturally, the Corporation is subject to a series of raids accomplished by individuals or hastily assembled gangs of criminals. Despite cyberpunk's reliance on and fascination with technology, the genre is deeply conservative and anti-technology, implacably hostile to any further erosion between the human and the mechanical. In the 'face' of increasing mechanization, cyberpunk's Cartesian privileging of mind allows its readers to reassert their supremacy over the machine. While Turner argues that human beings both have bodies and are bodies, cyberpunk narratives suggest that machines may have minds, but human beings *are* minds.

Although it seems reasonable to note that cyberpunk queries the concept of humanness by opposing it with the inhuman, Gibson's trilogy does become increasingly preoccupied with reaffirming the importance of the body, indeed, of humanity. The titles say a good deal. *Neuromancer* is, after all, an eponymous novel but the protagonist, so to speak, is not Case, but an Artificial Intelligence. *Count Zero* is an alias, a *nom de guerre*, but the subject is not an object, while in *Mona Lisa Overdrive* the human is fully reinstated. *Virtual Light*, Gibson's new novel, published in 1993, is the most socially mimetic of any of Gibson's novels. It is a conventional dystopia set in San Francisco in 2005 and it utilizes a female character, Chevette, to once again dramatize the conflict between the individual and the brutal power of 21st-century capitalism, a conflict which is also central to such dystopian films as *Total Recall* and *Robocop*.

Rosemary Jackson has suggested that the modern fantastic is the form of literary fantasy written within the secularized culture produced by capitalism. It is ironic to think that if capitalism is responsible for the modern fantastic, then the modern fantastic is more than happy to bite the hand that feeds it, and to bite the hand, moreover, with a prosthetic mouth.

References

Baudrillard, Jean (1993) *Symbolic Exchange and Death*. London: Sage.

Bonner, Frances (1992) 'Separate Development: Cyberpunk in Film and TV', in G. Slusser and T. Shippey (eds) *Fiction 2,000*. Athens, GA: University of Georgia Press.

Brautigan, Richard (1968) *The Pill versus the Springhill Mine Disaster*. New York: Delta Books.

Christie, John (1992) 'Of AIs and Others: William Gibson's Transit', in G. Slusser and T. Shippey (eds) *Fiction 2,000*. Athens, GA: University of Georgia Press.

Deery, June (1994) 'Ectopic and Utopic Reproduction: *He, She and It*', *Utopian Studies* 5(2): 36–49.

Descartes, René (1975) *A Discourse on Method*. London: Dent.

Dick, Philip K. (1972) *Do Androids Dream of Electric Sheep?* London: Granada.

Featherstone, Mike (1982) 'The Body in Consumer Culture', *Theory, Culture & Society* 1(3): 18–33.

Fitting, Peter (1994) 'Beyond the Wasteland: A Feminist in Cyberspace', *Utopian Studies* 5(2): 5–15.

Gibson, William (1986) *Neuromancer*. London: Grafton.

Gibson, William (1987) *Count Zero*. London: Grafton.

Gibson, William (1988) *Mona Lisa Overdrive*. London: Grafton.

Gibson, William (1993a) *Burning Chrome*. London: Grafton.

Gibson, William (1993b) *Virtual Light*. London: Penguin.

Haraway, Donna (1990) 'A Manifesto for Cyborgs: Science, Technology, and Socialist Feminism in the Last Quarter,' in Karen Hansen and Ilene Philipson (eds), *Woman, Class, and the Feminist Imagination: A Socialist-Feminist Reader*. Philadelphia: Temple.

Jackson, Rosemary (1988) *Fantasy: The Literature of Subversion*. London: Routledge.

Jameson, Frederic (1994) *The Seeds of Time*. New York: Columbia University Press.

Landon, Brooks (1992) 'Not What It Used To Be: The Overloading of Memory in Digital Narrative', in G. Slusser and T. Shippey (eds) *Fiction 2,000*. Athens, GA: University of Georgia Press.

McGurk, Carol (1992) 'The "New" Romancers: Science Fiction Innovators From Gernsback to Gibson', in G. Slusser and T. Shippey (eds) *Fiction 2,000*. Athens, GA: University of Georgia Press.

Neverow, Vara (1994) 'The Politics of Incorporation and Embodiment: *Woman on the Edge of Time* and *He, She and It* as Feminist Epistemologies of Resistance', *Utopian Studies* 5(2): 16–35.

Piercy, Marge (1976) *Woman on the Edge of Time*. New York: Ballantine.

Piercy, Marge (1991) *Body of Glass*. London: Penguin. (US edition retitled as *He, She and It*.)

Porush, David (1992) 'Frothing the Synaptic Bath: What Puts the Punk in Cyberpunk?', in G. Slusser and T. Shippey (eds) *Fiction 2,000*. Athens, GA: University of Georgia Press.

Shiner, Lewis (1992) 'Inside The Movement: Past, Present, and Future', in G. Slusser and T. Shippey (eds) *Fiction 2,000*. Athens, GA: University of Georgia Press.

Sterling, Bruce (ed.) (1986) *Mirrorshades: The Cyberpunk Anthology*. London: Grafton.

Sterling, Bruce (1980) *The Artificial Kid*. London: Penguin.

Turner, Bryan S. (1984) *The Body and Society: Explorations in Social Theory*. Oxford: Blackwell.

Kevin McCarron teaches in the English Department at the Roehampton Institute. His publications include *William Golding* (Northcote House, 1994) and *The Coincidence of Opposites* (Sheffield Academic Press, 1995).

Index